The summer course in theological German at the Johannes G[utenberg University] Mainz is internationally famous, and unique in kind. This book is specifically designed for that course. It provides basic German grammar and an extensive reader of German theological texts, from Martin Luther to Ruben Zimmermann. It is a wonderful resource not only for students who take the summer course but for theological students all the world over.

> **JOHN J. COLLINS,** Holmes Professor of
> Old Testament, Yale University

Oh, how I would have loved to have had a book like *Handbook of Reading Theological German* as I pursued a PhD and prepared to interact primarily with a German theologian on the use of the Old Testament in the New in Luke-Acts. Rather than trying to teach myself German, I could have sat at the feet of clear instructors who also offered me samples of the array of texts I would encounter. It would have been a God-sent gift. So to anyone struggling to learn German, this book is for you.

> **DARRELL L. BOCK,** executive director for cultural
> engagement, senior research professor of New
> Testament studies, Dallas Theological Seminary

A wonderful book for students learning how to read scholarly articles and books in German. The pedagogy that Jones and Hirt employ is thoughtful, practical, and accessible. They provide a user-friendly approach for working through the often complex sentences found in German-language scholarship. They also provide helpful (and often quite interesting) background for the selections in the book. While geared especially to people studying religion and theology, this book will be useful for any scholar in the humanities who needs to develop a reading knowledge of German.

> **BENJAMIN D. SOMMER,** professor of Bible and ancient Semitic
> languages, Jewish Theological Seminary, senior fellow, Kogod Center
> for Contemporary Jewish Thought of the Shalom Hartman Institute

The *Handbook of Reading Theological German* is an excellent source for graduate and postgraduate students to learn the nuances of theological German. I highly recommend it.

> **ED HINDSON,** dean emeritus and distinguished professor
> of religion, school of divinity, Liberty University

All theological students know about the massive influence of German scholarship on modern theology. What too few of them do is learn German well enough to read the sources of this influence. Jones and Hirt have provided a timely help to that task, as well as well-chosen passages that reinforce both the grammatical lessons learned and the substance of theological debate. Moreover, they provide translations of the passages from the various authors so that the students can check their work and, as important, easy-to-use appendices on critical topics students will often need to consult. All in all, a wonderful resource.

> **L. GREGORY JONES,** dean of the divinity school, and
> Ruth W. and A. Morris Williams Jr Distinguished Professor of
> Theology and Christian Ministry, Duke Divinity School

Road-tested with the highly successful Mainz summer school for German Language and Theology, this book now takes the reader gently by the hand to consider the salient points of written academic theological German, with a wide confessional sweep and helpfully annotated texts. It integrates an appreciation of the key outlines of German religious history and culture, German thought, as well as the word-forms. This is done not just to sweeten the grammatical pill but also to help students to fall in love with the language and culture. I have seen students benefit from this, and I look forward to using it in place of Ziefle's *Modern Theological German* of 1986.

> **MARK ELLIOT,** professor of divinity and biblical criticism,
> school of critical studies, University of Glasgow

Generally, when an acquired language is not used, it is eventually and gradually forgotten. The *Handbook of Reading Theological German* is an excellent vehicle for students and scholars of German theology and related areas who wish to either enhance their German reading skills or reawaken them. It offers a clear and easy-to-follow reading approach. The authors of this volume wisely touch upon the essentials of German grammar and syntax, and provide helpful paradigms of verb conjugations, adjective endings, article declensions, etc. The German texts offered as a corpus for practicing the Mainz translation method are authored by a carefully selected and diverse list of German theologians. Hence, while improving your German translation abilities, you just might find yourself adding bibliographic items for your next article.

> **TALIA SUTSKOVER,** chair, department of
> biblical studies, Tel Aviv University

German remains one of the key languages of theological research, and many of the seminal texts of Christianity have been written in German. In this carefully constructed volume, Jones and Hirt guide students through the task of reading theological German. Not only do they provide helpful tips on German theology and its grammar, but they also lead students through key texts to deepen understanding and expertise in reading theological German. This is a rich and invaluable tool that is highly recommended to all students of theology.

> **PAUL FOSTER,** professor of New Testament and early
> Christianity, school of divinity, University of Edinburgh

HANDBOOK
of READING
THEOLOGICAL
GERMAN

**CHRISTOPHER RYAN JONES
AND KATHARINA HIRT**

**ZONDERVAN
ACADEMIC**

This book is affectionately dedicated to all the students who desire to interact with the original German sources and incorporate them into their research. May this book prove to be a useful tool in your pursuit of academic excellence and help to elevate your scholarship.

Contents

APPENDICES

Acknowledgments

With heartfelt gratitude we acknowledge Prof. Dr. Ulrich Volp, who not only established the yearly International Summer School of German (and) Theology and provided the foreword for this volume, but encouraged and supported its production.

This project would not have been possible without Prof. Dr. Wolfgang Zwickel, who went above and beyond to provide assistance, advice, help, and encouragement every step of the way. Words cannot convey how humbly thankful we are.

Special thanks goes to Ms. Alicia Ward who had the special "honor" of reading over this manuscript multiple times as we prepared it for publication.

To each of the publishers and authors who agreed to allow their text to be included in this work, we appreciate your contribution and willingness to be a part of these efforts.

Additionally, this manuscript would not be what it is without the generous help of Beate Karst, Rafaela de Abreu Mathias, and Anna Mulcahy. We are grateful for your efforts and assistance. This project would not have been completed on time without your help. Thank you!

Finally, we are thankful for the PhD and graduate students from all over the globe who worked through some of these chapters and provided feedback. Your efforts have helped develop a tool which will undoubtedly assist other students who will not be limited as you were by a lack of resources.

Foreword

By Prof. Dr. Ulrich Volp

The book which you have in front of you is not the result of a solitary scholarly research project like many other academic publications today, but emerged more or less directly from the classroom at my university. It is a university that was founded in 1477 when Mainz was a seat of the Holy Inquisition, and one of the political centers of Germany, ruled by an archbishop who was one of the constitutional electors of the emperor of the Holy Roman Empire. Martin Luther started his theological career as one of his subjects, and it was not long before our university's theologians were officially asked to write their first Gutachten, a carefully written opinion, about Luther's teachings.

Our city also witnessed the invention of the printing press by its most famous son, Johannes Gutenberg, in the fifteenth century, and the subsequent media revolution which enabled the fast exchange of scholarly ideas and teaching, which we have since become so accustomed to. German-speaking theologians and their writings have since been studied worldwide and still have an impact on academic theological work in other countries. The rich and varied academic landscape in the Germany of the nineteenth and twentieth centuries with dozens of well-funded theological departments and many outstanding professorial minds produced a myriad of scholarly works in biblical, patristic and liturgical studies, church history, dogmatics, ethics, and many other fields—many of which are still worth consulting and provide for fruitful reading.

Today, well over one hundred German, Austrian, and Swiss universities offer courses in Christian theology taught in German. They also provide a research environment which makes this a flourishing part of scholarly production in these countries. One might not agree with the theological positions of Luther, Schleiermacher, Barth, Bonhoeffer, or Rahner, but my experiences of studying their ideas together with international students have been and continue to be some of the most rewarding of my own academic career. I feel privileged, because after more than half a millenium of theological studies at Mainz, I was given the resources to start the project of a theological summer school coupled with a German language course, which made many of these experiences possible.

The participants of the school came from practically all over the world: from the United States, Canada, Mexico, Peru, England, Scotland, Australia, Egypt, Ethiopia, Nigeria, South Africa, the Czech Republic, Denmark, Italy, the Netherlands, Russia, China, India, Indonesia, and South Korea. They spoke many different languages (up to eleven in one case) and brought with them very diverse learning experiences. For the Germans on the team, this made the course linguistically as interesting for them as for anybody else—indeed we sometimes felt we were learning and appreciating our own language all over again.

At the same time, we found that there was a surprising lack of helpful material on the subject and what was available felt not ideally suitable for the purpose: to enable students with some existing background in theology to efficiently and painlessly decode written German theological texts from different periods, and at the same time improve their linguistic skills. This book is designed to fill the gap and I wish for it to be useful for many who are not able to participate in the Mainz summer school. I have known both authors for some time now and I am confident that the expectations which we all have for this project will not be disappointed.

Having been at the receiving end of language instruction in more than half a dozen languages myself—some of it more, some less successful—I know that learning a foreign language can be frustrating at times, but I also know that the rewards far outweigh any sacrifices one may have to make. I sincerely hope that this book will enable you to reap these rewards much sooner than would have otherwise been possible.

Ulrich Volp
Mainz, May 2020

Introducing the
Handbook of Reading
Theological German

The rigorous academic work completed by students within the fields of biblical, Judaic, and theological studies comprises a diverse and robust curriculum—just ask any student. The journey from bachelor's to doctorate includes not only classes on biblical texts and theological categories, but, depending on the student's concentration, the program can also include courses on biblical archaeology, church history, cultural backgrounds, exegesis, hermeneutics, ministry, Talmud, textual criticism, and of course, in most universities, students must acquire certain language skills—primarily in Hebrew and Greek. In fact, these language skills are so essential that most students must complete a comprehensive examination in both areas before completing their doctorate.

In most countries, students are often required to demonstrate proficiency in a secondary research language, typically French, German, or Latin. For many students, German is an obvious choice, due to the vast amount of academic literature produced in German and, of course, the influential role German theologians have had for over five hundred years. Yet, when observing the development within any language over a period of five hundred years, noticeable changes can be seen between the older texts and the modern texts. This can be observed in any language. After all, no one goes around speaking the English used in the King James Bible; nor do modern Israelis speak Biblical Hebrew.

Students who observe this phenomenon when trying to work with the original German sources notice that it is extremely difficult to translate the texts. Not to mention, the German used in theological texts is very specific and not used, discussed, or mentioned in basic grammars or German dictionaries. This can make the student feel overwhelmed. Unfortunately, there is a lack of relevant and useful material that can be used in the development of courses in theological German, as the last notable text on this subject was originally published in 1986 by Helmut W. Ziefle.[1] This scarcity of materials can discourage many students from pursuing this specific focus.

Recognizing the necessity of theological German in the academic work of emerging biblical scholars and realizing the void in up-to-date resources, Prof. Dr. Ulrich Volp began an international summer school program, "German and Theology," at the University of Mainz in 2015. The purpose of the program was to provide visiting scholars with hands-on experience in both German theology and theological German. Professor Volp utilized the Protestant Theological Faculty of the University to lecture on areas relevant to German theology and enlisted Mrs. Christina Ersch to develop the linguistic part of the program.

Over the past five years, Christina and her colleague Katharina Hirt have worked each year to further develop the program in a way that meets the needs of international students and provides an exciting and challenging classroom experience. However, not everyone who would benefit from such a program is able to travel to Germany for three weeks. And while the program does a fantastic job of teaching both German theology and theological German, it does not fill the void in contemporary publications. It is with this need in mind, and with the inspiration of the summer school, that this book was conceived.

The purpose of this text is to fill the gap in modern scholarship and to offer a beneficial tool for understanding theological German. Due to her experience teaching at and helping to develop the international summer school program each year, and because of its unique and innovative methodology, I asked Katharina Hirt to write the grammar portions of this text. I will focus on aspects of German theology, pointing out the importance of not only the texts presented in this volume but also the importance of each respective author. It is our hope that this book will not only be helpful to those learning theological German on their own, but that it will also inspire the development of theological German courses.

The material presented in this volume is unique in that it focuses on reading and translating, as opposed to communication skills, which is typical in most contemporary German grammars. In addition, while we have tried to provide a very thorough foundation for German grammar, we only present materials that are relevant to theological German. This way, the student is not overwhelmed by unnecessary material that is not applicable to their studies.

The book is divided into three parts. In the first part, you will become familiar with German theology, its development, and the influential role it plays in contemporary and modern theology. You will also be introduced to the Mainz Method of reading and translating texts, using authentic examples from Martin Luther's *Von der Freiheit eines*

---

1. Ziefle published *Theological German: A Reader* in 1986 and *Dictionary of Modern Theological German* in 1992. Both volumes were later combined and published as *Modern Theological German: A Reader and Dictionary* (Grand Rapids: Baker, 1997).

Christenmenschen. Chapters 2–4 of this book are structured according to the ten steps of the Mainz Method and include:

1. Find all the verb forms.
2. Find all commas.
3. Find all conjunctions.
4. Mark the main clause.
5. Identify case and number of all nouns; establish noun phrases.
6. Locate all referent nouns.
7. Look out for participles used as adjectives.
8. Look up all new words and try combining the verb with phrases.
9. Perform a rough translation of the sentence.
10. Polish up the sentence to ensure readability.

In part two of this book, you will be able to apply the skills you learned in part one. In each chapter you will be introduced to one of the great minds that have been instrumental in the development of German theological thought. In each case, you will be given a short biography of each historical figure that explains the significant role they have played. We will also help you to recognize the uniqueness of each of their writing styles. You will then be presented with one of their well-known texts, which we will then help you translate.

Part three of this book is more advanced. It is divided up into areas of discipline. You will find texts related to the Hebrew Bible and biblical archaeology, New Testament studies, Judaic studies, church history, and theology. Two texts within each of these concentrations will be provided. The purpose of this section is to introduce you to a greater number of modern scholars[2] and to advance your reading and translation skills by offering less assistance than was provided in previous chapters. The texts were selected based on a number of factors, including the author's significance in the field and the general reception of their work within their area of study, to name a few. While on first glimpse it may appear to be heavily biased toward male authors, that is not our intent. In Germany, the concept of a woman having a career in academia is still relatively new and mostly emerged in the 1970s. Still, we made great efforts to include a broader range of authors and were only hindered by copyright issues.

Finally, in the appendix you will find a number of resources that we feel will be helpful to you. Included you will find an explanation of basic grammar terms, which has been designed for those who have not had a solid foundation of grammatical concepts

---

2. With the exceptions of Frankel and Geiger. The two texts are presented based on the significance of their authors on Modern Judaism and the lack of English translations available for their writings.

in the past. There are lists of irregular verbs and verbs with prepositions, which may be helpful to you. You will also find a glossary of terms; while it is not exhaustive, we do hope that it will be helpful, since many of the terms used in theological German are absent from most German-English dictionaries. The appendix also contains solutions to the exercises in the book and most importantly, you will find a copy of the Mainz Method Checklist. We recommend that you photocopy this checklist so that you can keep it beside you whenever you are doing translation work.

Additionally, I would like to say a few words about translations. One of the reasons why interacting with original texts is so important is that translations rely on the interpretation of the translator. You can give multiple people the same text and they will all come up with a different translation. This is often observed by the teachers of the Summer School. In the appendix you will also notice that there are translations of the texts presented in Parts II and III of this book. We felt it beneficial to offer these so that you could check your own translations. In order to provide translations that could be similar to your own, we have created these translations with heavy reliance on the footnotes within the chapter that you will be using to create your translation. Intentionally, these translations are not well polished, since with several of the texts, published English translations are already available. Instead, these translations are solely as a reference for checking your progress.

So, whether you're proficient in German or studying the language for the first time, it is my hope that this book will excite and encourage you to interact more frequently with German texts on a scholarly level. To be able to work with a text in its original language is a great gift and allows for much deeper and more meaningful interaction with the source. It is my hope that, in some small way, this book will help you produce the best scholarship possible.

Christopher Ryan Jones
Mainz, May 2020

PART I

Introduction to German Theology and Grammar

Overview

As you begin your journey into German theology and the grammar of the German language, you will receive an overview of the development of theology within Germany and its global influence over approximately a thousand years. Over the next four chapters, you will be given the tools necessary to appreciate original German sources and incorporate them into your research. Within chapters 2–4, you will develop a firm foundation of German grammar that is centered on the Mainz Method, presented in a ten-step checklist. Exercises will be provided for each step to reinforce the materials presented, enabling you to excel in parts II and III of this book.

Learning Objective

- Learners will discover the development and influence of German theology.
- Learners will only be introduced to essential grammatical concepts for reading and translating theological German texts.
- Learners will become familiar with the Mainz Method Checklist.
- Learners will begin to apply the Mainz Method Checklist to authentic materials.

Introduction to German Theology 1

Normally when the concept of theology is considered, the mind equates it with the theological perspectives held by members of particular religious communities, whereby it is possible to compare and contrast the theological ideologies of one particular faith group to those held by a different religious tradition. That is to say, it is possible to analyze the differences between sects within a religion, such as comparing Protestant and Catholic theology, or examining the theological differences between two different religions, such as Judaism and Christianity. In each of these instances, theology is always thought of in terms of its association with religion.

There are but a few examples of theology becoming linked to a nation. Israel, of course, would be the prime example, since the entire development of the nation is connected to a theological concept. Some may argue that the United States should be considered, as well, since its founding was based upon theological freedom. However, people do not speak in terms of "Israeli theology" or "American theology"; however, the term "German theology" is used. What then is German theology, and what is its significance? Within this chapter we will attempt to introduce the concept of German theology, its importance, and its influence both past and present. The term "German theology" does not speak to a concise set of beliefs or practices; instead it speaks to the massive impact Germany and its scholars have had on the development of theology worldwide. Regardless of your religious tradition or theological position, the influence that German scholars have had throughout the centuries within the theological sphere is irrefutable.

Theology and Its Development

In order to comprehend how and why there are so many different theological perspectives in the world, it is important to understand what theology is and how it evolved throughout time based upon a number of variables. The term "theology" comes from the Greek words θεός (theos, "God"), and λόγος (logos, "word," "speech," or "expression"). Thus, the term "theology" means a word about God. Or to put it in more common terms, it is a conversation about God. Therefore, when anyone dialogues about their perspective or conception of God, they are in fact doing theology, regardless of their educational or religious background (even if they have neither). As Charles Ryrie stated, "Even an atheist has a theology."[1]

---

1. Charles Caldwell Ryrie, *Basic Theology: A Popular Systematic Guide to Understanding Biblical Truth* (Chicago: Moody, 1999), 9.

Since theology is a composite of our thoughts about God that are then expressed, as our thoughts about God change, so then does our theology. Yet while theology may change over time, God does not; for it is not God who changes but rather our perspective and understanding of God that changes. This evolution in our cognition is the primary result of our environment and experiences. When we learn something new about God, it is not God who changed but our knowledge about God, which allows us to think and reflect on an entirely new level. Likewise, when our environmental realities differ from our current theological perspective, it causes us to reevaluate and reconsider our theological stance. Thus, our theology is constantly evolving and developing.

Søren Kierkegaard is quoted as having said, "In order to experience and understand what it means to be a Christian, it is always necessary to recognize a definite historical situation."[2] This statement is true of the theological perspective held by any religion. Considering this notion that environmental realities affect the evolution of theology, it is no wonder that Germany has played such a massive role in the development of modern theology. Regardless of religious tradition, the historical events that have taken place within the borders of the German nation have not only caused German theologians to reconsider their theological perspectives but have also challenged scholars from all over the world.

German History and Theology

While it would be impossible to examine every event that has taken place within Germany and influenced Christian theology, it is important that we point out three major events—the Reformation, the Enlightenment, and the Holocaust. It may come as a surprise to many that the global theological advancements made by German thinkers were not only felt within Christianity but also within Judaism. Jewish life in Mainz dates back to the tenth century, making it one of the oldest Jewish communities in the German-speaking world. Some of modern Judaism's most notable traditions and divisions trace their origins to German soil. Yet, before we discuss these events in detail, we must go back to the Renaissance, to the year 1440 in the city of Mainz, where Johannes Gutenberg invented the printing press. While scholars today believe printing presses were developed in Asia as early as 1060 AD,[3] it was Gutenberg's invention that took the European continent by storm. His printing press changed the way knowledge was spread and allowed for the advancement of ideas to circulate to broader audiences much more quickly than had previously been possible. Without Gutenberg's invention, the Reformation would not have had the opportunity to capture the masses the way it did.[4]

---

2. Eliseo Perez-Alvarez, *A Vexing Gadfly: The Late Kierkegaard on Economic Matters* (Eugene, OR: Pickwick, 2009), 110.

3. Raymond A. Lajoie, "What Tyndale Owed Gutenberg," *Christian History* 16 (1987).

4. Kevin Miller, ed., "Gutenberg Produces the First Printed Bible (1456)," *Christian History* 28 (1990).

The Reformation

Approximately forty-six years after the death of Gutenberg, Albert von Brandenburg became the Archbishop of Mainz. To pay for his elevated status, Albert borrowed around 20,000 gold gulden from a wealthy Austrian merchant named Jakob Fugger.[5] In order to pay back the loan, Albert received permission from Pope Leo X to sell indulgences within his diocese, under the condition that half of the money raised would be sent to Rome. Three years after assuming the Electorate of Mainz in 1514, Albert received a letter from a professor at the University of Wittenberg. The letter was sent on October 31, 1517 and was written primarily as an objection to the sale of indulgences. The letter, which is now known as the Ninety-Five Theses, was written by Martin Luther and ultimately led to the Reformation.

The Reformation was such a monumental event that it would be hard to evaluate the full extent of its impact. The Catholic Church had been subject to internal schisms prior to Martin Luther, but the Reformation caused such a staunch theological separation that it divided the Church and radically shifted the political landscape of the European continent. The impact of the Reformation affected not only the history of Christianity but changed the course of world history. Both the Church and the culture were subject to a cataclysmic shift, due in large part to Martin Luther.[6] In chapter 5 of this book, we will discuss Luther in greater depth and examine a portion of his writings.

Without the Reformation, it is possible that many of the theologians presented in this book would never have found their place in history. As you will come to recognize in part II, many of the most influential figures were either influenced by or debated with their predecessors and peers. Reading these texts, you will follow the thought processes that led to the development and evolution of theology into what it is today. While many consider the Swiss theologian Karl Barth the greatest theologian of the twentieth century, what contributions would he have been able to make without the influence of Kant and the

The Marktbrunnen was donated by Albert of Mainz in 1526.
© Hannah Wolf

---

5. Samuel Macauley Jackson, ed., *The New Schaff-Herzog Encyclopedia of Religious Knowledge: Embracing Biblical, Historical, Doctrinal, and Practical Theology and Biblical, Theological, and Ecclesiastical Biography from the Earliest Times to the Present Day* (New York; London: Funk & Wagnalls, 1908–1914), 105.

6. Yvanka B. Raynova, "Reformation der Kirche oder Reformation durch Kultur?," *Labyrinth* 20.2 (2018): 5–13.

foundation provided by Martin Luther and the Reformation?[7] The Reformation was such a momentous event that it would be exceptionally difficult to measure its impact on the history of the world and within the world of theology.

Enlightenment and Idealism

The association between the Age of Enlightenment and philosophy is so strong that it is easy to overlook the direction the movement took the theological world. One particular individual, Immanuel Kant, whom we discuss in chapter 6 of this book, has had exceptional influence on religious thought. Two hundred years after his death, many topics that are debated within the religious world are based upon the questions he formulated.[8] One area of exploration Kant focused on that continues to be heavily analyzed is the relationship between science and religion. As such, it should come as no surprise that his work is heavily relied upon in apologetics. Perhaps Nietzsche was correct to consider Kant as a sort of Christian apologist.[9]

The degree of Kant's influence was only fully realized centuries after his death. His book *Kritik der reinen Vernunft* (1781) was the first of his publications to gain notoriety. While the book did receive positive reception by many, there were also those who were very critical of the text. This led to the development of another philosophical movement in the eighteenth and nineteenth centuries, known as German Idealism. One of the most prominent voices in that movement was Georg Wilhelm Friedrich Hegel. His *Wissenschaft der Logik* was heavily influenced by Kant's *Kritik der reinen Vernunft*.

Though known primarily as a philosopher, Hegel attended the Protestant seminary in Tübingen early in his academic career.[10] Despite the fact that he did not seem to be too interested in his theological training at the time, theological subjects were often popular topics in his lectures later in his career.[11] His analysis and presentation of these ideas were so well crafted that Karl Barth once pondered why Hegel had not become for the Protestant world what Thomas Aquinas had become for the Catholic world.[12] This is not to say that all of the Protestant world has been as accepting of Hegel as Barth was. The contention between Hegel and his colleague at Berlin University, Friedrich Schleiermacher, was widely known by those living in Berlin at the time.[13] In particular, Hegel ridiculed Schleiermacher on his principle that religious faith was based upon a

---

7. Roger E. Olsen, *The Journey of Modern Theology: From Reconstruction to Deconstruction* (Downers Grove, IL: InterVarsity Press, 2013), 90.

8. Edward Scribner Ames, "The Religion of Immanuel Kant," *JSTOR* 5.2 (1925): 172.

9. Friedrich Nietzche, *The Portable Nietzsche*, ed. and trans. Walter Kaufmann (New York: Penguin, 1977), 96.

10. Terry Pinkard, *Hegel: A Biography* (Cambridge: Cambridge University Press, 2000), 20.

11. See Peter C. Hodgson, ed., *Hegel: Lectures on the Philosphy of Religion: One-Volume Edition, the Lectures of 1827* (Berkeley, CA: University of California Press, 1988).

12. Andrew Shanks, *Hegel's Political Theology* (Cambridge: Cambridge University Press, 1991), 71.

13. Pinkard, 447.

"feeling of dependence," asserting that this indicated that a hungry dog would make the best Christian, since it would experience feelings of salvation when it's hunger was satisfied.[14]

The Holocaust

Most recognize the impact that the Holocaust had on the political landscape of Europe, which changed drastically after the Second World War. Yet, many fail to consider the impact this tragedy had on theology within the Christian church. Catholic theologian Johann Baptist Metz made the assessment that in modern times it is impossible to do theology with a back turned to Auschwitz.[15] In other words, Christian theologians today must reconcile the realities of the Holocaust with their theological perspectives concerning the character of God, the nature of humanity, and the role of the church.

It is not only the aftermath of the Holocaust that has caused theologians to reflect critically on their theological perspectives, but also events preceeding and transpiring during World War II gave cause for reflection. Questions concerning the Christian's obligation to submit to government and how a Christian should respond to the injustices they see in the world around them are just a few of the topics that demanded attention. While history has largely ignored those who answered these questions incorrectly, the legacy of notable figures like Karl Barth and Dietrich Bonhoeffer (both of whom will be addressed in later chapters)—who were each forced to make vital decisions that impacted their careers and their lives—lives on, not only in their writings but in the examples they set.

The implications of the Holocaust among the Jewish people are devastating to say the least. The genocide of six million innocent people has caused serious reflection among the Jewish people, which is observed every year during Yom HaShoah. While we must never forget these events, we must also simultaneously recognize that these are not the first historical events in Germany that have impacted the Jewish people. While we look at the Holocaust in absolute horror, we cannot forget the great Jewish-German theological thinkers whose ideas and writings helped shape Judaism into what it is today.

The ShUM Cities, Unetanneh Tokef, and the Rhineland Massacres

The German cities of Speyer, Worms, and Mainz are known as the ShUM cities and played a pivotal role in Jewish life during the Middle Ages. The fingerprint of Mainz in particular can still be seen on worldwide Jewry. The city became an important location for Jewish study during the Middle Ages under the leadership of Rabbi Gershom ben Judah (ca. 960–1028), which differed greatly from the style of learning common in a

---

14. Pinkard, 500.

15. J. B. Metz, "Kirche nach Auschwitz," in *Kirche und Israel, Neukirchener Theologische Zeitschrift* 5 (1990): 99–108.

Babylonian model yeshiva. Gershom was known as the "light of the exile."[16] Under his leadership, there were three major rulings on Jewish law that have become standard practice. First, it was declared that a man could only have one wife at a time. Second, women had to agree to a divorce before a man could give her a *get*.[17] And finally, it was forbidden to open and read someone else's mail. While these may all sound common today, these were revolutionary (and rather liberal) positions in the eleventh century.

The *Unetanneh Tokef* (ונתנה תוקף)[18] is part of the liturgy recited during the High Holidays. According to the legend of Amnon of Mainz, the liturgy was the result of the martyrdom of Amnon, whom the archbishop of Mainz tried to convert. After multiple tries, Amnon told the archbishop that he needed three days to consider. Amnon then regretted wavering in his Jewish faith and told the archbishop that he would not convert and that his tongue should be removed for expressing doubts about Judaism. As punishment, the archbishop had Amnon's hands and feet cut off.[19]

Gravestone of Gershom ben Judah, Cemetery Judensand, Mainz
© Hannah Wolf

A few days later, Amnon asked to be carried to the synagogue where Rosh Hashanah services were being held. As one of the attendees began the Kedushah, Amnon asked him to wait as he recited what is now known as the *Unetanneh Tokef*. The legend has it that Amnon died as soon as he finished the prayer and appeared to Rabbi Kalonymus three days later in a dream asking him to spread the prayer throughout all Jewry. While there are no records of Amnon, the *Unetanneh Tokef* has continued to be an inspirational and moving portion of the High Holiday services.[20]

Some scholars believe that it was Rabbi Kalonymus ben Meshullam who wrote the liturgy. Kalonymus was the head of the Jewish community in Mainz during the Rhineland massacres. The massacres were a product of the First Crusades, as French and German Christians brutally slaughtered Jews in the Rhineland who refused to convert to Christianity. While some Jews converted to avoid persecution, thousands were killed by the crusaders. Rabbi Kalonymus sent a letter to King Henry IV, who later issued an order that Jews were not to be murdered. Nevertheless, Kalonymus, along with fifty-three others of the Jewish

---

16. H. H. Ben-Sasson, ed., *A History of the Jewish People* (Cambridge, MA: Harvard University Press, 1976), 433.

17. A *get* is a Jewish divorce. See Ronald L. Eisenberg, *The JPS Guide to Jewish Traditions* (Philadelphia: Jewish Publication Society, 2004), 67.

18. Translated as, "Let us speak of the awesomeness."

19. Eisenberg, *JPS Guide*, 200.

20. Ronald L. Eisenberg, *Essential Figures in Jewish Scholarship* (New York: Jason Aronson, 2014), 49–50.

community, were forced to take their own lives rather than be subjected to the hands of the enemy during the Worms massacre.[21] The attack on the Jewish community of Mainz was brutal and, at that time, was considered the largest act of violence committed against a Jewish community in Europe.[22]

Gravestone of Kalonymus ben Meshullam, Cemetery Judensand, Mainz
© Hannah Wolf

It has been reported that many of the Jews who converted during the threat of the crusaders later returned to Judaism. However, the events of the Rhineland massacre presented a number of issues to Jewish theologians and scholars on the issue of suicide. Some have tried to link the events to the suicide of King Saul in 1 Samuel 31, as well as to the actions of those in Masada and the Bar Kochba revolts. While the closest similarities of the Rhineland massacre are those of Masada, the events of Masada are largely ignored by Rabbinic scholars; thus the events of the Rhineland Massacre brought the topic to the forefront of discussion and debate.

The Birth of Modern Judaism

Nineteenth-century Germany is a crucial period in Jewish history, especially as it relates to how Judaism is studied and practiced today. The discipline of Judaic studies owes its founding to Leopold Zunz who, in 1819, established the Society for the Culture and Science of Judaism. The purpose of the organization was to advance the academic study of Judaism.[23] Yet it was not only the study of Judaism that was important in the nineteenth century but also the future of Judaism and how the religion should be lived. Competing ideas about how Judaism should be practiced caused serious debate between three German rabbis whose ideas form the foundation of modern Judaism.

Rabbi Abraham Geiger (ca. 1810–1874) believed that Judaism was always evolving and should continue to do so. For Geiger, it was important to do away with outdated traditions and prayers that he thought were no longer important to living a Jewish life in the modern world. He also felt that men and women should be equal in their standing

---

21. Siegmund Salfeld, *Das Martyrologium des Nürnberger Memorbuches* (Berlin: L. Simion, 1898), 116.

22. Matthew Gabriele, "Against the Enemies of Christ: The Role of Count Emicho in the Anti-Jewish Violence of the First Crusade," in *Christian Attitudes Toward the Jews in the Middle Ages: A Casebook*, ed. Michael Frassetto (New York: Routledge, 2007), 70.

23. Eisenberg, *Essential Figures in Jewish Scholarship*, 301–2.

within the Jewish community,[24] although he never explicitly referred to the inclusion of women in a minyan.[25]

Nevertheless, these ideas totally contradicted those which were standard in the Jewish world and drew great criticism from Rabbi Samson Raphael Hirsch (ca. 1808–1888). While Hirsch agreed that Judaism needed to engage with the culture, he also contended that the truth and laws of Judaism were eternal and therefore could not change. Rabbi Zacharias Frankel (ca. 1801–1875) opted for a more moderate approach to the reform of Judaism. He believed that Judaism should evolve to meet the needs of the current society and yet famously stormed out of the Frankfurt meeting when they began to discuss the elimination of Hebrew from the service's liturgy.[26]

The approaches of these three men form the foundation of the modern Reform, Orthodox, and Conservative movements. Geiger, though he was eventually appointed the chief rabbi of Breslau, is the father of the Reform movement and spent his final days on the faculty of the Hochschule für die Wissenschaft des Judentums, a Reform rabbinical college that was founded in Berlin in 1871. He had a number of notable publications including *Urschrift und Uebersetzungen der Bibel in ihrer Abhängigkeit von der innern Entwickelung des Judentums* (1857) and *Das Judentum und seine Geschichte* (1864–1871).

Earlier in life, Geiger had studied at the University of Bonn with Sampson Raphael Hirsch. The two started out as friends before eventually becoming enemies.[27] Hirsch is considered the father of the Orthodox movement and spent his final days establishing the "Freie Vereinigung für die Interessen des Orthodoxen Judentums."[28] The father of the Conservative movement, Zacharias Frankel, advocated the positive-historical approach to studying Judaism.[29] He published his ideas in a number of books and magazines, including his own monthly publication, *Zeitschrift für die Religiösen Interessen des Judenthums*. The Conservative movement college located in Berlin is named in Frankel's honor.[30] In chapters 15 and 16 of this book you will have the opportunity to engage with texts written by Geiger and Frankel and gain a greater appreciation for the two leaders' different approaches to Judaism.

---

24. See Max Wiender, ed., *Abraham Geiger and Liberal Judaism: The Challenge of the Nineteenth Century* (Cincinnati: Hebrew Union College Press, 1981).

25. Benjamin Maria Baader, *Gender, Judaism, and the Bourgeois Culture in Germany: 1800–1870* (Bloomington, IN: Indiana University Press, 2006), 61.

26. See W. Gunther Plaut, *The Rise of Reform Judaism: A Sourcebook of Its European Origins* (Philadelphia: Jewish Publication Society, 2015).

27. Moshe Aberbach, ed., *Jewish Education and History: Continuity, Crisis, and Change*, trans. David Aberbach (New York: Routledge, 2009), 89.

28. Free Union for the Interests of Orthodox Judaism was founded in 1885.

29. Neil Gillman, *Conservative Judaism: The New Century* (West Orange, NJ: Behrman, 1993), 18–31.

30. Ismar Schorch, "Zacharias Frankel and the European Origins of Conservative Judaism," *Judaism* (1991): 344–54.

Christian Theology in the Nineteenth and Twentieth Centuries

It would be unjust not to mention the influence of German-speaking theologians in the nineteenth and twentieth centuries and the impact they had globally on Christian thought. Roger E. Olsen, in his book, *The Journey of Modern Theology: From Reconstruction to Deconstruction* (2013) does an incredible job noting not only the prominent scholars but also those who influenced them, thus demonstrating how theology develops over time. There is no doubt that two major World Wars upon the continent caused many theologians to pause for reflection, thus creating major shifts in the theological beliefs that had previously been held. Two individuals are worth noting here—Adolf von Harnack and Rudolf Bultmann, considered two of the most notable advocates of liberal Protestantism in the twentieth century.[31]

Both Karl Barth and Dietrich Bonhoeffer were students of Adolf von Harnack, though they had different reactions to their teacher. Barth cites Harnack's signing of the *Manifesto of the Ninety-Three* as one of the reasons he rejected liberal theology. Bonhoeffer, on the other hand, was greatly impacted by the idea of the Social Gospel, which Harnack promoted.[32] Bonhoeffer presented a eulogy on behalf of Harnack's students at his funeral in 1930 and years later, while in prison, would still read the words of his teacher.[33] Harnack argued that much of the New Testament was influenced by Hellenism and, as such, Christians should question the authenticity of these doctrines. He also rejected the historicity of the Gospel of John and denied the possibility of miracles.[34] Harnack's works were not only influential to German theologians but were a major influence on American scholar Arthur Cushman McGiffert. McGiffert, who studied as a graduate student in Germany, later became professor at Union Seminary, where he required his students to read Harnack's work.[35]

Rudolf Bultmann was one of Harnack's students.[36] Bultmann would later become professor of New Testament at the University of Marburg and is considered one of the major figures in the field of biblical studies in the early twentieth century.[37] Many of his writings are still influencial, including *Geschichte der synoptischen Tradition* (1921), *Das Evangelium des Johannes* (1941), *Kerygma and Mythos* (1948), and *Theologie des Neuen*

---

31. Paul Barry Clarke and Andrew Linzey, *Dictionary of Ethics, Theology and Society* (New York: Routlege, 1996), 510.

32. Hans Schwarz, *Theology in a Global Context: The Last Two Hundred Years* (Grand Rapids: Eerdmans, 2005), 133.

33. Michael Mawson and Philip G. Ziegler, eds., *The Oxford Handbook of Dietrich Bonhoeffer* (Oxford: Oxford University Press, 2019), 13.

34. Schwarz, 131.

35. Elizabeth A. Clark, *The Fathers Refounded: Protestant Liberalism, Roman Catholic Modernism, and the Teaching of Ancient Christianity in Early Twentieth-Century America* (Philadelphia: University of Pennsylvania Press, 2019), 77–79.

36. William D. Dennison, *The Young Bultmann: Context for His Understanding of God, 1884–1925* (New York: Peter Lang, 2008), 30.

37. F. L. Cross and Elizabeth A. Livingstone, eds., *The Oxford Dictionary of the Christian Church* (Oxford: Oxford University Press, 2005), 252.

Testaments (1948). Within his work Bultmann utilized a history-of-traditions method, also known as form criticism, and often called the historical value of the Gospels into question.[38] While Bultmann's work has been influential in the research into the historical Jesus, many conservative scholars also interact with his work, often rejecting and criticizing his theories.[39]

Conclusion

Germany has played a significant role in the development of theology for both Jews and Christians. What would Christianity look like today without the likes of Luther, Schleiermacher, and Barth? What would Judaism look like today without the likes of Hirsch, Geiger, and Frankel? There is little doubt that the current theological framework of each of these two world religions is shaped in significant ways by these men.

The unique role that Germany has had in the development of modern religion outside its nation's borders is profound. One need only to look at the reverberation of Gutenberg's printing press and the essential role that it has played to note this. Not only was his invention important for Martin Luther, but also for other important figures during the Reformation who lived outside of the borders of Germany, such as William Tyndale. Gutenberg's invention made providing copies and translations of the Bible to the average citizen possible.

Recognizing important historical events and the impact these events have had on theologians and scholars alike helps us to realize the true value of German theology. It is astonishing to consider the centuries of contributions made by German scholars and how those contributions play a vital role in the development of contemporary and modern theology. The amount of scholarly literature written in German on the topics of biblical studies, theological studies, and Judaic studies is massive. It comes as no surprise, then, that scholars of all levels, from all religious backgrounds, and from all over the globe seek to improve their German skills in order to better interact with the original German texts of some of these influential minds. By learning to interact with these original sources, scholars are better equipped to examine and analyze these important writings in a more intimate way and are able to gain an appreciation for the intent and thought process of each author in a way that is impossible in translation. In the following three chapters, we will introduce important grammatical concepts that will help you on your journey toward reading and translating theological German texts.

---

38. Cross and Livingstone, 252.

39. Craig L. Blomberg, *The Historical Reliability of the Gospels* (Downers Grove, IL: InterVarsity Press, 2007), 23.

When learning any language, it is important to develop some fundamentals of the language's grammar and structure. This is intimidating for most students, but there is good news! German and English both belong to the Germanic language family, a subcategory of the Indo-Germanic languages. Their grammars share a lot of similarities, especially in the formation of tenses. Word categories such as verb, noun, and adjective correspond in both languages. Also, both languages conjugate verbs using first, second, and third person and use plurals in conjugation (verbs) as well as declination (nouns), even if this is less visible in English. English and German both recognize coordinate and subordinate clauses. Anyone who has studied a language that does not belong to the Indo-Germanic language family, like Japanese, can appreciate the advantages these similarities provide.

Now for the bad news: while English lost a lot of grammatical structures due to syncretism and a fixed word order, German retained most of its grammatical structures. German has a gender system with three categories and articles, adjectives, and pronouns all showing gender agreement with the controlling noun. German also has a case system with four cases, which are mainly marked by articles, adjectives, and pronouns. The word order[1] in German is not fixed as in English but is guided by a complex set of rules that allow for an extremely varied sentence structure. We will discuss the concept of word order in detail throughout the book as it is a concept that permeates German grammar.

Translating complex German sentences is comparable to translating Latin texts. The three grammatical chapters in this book will provide you with step-by-step instructions on how to translate theological German texts and give you the necessary grammar input to perform these steps. But before we dive deep into grammar, we will take a short look at German spelling and pronunciation in contrast to English.

Spelling and Pronunciation

Spelling and pronunciation are very close in German. All written letters are pronounced, with a few exceptions that we will point out here. In addition, there is close to no variation of pronunciation for the same spelling, which makes pronunciation predictable, a clear advantage compared to English.

---

1. "Word order" is simply the order of words in a phrase, clause, or sentence.

1. Long and Short Vowels
   - ie = long i as in *sie* (she) or *liegen* (lay) is pronounced like the English "see"
   - vowel + h = long vowel and the h is not pronounced as in *ihn* (him) or *stehen* (stand)
   - vowel in front of a double consonant (tt, ll, nn, etc.) = short vowel as in *Hölle* (hell)
   - double vowel = long vowel as in *Boot* (boat)
   - e at the end as in *Straße* (street) is pronounced [ə] as in English "s**e**vere" or "**e**nemy"
   - -er at the end as in *Lehrer* (teacher) or *Teller* (plate) is pronounced like the a in "father"
2. Consonants
   - st at the beginning of a word or syllable is pronounced scht as in *stellen* (put) or *stehen* (stand)
   - sp at the beginning of a word or syllable is pronounced schp as in *Sport* (sport) or *Spaß* (fun)
   - v is pronounced like f as in *Vogel* (bird) or *vergessen* (forget)
   - ck is mainly pronounced like k as in *Zucker* (sugar) or *zurück* (back)
3. Umlaut ä, ö, and ü
   - ä like in *Äpfel* (apples) is pronounced like the e in English "get"
   - ö like in *Söhne* (sons) is pronounced as follows: first articulate a long German e sound in a word such as *Sehne* (tendon). As you say it, gradually purse your lips and the word that emerges is *Söhne* (sons).
   - ü like in *Tür* is pronounced as follows: first articulate the German sound ie in a word such as *Tier* (animal). As you say it, gradually purse your lips and the word that emerges is *Tür* (door).
4. Diphthongs au, ei, and eu/äu
   - au as in *auch* (too) is pronounced like the ow in "wow"
   - ei as in *mein* (my) is pronounced like the English pronoun "I"
   - eu/äu as in *Leute* (people) or *Häuser* (houses) is pronounced like oi/oy in "boiling" or "toy"

ß or Double S

German children learn to call the letter ß *Buckel-S* (hunchback S) due to its shape, but the official term is *Esszett* or *scharfes S* (sharp S), due to its pronunciation. After the orthography reform in 1996, ß is substituted by double s if it follows a short vowel as in *dass* (that), *Fluss* (river), or *muss* (must). Most of the theological texts we are using in this book were written before the reform and therefore still use ß instead of double s.

However, you should be aware of the possible change when selecting texts for your own study.

Capitalized Nouns and Pronouns

All nouns in German start with a capitalized letter and are therefore easily recognized. In addition, German differentiates between a formal and an informal form when addressing someone. The formal address is always capitalized. This rule applies to the personal pronoun *Sie* (nominative and accusative; "you"), *Ihnen* (dative; "[to] you"), and the possessive pronoun *Ihr* (your) with its respective endings. It can refer to one or more people, depending on the context. In theological texts, we also find capitalized pronouns in the third-person singular *Er, Ihn, Ihm* (he, him) or the possessive pronoun *Sein* (his) with its respective endings when it is referring to God.

Frequent Abbreviations

In German texts you will encounter abbreviations that look different than their English equivalents and are therefore shown in the list below.

General abbreviations:

- *Anm.* → *Anmerkung* (explanatory note)
- *bspw.* → *beispielsweise* (for example)
- *bzw.* → *beziehungsweise* (translate as "respectively" or simply as "or")
- *ca.* → *circa* (translate as "approximately")
- *v. Chr.* → *vor Christus* (before Christ)
- *n. Chr.* → *nach Christus* (after Christ)
- *d.h.* → *das heißt* (literally "that means," equivalent to the abbreviation "i.e.," meaning "that is," used in English)
- *etc.* → *et cetera* (same as in English)
- *Jh.* → *Jahrhundert* (century)
- *Jhs.* → *Jahrhunderts* (century but in the genitive case)
- *Jt.* → *Jahrtausend* (millennium)
- *Jts.* → *Jahrtausends* (millennium but in the genitive case)
- *u. a.* → *unter anderem, unter anderen* (literally "among other or others"; translate as "i.a.")
- *usw.* → *und so weiter* (literally "and so on"; translate as "etc.")
- *z.B.* → *zum Beispiel* ("for example," equivalent to the abbreviation "e.g." used in English)
- *z.T.* → *zum Teil* (partly)

Abbreviations used when marking quotations:

- *et al.* → *et alii* (same as in English)
- *f.* → *folgend* (literally "following," used in references to indicate that the quote is taken from one more page following the referenced page)
- *ff.* → *fortfolgend* (literally "continuously following," used in references to indicate that the quote is taken from several pages following the referenced page)
- *vgl.* → *vergleiche* (literally "compare," used for references; translate as "see"; equivalent to the abbreviation "cf." in English)

After this short overview, we now come to the grammatical content needed to translate and understand theological German texts. As previously mentioned, we structured it according to our checklist. In this chapter we will discuss the first step on the checklist, which concerns verbs and all their features—tenses, passive and active voice, etc.

2.1 Step One: Find All the Verb Forms

The only fixed word in the German word order is the verb. In a main clause, it is always in the second position,[2] whereas in a subclause it is always in the last position.[3] Note that if the sentence forms a question, the verb is in the first position, like in English (see section 3.4 on word order).

When reading and translating complex German sentences, you should always start with the main clause!

As soon as you have found the verb, you will know the type of clause you are working with. To find the verb, you need to know the following:

1. Nouns are always capitalized in German.
2. Verbs are conjugated.
3. Verbs are often composed of two parts.

2.1.1 Verb Conjugation: Regular Verbs

For example, in the present tense (for use and function see section 2.2.1) the verb endings are as follows:

---

2. Note that the second position in a sentence is not the same as the second word in a sentence. We will discuss this further in chapter 3.

3. Note that this rule applies to finite verb forms only. Infinitives and participles are so-called infinite verb forms and their position in the sentence is determined by other factors. (See verbal bracket at the end of section 2.1.2.)

TABLE 1: Verb Conjugation: Present Tense Regular Verbs

Singular	Personal Pronoun	Verb gehen (to go)
First Person	ich	geh-e
Second Person	du	geh-st
Third Person	er/sie/es	geh-t
Plural		
First Person	wir	geh-en
Second Person	ihr	geh-t
Third Person	Sie[1]/sie	geh-en

[1] Note the formal address is capitalized in German. For more details go to the section on spelling at the beginning of this chapter.

1. If the stem[4] of the verb ends in a *t* or *d* like arbei*t*-en or an *m* or *n* after a consonant like at*m*-en, an *e* is added in the second person (singular and plural) to make it pronounceable:
   - du arbeit-e-st (you work), ihr arbeit-e-t (you [pl.] work)
   - du atm-e-st (you breathe), ihr atm-e-t (you [pl.] breathe)
2. If the stem of a verb ends in -s, -ß, -x, or -z like *sitzen* (to sit), the second-person singular is formed by adding a -t (instead of -st) and can be mistaken for the third-person singular as in:
   - du sitz-t (you sit), er/sie/es sitz-t (he/she/it sits)

The first- and third-person plural have the same ending (*-en*) as the infinitive. Therefore, it might be more difficult to distinguish the finite[5] from the infinite verb form, especially in a subordinate (sub) clause. Infinitive constructions will be discussed in chapter 3 (see section 3.1).

2.1.2 Verb Conjugation: Irregular Verbs

A notable number of verbs show a vowel change in the second- and third-person singular.

The conjugation of *haben* and *sein* should be memorized, due to their frequency and use as auxiliary verbs (see formation of tenses in section 2.2).

---

4. You get the stem of a verb by deleting *-en* from the infinitive →lesen
5. Finite verb forms are conjugated verb forms: they show different endings according to the person and the number (see tables above).

TABLE 2: Verb Conjugation: Present Tense Irregular Verbs

Singular	Personal Pronoun	Verb sehen (to see)
First Person	ich	seh-e
Second Person	du	sieh-st
Third Person	er/sie/es	sieh-t
Plural		
First Person	wir	seh-en
Second Person	ihr	seh-t
Third Person	Sie/sie	seh-en

Online dictionaries usually recognize the third person and provide the corresponding infinitive form.

Two very common irregular verbs in German are *haben* (to have) and *sein* (to be).

TABLE 3: Verb Conjugation: Present Tense *haben*

Singular	Personal Pronoun	Verb haben
First Person	ich	hab-e
Second Person	du	ha-st
Third Person	er/sie/es	ha-t
Plural		
First Person	wir	hab-en
Second Person	ihr	hab-t
Third Person	Sie/sie	hab-en

TABLE 4: Verb Conjugation: Present Tense *sein*

Singular	Personal Pronoun	Verb sein
First Person	ich	bin
Second Person	du	bist
Third Person	er/sie/es	ist
Plural		
First Person	wir	sind
Second Person	ihr	seid[1]
Third Person	Sie/sie	sind

[1]Note that *seit* is a temporal preposition as well as conjunction in German. Mnemonic: T for Time

---

Verbal Bracket

An important feature of the German word order is the so-called verbal bracket. As mentioned, the finite verb form takes the second position in the main clause. However, if the verb consists of two parts, the second part goes to the very end of the sentence.

- *Gott <u>hat</u> uns seinen Sohn <u>ausgesandt</u> (. . .).* (God has sent us his son.)

The verb has two parts in the following instances:

- Separable verbs
- Modal verbs
- All tenses except past tense[*]
- Passive
- *Würden*-subjunctive.

---

[*] Following *Martin Durell Hammer's German Grammar and Usage*, the term past tense is preferred to imperfect tense.

2.1.3 Separable Verbs

In German, the meaning of a verb can be altered by separable or inseparable prefixes: for example, *lesen* (to read) and *vorlesen* (to read to somebody). It is comparable to phrasal verbs ("to bring about") in English as many of the separable prefixes look like prepositions and often have the same meanings.

> Note that in a subordinate clause (see section 3.2) the first and second part of the verb are at the end of the clause. If the verb is a separable verb, the prefix is not separated (see *anlegt* in the example below).

In a sentence, the separable prefix goes to the end, as with the verb *anweisen* (to instruct) in *Sie <u>weisen</u> wohl <u>an</u>.* (They seem to[6] instruct.) It is therefore essential to look at a sentence as a whole and take a close look at the last position of the sentence.

In comparison, a sentence with an inseparable verb like *befehlen* (to command) looks as follows: *Er befiehlt allein.* (He alone commands.)

> Ebenso hilft es der Seele nichts, wenn der Leib heilige Kleider <u>anlegt</u>.
> Likewise, it does not help the soul, if the body dons holy clothing.

---

6. The German modal particle *wohl* is best translated as seem to + verb. For more detail on modal particles, see section 4.2.

There are a lot of separable prefixes, but a limited number of inseparable prefixes. To differentiate between separable and inseparable verbs, the easiest way is to memorize the following list of inseparable prefixes: *be-, emp-, er-, ent-, ge-, ver-, and zer-*.

While translating German texts, it is helpful to remember variable prefixes and to check with the dictionary if there is more than one meaning to the verb in question.

The most common separable prefixes look like prepositions (*ab-, an-, auf-, aus-, mit-, nach-, vor-, zu-*) but can, in their separated state, be recognized by their position in the sentence (namely, the last position). Other separable prefixes are *los-, heim-, zurück-, weg-, ein-*, and *her-*.

A few prefixes can be either separable or inseparable, depending on the meaning of the verb. The most striking example is *um-* as in *umfahren*.

Er umfährt das Schild.	He bypasses the sign.
Er fährt das Schild um.	He runs the sign down.

The most common variable prefixes are *durch-, über-, unter-, wider-*, and *wieder-*.[7] Any reliable dictionary marks if the prefix is separable. For example: um|fahren vs. umfahren

2.1.4 Modal Verbs

As mentioned above, the modal verbs form a verbal bracket as well, because they are always used in combination with a full verb in the infinitive form.

> *Denn kein anderes Werk kann einen Christen machen.*
> Because no other work can make a Christian.

Kann is the modal verb, and therefore the infinitive form of the second verb (*machen*) goes to the end of the sentence. So, every time you encounter a modal verb, look for the infinitive form that goes with it at the end of the sentence.

The modal verb *können* corresponds to the English "can" in the sense of "to be able to."

> *dass keine äußerliche Sache ihn frei und rechtschaffen machen kann.*
> that no external thing can make him free and righteous.

In this example, the modal verb is at the end of the sentence because it is in a subclause. But depending on the context, it can also mean "to know" as in *Er kann Englisch* (he knows English) or can express a possibility as in *Das kann sein* (that may be).

---

7. Note the change in meaning that is only marked by the different spelling (wieder = again; wider = against).

The modal verb *müssen* matches the English "to have to" or "must."

> *Es muss allemal noch etwas anderes sein.*
> It has to be something else.

The modal verb *dürfen* translates to the English "to be allowed to" or "may." Negated, it corresponds to the English "must not."

> *Hier darf er nicht müßig bleiben.*
> Here, he must not stay idle.

The modal verb *wollen* is used like the English "to want to." Its polite equivalent is *möchten* (see below).

> *Willst du alle Gebote erfüllen?*
> Do you want to fulfill all the commandments?

In this example the modal verb is in the first position of the sentence because it is a question.

The modal verb *sollen* corresponds best to the English "to be supposed to." The use of *sollen* implies the notion of a third party imposing an obligation.

> *Man soll die Werke eines Christenmenschen nicht anders ansehen.*
> You are not supposed to consider the works of a Christian any differently.

The verbs *können*, *müssen*, *dürfen*, and *wollen* change their vowel in the singular.

TABLE 5: Verb Conjugation: Present Tense Modal Verbs

Singular	Personal Pronoun	können	müssen	dürfen	wollen	sollen
First Person	ich	kann	muss[1]	darf	will	soll
Second Person	du	kannst	musst	darfst	willst	sollst
Third Person	er/sie/es	kann	muss	darf	will	soll
Plural						
First Person	wir	können	müssen	dürfen	wollen	sollen
Second Person	ihr	könnt	müsst	dürft	wollt	sollt
Third Person	Sie/sie	können	müssen	dürfen	wollen	sollen

[1]Note the alternative spelling *muß*, which can be found in texts published before the orthography reform in 1996. For more detail on spelling and pronunciation, refer to the beginning of the chapter.

Mögen means "to like" but is only used with nouns as a complement as in *er mag Theologie* (he likes theology); in modern German, it is not used as a modal verb, but it can be found in older German texts and should then be translated as "may."

However, its *Konjunktiv II*[8] form *möchten* is used frequently as a modal verb to express a polite request. Because of its frequency, grammar books for learners of German usually list *möchten* as one of the modal verbs, although it is originally a form of the full verb *mögen*.

TABLE 6: Verb Conjugation: Present Tense *möchten*

Singular	Personal Pronoun	Verb möchten (to want)
First Person	ich	möchte
Second Person	du	möchtest
Third Person	er/sie/es	möchte
Plural		
First Person	wir	möchten
Second Person	ihr	möchtet
Third Person	Sie/sie	möchten

2.1.5 Imperative Form

The imperative form is used for commands, suggestions, and for giving advice.

Lies Luthers Text!
Read Luther's text! (addressing one person)

Lest Luthers Text!
Read Luther's text! (addressing more than one person)

Lesen Sie Luthers Text!
Read Luther's text! (addressing one or more than one person formally)

It is easily recognizable because of three characteristics: first, its position, namely, the first position, as in questions; second, the personal pronoun is missing unless the formal form is used (see last example above); and, finally, the sentence usually ends with an exclamation mark. There are three different forms depending on the person

---

8. German for subjunctive, for details see section 2.2.5.

addressed, but the English translation is the same for all three of them (see examples above). The second-person singular is formed by deleting the ending -(s)t from the present tense form (*du liest – Lies!*); the second-person plural is formed by using the present tense form without personal pronoun (ihr lest – Lest!); and the formal version is formed by simply changing the word order and adding an exclamation mark (*Sie lesen – Lesen Sie!*).

2.2 Tenses

This section gives an overview of the use and formation of German tenses. It is meant to enable you to recognize the different tenses and to be able to translate them correctly. You will notice that the formation of tenses in English and German is very similar. For all verb forms that are built by using two parts (auxiliary verb + participle or infinitive), the aforementioned verbal bracket applies. That means in main clauses the finite verb form is in the second position, while the infinite verb form (participle or infinitive) goes to the very end of the sentence.

2.2.1 Present Tense

In German the present tense is used like the present tense (simple or progressive[9]) in English to express events or actions that happen in the present or are habitual. It is also used for actions or events that are timeless. For the conjugation of the present tenses, please refer to the beginning of this chapter (see section 2.1.1 and 2.1.2). When translating German texts, you need to decide if the verb expresses a simple present or present progressive meaning and translate accordingly.

2.2.2 The Past and Perfect Tenses

German, like English, has a past, perfect, and pluperfect tense. The formation of the perfect and pluperfect tense is similar to English. However, the use of past and perfect tense differs. In German past and perfect tense convey the same meaning but are used in different contexts. Present perfect is mainly used in spoken German, while the past tense is used in written German. Both describe an action or event in the past. The pluperfect is mainly used with the conjunction *nachdem* to describe an action or event that happened before another action or event in the past. It expresses anteriority.

> *Nachdem er drei Jahre in Mainz gelebt hatte, verließ er Mainz.*
> After he had lived in Mainz for three years, he left Mainz.

---

9. German has no equivalent to the English progressive form with "-ing."

As in English, German irregular verbs change their stem in the past tense and the participle II[10] that is used to form present perfect, pluperfect, and passive verb forms. For example:

gehen–g**i**ng–geg**a**ngen (go–went–gone)
denken–d**ach**te–ged**ach**t (think–thought–thought)

It is useful to learn the stem forms of the most common verbs (see list in the appendix). It is essential to recognize the participle II (past participle) of a verb to be able to identify the tense. For regular verbs, you need to know the following:

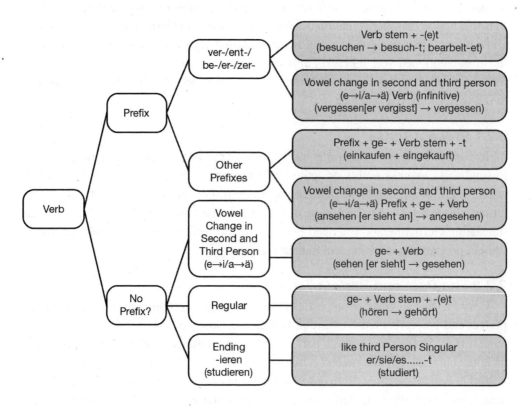

The chart above shows how the different verb types mentioned in paragraph 2.1 form the participle II. It is meant to give you an overview of the types of participle II formation. If you come across a verb form with a *ge-* at the beginning or in between a prefix and the stem, it is most likely a participle II. However, verbs ending in *-ieren*

---

10. Participle I is the present tense participle as in *lernend* (learning) that is used as an adjective; for more information, see section 4.2.

look the same in the third-person singular and in the participle II, but both forms can be distinguished by their position in the sentence:

> Er **studiert** Theologie in Mainz.
> He studies theology in Mainz.

> Er <u>hat</u> drei Jahre Theologie in Mainz **studiert**.
> He studied theology in Mainz for three years.

The position of a verb form is an important indicator of its tense.

Formation of the Past Tense

Regular verbs add the endings *-te, -test, -te, -ten, -tet, -ten* (listed in order of the person; see table below) to their stem to form the past tense. So as soon as a verb has an additional *-t* at its ending, you are most likely dealing with the past tense. Note that in the past tense, the first- and third-person singular look the same as in the present tense; the first- and third-person plural look alike, as well.

TABLE 7: Verb Conjugation: Past Tense Regular Verbs

Singular	Personal Pronoun	Verb lachen (to laugh)
First Person	ich	lach-te
Second Person	du	lach-test
Third Person	er/sie/es	lach-te
Plural		
First Person	wir	lach-ten
Second Person	ihr	lach-tet
Third Person	Sie/sie	lach-ten

> daß sie sich das Wort und Christus gut <u>einprägten</u> und diesen Glauben ständig <u>übten</u> und <u>stärkten</u>
> <u>that they memorized the word and Christ well and constantly practiced and strengthened this faith</u>

The past tense of *haben* and *sein* is as irregular as the present tense and should be memorized, as well. These verbs occur frequently and are used as auxiliary verbs to form other tenses.

TABLE 8: Verb Conjugation: Past Tense *sein* and *haben*

Singular	Personal Pronoun	Verb sein (to be)	Verb haben (to have)
First Person	ich	war	hatte
Second Person	du	warst	hattest
Third Person	er/sie/es	war	hatte
Plural			
First Person	wir	waren	hatten
Second Person	ihr	wart	hattet
Third Person	Sie/sie	waren	hatten

The past tense of the modal verbs is presented below. *Können, müssen,* and *dürfen* form the past tense without *Umlaut* (here: ö and ü; for more information, see the section on pronunciation at the beginning of the chapter), whereas *wollen* shows no vowel change. *Möchten* has no past tense due to it being derived from *mögen* (see section 2.1.4). Instead we use *wollen* to express a wish or desire in the past tense. The past tense of *mögen* is *ich mochte, du mochtest,* etc. and is only used as a full verb as in *er mochte Luthers Schriften* (he liked Luther's texts).

TABLE 9: Verb Conjugation: Past Tense Modal Verbs

Singular	Personal Pronoun	können	müssen	dürfen	wollen	sollen
First Person	ich	konnte	musste	durfte	wollte	sollte
Second Person	du	konntest	musstest	durftest	wolltest	solltest
Third Person	er/sie/es	konnte	musste	durfte	wollte	sollte
Plural						
First Person	wir	konnten	mussten	durften	wollten	sollten
Second Person	ihr	konntet	musstet	durftet	wolltet	solltet
Third Person	Sie/sie	konnten	mussten	durften	wollten	sollten

Formation of Present Perfect

The present perfect is formed with the present tense forms of the auxiliary verbs *haben* or *sein* (see section 2.1.2) depending on the verb and the participle II of the full verb.

> *Er <u>hat</u> ihnen <u>gegeben</u>, dass . . .*
> He has given them that . . .

Verbs of movement, verbs expressing a change of state,[11] and a few exceptions take *sein*, while all other verbs take *haben*.

Exceptions that take *sein*: *bleiben* (stay), *werden* (become), *sein* (be), *gelingen* (succeed), *geschehen* (happen), *passieren* (happen).

In order to understand and translate German texts, you have to be aware of this: one type of passive is also formed with *sein* + participle II (for more detail see section 2.2.3), and it is difficult to differentiate between these two structures.

The Verb Werden

Werden can be used as a full verb meaning "to become."

> *auf daß ich nicht selbst verwerflich werde*
> so that I don't become condemnable myself

However, it is mostly used as an auxiliary verb to form the future tense and the passive. In the perfect and pluperfect, it takes *sein* as an auxiliary verb. The participle II of werden is *worden* if it is used as an auxiliary verb. The full verb *werden* uses *geworden* as participle II, as in *Er ist alt geworden* (He has become old).

If *werden* occurs with an infinitive (= future tense) or a participle II (= passive), it does not mean "to become."

Formation of the Pluperfect

The pluperfect is formed similar to the present tense but with the past tense form of the auxiliary verbs *haben* or *sein* (see above).

> *Nachdem er Luther gelesen hatte, verstand er seine Bedeutung für die Theologie.*
> After he had read Luther, he understood his meaning for theology.

Future Tense or Future I

Unlike English, German has only one type of future tense, and it is usually only used if the context does not already convey a future time. Future meaning is rather expressed with temporal adverbs like *morgen* (tomorrow) or time specifications like *nächste Woche* (next week) or *am 23. April* (on April 23).

It is formed with the present tense of the auxiliary verb *werden* (see table below) and the infinitive of a full verb.

---

11. For example, the change from being asleep to being awake; thus the verb *aufwachen* "to wake up," takes *sein*.

TABLE 10: Verb Conjugation: *werden*

Singular	Personal Pronoun	Verb werden (here: will)
First Person	ich	werde
Second Person	du	wirst
Third Person	er/sie/es	wird
Plural		
First Person	wir	werden
Second Person	ihr	werdet
Third Person	Sie/sie	werden

Gott <u>wird</u> auf der Erde ein kurzes Fazit <u>ziehen</u>.
God will draw a short conclusion on earth.

Future Perfect or Future II

The future perfect is similar to the pluperfect because it describes an event that happens before another event, but in this case it is another event or action that will happen in the future. It is not used often, but that makes it even harder to recognize. It is formed by the present tense of *werden* + participle II + infinitive of *haben* or *sein* as in *er wird gelesen haben* (he will have read) or *er wird gelaufen sein* (he will have run).

Ich frage mich, ob er Luther <u>gelesen haben wird</u>.[12]
I wonder if he will have read Luther.

2.2.3 Passive

The passive verb form is used to emphasize the action of an event. The person or thing responsible for the action is either not important or unknown, and it is therefore not mentioned. Passive is not a tense and can be used in all tenses, even in the subjunctive (see section 2.2.5).

German has two types of passive. The first type is called *werden*-passive, due to its formation or *Vorgangspassiv* due to it expressing a process (*Vorgang*). Correspondingly, the second type is called the *sein*-passive or the *Zustandspassiv* (*Zustand* "state of being").

---

12. Verb parts here in the word order of a subclause.

The *werden*-passive is formed with the present tense of *werden* and the participle II of a full verb.

> *Nach der Seele <u>wird</u> er ein geistlicher, neuer, innerlicher Mensch <u>genannt</u>.*
> According to the soul, he is called a spiritual, new, inward person.

Using the appropriate tense of *werden* forms the different tenses.

Past Tense:

> *Nach der Seele <u>wurde</u> er ein geistlicher, neuer, innerlicher Mensch <u>genannt</u>.*
> According to the soul, he was called a spiritual, new, inward person.

Perfect Tense:

> *Nach der Seele <u>ist</u> er ein geistlicher, neuer, innerlicher Mensch <u>genannt worden</u>.*
> According to the soul, he has been called a spiritual, new, inward person.

Pluperfect:

> *Nach der Seele <u>war</u> er ein geistlicher, neuer, innerlicher Mensch <u>genannt worden</u>.*
> According to the soul, he had been called a spiritual, new, inward person.

Future Tense:

> *Nach der Seele <u>wird</u> er ein geistlicher, neuer, innerlicher Mensch <u>genannt werden</u>.*
> According to the soul, he will be called a spiritual, new, inward person.

Future Perfect:

> *Nach der Seele wird er ein geistlicher, neuer, innerlicher Mensch <u>genannt worden sein</u>.*
> According to the soul, he will have been called a spiritual, new, inward person.

Passive is usually used to avoid mentioning the person or thing performing an action but, if necessary, the person or thing can be added by using *von* (mainly for persons) or *durch* (mainly for things).

> *Die deutsche Theologie <u>wurde von</u> Luther <u>geprägt</u>.*
> German theology was shaped by Luther.

The *sein*-passive is formed with the present tense of *sein* and the participle II of a full verb. *Sein* is used for all verbs, unlike with the perfect and pluperfect tenses where it is only used for verbs of movement and a few exceptions.

> *Ohne das Wort Gottes <u>ist</u> ihr mit keinem Ding <u>geholfen.</u>*
> Without God's word she is not being helped by anything.

It can be used in other tenses as well by changing the tense of *sein*, but it is mostly used in the present or the past tense.

> *Ohne das Wort Gottes <u>war</u> ihr mit keinem Ding <u>geholfen</u>.*
> Without God's word she was not being helped by anything.

2.2.4 Passive-Like Constructions

Apart from the *werden-* and *sein*-passive, German has other constructions to convey passive meaning. By using these active voice constructions, an overload of passive sentences is avoided. Here, we will only discuss constructions that can be found in theological texts.

1. The impersonal pronoun *man* is used to express passive meaning. *Dass <u>man</u> von Herzen glaubt* (That one believes from one's heart)
2. An infinitive construction in the form of *sein + zu +* infinitive is called a modal infinitive construction because it conveys possibility (like the modal verb *können*), obligation (like the modal verb *müssen*), or necessity (like the modal verb *sollen*). You have to choose a modal verb depending on the context when translating the construction and put it in the passive in English. *Diese zwei Sätze <u>sind</u> klar bei Sankt Paulus <u>zu finden</u>.* (These two sentences can clearly be found with Saint Paul.)
3. The use of the verb *(sich) lassen* with an infinitive expresses passive meaning and has to be translated as a passive in English:

   > *und <u>lässt</u> <u>dir</u> durch sein lebendiges, tröstliches Wort <u>sagen</u>*
   > and lets you be told by his lively, comforting word

4. Adjectives ending in *-bar* (-able/-ible) as in *lesbar* (readable) also express passive meaning and can be translated either by the equivalent adjective or by using the modal verb "can." The negation of the adjective is achieved with the prefix *un-*.

   > *So sind auch alle andern Gebote für uns <u>unerfüllbar</u>.*
   > Therefore, all other commandments cannot be fulfilled by us either.

2.2.5 Subjunctive (Konjunktiv I + II)

German subjunctive types are divided into two types according to their function and called *Konjunktiv I* and *Konjunktiv II*. *Konjunktiv I* is used for indirect speech whereas *Konjunktiv II* expresses an unreal condition or a possibility.

Konjunktiv I

This type is formed by adding the following endings to the stem of the verb.

TABLE 11: Verb Conjugation: *Konjunktiv I*

Singular	Personal Pronoun	geben (to give)
First Person	ich	geb-e
Second Person	du	geb-est
Third Person	er/sie/es	geb-e
Plural		
First Person	wir	geb-en
Second Person	ihr	geb-et
Third Person	Sie/sie	geb-en

The endings of the first-person singular and the first- and third-person singular look the same as the indicative present tense endings. In these cases, *Konjunktiv II* forms are used instead.

> Verbs in *Konjunktiv I* simply indicate indirect speech and should be translated as indicative in English.

TABLE 12: Verb Conjugation: *Konjunktiv I* Modal Verbs

Singular	Personal Pronoun	können	müssen	dürfen	wollen	sollen
First Person	ich	könne	müsse	dürfe	wolle	solle
Second Person	du	*könnest*	*müssest*	*dürfest*	*wollest*	*sollest*
Third Person	er/sie/es	könne	müsse	dürfe	wolle	solle
Plural						
First Person	wir	können	müssen	dürfen	wollen	sollen
Second Person	ihr	*könnet*	*müsset*	*dürfet*	*wollet*	*sollet*
Third Person	Sie/sie	können	müssen	dürfen	wollen	sollen

The same applies to the modal verbs; the marked forms in the table below are obsolete but may be found in theological texts.

The *Konjunktiv I* of the verb *sein* is irregular and is used frequently. The forms of *haben* and *werden* are used to build other *Konjunktiv I* tenses (see below).

TABLE 13: Verb Conjugation: *Konjunktiv I* of Auxiliary Verbs

Singular	Personal Pronoun	sein (to be)	haben (to have)	werden (will)
First Person	ich	sei	habe	werde
Second Person	du	seist	habest	werdest
Third Person	er/sie/es	sei	habe	werde
Plural				
First Person	wir	seien	haben	werden
Second Person	ihr	sei(e)t	habet	werdet
Third Person	Sie/sie	seien	haben	werden

Future Tense of Konjunktiv I

The future tense is formed with the *Konjunktiv I* form of the auxiliary verb *werden* and the infinitive of the full verb.

> *Er sagte, er <u>werde</u> Luther <u>lesen</u>.*
> He said, he would read Luther.

Past tense of Konjunktiv I

The past tense is formed by using the *Konjunktiv I* form of *haben* or *sein* and the participle II.

> *Er sagte, er <u>habe</u> Luther <u>gelesen</u>.*
> He said, he had read Luther.

Konjunktiv II

This type of *Konjunktiv* expresses unreal or hypothetical conditions and possibilities. It is used in *wenn*-sentences (if-clauses), only if they state a hypothetical condition or a wish. For regular verbs, the forms of the *Konjuntiv II* and of the past tense are identical, and therefore the so-called *würden*-subjunctive is used. *Würden* is the *Konjunktiv II* form of the auxiliary verb *werden*. Würden + infinitive form the *würden*-subjunctive, and it is translated with "would" in English.

> *Wenn er Deutsch <u>verstehen würde</u>, <u>würde</u> er Luther <u>lesen</u>.*
> If he understood German, he would read Luther.

Irregular and modal verbs build *Konjunktiv II* with *Umlaut* (*ä, ü, ö*) and the past tense conjugation. For *wollen* and *sollen*, *Konjunktiv II* and past tense forms are identical. The context will provide clues as to how to translate it.

> als <u>wollte</u> er sagen:
> as if he wanted to say:

Note that the modal verb *dürfen* used in the *Konjunktiv II* can express probability, and to convey this meaning, you need to add the adverbs "probably" or "surely" to your translation (see example below taken from Zwickel).

> *Seit dem 8. Jh. v. Chr. <u>dürften</u> die fremden Strömungen noch nachhaltiger gewesen sein.*
> Since the eighth century BC, the foreign trends would surely have been even more sustainable.

TABLE 14: Verb Conjugation: *Konjunktiv II* Modal Verbs

Singular	Personal Pronoun	können	müssen	dürfen
First Person	ich	könnte	müsste	dürfte
Second Person	du	könntest	müsstest	dürftest
Third Person	er/sie/es	könnte	müsste	dürfte
Plural				
First Person	wir	könnten	müssten	dürften
Second Person	ihr	könntet	müsstet	dürftet
Third Person	Sie/sie	könnten	müssten	dürften

> *wodurch er rechtschaffen werden könnte*
> whereby he could become righteous

TABLE 15: Verb Conjugation: *Konjunktiv II sein* and *haben*

Singular	Personal Pronoun	sein (to be)	haben (to have)
First Person	ich	wäre	hätte
Second Person	du	wärest	hättest
Third Person	er/sie/es	wäre	hätte
Plural			
First Person	wir	wären	hätten
Second Person	ihr	wäret	hättet
Third Person	Sie/sie	wären	hätten

So hätte keins von diesen Werken einen Wert und sie wären lauter Narrenwerk.

Therefore, none of these works would have any worth, and they would be purely fools work.

Past tense of Konjunktiv II

The past tense is formed by using the *Konjunktiv II* form of *haben* or *sein* and the participle II.

Er hätte Luther gelesen.
He would have read Luther.

Exercises

Underline all verb forms in the following paragraphs from Luther's *Von der Freiheit eines Christenmenschen*. Then identify the first and the second part of each verb. Doing so will help you determine its tense and to distinguish between passive and active or subjunctive and indicative forms. Fill in the table below with the missing information. In the second column, write the infinitive form of the verb. This step is important for identifying the tense and will help you find the correct translation.

If the verb form is an infinitive form, put "infinitive" in the column "person." The number of lines indicates the number of verb forms in the paragraph.

Example

Ich <u>bin</u> frei in allen Dingen und <u>habe</u> mich zu jedermanns Knecht <u>gemacht</u>.

Verb form	Infinitive	Verb type (irregular or regular)	Person	Tense	*Konjunktiv* or Indicative	Passive or Active
bin	sein	irregular	1.Pers. Sg.	Present tense	Indicative	Active
habe . . . gemacht	machen	regular	1.Pers. Sg	Perfect tense	Indicative	Active

 LEICHT

Paragraph 1

Und um dieses Unterschieds willen werden von ihm in der Schrift Dinge gesagt, die sich vollständig widersprechen wie das, was ich jetzt von der Freiheit und Dienstbarkeit gesagt habe.

Verb form	Infinitive	Verb type (irregular or regular)	Person	Tense	Subjunctive or Indicative	Passive or Active
witten	*witten*	*regular*	*3.pl.*			
werden gesagt	*sagen*	*"*	*3.pl.*	~~*Past Perfect*~~		
gesagt habe	*sagen*	*"*	*1.sg.*	*Perfect*		

find seduction in pg. 207

┤├ MITTEL

Paragraph 2

Hier beginnt nun der fröhliche Tausch und Streit: weil Christus Gott und Mensch ist, der noch nie gesündigt hat, und seine Rechtschaffenheit unüberwindlich, ewig und allmächtig ist, so müssen die Sünden in ihm verschlungen und ersäuft werden, wenn er die Sünden der gläubigen Seele durch ihren Brautring, d. h. den Glauben, sich selbst zu eigen macht und so handelt, wie er gehandelt hat.

Verb form	Infinitive	Verb type (irregular or regular)	Person	Tense	Subjunctive or Indicative	Passive or Active
beginnt	*beginnen*	*irregular*	*3.sg.*	*Pres. Tens*	*ind.*	*a.*
ist	*sein*	*irregular*	*3.sg.*	*"*	*"*	*a.*
gesündigt hat	*gesündigt sündig*	*regular*	*3.sg.*	*Pres. Perf*	*"*	*a.*
ist	*sein*	*irregular*	*3.sg.*	*Pres. Tens*	*"*	*a*
müssen verschlungen	*verschlingen*	*irregular*	*3.pl*	*"*	*"*	*pass.*
ersäuft	*ersäufen*	*irregular*	*3.pl*	*"*	*"*	*pass.*
macht	*machen*	*regular*	*3.sg.*	*"*		*act*
handelt	*handeln*	*regular*	*3.sg.*	*"*	*"*	*act.*
hat gehandelt	*handeln*	*regular*	*3.sg.*	*Pres Perf.*	*"*	*act.*

┤├ SCHWER

Paragraph 3

Aber damit er nicht müßig ginge, gab ihm Gott etwas zu schaffen, das Paradies zu bepflanzen, zu bebauen und zu bewahren. Und dies wären lauter freie Werke gewesen, *die sonst nichts zuliebe getan worden wären als nur Gott zu Gefallen und nicht, um die Rechtschaffenheit zu erlangen, die er schon vorher besaß, und die auch uns allen von Natur angeboren gewesen wäre.*

Verb form	Infinitive	Verb type (irregular or regular)	Person	Tense	Subjunctive or Indicative	Passive or Active

vnd leer/vnd es war finster auff der tief-
fe/vnd der Geist Gottes schwebet auff
dem wasser.

Vnd Gott sprach/Es werde liecht/
...sahe das
liecht fur gut an/Da scheidet Gott das
...net...
liecht/Tag/vnd die finsternis/Nacht/
Da ward aus abend vnd morgen der

German Grammar: Sentence Structure and Case System 3

While the second chapter covered the first step on our "How to Translate Complex German Sentences" checklist, the third chapter covers the following steps:

2. Find all commas.
3. Find all conjunctions.
4. Mark the main clause.
5. Identify case and number of all nouns; establish noun phrases.

These steps will help you to figure out the sentence structure (main vs. subclause) and structure within the sentence. It is important to understand the relationship of the main clause to the subclauses before you start translating. It will help you to make assumptions about the content, which speeds up the process of translating. Establishing noun phrases is key to decoding the elements in the sentence.

3.1 Step Two: Find All Commas

In German, commas are important and mandatory. They mark subclauses, series, infinitive constructions with *zu* and *um . . . zu* as well as explanatory phrases and phrases in apposition. To complete step 2, you have to circle all commas in your sentence, as demonstrated below.

Um diese zwei sich widersprechenden Aussagen von der Freiheit und Dienstbarkeit zu verstehen, müssen wir bedenken, daß jeder Christenmensch zwiefacher Natur ist, einer geistlichen und einer leiblichen.

In this sentence, we have an infinitive construction with *um . . . zu*, a subclause introduced by the conjunction *dass* (here with the outdated spelling *daß*), and a phrase in apposition (*einer geistlichen und einer leiblichen*). Infinitive constructions can easily be identified by the *zu* + infinitive and should be translated with an infinitive with a "to" in English.

Er beginnt Luthers Texte <u>zu lesen</u>.
He begins to read Luther's texts.

If they occur with an *um* in the beginning as in the example above, the phrase should be translated with *in order to* + infinitive.

> *Um diese zwei sich widersprechenden*[1] *Aussagen von der Freiheit und der Dienstbarkeit zu verstehen*
>> In order to understand these two contradicting statements on freedom
>> and servitude

Explanatory phrases and phrases in apposition separated by a comma can be recognized by eliminating all other options. If the phrase separated by commas does not include a subclause introduced by a conjunction or an infinitive with *zu* construction, it is most likely an explanatory phrase or a phrase in apposition, as in *einer geistlichen und einer leiblichen* (a spiritual and a bodily) in the example at the beginning of this section. In these cases, the commas simply help to structure the sentence by separating a noun phrase from the rest of the sentence and are less meaningful than commas separating clauses. Note that explanatory phrases and phrases in apposition are often not separated by a comma and are therefore harder to identify.

> With separable verbs (see section 2.1.3), the *zu* is placed between the prefix and the stem as in *mitzunehmen* (*mitnehmen*: "to take with").

Although relative clauses are also easily recognized by finding the commas, they will be explained in greater detail in chapter 4 (see section 4.1.4), as they are introduced by relative pronouns. These pronouns are declined like nouns and other pronouns, which are also explained in chapter 4.

Exercise

 **LEICHT**

Find and mark all verb forms and commas.

> *Umgekehrt schadet es der Seele nichts, wenn der Leib unheilige Kleider trägt, sich an unheiligen Orten befindet, wenn er ißt und trinkt, nicht wallfahrtet und betet und all die Werke unterläßt, die die genannten Gleißner tun.*

> *Und wenn du das wirklich glaubst, wie du verpflichtet bist, so mußt du an dir selbst verzweifeln und bekennen, daß der Spruch Hoseas wahr sei.*

---

1. Participle I used as adjective, see section 4.2.

3.2 Step Three: Find All Conjunctions

The third step is necessary to differentiate between types of subclauses as well as subordinating and coordinating conjunctions. You will find an alphabetical list in the appendix. However, we recommend that you memorize the frequently used conjunctions to expedite your reading. Less frequently used conjunctions are marked with an asterisk (*).

3.2.1 Coordinating Conjunctions

Coordinating conjunctions connect clauses or phrases of the same kind. The following conjunctions are not separated by a comma:

> *und* (and), *sowie*[2] (and), *oder* (or), *sowohl . . . als auch* (as well as), *teils . . . teils** (partly . . . partly), *entweder . . . oder* (either . . . or), *weder . . . noch* (neither . . . nor)

Whereas the coordinating conjunctions listed here are separated by a comma:

> *aber* (but), *sondern* (but), *jedoch** (but), *denn* (because)

If there are several coordinating clauses or phrases, we have a so-called series. The coordinating conjunction is omitted until the last part of the series; all other parts are separated by a comma.

> *Nach dem Fleisch und Blut wird er <u>ein leiblicher, alter</u> und <u>äußerlicher</u> Mensch genannt.*
> According to the flesh and the blood he is called a bodily, old, <u>and</u> external person.

3.2.2 Subordinating Conjunctions

As already mentioned, subordinating conjunctions introduce a subclause, which is always separated by comma (as in the example below) and has the finite verb (verb part 1, see verbal bracket in section 2.1) in the last position.

> *Das ist noch viel mehr als König sein, <u>weil</u> das Priestertum uns würdig macht, vor Gott zu treten und für andere zu bitten.*
> This is much more than being a king, <u>because</u> the priesthood makes us worthy of coming before God and interceding for others.

The conjunction *während* has two different meanings, depending on context. It is either used in a temporal sense, meaning "while" or in an adversative sense, meaning "whereas."

---

2. The word *sowie* can also be used as a subordinating conjunction with a temporal meaning (as soon as).

Temporal conjunctions

als (when), *bevor* (before), *ehe** (before), *nachdem* (after), *seit(dem)* (since), *sobald/ sowie* (as soon as), *solange* (as long as), *sooft* (as often as, whenever)

Causal conjunctions

weil (because), *da* (because, since, as), *zumal** (especially as)

Final conjunctions (clauses of purpose)

damit[3] (so that), *auf dass** (so that)

Consecutive conjunctions (clauses of result)

so dass[4] (so that), *derart dass** (so that)

Concessive Conjunctions

obwohl (though, although), *obgleich* (though, although), *obschon/wenngleich/wiewohl/ obzwar** (though, although)

The combination *zwar . . . , aber* relates a concessive meaning, as well (see example below):

> *Jede Erzählung ist <u>zwar</u> faktual auf das Passafest bezogen, <u>aber</u> zugleich zeigt sie einen theologischen Gestaltungswillen.*[5]

Although each narration factually relates to the Passover, it also shows a theologically creative drive at the same time.

Comparative Clauses

Als and *wie* introduce comparative clauses or phrases. A clause <u>must</u> be marked by a comma, whereas a phrase <u>may</u> be marked by a comma. A clause is characterized by containing a subject and a verb. *Als* and *wie* can both be translated as "like" or "as." *Als* is also used for comparison with adjectives, as in *er ist größer als du* (he is taller than you), and should be translated with "than" in this context. The example below contains a *wie*-subclause followed by an *als*-clause, but here the *als* is the temporal conjunction meaning "when" (see above).

> *Denn kein anderes Werk kann einen Christen machen, wie Christus zu den Juden sagt, als sie ihn fragten, was sie für Werke tun sollten* (indirect question), *um göttliche und christliche Werke zu tun* (um . . . zu + infinitive construction).

---

3. Do not mistake it for the *da*-compound with the preposition *mit* ("with").

4. Sometimes the *so* occurs in the main clause before the *dass*-sentence.

5. Example from Ruben Zimmermann, "Fiktion des Faktischen: wie der historische und der erinnerte Jesus zusammengehören," *Zeitzeichen* 16 (2015): 17–19.

Because no other work can make a Christian, as Christ says to the Jews when they asked him what kind of works they should do in order to do godly and Christian works.

Conditional Sentences

Wenn (if) is used to introduce conditional sentences. In German, subclauses and main clauses are either in the indicative or both are in *Konjunktiv II* (see section 2.2.5). The latter expresses a remote or unreal condition.

> *Ebenso hilft es der Seele nichts, <u>wenn</u> der Leib heilige Kleider anlegt.*
> Similarly, it helps the soul nothing, if the body puts on holy clothing.

> *So wäre (Konjunktiv II) es wohl, <u>wenn</u> du nur ein innerlicher Mensch und ganz geistlich und innerlich geworden wärest.*
> It would be like this if you had become only an inner man and had become completely spiritual and internal.

But the conjunction *wenn* can be omitted, as in the example below.

> *<u>Willst du</u> etwas stiften, beten oder fasten, so tu es nicht in der Absicht, dir damit etwas Gutes anzutun.*
> If you want to give something to charity, pray or fast, do not do it with the intent to do something good with it for yourself.

The conditional meaning is conveyed by placing the verb in the first position, as if you were posing a question, and it is often followed by a *so* or a *dann* in the main clause. In this construction, the conditional sentence must come before the main clause.

Another less frequent conjunction, which introduces conditional sentences is *sofern*, which should be translated as "if" as well.

Complement Sentences

A clause introduced by the conjunction *dass* (that) is called a complement sentence. Complements are elements ruled by the so-called verb valency, a complex concept that will be explained in detail in section 3.6.4. In short: the verb requires certain elements to be complete. These elements can either be words, noun phrases, or complement sentences introduced by *dass*. Verb valency determines the grammatical case of the complement and thereby its function in a sentence. A *dass*-sentence can therefore have the role of a subject, a direct object, etc. In the example below, *dass* marks the object clause of the verb *lesen*.

So <u>lesen</u> wir auch im Psalter, <u>daß</u> der Prophet nach nichts so sehr schreit wie nach Gottes Wort.

Therefore, we read as well in the Psalter that the prophet cries for nothing as much as for God's word.

Note that the *dass* can be omitted with verbs introducing indirect speech and with verbs or other expressions of perceiving, feeling, hoping, and believing.

Er sagte, er habe in Mainz studiert.
He said that he had studied in Mainz.

Er denkt, Mainz ist eine schöne Stadt.
He thinks that Mainz is a beautiful city.

Due to the position of the verb in these types of clauses, sentences look like a main clause, but should be translated with a that-sentence.

Indirect questions

Indirect questions are introduced either by *ob* (if, whether) or by an interrogative pronoun (see 4.1.3). The word order is the same as in any subclause (the verb is in the last position).

Less Frequently Used Conjunctions

Indem[6] and *dadurch dass* convey an instrumental meaning and should be translated with a construction of "by" and "-ing."

Er übt Deutsch, indem er theologische Texte übersetzt.
He practices German by translating theological texts.

The two-part conjunction *je* + comparative form . . . *desto* + comparative form is used for comparative sentences but is less frequent. It should be translated as demonstrated in the example below.

<u>Je länger</u> er in Mainz studiert, <u>desto besser</u> gefällt ihm die Stadt.
The longer he studies in Mainz, the better he likes the city.

---

6. You may also encounter sentences introduced by *in dem*, which is the preposition *in* with a relative pronoun in the dative case and therefore introduces a relative clause.

insofern (als) or *soweit* (in so far as/as far as)

insoweit (als) (inasmuch as)

soviel is mostly used in the phrase *soviel ich weiß* (as far as I know)

Exercise

Find and translate all conjunctions.

> *Umgekehrt schadet es der Seele nichts, wenn der Leib unheilige Kleider trägt, sich an unheiligen Orten befindet, wenn er ißt und trinkt, nicht wallfahrtet und betet und all die Werke unterläßt, die die genannten Gleißner tun.*

> *Und wenn du das wirklich glaubst, wie du verpflichtet bist, so mußt du an dir selbst verzweifeln und bekennen, daß der Spruch Hoseas wahr sei.*

3.3 Step Four: Mark the Main Clause

After you have completed steps 2 and 3, this step will be very easy to accomplish. You can identify the main clause through elimination. Whatever is not a subclause is the main clause.

> <u>*Das ist die christliche Freiheit, allein der Glaube*</u> (main clause), *der nicht bewirkt* (relative clause), *daß wir müßig gehen oder Böses tun können, sondern daß wir kein Werk nötig haben* (dass-sentence), *um das Gutsein und die Seligkeit zu erlangen* (infinitive with *um . . . zu* construction).
> This is the Christian freedom, the faith alone, which does not effectuate that we can go idle or do bad things but that we do not need any work in order to reach being good and blessedness.

If the clause starts with or is followed by an infinitive construction with *zu*, it should be considered part of the main clause. Another identifying feature of the main clause is the position of the verb (see section 2.1). It is always in the second position unless it is part of a subclause, in which case it is always in the final position. We will talk about word order in more detail in the next paragraph. Later on, when you start translating, always begin with the main clause.

Before we start with step 5, a short introduction to German word order and the German gender system is in order. It will help you to understand steps 5 and 6 on our checklist.

Exercise

 **MITTEL**

Mark the main clause:

Umgekehrt schadet es der Seele nichts, wenn der Leib unheilige Kleider trägt, sich an unheiligen Orten befindet, wenn er ißt und trinkt, nicht wallfahrtet und betet und all die Werke unterläßt, die die genannten Gleißner tun.

Und wenn du das wirklich glaubst, wie du verpflichtet bist, so mußt du an dir selbst verzweifeln und bekennen, daß der Spruch Hoseas wahr sei.

3.4 German Word Order

In chapter 2 we already discussed one fundamental principle of German word order—the position of the verb, which is in the second position in the main clause and the last position in a subclause.[7] The position of the verb in a main clause also constitutes the so-called verbal bracket (see section 2.1). Next to the verb, the subject plays a very important role in a sentence, and it is always placed in front of or next to the verb in a main clause. The German sentence is divided into three "fields" according to the verbal bracket: the *Vorfeld*, the *Mittelfeld*, and the *Nachfeld*.

	Vorfeld	Bracket	*Mittelfeld*			
		Verb 1	Pronouns N A D	Subject	Dative Object	Most adverbials
Main Clause	Ich	habe				kurzweg
Main Clause	Er	hat	ihnen			
Main Clause	Umgekehrt	kann	man		Gott	
Question		Ist		das		nun
Question	Was	hilft	es		der Seele?	

---

7. Keep in mind that the second position in a sentence is not the same as the second word in a sentence.

The *Vorfeld* is located in front of the first part of the verbal bracket, the *Mittelfeld* lies in between the brackets, and the *Nachfeld* describes all elements after the second verbal bracket (here clarified by actual brackets [...]).

> *Da (Vorfeld) muß [der Leib in der Tat mit Fasten, Wachen, Arbeiten und mit jeder Art maßvoller Zucht (Mittelfeld)][8] angetrieben und geübt werden.* [*Nachfeld* would be everything after the second part of the verb and is often made up of infinitive with *zu* constructions.]

The most complex part is the *Mittelfeld*, and it is important to know its word order to be able to identify all elements in a sentence. Knowing the case system is insufficient because form syncretism has led to many ambiguities, as you will see in step 5. The following table shows the basic word order in main clauses, questions, and subclauses.

As we continue going down our checklist, we will refer back to this table when explaining how to recognize the above-mentioned elements in a sentence.

The order of the adverbials (see verb valency in section 3.6.4) can easily be memorized by the following rule: TE-KA-MO-LO

TE-temporal (when?)
KA-kausal (why?)
MO-modal (how?)
LO-lokal (where?)

Mittelfeld (cont.)			Bracket	Nachfeld	
Accusative Object	**Manner Adverbials**	**Complements**	**Verb 2**		
alles		auf den Glauben	gestellt		*Main Clause*
			gegeben		*Main Clause*
keine größere Schmach			antun		*Main Clause*
		nicht ein fröhlicher Hausstand?			*Question*
					Question

---

8. Verbal bracket: *muß* (verb part 1), *angetrieben und geübt werden* (verb part 2).

3.5 The German Gender System

A key structure of German grammar is the gender system, as all nouns bear a gender and all elements agreeing with a noun reflect its gender. Elements showing gender agreement include articles, adjectives, and all types of pronouns. German has three genders: masculine, feminine, and neuter. In general, the noun itself displays no gender markers; the gender becomes visible only through its agreeing elements.

The best and most commonly used gender indicator is the definite article in the nominative case as it is different for each gender (see examples below).

- *der Tisch* (the table, masculine)
- *die Tür* (the door, feminine)
- *das Haus* (the house, neuter)

Gender is only marked in the singular; there is no gender differentiation in the plural, meaning that there is no specific plural form used only for the masculine, feminine, or neuter nouns.

Be aware that sometimes the grammatical gender does not reflect the biological gender when referring to a person, as you can see in the following example:

- das Mädchen (girl)

It is neuter (therefore the article *das*) due to the suffix *-chen*, but it refers to a female person. Examples like this demonstrate that the gender assignment in German is governed by a set of morphological (mainly suffixes), phonological (regarding monosyllabic words), and semantic (biological gender, semantic noun clusters) rules, which sometimes contradict each other.

TABLE 16: Gender Assignment Rules

Morphologi-cal rules	Masculine	Feminine	Neuter
	-er, -or, -us, -ismus	-heit, -keit, -schaft, -tät, -ung, -sion, -tion, -in	-chen, -tum,
Phonological rules	most mono-syllabic nouns	nouns ending in -e (pronounced [ə] as in "enemy")	
Semantic rules	a male person (der Mann) professions (der Lehrer)	a female person (die Frau)	languages (das Deutsche) names of cities and continents (das Mainz, das Europa), umbrella terms (das Obst)

The following gender assignment rules have been selected because they can easily be remembered and cover a reasonable number of nouns.

In compound nouns, the gender of the last noun determines the gender of the whole compound noun. Note that the use and formation of compound nouns is very common in German and can lead to long and complex nouns, such as:

> *Billigungs- und Mißbilligungsvermögen*[9]
> Capability of approval and disapproval

Learning the genders of frequent words speeds up the process of reading and translating German texts because it helps the reader recognize the grammatical case, and with that the role of each noun in a sentence. Gender helps to keep track of references in complex sentences, especially pronouns. It has been argued that this function of gender is one of the main reasons why German still has a gender system, while English, with its fixed word order, has lost its gender system (except in relation to personal and possessive pronouns). As shown in the following example, German gender dissolves ambiguities:

> The jug fell into the bowl, but it did not break.

This sentence is ambiguous because it raises the question about which item did not break. In German, the gender of the pronoun clarifies the event.

> *Der Krug fiel in die Schale, aber **sie*** [referring to the feminine noun *Schale*] *zerbrach nicht.*
> *Der Krug fiel in die Schale, aber **er*** [referring to the masculine noun *Krug*] *zerbrach nicht.*

Another function of German gender is the so-called framing principle, which is useful in complex word groups:

> ***der** besonders an den Ergebnissen unserer Arbeitsgruppe interessierte **Minister***
> the Minister, who is especially interested in the result of our work group

The noun and its agreeing article frame the attributes and thereby state how they relate to each other. While reading and translating German texts, you should be aware of these principles, as they help you to untangle various syntactic relations and structures. Step 5 on our checklist aims at discovering precisely these syntactic relations.

---

9. Example taken from Mendelssohn's text in chapter 7.

3.6 Step Five: Identify Case and Number of All Nouns; Establish Noun Phrases

German has four cases (nominative, genitive, dative, and accusative),[10] which are marked in nouns and in their agreeing elements like articles, pronouns, and adjectives. In order to read and translate German texts, you will need to be aware of these cases. The following example demonstrates the importance of understanding these cases.

> *Der Hund beißt den Mann.* (The dog bites the man.)
> *Den Mann beißt der Hund.* (The dog bites the man.)

German word order allows every element in the sentence to be in the first position. Therefore, you need to know that *den Mann* is accusative and thereby is the direct object of the sentence in order to understand the meaning of the second sentence above. In complex sentences, the elements are often composed of more than one word, with the noun as the head of the phrase—so-called noun phrases. The noun phrase usually starts with a determiner and ends with the noun, except for genitive attributes, which follow the noun but are still considered part of the noun phrase. In the example below, the whole underlined part is the subject of the sentence connected by *und* as well as the corresponding case (nominative).

> *Damit ist dann <u>das ganze Verständnis der christlichen Gnade und Freiheit, des christlichen Glaubens und alles, was wir von Christus haben, und Christus selbst</u> aufgehoben.*

Under step 5, you will learn about the use and declension of determiners (articles and quantifiers), plural formation, and prepositions. With that knowledge you can then establish noun phrases and therefore the number of elements in the sentence. To complete this step, knowing the gender of the nouns in your sentence is essential. If you do not know the gender of a noun, you should look it up before continuing. We will also discuss verb valency and by that the function of complements, enabling you to identify the role of each element in a sentence.

---

10. We use the traditional case order as in Latin grammars. Current German grammars use the following order according to frequency of the cases in modern German: nominative, accusative, dative, genitive. But for our purposes, the traditional order is better suited. Theological texts do not display a decline in the dative and genitive, as modern German does.

3.6.1 The Declension and Use of Articles

The German definite article translates into English as "the" and is used when the noun has previously occurred in the text or is further specified by attributes. In the example below, *die* is used instead of *eine* because the relative clause defines the noun "freedom."

> *und wie es um <u>die</u> Freiheit stehe, <u>die ihm Christus erworben und gegeben hat</u>*
> and how about the freedom that Christ gained for him and gave to him

The table below shows the declension of the definite article. Please note that there is no gender in the plural (see 3.5), therefore the article displays no gender differentiation in the plural.

TABLE 17: Declension: The Definite Article

Case	Masculine	Feminine	Neuter	Plural
Nominative	der Tisch	die Tür	das Haus	die Tische
Genitive	des Tisches	der Tür	des Hauses	der Tische
Dative	dem Tisch	der Tür	dem Haus	den Tischen
Accusative	den Tisch	die Tür	das Haus	die Tische

Indefinite Article

The indefinite article translates into English as "a/an" and as such, no plural form exists. It is used when talking about something in general as in the example below:

> *Damit wir gründlich erkennen, was <u>ein</u> Christenmensch ist*
> So that we thoroughly recognize what a Christian is

TABLE 18: Declension: The Indefinite Article

Case	Masculine	Feminine	Neuter
Nominative	ein Tisch	eine Tür	ein Haus
Genitive	eines Tisches	einer Tür	eines Hauses
Dative	einem Tisch	einer Tür	einem Haus
Accusative	einen Tisch	eine Tür	ein Haus

Negative Indefinite Article

The negative indefinite article *kein/keine* is used to negate a noun, like the English "no," whereas the negation with *nicht* negates the whole sentence, like "not" in English.

Es ist dann offenbar, daß <u>keine</u> äußerliche Sache ihn frei oder rechtschaffen machen kann
It is then obvious that <u>no</u> external thing can make him free or righteous

Was hilft es der Seele, wenn der Leib <u>nicht</u> gefangen, frisch und gesund ist
What does it help the soul if the body is <u>not</u> caught, fresh and healthy

Kein/keine has a plural form, as is shown in the table below.

TABLE 19: Declension: Negative Indefinite Article

Case	Masculine	Feminine	Neuter	Plural
Nominative	kein Tisch	keine Tür	kein Haus	keine Häuser
Genitive	keines Tisches	keiner Tür	keines Hauses	keiner Häuser
Dative	keinem Tisch	keiner Tür	keinem Haus	keinen Häusern
Accusative	keinen Tisch	keine Tür	kein Haus	keine Häuser

Possessive Pronouns

Although the grammatical term is pronouns, they function as articles and are therefore often called *Possessivartikel* in German grammars. They carry the same endings as the negative indefinite articles. The basic forms of the possessives are as follows:

TABLE 20: Possessive Pronouns

Person	Basic Form
Singular	
First Person	mein
Second Person	dein
Third Person (masculine, feminine, neuter)	sein, ihr, sein
Plural	
First Person	unser
Second Person	euer
Third Person	ihr
Formal second Person (Sg. + Pl.)	Ihr

With the second-person plural *euer*, the second *e* gets dropped when the ending is added:

TABLE 21: Declension: Possessive Pronouns

Case	Masculine	Feminine	Neuter	Plural
Nominative	euer Tisch	eure Tür	euer Haus	eure Häuser
Genitive	eures Tisches	eurer Tür	eures Hauses	eurer Häuser
Dative	eurem Tisch	eurer Tür	eurem Haus	euren Häusern
Accusative	euren Tisch	eure Tür	euer Haus	eure Häuser

Note that the form of the third-person singular is determined by the grammatical (!) gender of the referent noun.

> *Der Tisch ist alt. Seine* [referring back to the masculine noun *Tisch*] *Farbe ist verblasst.*
> The desk is old. Its [lit., his] color has faded.

We will discuss this further when we talk about pronouns later in the chapter at checklist step 6.

Zero Article and Adjective Endings

If no article is used but the nominal phrase includes an adjective, the adjective carries the gender, number, and case information, as shown in the table below. This is called zero article declension or strong adjective declension.

TABLE 22: Adjective Endings with Zero Article

Case	Masculine	Feminine	Neuter	Plural
Nominative	schöner Tisch	schöne Tür	schönes Haus	schöne Tische
Genitive	schönen Tisches	schöner Tür	schönen Hauses	schöner Tische
Dative	schönem Tisch	schöner Tür	schönem Haus	schönen Tischen
Accusative	schönen Tisch	schöne Tür	schönes Haus	schöne Tische

If the noun phrase includes some kind of determiner (article, quantifier, numeral) indicating gender, case, and number, the adjective endings are less diverse. They end in "-en" except for in the nominative case (-e) and the feminine and neuter accusative singular (-e).

> If the adjective is used as a predicative for a copular verb (see section 3.6.4), it has no endings.
>
> *weil es wahr und recht ist*
> because it is true and just

für einen rechtschaffenen, wahrhaftigen Mann (accusative case)
for a righteous, truthful man

dem göttlichen Wort (dative case)
the godly word

In order to understand German texts, you only need to be aware of the adjective endings if the determiner does not indicate gender, case, or number. This holds true for the indefinite article (*ein*), the negative indefinite article (*kein*), and the possessive pronouns and is therefore frequent. The table below shows the declension for *kein*, but as mentioned before, *ein* and the possessive pronouns have the same endings, except that *ein* has no plural.

TABLE 23: Adjective Endings with Negative Indefinite Article

Case	Masculine	Feminine	Neuter	Plural
Nominative	kein neu**er** Tisch	keine neue Tür	kein neu**es** Haus	keine neuen Häuser
Genitive	keines neuen Tisches	keiner neuen Tür	keines neuen Hauses	keiner neuen Häuser
Dative	keinem neuen Tisch	keiner neuen Tür	keinem neuen Haus	keinen neuen Häuser
Accusative	keinen neuen Tisch	keine neue Tür	kein neu**es** Haus	keine neuen Häuser

You should at least memorize the endings marked in bold so you will be able to recognize gender, number, and case. For all other forms, being able to identify the form of the determiner is sufficient.

Quantifiers and Numerals

There are several quantifiers in German—most of them can be used as pronouns or determiners. This means they either stand alone (pronoun) or they are part of a noun phrase (determiner). If used as a determiner, most of them decline like the demonstrative pronoun *dieser* (see section 4.1.5). Depending on their meaning, some occur only in the singular or the plural. In order to understand German texts, you can look up their meaning, and if they are being used as a determiner, memorize the declension of *dieser* to recognize gender, number, and case. We have listed the most frequent quantifiers below:

- *beide* (both), *einige* (some, a few), *irgendwelcher* (some, some other), *jeder* (each, every), *viel* (many, much), *wenig* (few), *manche* (some)

- *irgendein(er)* (some) can be used as a determiner or a pronoun and refers only to singular nouns; when used as a determiner it declines like *ein*
- *alle* (all) when used without an article, as in *die Erfüllung aller Gebote* (the fulfillment of all commandments); it occurs especially frequently in the genitive *aller* in theological texts, as shown in the example above.

Ordinal numbers are formed by adding "-te" from 2–19 as in *zweite, dritte, vierte, fünfte,* and so on and "-ste" from 20 onward as in *zwanzigste* and take the same endings as adjectives (see above on zero article). The ordinal number for 1 is irregular and is called *erste*.

3.6.2 Plural Formation

While in English in most cases an "s" is added to form the plural, there are a number of possible plural endings in German. Plural formation is guided by a complex set of rules, and even these rules have exceptions—especially with frequent nouns. The best solution is to learn the plural ending for each noun. As we have already discussed (see section 3.5), the same applies to gender.

However, it is still useful to remember the following rules as they cover a large percentage of German nouns:

> Learn nouns with gender (e.g., the definite article der, die, das) and plural!

- Masculine and neuter nouns with the endings *-el, -en, -er* as in *der Esel* (donkey), or *das Rätsel* (riddle) have no endings and therefore look the same in the singular and the plural.
- Other masculine nouns add *-e* with Umlaut as *der Stuhl → die Stühle*
- Other neuter nouns add *-e* without Umlaut as in *das Jahr → die Jahre*
- Feminine nouns add *-(e)n* as in *die Aussage → die Aussagen*
- Many foreign words and all words ending in a vowel add *-s das Auto → die Autos*

When encountering a noun, check for an *Umlaut*[11] (often an indication of plural) and the article. The ending of the article can help you identify number. But be careful: *die* depicts either feminine gender or plural (all nouns) for the nominative and accusative cases. If the noun in question is the subject, the number of the verb will agree with the number of the subject. Therefore, the verb ending is a foolproof way to determine the number of the subject (see example below). So be sure to memorize verb endings (see 2.1).

> *daß <u>die</u> ganze heilige Schrift in zweierlei Worte <u>geteilt wird</u>*
> that the whole holy Scripture is being devided into two types of words

---

11. *Umlaut* means the letters Ö/ö, Ä/ä, and Ü/ü.

In this example, the verb is singular and therefore the subject has to be singular as well; *die* can only be nominative singular of the feminine gender.

3.6.3 Nominalizations

Adjectives and verbs can easily be turned into nouns by adding a determiner and capitalizing the initial letter.

Adjectives: The gender of a nominalized adjective depends on the meaning and is indicated by the article. If it refers to a male or female person, the appropriate article is added. If it refers to a general notion like abstract or collective ideas, a neuter determiner is added.

> *gut* → *das Gute*
> good → the good (things)
> *gut* → *der Gute*
> good → the good (male person)

Verbs: Verbs are used in the infinitive form and a neuter determiner is added. They typically translate into English with an "-ing" form and only occur in the singular.

> *lesen* → *das Lesen*
> read → the reading

Prepositions fused with the neuter definite article and used with nominalized verbs convey a specific meaning.

- *am* + nominalized verb expresses a continuous action and should be translated with a progressive form as in *Er ist am Lesen.* (He is reading.)
- *beim* + nominalized verb also conveys a progressive meaning and should be translated with "on" or "while" and an "-ing" form as in *Beim Lesen isst er einen Apfel.* (While reading he eats an apple.)
- *zum* + nominalized verb is used to convey a purpose and is best translated with "for" + an "-ing" form or an infinitive + "to" construction as in *Zum Lesen braucht er eine Brille.* (In order to read, he needs glasses.)

3.6.4 Verb Valency

In German the verb is basically the master of all other elements in the sentence. The verb determines the number of elements needed and their grammatical case. These elements are called complements because they complement the verb. In German, we call them *Ergänzungen*. Using a certain verb opens up slots that need to be filled in a sentence; the number of open slots make up the so-called valency of the verb. In the example below, the verb *aussenden* needs a subject and a direct object to form a grammatical sentence.

> *Er* [subject] *hat* [verb part 1] *sein Wort* [direct object, accusative case] *ausgesandt* [verb part 2, participle II].
> He has sent out his word.

There may be more elements in a sentence than demanded by the verb valency. They provide additional information and are called adverbials (*Angaben* in German). The word order of the adverbials has been explained at the beginning of this chapter (TE-KA-MO-LO). The difference between complements and adverbials is that a missing complement renders the sentence ungrammatical.

The first and largest group of verbs demands a subject (nominative case) and a direct object (accusative case). The subject agrees with the verb in number. If there are several nouns connected by *und*, *oder*, or other connectors, the verb is usually in plural, even if the individual nouns refer to singular entities.

> *Denn* <u>*alle diese genannten Dinge, Werke und Weisen*</u> [direct object] *können* [modal verb] *auch* <u>*ein böser Mensch, ein Gleißner und Heuchler*</u> [subject] *an sich* <u>*haben*</u> [verb] *und* <u>*ausüben*</u> [verb]
> because all these mentioned things, works, and manners can a bad person, a phony and a hypocrite have upon himself and carry out as well

The second most common group of verbs describes the action of someone (subject) giving in some form something (direct object) to someone or something (dative object, or indirect object). These verbs open up three slots that must be filled to make a grammatical sentence.

> <u>*was*</u> [direct object] *er* [subject] *mir*[12] [dative object] <u>*gebracht*</u> [participle of *bringen*] *und* <u>*gegeben*</u> [participle of *geben*] *hat*
> what he has brought and given me

The third significant group of verbs needs, next to the subject, a prepositional object in which the preposition is predetermined by the verb. These verbs are therefore called *verbs with prepositions*. Some verbs can be used with multiple prepositions, with each preposition conveying a different meaning. For example: *sich freuen auf* (to look forward to something) vs. *sich freuen über* (to be happy about something).

---

12. We will discuss pronouns and their declension in section 4.1.

We provide a list of verbs with prepositions in the appendix. In the example below, the verb is *auf jemanden vertrauen* (to trust in someone).

> *Du* [subject] *solltest* [. . .] *frisch <u>auf ihn</u>* [prepositional object] *vertrauen.*
> You should newly/freshly trust in him.

The next three groups of verbs are fewer in number but are nevertheless just as frequent.

1. Verbs with a subject and a locative complement like *fahren* (to drive) or *wohnen* (to live):

   > <u>*Der Student*</u> [subject] *wohnt <u>in Mainz</u>* [locative complement].
   > The student lives in Mainz.

2. Verbs with a subject and a dative object as a direct object like *helfen* (to help):

   > *Was hilft <u>es</u>* [subject] <u>*der Seele*</u> [direct object in dative, *Seele* is feminine]
   > what does it help the soul

3. Verbs with a subject and a predicate complement, also called copular verbs:
   The following copular verbs exist in German: *bleiben* (remain), *heißen* (to be called), *sein* (to be), *werden* (to become), and *scheinen* (to seem)
   Predicate complements are noun phrases or adjectives that describe the subject of the sentence.

   > <u>*Ein Christenmensch*</u> [subject] <u>*ist*</u> [verb to be] <u>*ein freier Herr*</u> [predicate complement].
   > A Christian is a free man.

   > *wenn <u>der Leib</u>* [subject] *nicht <u>gefangen, frisch und gesund</u>* [predicate complement] <u>*ist*</u> [verb to be]
   > if the body is not caught, fresh and healthy

A small group of verbs demands two objects in the accusative case to form a grammatical sentence: *kosten* (to cost), *lehren* (to teach), *abfragen/abhören* (to test somebody orally), *fragen* (to ask), and *bitten* (to beg/to ask)

> <u>*Der Tod*</u> [subject] *kostet <u>dich</u>* [accusative object] <u>*das Leben*</u> [accusative object].
> Death costs you your life.

Reflexive Verbs

Most reflexive verbs in German are used with a reflexive pronoun, and dictionaries list them like this: *sich anziehen* (to get dressed), *sich beschweren* (to complain), *sich bewerben für etwas* (to apply for something).

However, when translating the verbs into English, you usually drop the reflexive pronoun as the verb constructions are not equivalent in English and German.

> *auch nicht, wenn er <u>sich</u> mit heiligen Dingen <u>befaßt</u>* [verb: *sich befassen*]
> Not even, if he deals with holy things

It is important to properly identify reflexive verbs because in other contexts you have to translate the reflexive pronouns (see also section 4.1 on pronouns).

> *denn er bringt alle Seligkeit mit <u>sich</u>*
> because he brings all blessedness with him

> *die <u>sich</u> vollständig widersprechen*
> which contradict each other completely

Es as a Correlate

With a *dass*-clause as complement, the pronoun *es* is often used in the preceding main clause as a representative for the *dass*-clause (see examples below for subject and direct object). In English, it should be translated simply as "it."

Subclauses or Infinitive with zu Constructions as Complements

Complements can occur in the form of a subclause or an infinitive with *zu* construction (see section 3.2) but only as the subject, direct object (in the accusative case), or the prepositional object.

1. As a subject: infinitive with *zu* constructions or subclause with *dass* or with an interrogative (see section 4.1.3):

> <u>*Wer*</u> [interrogative] *nun nicht mit diesen Blinden in die Irre gehen will*
> [subject], <u>*muß auf mehr sehen als auf die Werke*</u>
> Who now does not want to go astray with these blind persons, has to look upon more than the works

In the second example, the pronoun *es* is used as a correlate (see box above):

> *Es* [subject] *ist dann offenbar, <u>daß keine äußerliche Sache ihn frei oder</u>*
> <u>*rechtschaffen machen kann*</u> [describes the previous *es*].
>   It is then obvious that no external thing can make him free or righteous.

If the *dass*-sentence is at the beginning of the complex sentence, the *es* will be omitted.

> <u>*Daß keine äußerliche Sache ihn frei oder rechtschaffen machen kann*</u>
> [subject]*, ist dann offenbar.*
>   That no external thing can make him free or righteous is then obvious.

2. As a direct object in the accusative case: infinitive with *zu* constructions or subclause with *dass* and *ob*[13] or with an interrogative.

> *So <u>lesen</u>* [verb] *<u>wir</u>* [subject] *auch im Psalter* [locative adverbial]*, <u>daß der</u>*
> <u>*Prophet nach nichts so sehr schreit wie nach Gottes Wort*</u> [direct object].
>   Thus we also read in the Psalter that the prophet cries for nothing as much as for the Word of God.

In the second example, the pronoun *es* is used as a correlate (see box above).

> *Wie ist das aber möglich, daß <u>es</u> der Glaube allein vermag, <u>rechtschaffen</u>*
> <u>*zu machen und ohne alle Werke so überschwenglichen Reichtum zu geben*</u>
> [specification of the direct object *es*]
>   But how is it possible that faith alone is able to make righteous and to give such exuberant riches without any works

3. As a prepositional object: subclause with *dass*, *ob*, or an interrogative and infinitive with *zu* construction, which is often preceded by a da-compound (see box below).

> *denn sie zweifelt* [verb: *an etwas zweifeln*] *nicht <u>daran</u>, daß er rechtschaffen*
> *und wahrhaftig sei in allen seinen Worten* [prepositional object]
>   because it (the soul) doesn't doubt that He is righteous and true in all His words

---

13. Used to pose an indirect question; compare to "if" in English.

Da-Compounds

A *da*-compound is formed with *da* and a preposition as in *dazu*. If the preposition starts with a vowel, which is often the case, an *r* is added in between as in *darauf* or *daran*. Da-compounds occur frequently with verbs with prepositions. They can either refer back to something mentioned in a previous sentence or precede a prepositional object in the form of a clause (see examples above). They should only be translated if a prepositional object is needed to form a grammatical sentence in English. If so, translate *da* as "that" and add an appropriate preposition (see section 3.6.5 on prepositions).

Note that *damit* can be a da-compound meaning "with/by that" or a conjunction meaning "so that." If used as a conjunction, it introduces a subclause, which is separated by a comma. *Darum* is equally used to express two meanings. It can either function as an adverb, meaning "therefore" (synonym of *deshalb*) or as a da-compound with the preposition *um*. The same applies to *daher*. It is either a da-compound with *her*, or it functions as an adverb meaning "therefore" (synonym of *deshalb*).

The Genitive Case

The genitive is mostly used for attributes as in the following examples:

- *Zorn Gottes* or *Gottes Zorn* (both grammatically correct) (God's wrath)
- *auf den Reichtum dieses Glaubens* (on the wealth of this faith)
- *mit allen Werken der Gebote* (with all the works of the commandments)

The attribute follows the nouns it is describing unless a proper name is used with an s-genitive[14] as in the example above of *Gottes Zorn* (God's wrath). In this case it is translated with an s-genitive in English, as well. In all other cases (see examples above) the English translation is made with "of."

A few verbs take a genitive object. They are less common in modern German but can be found in theological texts.

> *So bedarf sie* [subject] *auch keines anderen Dings* [direct object in the genitive case] *mehr.*
> Therefore she also does not require any other thing anymore.

The following verbs take the genitive object as their only complement along with the subject.

---

14. Note that with the nouns *Gott*, *Christus*, and *Jesus*, the genitive attribute often follows the referent noun as in *Sohn Gottes* instead of *Gottes Sohn*.

- *bedürfen* (need, require), *entbehren* (lack), *ermangeln* (lack), *gedenken* (remember), *harren* (await)

As do the following reflexive verbs:

- *sich annehmen* (to look after), *sich bemächtigen* (to seize), *sich entsinnen* (to remember), *sich erfreuen* (to enjoy), *sich erwehren* (to refrain from), *sich rühmen* (to boast about/of), *sich schämen* (to be ashamed of), *sich vergewissern* (to assure oneself)

For the purpose of reading German theological texts, you do not need to memorize the verbs listed above, but you should be aware of the existence of this kind of verb. If the sentence you are reading contains a noun in the genitive case and you cannot find a referent noun, it might be a genitive object instead of an attribute. If it is a genitive object, it should be translated as a direct object and not as a genitive (see examples above).

3.6.5 Prepositions

In order to understand and translate German texts, the case a preposition takes is not relevant. The case does not change the meaning. All you need to know is how the German prepositions relate to the English prepositions. However, you should be aware that prepositions govern cases and, in particular, that there is a group of prepositions that changes their case depending on context. The following prepositions are called *Wechselpräpositionen* (changing prepositions) because they take the accusative when indicating a direction and the dative when indicating a location:

> Contractions of prepositions and definite articles are used in written and spoken German: *ans* (*an das*), *am* (*an dem*), *beim* (*bei dem*), *ins* (*in das*), *im* (*in dem*), *vom* (*von dem*), *zum* (*zu dem*), *zur* (*zu der*)

- *in* (in/into), *an* (on/at), *auf* (on/on top of), *unter* (under), *neben* (next to), *über* (over), *hinter* (behind), *vor* (in front of), *zwischen* (between)

For the purpose of reading German, this change in case is less important because the verb already implies the notion of direction or location.

> *Der Student geht in die Bibliothek* [accusative case].
> The student goes into the library.

> *Der Student ist in der Bibliothek* [dative case].
> The student is in the library.

The following list of prepositions provides the basic meaning of each preposition and the case it takes. When reading German texts, you need to be aware of all possible meanings and use the appropriate English preposition, depending on the context. As mentioned before, prepositions are often determined by the verb, and it is often useful to look up the verb with the preposition. We will discuss this further in step 8 on our checklist.

TABLE 24: Prepositions

bis + Akk	up to/as far as, until/by	aus + Dat	out of, from
durch + Akk	through, by	außer + Dat	besides
für + Akk	for	bei + Dat	by, at
gegen + Akk	against	gegenüber[1] + Dat	opposite, compared to
ohne + Akk	without	mit + Dat	with, by
um + Akk	(a)round, at	nach + Dat	after, to, according to
wider + Akk	against		
seit + Dat	since, for	ab + Dat	from
von + Dat	from, of	dank + Dat	thanks to
zu + Dat	to	laut + Dat	according to
entgegen + Dat	contrary to	binnen + Dat	within (time)
entsprechend + Dat	according to	fern + Dat	far from
(mit)samt + Dat	together with	nahe + Dat	near (to)
nebst + Dat	in addition to	per + Dat	by, per
zufolge[2]* + Dat	according to	zuliebe* + Dat	for the sake of
zuwider* + Dat	contrary to	(an)statt + Gen	instead of
trotz + Gen	despite	während + Gen	during
wegen + Gen	because of	entlang + Gen	along

[1] *Gegenüber* can be placed in front of or after the noun.
[2] Prepositions marked with an asterisk (*) always follow the noun.

Less frequent prepositions with the genitive case denoting a location in relation to something include:

> *außerhalb* (outside), *innerhalb* (within), *oberhalb* (above), *unterhalb* (below), *diesseits* (on this side), *jenseits* (beyond),[15] *unweit* (not far from)

---

15. Note that the nouns *das Diesseits* (this world) and *das Jenseits* (beyond, afterlife) are written with a capital letter (as are all nouns in German) and should not be mistaken for the preposition.

Another preposition that you will encounter frequently in the texts in part II and III of this book is the two-part preposition *von . . . her* + dative.

> **Von** *dem Studium* **her** *ist Mainz eine gute Wahl.*
> **In respect to** the course of studies, Mainz is a good choice.

Its basic meaning is "in respect to," but as mentioned before, translating prepositions requires a certain amount of flexibility; we provide footnotes in the texts to support your translations.

The list provided above is not exhaustive but lists the most frequently used prepositions.

Now you have become familiar with five of the ten steps necessary for reading and translating German. It is very important that you complete all the exercises provided in order to reinforce what you have learned. By doing these practical exercises you will apply the information you have learned thus far and create a mental roadmap so you can apply this system to future texts you may encounter. The effort you invest now will make part II and part III of this book much easier.

Exercise

 **SCHWER**

Perform the following steps with all examples below.

1. Find all verbs.
2. Establish noun phrases and determine their respective cases.
3. Identify the complements of all verbs.

> *Gott wird auf der Erde ein kurzes Fazit ziehen, und dem kurzen Fazit wird wie eine Sintflut die Gerechtigkeit entströmen.*

> *Denn kein gutes Werk hängt an dem göttlichen Wort so wie der Glaube.*

> *So wird die Seele von all ihren Sünden einzig durch ihr Brautgeschenk, d. h. um des Glaubens willen, frei und los und mit der ewigen Gerechtigkeit ihres Bräutigams Christus beschenkt.*

Use colored pencils for the cases.
We suggest the following color scheme:

nominative → green
genitive → orange
dative → blue
accusative → red
prepositional complement → yellow

I n the previous chapter we discussed the following steps on our checklist:

6. Locate all referent nouns.
7. Look out for participles used as adjectives.
8. Look up all new words and try combining the verb with phrases.
9. Perform a rough translation of the sentence.
10. Polish up the sentence to ensure readability.

This chapter contains explanations regarding various kinds of pronouns and their declension. We will also be discussing adjectives in general and participles used as adjectives, as well as special features of German, such as modal particles. In the final two steps, we will advise you on how to translate the sentence. At the end of this chapter, you will have completed section one of the *Handbook of Reading Theological German* and will be prepared to apply these methods to the texts that are presented in the remainder of this book.

4.1 Step Six: Locate All Referent Nouns

Understanding the references in a complex German sentence is crucial to understanding the sentence. As mentioned before, all pronouns agree in gender and number with their referent noun. You need to know the declension of the pronouns to match them with their referent noun and to identify their role in the sentence. Under step 6, you will learn about the various kinds of pronouns and their forms as far as they are crucial for reading German.

As mentioned before, the masculine and feminine pronouns are used to refer to inanimate nouns as well as animate nouns because they agree with the grammatical gender of the noun. This might feel wrong to you at the beginning, and you might look for a person as a referent noun when you encounter *sie*, when it actually refers to *die Seele* (soul) (see example in the next paragraph). Therefore, it is important to remember this feature of German grammar while reading and translating German texts.

4.1.1 Personal Pronouns

It is important to recognize the different cases of the personal pronouns to identify their role in the sentence (see verb valency in 3.6.4).

	Nominative	Genitive[1]	Dative	Accusative
Singular				
First Person	ich	meiner	mir	mich
Second Person	du	deiner	dir	dich
Third Person (Masculine, feminine, neuter)	er sie es	seiner ihrer seiner	ihm ihr ihm	ihn sie es
Plural				
First Person	wir	unser	uns	uns
Second Person	ihr	euer	euch	euch
Third Person	sie	ihrer	ihnen	sie
Second Person Formal Sg./Pl.	Sie	Ihrer	Ihnen	Sie

[1] This case is rarely used, but it may occur in older texts.

Note that the grammatical gender determines only the form of the third-person singular pronouns as there is no gender differentiation in the plural.

> *So hält die Seele, wenn sie Gottes Wort fest glaubt, Gott für wahrhaftig, rechtschaffen, und gerecht.*
> Thus the soul takes God as truthful, righteous, and just if it believes strongly [in] God's word.

Note that the form *sie* has several meanings. If the sentence contains *sie*, you should check for a subject to differentiate between the accusative and the nominative *sie*. If it is the subject, it is helpful to check for the number of the verb. It helps you to differentiate between the third-person singular *sie* and the third-person plural *sie*. If it is the direct object, look for referent nouns in the previous sentence to differentiate between the third-person singular *sie* and the third-person plural *sie*. In the example below, *sie* is the direct object of the verb *verdammen* in the *dass*-clause. To identify its number and how to translate it, you need to search in the previous sentence for a referent noun that is either in plural or of the feminine gender. Possible translations would be "she" (referring to a female person), "it" (referring to an inanimate object or notion), or "they" (referring to a plural noun). Here it refers to a feminine noun, *die Erstgeburt*, literally "the first birth" mentioned in the first clause.

So wie nun Christus die Erstgeburt mit ihrer Ehre und Würde besitzt, teilt er sie auch mit all seinen Christen, daß sie durch den Glauben auch alle mit Christus Könige und Priester sein müssen.

As now Christ possesses the first birth/firstborn with its honor and dignity, so he also shares it with all his Christians, so that through faith they all have to be kings and priests with Christ.

The impersonal pronoun *man* takes the same verb endings as the third-person singular and conveys a passive meaning. It is used for rules or general statements and translates to the English "one" or "you." It can only be used in the nominative case. For other cases the indefinite article is used as a pronoun. *Man* takes the possessive pronoun *sein* and the reflexive pronoun *sich*.

Daß <u>man</u> von Herzen glaubt, das macht <u>einen</u> [accusative] gerecht und rechtschaffen.
That a person believes from the heart, that makes one just and righteous.

4.1.2 Reflexive Pronouns

As mentioned before, in the context of reflexive verbs, German reflexive pronouns do not have to be translated. However, *sich* can be used as a reciprocal pronoun and should then be translated as "each other" or some form of "-self" (himself, herself . . .) according to the context. As shown in the table below, they only occur in the accusative and the dative cases.

TABLE 25: Declension: Reflexive Pronouns

	Accusative	Dative
Singular		
First Person	mich	mir
Second Person	dich	dir
Third Person (masculine, feminine, neuter)	sich	sich
Plural		
First Person	uns	uns
Second Person	euch	euch
Third Person	sich	sich
Second Person formal	sich	sich

For the purpose of reading German texts, you need to be able to recognize reflexive pronouns in order to fully understand a sentence. The reflexive pronoun agrees in person with the subject of the sentence. When used with a preposition, as in *zu sich*, it refers back to the subject and should be translated as a pronoun ("to him," "to her," "to it," or "to them," depending on the subject). If the sentence contains a reflexive pronoun, you should always look up the verb with the reflexive pronoun *sich* to check if it is a reflexive verb.

Da-compounds instead of Pronouns

When referring to things, *da*-compounds are used instead of a pronoun with preposition. This is especially common in answers and usually the case with verbs with prepositions.

When referring to a thing:

> *Denkst du <u>an</u> das Buch? Ja, ich denke <u>daran</u>.* (verb: *denken an*)
> Are you thinking of the book? Yes, I am thinking of it.

When referring to a person:

> *Denkst du <u>an</u> deinen Freund? Ja, ich denke <u>an</u> ihn.* (verb: *denken an*)
> Are you thinking of your boyfriend? Yes, I'm thinking of him.

4.1.3 Interrogative Pronouns

Interrogative pronouns introduce a question. When asking after a complement, the pronoun takes the case of that complement (see table below).

TABLE 26: Declension: Interrogative Pronouns

Case	Referring to a person	Referring to a thing or a notion
Nominative	wer	was
Genitive	wessen	wessen
Dative	wem	-
Accusative	wen	was

The other interrogative pronouns are: *wo* (where), *woher* (from where), *wohin* (where to), *wann* (when), *wie* (how), *warum* (why), and *weshalb* (why).

Wo-compounds: Like the *da*-compounds already mentioned, wo-compounds are formed with *wo*- and a preposition like *wovon*, and an "r" is added if the preposition starts with a vowel, as in *worauf*. They are used when asking after a prepositional complement and occur mostly when a verb with a preposition is involved.

Contrary to the interrogative pronouns mentioned so far, *welch-* (which) is followed by a noun and has endings like other articles. Gender, number, and case are determined by the referent noun.

TABLE 27: Declension: Interrogative Pronoun *welch-*

Case	Masculine	Feminine	Neuter	Plural
Nominative	welcher	welche	welches	welche
Genitive	welches	welcher	welches	welcher
Dative	welchem	welcher	welchem	welchen
Accusative	welchen	welche	welches	welche

4.1.4 Relative Pronouns

A relative clause is introduced by a relative pronoun and separated by a comma. The relative pronoun refers back to a noun in the previous sentence and the relative clause provides additional information on the noun. The most common relative pronouns are shown in the table below. They are almost identical to the definite article except for the forms colored in red.

Relative pronouns can be used with prepositions, as in the following example:

> *d.h. der Glaube, in dem kurz die Erfüllung aller Gebote besteht*
> that is, faith, in which lies in short the fulfillment of all commandments

The pronoun agrees in gender and number with its referent noun outside the clause, but the case is governed by its role in the clause or the preposition it is used with.

TABLE 28: Declension: Relative Pronouns

Case	Masculine	Feminine	Neuter	Plural
Nominative	der	die	das	die
Genitive	**dessen**	**deren**	**dessen**	**deren**
Dative	dem	der	dem	**denen**
Accusative	den	die	das	die

The interrogative pronoun *welch-* (see table above on interrogative pronouns) can be used as a relative pronoun and as such is not followed by a noun.

Denn du siehst hier, daß er allein das erste Gebot erfüllt, in welchem geboten wird . . .

Because you see here that he alone fulfills the first commandment in which is commanded . . .

The interrogative pronouns *was, wo, wie* and the *wo*-compounds (see explanation above on interrogative pronouns) can be used as relative pronouns, as well.

Es muß allemal noch etwas anderes sein, was der Seele Rechtschaffenheit und Freiheit bringen und geben kann.

It certainly has to be something else that can bring righteousness and give freedom to the soul.

4.1.5 Demonstrative Pronouns

The meaning of demonstrative pronouns differs slightly from the meaning of definite articles. As the name suggests (derived from the Latin *demonstrare* = to point to sth.), they point to a specific referent that has been mentioned before in the text. The English equivalent to *dieser* (and its various forms) is "this," or in the plural "these." As with the articles, the gender, number, and case depend on the referent noun. The endings correspond to the endings of the definite article (*dies-* + ending).

TABLE 29: Declension: Demonstrative Pronoun *dieser*

Case	Masculine	Feminine	Neuter	Plural
Nominative	dieser	diese	dieses	diese
Genitive	dieses	dieser	dieses	dieser
Dative	diesem	dieser	diesem	diesen
Accusative	diesen	diese	dieses	diese

The demonstrative pronoun *jener* (jen- + ending) takes the same endings as *dieser* and is the equivalent to the English "that" or in the plural "those." It is less frequent than *dieser*. Another demonstrative pronoun with the same meaning is *derjenige*. It is a compound of the definite article and its various forms (see section on articles) and *-jenige(n)*.

In order to read and understand German texts, you just need to be aware of the construction and memorize the definite article (a point we cannot stress enough) in order to recognize the gender, case, and number.

TABLE 30: Declension: Demonstrative Pronoun *derjenige*

Case	Masculine	Feminine	Neuter	Plural
Nominative	derjenige	diejenige	dasjenige	diejenigen
Genitive	desjenigen	derjenigen	desjenigen	derjenigen
Dative	demjenigen	derjenigen	demjenigen	denjenigen
Accusative	denjenigen	diejenige	dasjenige	diejenigen

The next demonstrative pronoun we will discuss has a similar construction. *Derselbe* is a compound of the definite article and *-selbe(n)* and it means "the same."

TABLE 31: Declension: Demonstrative Pronoun *derselbe*

Case	Masculine	Feminine	Neuter	Plural
Nominative	derselbe	dieselbe	dasselbe	dieselben
Genitive	desselben	derselben	desselben	derselben
Dative	demselben	derselben	demselben	denselben
Accusative	denselben	dieselbe	dasselbe	dieselben

Another less frequent demonstrative pronoun is *solch-*. It takes the same endings as *dies-* (see above) and means "such."

The relative pronoun *der, die, das* with its declined forms can be used as a demonstrative pronoun. Note that instead of *deren*, the form *derer* can occur (see table above for the relative pronoun). If *der, die, das* is not followed by a noun, it is either used as a relative or as a demonstrative pronoun. You can differentiate between both pronoun types by looking at the position of the verb. If *der, die, das* is used as a relative pronoun, it is introducing a subclause and the verb will be in the last position.

Compounds of Prepositions and Pronouns

There are two prepositions that can be combined with pronouns. It is hard to find them in the dictionary in their various forms if you do not understand their construction. We mention them here because they can be found in theological texts. Both mean "for the sake of."

> *halber*: as a preposition, it follows the noun; combined with a pronoun it becomes *-halben* as in *meinethalben* (for my sake). In between the pronoun and *-halben*, a "t" is inserted.

um . . . willen: as a preposition, the noun is in between the two parts of the preposition as in *um dieses Unterschieds willen* (for the sake of this difference).
In combination with a pronoun a "t" is inserted as in *um meinetwillen* (for
my sake).

After completing steps 1 through 6, your sentence should look similar to this:

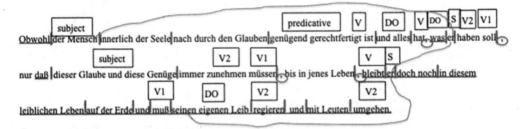

So far, we have concentrated on verbs, nouns, and function words like prepositions
and conjunctions to untangle the relationship between clauses and between the parts
inside a clause. To understand German texts, you need to know how to look up new
words. In steps 7 and 8, you will learn how to recognize adjectives, modal particles,
and adverbs.

Exercises

Find all pronouns and determine the type of the pronoun (personal, demonstrative,
etc.). Identify their case and the noun to which they refer, if possible.

> *Wenn Gott daher sieht, daß ihm die Seele Wahrhaftigkeit zugesteht und ihn so durch
> ihren Glauben ehrt, so ehrt er sie ebenfalls und hält sie auch für rechtschaffen und
> wahrhaftig, und durch so einen Glauben ist sie auch rechtschaffen und wahrhaftig.*

> *Damit wir gründlich erkennen, was ein Christenmensch ist, und wie es um die
> Freiheit stehe, die ihm Christus erworben und gegeben hat, wovon Sankt Paulus viel
> schreibt, will ich diese zwei Sätze aufstellen:*

4.2 Step Seven: Look Out for Participles Used as Adjectives

We have already discussed the use and the declension of adjectives. In step 7, we focus
on the comparison of adjectives, word formation of adjectives, and participles used as
adjectives.

Adjectives can be used to compare the quality of one item with the quality of another item. This form of the adjective is called the comparative, or the superlative if the comparison is made between more than two items. The comparative occurs mostly in comparisons with *als* (than) but also after the modal particle (see section 4.3) *noch* as in *noch besser* (even better). The regular formation of the forms is shown below.

- nett-nett**er**-am nett**esten**/der[1] nett**este** (nice-nicer-the nicest)

When the superlative is used as an attribute, it declines as shown in section 3.6.1 on adjective declension. As in English, the superlative is then placed together with the definite article. All adjectives form the comparative forms the same way, but there are a few irregular formations.

Most of them have *Umlaut* in the comparative and the superlative as in *klug-klüger-am klügsten/der klügste* (smart-smarter-the smartest). However, the very common adjective *gut* (good) takes the comparative *besser* (better) and the superlative *am besten/der beste* (the best), similar to the English forms. Online dictionaries give you the appropriate translations of the comparative forms, so that memorizing the irregular forms is unnecessary. Nonetheless, knowing the principles of their formation helps you to identify adjectives. The same holds for word formation of adjectives.

The endings *-ig*, *-lich*, *-isch*, *-bar*, *-haft*, *-los* are most common and are worth memorizing as an indicator for adjectives. The following prefixes negate the meaning of the adjective: *a-*, *des-/dis-*, *il-*, *in-*, *ir-*, *miss-*, *non-*, *un-*[2] (this one is most common) as in *möglich – unmöglich* (possible-impossible) and are equally worth memorizing to speed up your reading process.

There are, however, a few endings that are used especially in academic texts to form new adjectives by adding the suffix to a noun and have to be translated with a prepositional phrase in English. These are *-bedingt* as in *situationsbedingt* (depending on the situation), *-gemäß* as in *situationsgemäß* (according to the situation), and *-halber* as in *informationshalber* (for the sake of information).

Note that adjectives can be modified by adding *so* (so) as in *so klein* (so small) or *zu* (too) as in *zu klein* (too small), equivalent to English.

The present and perfect participles, also called participle I and II, are frequently used as adjectives. The participle I is formed by adding the -(e)nd to the stem[3] of the verb, as in *lesend*. When used as an adjective, it declines the same as all adjectives (see section

---

1. The gender of the article and the ending of the adjective depend on the referent noun; e.g., *das netteste Mädchen, der netteste Mann, die netteste Frau* (the nicest girl, the nicest man, the nicest woman).
2. The prefix *un-* is also used to negate nouns; so, e.g., the word *Glaube* means "faith," but *Unglaube* means "unbelief."
3. You get the stem of a verb by deleting the "-en" of the infinitive form *lesen* (*les-*).

3.6.1) and is part of the noun phrase. The translation depends on the complexity of the noun phrase.

> *diese zwei sich <u>widersprechenden</u> Aussagen*
> these two statements contradicting each other // these two statements which contradict each other

> *diese zwei dem Wort Gottes <u>widersprechenden</u> Aussagen*
> these two statements which contradict God's word

The more words the participle I construction contains, the better it is translated into English by a relative clause in the present tense in English. Simple constructions should be translated with an "-ing" form.

If the participle II[4] is used as an adjective, it should be translated with a past participle or, for more complex constructions, with a relative clause in the past tense.

Participles used as adjectives can be turned into nouns (see section 3.6.3 on nominalization) by adding a determiner and capitalizing the first letter.

> *für <u>das</u> hier <u>Gelehrte</u> (lehren → gelehrt → das Gelehrte)*
> for the here taught (things)

Exercises

1. Mark the participles used as adjectives.
    ○ *Der erinnerte Jesus ist zugleich der erzählte Jesus.*[5]

2. Answer the following questions for each participle in the sentence above:
    What kind of participle is it? What is the infinitive of the verb?

3. Translate the sentence!

---

4. For its formation, see section 2.2.2.
5. Example taken from Zimmermann, "Fiktion des Faktischen."

 **MITTEL**

4. Fill in the comparative forms of the adjectives:

schlecht		
rechtschaffen		
treu		
gläubig		

4.3 Step Eight: Look Up All New Words and Try Combining the Verb with Phrases

After completing the previous seven steps, you have almost decoded the sentence. Only the words that are neither part of a noun phrase (determiners, adjectives, nouns) or function words (pronouns, conjunctions, prepositions) are left. We will also discuss compound words again, as they can be created by the author of a text and therefore may not be found in any dictionary.

We will not discuss adverbs in detail as they are easily found in any dictionary and do not decline. Note that some have comparative forms that are also listed in every dictionary. However, it is important to know that their position in the sentence is variable and that they are very common.

A more important and very special feature of German is the so-called modal particles such as *ja, schon,* or *bloß.* They do not change the meaning of the sentence but rather alter the tone of the sentence. There are many of them, and they are very common in spoken as well as in written German.

Our advice is to memorize the most common ones along with their basic meanings and to ignore them while doing your first rough translation of the sentence (see step 9 on our checklist). The meaning of modal particles depends very much on the context they are used in, and you will need to know the context first in order to choose the appropriate translation. If you are unsure about the modal particle, leave it out of your translation. So-called scalar or focus particles refer to a noun or noun phrase only, not to the whole sentence, like the rest of the modal particles.

The table below shows modal particles and their use, as commonly found in theological texts. It is, however, not an exhaustive list but rather a list of the most common modal particles. You may notice that some of the words listed below are also used as conjunctions or adverbs. Their function in the sentence depends mostly on their position in it. If *aber,* for example, is not placed directly after a comma, it is most likely used as a modal particle.

TABLE 32: List of Modal Particles

aber	can express a contradiction, close to "though"
allerdings/freilich	close to *aber*, can be translated with "admittedly", "all the same"
bloß	expresses a restrictive sense, can be translated with "simply" or "merely"
doch	expresses a contradiction or a disagreement, can be translated as "though"
eben[1]	expresses a confirmation, can be translated as "just"
eigentlich	can be translated as "actually"
erst	As a focus particle in front of a word or a phrase, it expresses the notion of "less than expected" and can be translated as "only" in that sense.
etwa	As scalar particle, it expresses approximation or possibility.
gar	intensifies a negation (omit in translation) or emphasizes the word it is preceding, translate as "even" or "possibly"
ja	expresses that the sentence contains something the reader already knows
jedenfalls	emphasizes why something should be the case, can be translated as "at least"
noch	In expressions of time it expresses that something takes longer than expected.
nur/lediglich	As a focus particle, it expresses a restriction, can be translated with "only."
schon	As a focus particle, it expresses that something happened sooner than expected (opposite to erst) and can be translated with "already."
wohl	expresses a presumption and can be translated with "probably" or "seems to be"

[1] As an adverb, it means "just now"; as an adjective, it means "level."

We will point out modal particles in the texts in part II of this book, and you will have mastered their recognition and translation by the end of this book.

Another feature of German is the so-called *Funktionsverbgefüge*,[6] which are set phrases containing a verb, as in *eine Entscheidung treffen*, which translates literally as "to meet a decision" but should be translated as "to make a decision." If you are unaware of their existence, you might translate the sentence incorrectly. They are too high in number

---

6. There is no equivalent term in English. Literally translated it means the functional combination of a verb with something else.

to be memorized. We will point them out in the texts in part II, so that you can learn to recognize them. But in general, you should heed the following: If your translation of a sentence does not fit the context, you should look up the verb with the subject or its prepositional complement to identify a *Funktionsverbgefüge*. A very frequent fixed phrase is *es gibt*, which is the German equivalent to the English "there is," except that it is always used in the singular, even when describing plural entities as in *es gibt viele Bücher über Theologie* (there are many books on theology). It exists in various tenses, so be aware of it whenever the verb *geben* and the pronoun *es* occur in a sentence.

Another typical feature of German grammar is the formation of compound nouns. Their formation is easy, and they are frequently used, especially in academic writing. For the purpose of reading and translating German texts, you need to be able to identify the parts of a compound. As mentioned in section 3.5, the grammatical gender is determined by the last part of the compound word. When encountering a compound word, first translate its parts separately; the last part is usually specified by the previous parts of the compound, much like a genitive attribute specifies the referent noun. Therefore, you can often translate them as such if there is no better equivalent in English. Another option is to put both words next to each other and thereby form the English equivalent of a compound word. A third option is to use an adjective for the first parts of the compound and a noun for the last part (see examples below).

- *Tugendlehren* → *die Tugend* + *die Lehren* (plural)
  "virtue" + "teachings" translate as "teachings of virtue" or "virtue teachings"
- *Vulgärethiken* → *vulgär* + *die Ethiken* (plural)
  "vulgar" + "ethics" translate as "ethics of vulgarity"[7]
- *Kontextbedingtheit* → *der Kontext* + *die Bedingtheit*
  "context" + "conditionality" translate as "conditionality of context" or "context conditionality"
- *Bezugstext*[8] → *der Bezug* + *der Text*
  "reference" + "text" translate as "reference text"

Understanding German compound words requires awareness, creativity, and practice. We will support you with footnotes in all our texts presented in parts II and III of this book and are confident that you will be well-equipped to handle compound words after completing all the exercises in this book.

---

7. Although *vulgär* is an adjective in German, in this compound phrase the author uses it as a catagory of ethics. When adjectives are used in a compound word in German, they should not be translated as an adjective in English. Therefore, "ethics of vulgarity" and not "vulgar ethics" is the proper way to translate this phrase.

8. All examples taken from Ulrich Volp (2019); see his text in part III of this book.

Exercises

 **MITTEL**

1. Find the modal particle in both examples.

> *Darum sollte das wohl für alle Christen das einzige Werk und die einzige Übung sein*

> *wenn der Glaube alles ist und allein schon als genügend gilt*

 **SCHWER**

2. Translate the sentence in both examples. Remember that the definite article can be used as a demonstrative pronoun.

4.4 Step Nine: Perform a Rough Translation of the Sentence

After completing the previous steps, you should be able to perform a rough, very literal translation of the whole sentence. Start with the main clause and relative clauses, depending on the main clause, and continue with the subclauses. Within a clause, start with the subject and the verb, and then continue with its other complements. If you encounter complex noun phrases, translate the head noun first and leave all attributes aside until you understand the basic meaning of the sentence. Leave out modal particles, as well. Stick to the grammar and do not get carried away by what you expect the sentence to say, based on context. After you have translated the basic elements, add all attributes to your translation. You might now realize that you need to look up a few words again to help you choose a more appropriate meaning.

If your goal is simply to understand the text, you can now go to the next sentence and start again with step 1 on the checklist. If you want a written translation as a result, go to step 10.

Exercise

 **SCHWER**

Perform a rough translation of the sentence by applying steps 1 through 8 on the checklist. (We provided an exemplary analysis of this sentence after step 6; you might want to use it to support your own analysis.)

Obwohl der Mensch innerlich der Seele nach durch den Glauben genügend gerechtfertigt ist und alles hat, was er haben soll, nur daß dieser Glaube und diese Genüge immer zunehmen müssen, bis in jenes Leben, bleibt er doch noch in diesem leiblichen Leben auf der Erde und muß seinen eigenen Leib regieren und mit Leuten umgehen.

4.5 Step Ten: Polish up the Sentence to Ensure Readability

If your goals is a written translation, you should reread your rough translation and ensure that it is a proper English sentence. You might need to change the word order or place clauses differently. At this point, your translation becomes an interpretation. You have understood its content, and you can now find the best translation for the individual words and revise your translation accordingly. Sometimes it helps to complete a rough translation of a whole paragraph first to fully understand the context, before polishing up the translation.

Exercise

 SCHWER

Revise your translation from the exercise in step 9.

Congratulations! You have completed section one of the *Handbook of Reading Theological German*. At this point, you have applied the ten steps of the Mainz Method for reading and translating theological German texts. As you continue into part II of this book, you will be introduced to important historical figures who made significant contributions to various areas of theology. You will not only become familiar with each of these individuals but you will also learn about their writing styles and have the chance to apply the steps you have just learned as you read and translate one of their texts.

PART II

Significant German Theologians and Their Texts

Overview

In this portion of the book, you will be introduced to important German theologians and have the opportunity to analyze portions of some of their most popular texts. For each chapter, you will be given a short biography of each notable figure, which will help you to understand their role and influence in the field of theology, and you will learn about each author's unique writing style. Exercises are provided to help you prepare for your analysis of the author's texts.

Do not be overly anxious about translating the original German source. Many native German speakers have difficulty reading and understanding the materials you are about to encounter. To ensure your success, we will assist you in your translations by providing you with a number of footnotes, aiding you in grammar concepts and vocabulary terms. Please refer to the bulletpoints below—they will help you understand how to effectively utilize these tools. Upon completion of this portion of the book you should have accomplished the learning objectives presented.

Lesson Bulletpoints

- For each text, we have selected the most difficult portions and pre-applied some of the checklist to help you in your translation.
- Remember to refer to the color scheme in section 3.6.
- Translations in footnotes are suggestions to help you understand the word in the context.
- The term "fixed phrases" is used loosely and refers to idiomatic expressions as well as *Funktionsverbgefüge* (see section 4.3).
- Additions to the text that have been made to aid clarity are indicated by brackets []. To modernize the text, the deletion of a letter is indicated as follows: stell[e]t.
- Abbreviations are given in the pre-analyzed sentences for nominative (NOM), dative (DAT), accusative (AKK), genitive (GEN), prepositional complement (PREP COMP), verb part 1 (v1), and verb part 2 (v2).

Learning Objectives

- Learners will become familiar with notable historical figures in German theology.
- Learners will understand the uniqueness of each author's contribution and writing style.
- Learners will be introduced to important theological texts.
- Learners will begin to utilize the Mainz Method Checklist.
- Learners will become proficient in selecting translation terms based upon context.

Martin Luther

The Protestant Reformer

5

While theologians and Bible scholars enjoy heated debate over many topics, very few, if any, would dispute the importance of Martin Luther. His influence radically divided Christendom and sent shockwaves throughout the European continent, the aftermath of which can still be seen around the world. His polarizing life has drawn both criticism and praise, and yet it would be hard to recall another person who has had as big an impact on theology and the German language as Martin Luther.

Though the year is uncertain,[1] Hans and Margarethe Luther had their first child on the evening of November 10th. The child was baptized the next morning on the feast day of St. Martin of Tours, in whose honor they would name their son.[2] The location was a growing city of more than 4,000 inhabitants known as Eisleben, located in the county of Mansfeld.[3] Although the child would grow up in a mining town, his parents invested in his education, hoping that one day he would study law.[4]

Growing up in a strict religious home, nothing about his background would have suggested the extraordinary future that would lie ahead.[5] Dealing with bouts of depression even at a young age, young Martin Luther was already terribly concerned with his status as a sinner.[6] As time passed, he would follow his parents' desires and study law at the University of Erfurt until July of 1505, when lightning struck the ground near him while he was traveling in a thunderstorm from Stutterheim to Erfurt. Luther cried, "Ich will ein Mönch werden!"[7] Vowing to become a monk should he survive the event, Luther entered an Augustinian monastery.[8]

As a monk, Luther's youthful terror of Jesus as judge continued. The Augustinian monks believed that salvation, while not impossible, was difficult to achieve. Luther became

---

1. The exact date on which Martin Luther was born is unknown. Luther and his mother believed his date of birth was 1484 (see Eric Metaxas, *Martin Luther: The Man Who Rediscovered God and Changed the World* [New York: Viking, 2017], 7), yet many hold to the year 1493, due to a statement by Melanchthon (see Martin Brecht, *Martin Luther: His Road to Reformation 1483–1521* [Minneapolis: Fortress, 1993], 1).

2. Arthur Cushman McGiffert, *Martin Luther: The Man and His Work* (New York: Century, 1911), 5.

3. Brecht, *Martin Luther*, 1.

4. Lyndal Roper, *Martin Luther: Renegade and Prophet* (New York: Random House, 2016), 6.

5. Erwin W. Lutzer, *Rescuing the Gospel: The Story and Significance of the Reformation* (Grand Rapids: Baker, 2016), 32.

6. Lutzer, 33.

7. Metaxas, 31.

8. Lutzer, 33.

increasingly zealous. He would spend many hours in prayer and fasted so often that his friends feared for his health. Additionally, he went to confession every chance he had and still feared for his eternal state, feeling utterly inadequate.[9]

As a monk, Luther studied theology, which focused not on the biblical text but on Aristotle, whom the bishop and Erfurt professor Johann Bonemilch Von Laasphe believed to be of primary importance.[10] Yet, while reading the works of early church fathers such as Augustine, Luther began to notice a discrepancy between what Augustine wrote and the words penned by Aristotle.[11] Between 1889 and 1890, the very books Luther had studied were discovered at the Ratsschul Library in Zwickau. Among the collection were some of Augustine's works, which contained writings and marginal notes penned by Luther.[12] His fervent study as a young monk led him to begin to question the teachings and practices of the Church to which he had devoted his life and service.

His questioning of Church teachings came to a climax in 1517 when his *Ninety-five Theses* were placed on the door of the Schlosskirche[13] in Wittenberg. Luther had hoped that his effort would produce an academic discussion surrounding the practice and efficacy of indulgences as they were being performed by the Church. Never had he imagined that such an action would cause him to be excommunicated by the Church and labeled an outlaw within the Holy Roman Empire.

His disagreement on the way the Church practiced indulgences was not his only contention with the Catholic Church. His major theological departure was the belief that justification was *sola fide* (by faith alone). Luther expressed these teachings in his 1525 publication of *De Servo Arbitrio* (*On the Bondage of the Will*). The following year, in 1526, he wrote a German liturgy known as *Deutsche Messe und Ordnung des Gottesdienstes* (German Mass and Order of Worship). Three years later he wrote *Der Große Katechismus* (the Large Catechism), which we will look at momentarily, followed by *Der Kleine Katechismus* (the Small Catechism). These texts were written to make worship more personal for the common man and to provide a guide for clergy.

Though notably identified as a theologian and reformer, Luther also helped to standardize the German language, which had been primarily a collection of various dialects. When he translated the Bible into German, it triggered the development of the standardization of the German language. Luther first translated the New Testament into German in 1522, yet it would be another twelve years before the Old Testament was completed. Today, Luther's translation of the Bible, though it has been revised multiple times, is still the most popular German translation of the Scriptures for the Protestant Church.

---

9. Metaxas, 47.
10. Brecht, 34.
11. Metaxas, 51.
12. Metaxas, 51.
13. Name of the church in Wittenberg, literally, "Castle Church."

Likewise, Luther's pivotal contributions to the development of the German language are still studied and expanded upon by linguists and grammarians.

Luther's contributions to Christendom have been very divisive—causing his supporters to label him a saint while his opponents considered him demon-possessed.[14] Yet it is hard to think of a historical figure who has impacted the direction of Christianity and the European continent as much as Luther. Despite any positive contributions he made, in order to give an accurate portrayal, one cannot ignore the negative.

Within the pages of Luther's writings, deeply rooted anti-Semitism can be found. In as early as 1515, Luther labeled the Jews as godless. Kalimi notes, "For Luther, the terms 'Judaism' and 'lies' are deeply connected, and they are one unit, standing in contrast to 'Christianity' and 'truth.'"[15] As Luther aged, his resentment toward the Jewish people only increased. In 1543, three years before his death, Luther published two volumes filled with anti-Semitic rhetoric. Both *Von den Juden und Ihren Lügen* (On the Jews and Their Lies) and *Vom Schem Hamphoras und vom Geschlecht Christi* (On the Holy Name of the Lineage of Christ) have been used to promote violence against Jewish communities and are considered by some scholars to be the justification for the Kristallnacht.[16]

As fate would have it, Martin Luther would die in Eisleben, the city of his birth.[17] Historians may argue over whether Luther's influence has been more positive or negative, yet his legacy is undeniable: he changed the direction of Christianity. Understanding Luther's life and work helps us to understand the Christian movement today by shedding light on its history and by allowing us to watch its development unfold. Within his catechism, originally published in 1529, Luther addressed the Ten Commandments and their implication and application within the Church, a discussion that still takes place within theological circles today. In this portion of text, we will examine what Luther has to say about the commandment to keep the Sabbath day holy.

Introduction to Luther's Writing Style

Dating back to the sixteenth century, vocabulary in this text is often archaic and cannot be found in modern German dictionaries. You will find footnotes for these words, which are not used in modern German. Additionally, the word order deviates from modern German. Verbs in main clauses are often in the last position rather than the second position. The best way to find the main clause is by way of elimination. Look for conjunctions and relative pronouns; a clause without one is most likely the main clause.

---

14. Lutzer, 32.
15. Isaac Kalimi, "Martin Luther, the Jews, and Easter: Biblical Interpretation in the Shadow of Judeophobia," *JOR* 100.1 (2020): 54.
16. Diarmaid MacCulloch, *Reformation: Europe's House Divided, 1490–1700* (New York: Penguin, 2004), 666–67.
17. Roper, 6.

Finally, Luther uses conjunctions frequently, and they differ in meaning depending on the context (see exercise 1).

The following exercises are meant to prepare you for reading and translating the text. You will find the solutions in the appendix.

Exercises

 **SCHWER**

1. Before reading and translating the text, circle all of Luther's uses of *so*! While reading and translating, decide which of the following uses fits the context best for each use of *so*.
   a. comparison, translate with "as" or "like"
   b. relative pronoun
   c. conditional, translate as "if"
   d. consecutive, translate as "then," "that," or "so that"
   e. concessive, translate as "although"

 **MITTEL**

2. Analyze the first paragraph labeled *Vorrede* by applying the checklist introduced in chapters 2–4. Mark all verb forms and circle all conjunctions. Use colored pencil to mark the subject, the accusative, and (if present) the dative object. Use a pencil to divide word groups by looking at the relationships between the words in the sentence (for example, to which noun does the genitive object belong?).

Excerpt from Der Große Katechismus (1529)

Vorrede

Diese Predigt ist dazu[18] geordnet und angefangen, dass es sei ein Unterricht für die Kinder und Einfältigen. Darum sie auch von alters her auf griechisch heißt[19] Katechismus, das ist eine Kinderlehre, so ein jeglicher Christ zur Not wissen soll, also dass [,] wer solches nicht weiß, nicht könnte[20] unter die Christen gezählt und zu keinem Sakrament zugelassen werden. Gleichwie man einen Handwerksmann, der seines Handwerks[21] Recht und Gebrauch nicht weiß, auswirft und für untüchtig hält.

---

18. *Da*-compound referring to the following *dass*-clause.
19. Verb in a grammatically incorrect position, translate as if in second position.
20. First part of the verb and should be at the end of the sentence. Translate as if it is at the end.
21. Genitive attribute to *Recht und Gebrauch*.

Derhalben[22] soll man junge Leute die Stücke, so in den Katechismus oder Kinderpredigt gehören, wohl und fertig lernen lassen und mit Fleiß darin üben und treiben. Darum auch ein jeglicher Hausvater schuldig ist,[23] dass er zum wenigstens die Woche einmal seine Kinder und Gesinde umfrage und verhöre,[24] was sie davon wissen oder lernen, und wo sie es nicht können, mit Ernst dazu[25] halte.

> Denn ich (NOM) [ge]denke (verb + dative) wohl der Zeit (DAT), ja es begibt (verb, befall/happen) sich noch täglich, dass man (NOM) grobe, alte, betagte Leute (AKK) findet (verb), die hiervon (referring to Katechismus) gar nichts gewusst (v2) haben (v1) oder noch wissen (verb), [die (NOM)] gehen (verb) doch gleichwohl zur Taufe und Sakrament und brauchen (verb)[26] alles (AKK), was (AKK) die Christen (NOM) haben (verb); so[27] doch, die (NOM) zum Sakrament gehen (verb), billig (reasonable) mehr wissen (verb) und völligern Verstand (AKK) (understanding) aller christlichen Lehre haben (v2) sollen (v1) denn (than) die Kinder (NOM) und neuen Schüler (NOM);

wiewohl wirs[28] für den gemeinen Haufen[29] bei den drei Stücken bleiben lassen, so von alters her in der Christenheit geblieben sind, aber wenig recht gelehrt und getrieben, so lange, bis man sich in denselben[30] wohl übe und geläufig werde, beide, jung und alt, was Christen heißen und sein will; und sind nämlich diese:

(. . .)

Das dritte Gebot
Du sollst den Feiertag heiligen

Feiertag haben wir genannt nach dem hebräischen Wörtlein Sabbat, welches eigentlich heißt „feiern", das ist müßig stehen von der Arbeit. Daher wir pflegen zu sagen „Feierabend machen" oder „heiligen Abend geben". Nun hat Gott im Alten Testament den siebenten Tag ausgesondert und aufgesetzt zu feiern und geboten, denselbigen[31] vor allen andern heilig zu halten.

---

22. Translate as *deswegen*.
23. Verb in a grammatically incorrect position, translate as if in second position.
24. Translate as *befragen* and *nachfragen*.
25. Refers back to the notion of *wissen und lernen*.
26. Subject to this verb is still *die* referring to *Leute*.
27. Luther uses *so* frequently as a concessive conjunction.
28. Abbreviation for *wir es*.
29. Translate *Haufe* or *Haufen* in theological texts as "common mass," omit *gemeinen*.
30. Referring back to *den drei Stücken*.
31. Referring back to *den siebenten Tag*.

> Und dieser äußerlichen Feier nach[32] ist (v1) dies Gebot (NOM) allein den Juden (AKK) gestellt (v2, *sein*-passive), dass sie (NOM) sollten (v1)[33] von groben Werken (plural) stillstehen (v2) und ruhen (v2), auf dass (so that) sich beide, Mensch und Vieh (NOM), wieder erholten[34] (v2) und nicht von steter Arbeit geschwächt (v2) würden (v1, *Konjunktiv II*).

Wiewohl sie es hernach allzu eng spannten und gröblich missbrauchten, dass sie auch an Christo lästerten und nicht leiden konnten solche Werke, die sie doch selbst daran taten, wie man im Evangelio liest.[35] Gerade als sollte das Gebot damit erfüllt sein, dass man gar kein äußerlich Werk täte;[36] welches doch nicht die Meinung war, sondern lediglich die, dass sie den Feier- oder Ruhetag heiligten, wie wir hören werden.

Darum geht nun dies Gebot nach dem groben Verstand[37] uns Christen nichts an, denn es ein ganz äußerliches Ding ist, wie andere Satzungen des Alten Testaments, an sonderliche Weise, Person, Zeit und Stätte gebunden,[38] welche nun durch Christum alle frei gelassen sind. Aber einen christlichen Verstand zu fassen für die Einfältigen, was Gott in diesem Gebot von uns fordert, so merke, dass wir Feiertage halten nicht um der verständigen und gelehrten Christen willen,[39] denn diese bedürfen nirgends zu,[40] sondern erstlich auch um leiblicher Ursache und Notdurft willen, welche die Natur lehrt und fordert für den gemeinen Haufen, Knechte und Mägde, so die ganze Woche ihrer Arbeit und Gewerbe gewartet,[41] dass sie sich auch einen Tag einziehen, zu ruhen und erquicken. Darnach[42] allermeist darum, dass man an solchem Ruhetage (weil man sonst nicht dazu kommen kann) Raum und Zeit nehme, Gottesdienstes zu warten;[43] also dass man zu Haufe[44] komme, Gottes Wort zu hören und handeln, darnach Gott loben, singen und beten. Solches aber (sage ich) ist nicht also an Zeit gebunden wie bei den Juden, dass es müsse eben dieser oder jener Tag sein; denn es ist keiner an sich selbst besser denn der andere: sondern sollte wohl täglich geschehen, aber weil es der Haufe nicht warten[45]

---

32. Here *nach* follows the noun and means "according to."
33. First part of the verb and should be at the end of the *dass*-clause; translate as if it were.
34. Reflexive verb in German; translate without reflexive pronoun.
35. This is an example of comments made by Luther that can be interpreted as anti-Semitic.
36. Main and sub-clause in *Konjunktiv II*, translate *gerade als* with "as if'" and use indicative in English.
37. Translate as "understanding."
38. The verb is *binden an* "to bind to": *ist . . . an . . . gebunden* (= *sein*-passive).
39. *um . . . willen* (preposition) means "for the sake of."
40. Translate as "they (referring to educated Christians) don't need anything like this."
41. Translate *warten* here as "maintain."
42. Same as *danach*.
43. Translate *warten* here as "maintain."
44. Translate *zu Haufe* as *zusammen* (together).
45. Translate *warten* here as "maintain."

kann, muss man je zum wenigsten einen Tag in der Woche dazu ausschießen.[46] Weil aber von alters her der Sonntag dazu gestellt ist, soll mans[47] auch dabei bleiben lassen, auf dass es in einträchtiger Ordnung gehe und niemand durch unnötige Neuerung eine Unordnung mache. Also ist das die einfältige Meinung dieses Gebotes: Weil man sonst Feiertag hält, dass man solche Feier anlege, Gottes Wort zu lernen; also dass dieses Tages eigentliches Amt sei das Predigtamt um des jungen Volkes und armen Haufens willen; doch das Feiern nicht so eng gespannt, dass darum andere zufälligen Arbeit, so man nicht umgehen kann, verboten wäre. Derhalben wenn man fragt, was da gesagt sei: Du sollst den Feiertag heiligen? so antworte: Den Feiertag heiligen heißt soviel als heilig halten. Was ist denn heilig halten? Nichts anders denn heilige Worte, Werke und Leben führen; denn der Tag bedarf für sich selbst keines Heiligens,[48] denn er ist an sich selbst heilig geschaffen; Gott will aber haben, dass er dir heilig sei. Also wird er deinethalben heilig und unheilig, so du heiliges oder unheiliges Ding daran treibst. Wie geht nun solches Heiligen[49] zu? Nicht also, dass man hinter dem Ofen sitze und keine grobe Arbeit tue oder einen Kranz aufsetze und seine besten Kleider anziehe, sondern (wie gesagt) dass man Gottes Wort handle und sich darin übe.[50] Und zwar wir Christen sollen immerdar solchen Feiertag halten, eitel heiliges Ding treiben, das ist, täglich mit Gottes Wort umgehen, im Herzen und Mund umtragen.[51] Aber weil wir (wie gesagt) nicht alle Zeit und Muße haben, müssen wir die Woche etliche Stunden für die Jugend oder zum wenigsten einen Tag für den ganzen Haufen dazu[52] brauchen, dass man sich allein damit bekümmere und eben die zehn Gebote, den Glauben und Vaterunser treibe und also unser ganzes Leben und Wesen nach Gottes Wort richte.[53] Welche Zeit nun das[54] in Schwang und Übung geht,[55] da wird ein rechter Feiertag gehalten. Wo nicht, so soll es kein Christenfeiertag heißen; denn feiern und müßig gehen können die Unchristen auch wohl, wie auch das ganze Geschwür unserer Geistlichen täglich in der Kirche steht, singt und klingt, heiligt aber keinen Feiertag, denn sie kein Gottes Wort predigen noch üben,[56] sondern eben dawider[57] lehren und leben.

Denn das Wort Gottes ist das Heiligtum über alle Heiligtümer, ja das einige, das wir Christen wissen und haben. Denn ob wir gleich aller Heiligen Gebeine oder heilige und

---

46. Translate as *auswählen*.
47. Abbreviation for *man es*.
48. Nominalized noun derived from the verb *heiligen*; translate with "ing"-form in English.
49. See above.
50. Whole sentence in *Konjunktiv I*; translate with indicative.
51. Translate as *tragen*.
52. *Da*-compound refers to *dass*-clause.
53. *Dass*-clause in *Konjunktiv I*, translate with indicative.
54. Here used as a demonstrative pronoun referring back to the previous sentence.
55. Translate *in Schwang und Übung gehen* as "to become customary."
56. Verb in a grammatically incorrect position; translate as if in second position.
57. Translate as *dagegen*.

geweihte Kleider auf einem Haufen hätten, so wäre uns doch nichts damit geholfen;[58] denn es ist alles totes Ding, das niemand heiligen kann. Aber Gottes Wort ist der Schatz, der alle Dinge heilig macht, dadurch sie selbst, die Heiligen alle,[59] sind geheiligt worden. Welche Stunde man nun Gottes Wort handelt, predigt, hört, liest oder bedenkt, so wird dadurch Person, Tag und Werk geheiligt, nicht des äußerlichen Werkes halber, sondern des Wortes halber,[60] so [es][61] uns alle zu Heiligen macht. Derhalben[62] sage ich allezeit, dass alle unser Leben und Werke in dem Wort Gottes gehen müssen, sollen sie Gott gefällig oder heilig heißen. Wo das geschieht, so geht dies Gebot in seiner Kraft und Erfüllung.[63] Wiederum, was für Wesen und Werk außer Gottes Wort geht, das ist vor Gott unheilig, es scheine und gleiße,[64] wie es wolle, wenn mans[65] mit eitel Heiligtum behinge, als da sind die erdichteten geistlichen Stände, die Gottes Wort nicht wissen und in ihren Werken Heiligkeit suchen. Darum merke,[66] dass die Kraft und Macht dieses Gebotes steht nicht im Feiern, sondern im Heiligen, also dass dieser Tag eine sonderliche heilige Übung habe. Denn andere Arbeiten und Geschäfte heißen eigentlich nicht heilige Übungen, es sei denn[67] der Mensch [ist] zuvor heilig. Hier aber muss ein solches Werk geschehen, dadurch ein Mensch selbst heilig werde, welches allein (wie gehört) durch Gottes Wort geschieht; dazu denn gestiftet und geordnet sind Stätte, Zeit, Personen und der ganze äußerliche Gottesdienst, dass solches auch öffentlich im Schwang gehe.[68]

Weil nun so viel an Gottes Wort gelegen ist, dass ohne dasselbige[69] kein Feiertag geheiligt wird, sollen wir wissen, dass Gott dies Gebot streng will gehalten haben[70] und strafen alle, die sein Wort verachten, nicht hören noch lernen wollen, sonderlich in der Zeit, so dazu geordnet ist. Darum sündigen wider dies Gebot nicht allein, die den Feiertag gröblich missbrauchen und verunheiligen,[71] als die um ihres Geizes oder Leichtfertigkeit willen Gottes Wort nachlassen zu hören, oder in Tavernen liegen, toll[72] und voll sind wie die Säue; sondern auch der andere Haufe, so Gottes Wort hören als einen andern Tand[73] und nur aus Gewohnheit zur Predigt und wieder herausgehen, und

---

58. Whole sentence in *Konjunktiv II* stating a hypothetical.

59. Specifies the *sie*.

60. Preposition + genitive after the noun meaning *wegen* (because of).

61. Add it (referring to *des Wortes*) here as subject.

62. Translate as *deswegen*.

63. Modern German: *tritt in Kraft und geht in Erfüllung* "takes effect and comes true."

64. Translate as "blaze."

65. Abbreviation for *man es*.

66. Imperative form.

67. Translate *es sei denn* as "unless."

68. Translate *in Schwang gehen* as "to become customary."

69. Translate as "the very same."

70. Special use of the modal verb *wollen*: if used with perfect infinitve form (*gehalten haben*), it usually expresses a claim, but here it conveys as passive meaning. Translate as "wants to be upheld."

71. Translate as *entheiligen* "to desecrate."

72. Translate as "mad."

73. Translate as "frills" or "froth."

wenn das Jahr um ist, können sie heuer so viel als fert.[74] Denn bisher hat man gemeint, es wäre wohl gefeiert, wenn man sonntags eine Messe oder das Evangelium hätte hören lesen;[75] aber nach Gottes Wort hat niemand gefragt, wie es auch niemand gelehrt hat.

Jetzt, weil wir Gottes Wort haben, tun wir gleichwohl den Missbrauch nicht ab, lassen uns immer predigen und vermahnen, hörens[76] aber ohne Ernst und Sorge. Darum wisse,[77] dass nicht allein ums[78] Hören zu tun ist, sondern auch soll gelernt und behalten werden, und denke[79] nicht, dass es in deiner Willkür stehe[80] oder nicht große Macht daran liege;[81] sondern dass Gottes Gebot ist, der es fördern wird, wie du sein Wort gehört, gelernt und geehrt habest.[82]

Desgleichen sind auch zu strafen die ekligen Geister, welche, wenn sie eine Predigt oder zwei gehört haben, sind sie es satt und überdrüssig,[83] als die es nun selbst wohl können und keines Meisters mehr bedürfen.

Denn das (NOM) ist (verb) eben die Sünde (NOM), so (which/that) man (NOM) bisher unter die Todsünden gezählt (v2) hat (v1) und heißet (verb, *Konjunktiv I*)[84] Akidia (AKK),[85] das (NOM) ist (verb) Trägheit oder Überdruss, eine feindselige, schädliche Plage (all NOM), damit (with that) der Teufel (NOM) vieler Herzen (AKK)[86] bezaubert (verb) und betrügt (verb), auf dass er (NOM) uns (AKK) übereile (verb, *Konjunktiv I*) und das Wort Gottes (AKK + GEN) wieder heimlich entziehe (verb, *Konjunktiv I*).[87]

Denn das lasse dir gesagt sein: Ob du es gleich aufs beste könntest und aller Dinge Meister wärest, so bist du doch täglich unter des Teufels Reich, der weder Tag noch Nacht ruhet, dich zu beschleichen, dass er in deinem Herzen Unglauben und böse Gedanken

---

74. Translate as *heute so viel wie damals* (today as much as before).

75. The perfect tense of *hören* can be formed with the infinitive form if constructed with a second verb. *ich habe ihn lesen hören* or *ich habe ihn lesen gehört* (I have heard him reading). *hätte lesen hören* (verbs put in correct order) is present perfect of *Konjunktiv II*. Translate as "would hear read."

76. Abbreviation for *hören es*.

77. Imperative form.

78. Abbreviation for *um das*.

79. Imperative form.

80. *Konjunktiv I* form.

81. *Konjunktiv I* form.

82. *Konjunktiv I* form.

83. Second part of the *welche*-clause.

84. Translate with indicative.

85. Derived from the Greek ἀκήδεια and used as a term in theology; Luther explains its meaning in the following sentence.

86. Genitive ending, but has to be translated as an accusative object.

87. Whole clause in *Konjunktiv I*; translate with indicative.

wider die vorigen und alle Gebote anzünde.[88] Darum musst du immerdar Gottes Wort im Herzen, Mund und vor den Ohren haben. Wo aber das Herz müßig steht und das Wort nicht klingt, so bricht er[89] ein und hat den Schaden getan, ehe mans[90] gewahr wird. Wiederum hat es[91] die Kraft, wo mans[92] mit Ernst betrachtet, hört und handelt, dass es nimmer ohne Frucht abgeht, sondern allzeit neuen Verstand, Lust und Andacht erweckt, reines Herz und Gedanken macht; denn es sind nicht faule noch tote, sondern geschäftige lebendige Worte. Und ob uns gleich kein anderer Nutz und Not triebe,[93] so sollte doch das jedermann dazu reizen, dass dadurch der Teufel gescheucht und verjagt, dazu dies Gebot erfüllt wird und Gott gefälliger ist denn alle anderen gleißenden Heuchelwerke.[94]

(. . .)

---

88. *Konjunktiv I*; translate with indicative.
89. Refers to *der Teufel*.
90. Abbreviation for *man es*.
91. Refers to *das Wort*.
92. Abbreviation for *man es*.
93. *Konjunktiv I*; translate with indicative.
94. Translate as "hypocritical works."

Immanuel Kant

Der Schöne Magister

6

Considered one of the most influential German philosophers during the Age of Enlightenment, Immanuel Kant was born on April 22, 1724 in Königsberg, Prussia. He was baptized Emanuel and was the fourth of nine children to his parents, Johann Georg and Anna Regina Cant. The spelling of both of his names would change as he grew. After learning Hebrew at the age of twenty-two, he changed the spelling of his first name to Immanuel. Likewise, he would also change the spelling of his surname to Kant so that it would better align with German spelling.[1]

Kant grew up in a strictly religious family. The family were Pietists, a devout sect of Lutherans. Religious thought, morality, and strict codes of behavioral conduct were instilled at a very young age and proved to be very influential. One of the theological beliefs instilled in Kant was that humanity was so corrupt that it was impossible for a human being to keep the commandments of God. This concept was something that remained in Kant's thoughts throughout his life.[2]

Although some consider the Pietist tradition to be anti-intellectual, in the late seventeenth century it was one of the primary factors for the spread of education in Germany.[3] Schools were set up throughout the Prussian Empire, including one in Königsberg. At the age of eight, Kant would be sent to this school to begin his studies. Very early on, Kant's brilliance was recognized. He entered university at the age of sixteen and graduated six years later.[4] He then worked as a local tutor and published some texts. Through this experience, he earned the title of *der schöne Magister*.[5] Yet, it would not be until 1754 that he would submit his doctoral thesis and another fifteen years before he would be appointed to a professorship.[6]

Throughout his academic career, Kant published a number of works. His 1781 publication of *Kritik der reinen Vernunft* is considered one of his most important works and is also one of the most important works on Western thought. Kant was fifty-seven years old at the time of its publication, and it is considered his first major publication.

---

1. Roger Scruton, *Kant: A Very Short Introduction* (Oxford: Oxford University Press, 2001), 1.
2. Anthony Kenny, *Immanuel Kant: A Very Brief History* (London: SPCK, 2019), 3.
3. Scruton, 1.
4. Scruton, 2
5. Scruton, 4
6. Kenny, 4.

It is concerning this title that he corresponded with Jewish Enlightenment Philosopher Moses Mendelssohn, stating that the book was a product of twelve years of reflection.[7]

Though Kant is primarily considered a philosopher, his impact on theology has been monumental. As Olsen observes, many nineteenth-century theologians have found Kant's 1793 text *Die Religion innerhalb der Grenzen der bloßen Vernunft* a valuable proposal to end the war of science with religion.[8] It is reasonable to assert that these theological underpinnings within Kant's writing are a product of his religious upbringing. Yet, not all philosophers welcome input from a theologian, nor do all theologians welcome input from a philosopher. Nietzsche, for example, was critical of Kant, questioning why many German scholars are delighted by the works of Kant when they themselves are the children of pastors. Ultimately, Nietzsche likened the work of Kant to that of Luther and called his success a theologian's success.[9]

Kant's greatest contribution (and perhaps the most controversial) to theological thought was his essay titled, "Was ist Aufklärung?"[10] It was within this essay that he declared the phrase, *Sapere aude*![11] Kant wrote of the importance of individuals thinking for themselves and rejecting the knowledge and ideologies that are imposed on them by both religious and political authorities.[12] Though the text was not a rejection of religion or religious ideas as a whole, just as Luther's writings challenged the authority of the Catholic Church, so too Kant's writings challenged both Catholic and Protestant authority and changed the way future theologians and apologists approached their fundamental beliefs.

Introduction to Kant's Writing Style

Reading Kant is difficult, even for native German speakers, because of the complex and interlaced sentence structure and the use of vocabulary that is no longer common in modern German or easy to locate in a dictionary. To support you in your effort to translate Kant's texts, we have provided more than two hundred footnotes explaining grammatical features as well as offering you translations of words and phrases embedded in the text.

You will encounter many modal particles, which will give you the chance to practice translating them in context. We will provide footnotes to the ones with a more obscure meaning. Kant uses *aber* frequently as a modal particle in the middle of the sentence.

---

7. Scruton, 9.

8. Olsen, *Journey of Modern Theology*, 23.

9. Aaron Ridley and Judith Norma, *Nietzsche: The Anti-Christ, Ecce Homo, Twilight of the Idols, and Other Writings* (Cambridge: Cambridge University Press, 2005), 9.

10. Translated as, "What is Enlightenment?"

11. Translated as, "Think for yourself."

12. Olsen, 45.

In most cases, you can translate it with "but" and put it at the beginning of the sentence. Also, he often refers back to a previous noun with the demonstrative pronouns *derselbe* or *derjenige* (see chapter 4 section 4.1.5 for more details). To ensure readability, it is often better to repeat the referent noun in the translation, as English does not have an equivalent to these pronouns and the noun in question has often been mentioned further back in text.

Exercises

 **LEICHT**

1. Kant uses very complex sentence structure. Steps 2 and 3 on our checklist are very important while reading Kant. Find all the commas, conjunctions, and relative pronouns in the following sentences from the text:

   > *Besonders ist hiebei: daß das Publikum, welches zuvor von ihnen unter dieses Joch gebracht worden [ist], sie hernach selbst zwingt, darunter zu bleiben, wenn es von einigen seiner Vormünder, die selbst aller Aufklärung unfähig sind, dazu aufgewiegelt worden [ist]*

   > *Faulheit und Feigheit sind die Ursachen, warum ein so großer Teil der Menschen, nachdem sie die Natur längst von fremder Leitung freigesprochen (naturaliter maiorennes) [hat], dennoch gerne zeitlebens unmündig bleiben; und warum es anderen so leicht wird, sich zu deren Vormündern aufzuwerfen*

 **SCHWER**

2. Another feature of Kant's writing style is the frequent use of modal particles, and this text presents a good opportunity to study their use.

   While reading the text, fill out the table below, using tallies to mark how often each respective meaning is used.

Modal particle	Meaning 1	Meaning 2	Meaning 3
bloß			
ja			
schon			
wohl			
sogar			

Excerpt from Beantwortung der Frage:
Was Ist Aufklärung? (1784)

Aufklärung ist der Ausgang des Menschen aus seiner selbstverschuldeten Unmündigkeit. Unmündigkeit ist das Unvermögen, sich seines Verstandes ohne Leitung eines anderen zu bedienen. Selbstverschuldet ist diese Unmündigkeit, wenn die Ursache derselben[13] nicht am Mangel des Verstandes, sondern [an] der Entschließung und des Mutes liegt, sich seiner ohne Leitung eines andern[14] zu bedienen. Sapere aude! Habe Mut, dich deines eigenen Verstandes zu bedienen! ist also der Wahlspruch der Aufklärung.

Faulheit und Feigheit sind die Ursachen, warum ein so großer Teil der Menschen, nachdem sie die Natur längst von fremder Leitung freigesprochen (naturaliter maiorennes[15]) [hat], dennoch gerne zeitlebens unmündig bleiben; und warum es anderen so leicht wird, sich zu deren Vormündern aufzuwerfen. Es ist so bequem, unmündig zu sein. Habe ich ein Buch, das für mich Verstand hat, einen Seelsorger, der für mich Gewissen hat, einen Arzt, der für mich die Diät beurteilt usw.,[16] so brauche ich mich ja[17] nicht selbst zu bemühen. Ich habe nicht nötig[18] zu denken, wenn ich nur bezahlen kann; andere werden das verdrießliche Geschäft schon[19] für mich übernehmen. Daß der bei weitem größte Teil der Menschen (darunter das ganze schöne Geschlecht[20]) den Schritt zur Mündigkeit, außer dem[21] daß er beschwerlich ist, auch für sehr gefährlich halte:[22] dafür sorgen schon[23] jene Vormünder, die die Oberaufsicht über sie gütigst[24] auf sich genommen haben.

> Nachdem sie (die Vormünder) (NOM) ihr Hausvieh (AKK) zuerst dumm gemacht (v2) haben (v1) und sorgfältig verhüteten (verb, prevented), daß diese ruhigen Geschöpfe (NOM) ja (here: in no case) keinen Schritt (AKK) außer dem (outside of) Gängelwagen (here: cage), darin (here: in which) sie (die Vormünder) (NOM) sie

---

13. Refers to *Unmündigkeit*.

14. Translate as "someone else."

15. Latin for *von Natur aus mündig* (of age by nature).

16. Conditional sentence without *wenn*; translate with an if-sentence.

17. Modal particle; expresses that the sentence refers to something already known to the reader.

18. Attention! There is a fixed phrase *etwas nicht nötig haben* "to not have to put up with something," but it does not fit in this context. Here, translate as "do not need to"!

19. Modal particle; here it expresses an exception and is best translated with "surely."

20. *schöne Geschlecht* (literally "beautiful sex") refers to women.

21. Although it is written as one word (*außerdem*) in modern German, it means the same and is best translated as "besides."

22. *Konjunktiv I*; translate with indicative.

23. Modal particle; translate here as "already."

24. Superlative to *gütig* (kind).

(die Geschöpfe) (AKK) einsperr[e]ten (verb), wagen (v2) durften (v1), <u>so zeigen (verb)</u> <u>sie (NOM) ihnen (GEN) nachher die Gefahr (AKK)</u>, die (NOM) ihnen (GEN) droh[e]t (verb), wenn sie (NOM) es (AKK) versuchen (verb), allein zu gehen (infinitive).

Nun ist diese Gefahr zwar eben so groß nicht, denn sie würden durch einigemal Fallen[25] wohl[26] endlich gehen lernen; allein[27] ein Beispiel von der Art macht doch[28] schüchtern und schreckt gemeiniglich[29] von allen ferneren Versuchen ab.

Es ist also für jeden einzelnen Menschen schwer, sich aus <u>der ihm beinahe zur Natur gewordenen Unmündigkeit</u>[30] herauszuarbeiten. Er hat sie sogar lieb gewonnen und ist vorderhand[31] wirklich unfähig, sich seines eigenen Verstandes zu bedienen,[32] weil man ihn niemals den Versuch davon machen ließ.[33] Satzungen und Formeln, <u>diese</u> <u>mechanischen Werkzeuge eines vernünftigen Gebrauchs oder vielmehr Mißbrauchs</u> <u>seiner Naturgaben</u>,[34] sind die Fußschellen[35] einer immerwährenden Unmündigkeit. <u>Wer</u> <u>sie auch abwürfe</u>,[36, 37] würde dennoch auch über den schmalesten Graben einen nur[38] unsicheren Sprung tun, weil er zu dergleichen freier Bewegung nicht gewöhnt ist. Daher gibt es nur wenige, denen es gelungen ist, durch eigene Bearbeitung ihres Geistes sich aus der Unmündigkeit heraus zu wickeln[39] und dennoch einen sicheren Gang zu tun.

Daß aber ein Publikum sich selbst aufkläre,[40] ist eher möglich; ja[41] es ist, wenn man ihm nur Freiheit läßt, beinahe unausbleiblich. Denn da[42] werden sich immer einige Selbstdenkende,[43] sogar[44] unter den eingesetzten Vormündern des großen Haufens

---

25. Nominalized verb; translate with an "-ing" form.
26. Modal particle; translate here as "probably."
27. Modal particle; translate here as "even."
28. Modal particle; translate here as "surely."
29. Translate as "commonly."
30. Complex noun phrase with participle II as adjective; translate *ihm beinahe zur Natur gewordene* with a relative clause.
31. Translate as "for the time being."
32. Verb with direct object in the genitive case.
33. Past tense of *lassen*, passive-like construction with impersonal pronoun *man* and verb + *lassen* (let).
34. Explanation to *Satzungen und Formeln*.
35. Literally "legcuffs," but "shackles" fits better in English.
36. *Konjunktiv II*; translate with "would + verb."
37. *Wer*-sentence is subject to the main clause.
38. Scalar particle; translate here as "merely."
39. *herauswickeln* literally "to unwrap"; translate here as "to put off."
40. *Konjunktiv I*; translate with indicative.
41. Modal particle; translate here simply as "yes."
42. Translate as "there."
43. Nominalized adjective derived from participle I of *selbst denken*; translate as "independent thinkers."
44. Modal particle; translate here as "even."

finden, <u>welche</u>, nachdem sie das Joch[45] der Unmündigkeit selbst abgeworfen haben, <u>den Geist einer vernünftigen Schätzung des eigenen Werts und des Berufs[46] jedes Menschen, selbst zu denken, um sich verbreiten werden.</u>[47] Besonders ist hiebei:[48] daß das Publikum, welches zuvor von ihnen[49] unter dieses Joch gebracht worden [ist], sie[50] hernach[51] selbst zwingt, darunter[52] zu bleiben, wenn es von einigen seiner[53] Vormünder, die selbst aller Aufklärung unfähig sind, dazu aufgewiegelt worden [ist]; so schädlich ist es, Vorurteile zu pflanzen, weil sie[54] sich zuletzt an denen selbst rächen, die oder deren[55] Vorgänger ihre[56] Urheber gewesen sind. Daher kann ein Publikum nur langsam zur Aufklärung gelangen.

> Durch eine Revolution wird (v1) vielleicht wohl[57] ein Abfall von persönlichem Despotism (NOM)[58] und gewinnsüchtiger oder herrschsüchtiger Bedrückung (NOM), aber niemals wahre Reform der Denkungsart (NOM) zustande kommen[59](v2); sondern neue Vorurteile (NOM) werden (v1), ebensowohl als[60] die alten [Vorurteile] (NOM), zum Leitbande des gedankenlosen großen Haufens (PREP COMP) dienen (v2, "serve as").

Zu dieser Aufklärung aber wird nichts erfordert als[61] Freiheit; und zwar[62] die unschädlichste[63] unter allem, was[64] nur[65] Freiheit heißen mag,[66] nämlich die:[67] von seiner[68] Vernunft in allen Stücken öffentlichen Gebrauch zu machen. Nun höre ich aber

---

45. Translate as "yoke."
46. Translate here as "mission" or "vocation."
47. The underlined part is one relative clause in the future tense which refers to *Selbstdenkende*.
48. Outdated for *hierbei*; translate whole phrase as "it is here exceptional that . . ."
49. Refers back to *Vormündern*.
50. Refers back to *Vormündern*.
51. Outdated for *danach*; translate as "afterward."
52. Refers back to *Joch*; translate as "underneath it."
53. Refers back to *Publikum*.
54. Refers back to *Vorurteile*.
55. The relative pronouns *die* and *deren* refer back to *an denen* and it all refers back to *Vormünder*.
56. Refers back to *Vorurteile*.
57. *Vielleicht* and *wohl* are both modal particles expressing the same thing ("probably"). Used together they convey a weak probability.
58. The same as in English, usually *Despotismus* in German.
59. Future tense of the verb *zustande kommen*; translate as "will come about."
60. Outdated for *ebenso wie*; translate as "as well as."
61. *aber. . . als* translate as "but."
62. Modal particle; translate *und zwar* together as "namely."
63. Superlative to *unschädlich* (harmless).
64. Refers back to *allem* (here: "all").
65. Modal particle; translate here as "ever."
66. Verb *mögen*, here used like a modal verb; translate as "may."
67. *die* functions here as a demonstrative pronoun and is specified in the part after the colon.
68. Not referring to a noun; translate here as "one's."

von allen Seiten rufen: räsonniert[69] nicht! Der Offizier sagt: räsonniert nicht, sondern exerziert! Der Finanzrat: räsonniert nicht, sondern bezahlt! Der Geistliche: räsonniert nicht, sondern glaubt! (Nur ein einziger Herr in der Welt sagt: räsonniert, soviel ihr wollt und worüber ihr wollt, aber gehorcht!) Hier ist überall Einschränkung der Freiheit. Welche Einschränkung aber[70] ist der Aufklärung hinderlich, welche nicht, sondern ihr wohl[71] gar[72] beförderlich?[73]–Ich antworte: Der öffentliche Gebrauch seiner[74] Vernunft muß jederzeit frei sein, und der[75] allein kann Aufklärung unter Menschen <u>zustande bringen</u>;[76] der Privatgebrauch derselben[77] aber darf öfters <u>sehr enge eingeschränkt</u>[78] sein, ohne doch[79] darum[80] den Fortschritt der Aufklärung sonderlich zu hindern. Ich verstehe[81] aber unter dem öffentlichen Gebrauche seiner eigenen Vernunft denjenigen,[82] den[83] jemand als Gelehrter von ihr[84] vor dem ganzen Publikum der Leserwelt macht. Den Privatgebrauch nenne ich <u>denjenigen, den</u>[85] er <u>in einem gewissen ihm anvertrauten bürgerlichen Posten oder Amte</u>[86] von seiner Vernunft machen darf. Nun ist zu manchen Geschäften, die in das Interesse des gemeinen Wesens laufen,[87] ein gewisser Mechanism[88] notwendig, vermittelst dessen[89] einige Glieder des gemeinen Wesens sich bloß[90] passiv verhalten müssen, um durch eine künstliche Einhelligkeit von der Regierung zu öffentlichen Zwecken gerichtet[91] [zu werden] oder wenigstens von der Zerstörung dieser Zwecke abgehalten zu werden. Hier ist es nun freilich[92] nicht erlaubt zu räsonnieren; sondern man muß gehorchen. Sofern sich aber dieser Teil der

---

69. Verb derived from *Räson* (reason, intellect, sense); best translated as "reason."
70. Modal particle; translate as "but" and place at the beginning of the sentence.
71. Modal particle; translate as "presumably."
72. Modal particle; translate as "even."
73. Adjective derived from the verb *befördern* "to promote," here in opposition to *hinderlich* "obstructive"; translate as "promoting."
74. Not referring to a noun; translate here as "one's."
75. *Der* functions here as a demonstrative pronoun and refers back to *Gebrauch*.
76. Translate as "achieve."
77. Refers back to *Vernunft* (only feminine noun close by); translate as "of the same."
78. Translate as "very tightly restricted."
79. Here used in the sense of *jedoch*; translate as "though."
80. Here used in the sense of *damit*, translate as "by it" or "with it."
81. Verb with preposition *verstehen unter* "to recognize as."
82. Refers back to *Gebrauche*; translate as "the kind of use"; further specified by the following relative clause.
83. Refers back to *denjenigen* (meaning *Gebrauch*, "use").
84. Refers back to *Vernunft*.
85. Refers back to *Gebrauche*.
86. One complex noun phrase.
87. Translate *in etwas laufen* as "to affect."
88. The same as in English, usually *Mechanismus* in German.
89. Relative clause in the genitive case, because the preposition *vermittelst* (modern German *mittels* "by means of") takes the genitive.
90. Modal particle; translate as "simply."
91. Translate as "directed."
92. Modal particle; translate as "of course."

Maschine zugleich als Glied eines ganzen gemeinen Wesens, ja sogar[93] [als Glied] der Weltbürgergesellschaft ansieht, mithin[94] in der Qualität eines Gelehrten, der sich an ein Publikum im eigentlichen Verstande durch Schriften wendet, kann er allerdings räsonnieren,[95] ohne daß dadurch die Geschäfte leiden, zu denen[96] er zum Teile[97] als passives Glied angesetzt[98] ist. So würde es sehr verderblich sein, wenn ein Offizier, dem von seinen Oberen etwas anbefohlen[99] wird, im Dienste über die Zweckmäßigkeit oder Nützlichkeit dieses Befehls laut vernünfteln[100] wollte; er muß gehorchen. Es kann ihm aber billigermaßen[101] nicht verwehrt werden, als Gelehrter über die Fehler im Kriegsdienste[102] Anmerkungen zu machen und diese seinem Publikum zur Beurteilung vorzulegen. Der Bürger kann sich nicht weigern, die ihm auferlegten Abgaben zu leisten; sogar kann ein vorwitziger[103] Tadel solcher Auflagen, wenn sie von ihm geleistet werden sollen, als ein Skandal (das[104] allgemeine Widersetzlichkeiten[105] veranlassen könnte) bestraft werden. Ebenderselbe[106] handelt demohngeachtet[107] der Pflicht eines Bürgers nicht entgegen, wenn er als Gelehrter wider[108] die Unschicklichkeit oder auch Ungerechtigkeit solcher Ausschreibungen[109] öffentlich seine Gedanken äußert. Ebenso ist ein Geistlicher verbunden,[110] seinen Katechismusschülern und seiner Gemeine[111] nach dem Symbol der Kirche, der er dient, seinen Vortrag[112] zu tun, denn er ist auf diese Bedingung angenommen worden. Aber als Gelehrter hat er volle Freiheit, ja sogar den Beruf[113] dazu, alle seine sorgfältig geprüften und wohlmeinenden Gedanken über das Fehlerhafte in jenem Symbol und [seine] Vorschläge wegen besserer Einrichtung des Religions- und Kirchenwesens dem Publikum mitzuteilen.[114] Es ist hiebei[115] auch[116]

---

93. Both are modal particles; translate as "yes even."

94. Translate here as "at times."

95. Main clause.

96. Relative clause with *zu*; refers back to *Geschäfte.*

97. Translate as "partly."

98. Translate here as "attached."

99. Outdated for *befehlen* "order," here in the passive voice.

100. Verb derived from *Vernunft*; translate as "reason."

101. Outdated; translate as *mit Recht* "rightly" or "justly."

102. Outdated for *Kriegsdienst* "military service."

103. Translate here as "hasty."

104. Relative clause specifying *Skandal*, although the gender does not match.

105. Outdated for *Widerstand* "protest" or *Aufstand* "uprising"; be aware that the noun is here used in the plural.

106. Outdated demonstrative pronoun; translate as "exactly the same," and you could add "person" for readability.

107. Outdated for *demungeachtet* "notwithstanding."

108. Preposition meaning "against."

109. Translate as "announcements." Kant refers here to the obligations (*Auflagen*) in the sentence before.

110. Translate as "bound."

111. Usually *Gemeinde* "congregation."

112. Translate here as "sermon."

113. Translate here as "mission" or "vocation."

114. Verb *mitteilen* "to inform" takes three complements (subject, direct object, and dative object).

115. Usually *hierbei*; translate here as "with this." It refers back to the notion expressed in the previous sentence.

116. Modal particle; translate as "anyway."

nichts, was dem Gewissen zur Last gelegt[117] werden könnte. Denn was er zufolge[118] seines Amts als Geschäftträger[119] der Kirche lehrt, das[120] stellt er als etwas vor, in Ansehung dessen[121] er nicht freie Gewalt hat, nach eigenem Gutdünken[122] zu lehren, sondern das er nach Vorschrift und im Namen eines andern vorzutragen angestellt ist. Er wird sagen: unsere Kirche lehrt dieses oder jenes; das sind die Beweisgründe, deren sie[123] sich bedient. Er zieht alsdann allen praktischen Nutzen für seine Gemeinde aus Satzungen, die er selbst nicht mit voller Überzeugung unterschreiben würde, zu deren[124] Vortrag er sich gleichwohl[125] anheischig machen[126] kann, weil es doch[127] nicht ganz unmöglich ist, daß darin Wahrheit verborgen läge,[128] auf alle Fälle aber wenigstens doch [,daß] <u>nichts der innern Religion Widersprechendes</u>[129] darin angetroffen wird. Denn glaubte er das letztere darin zu finden,[130] so würde er sein Amt mit Gewissen nicht verwalten können; er müßte[131] es niederlegen. Der Gebrauch also, den ein angestellter Lehrer von seiner Vernunft vor seiner Gemeinde macht, ist bloß[132] ein Privatgebrauch, weil diese immer nur eine häusliche, <u>obzwar noch so</u>[133] große Versammlung ist; und <u>in Ansehung dessen</u>[134] ist er als Priester nicht frei und darf es auch nicht sein, weil er einen fremden Auftrag ausrichtet. Dagegen als Gelehrter, der durch Schriften zum eigentlichen Publikum, nämlich der Welt spricht, mithin[135] der Geistliche im öffentlichen Gebrauche seiner Vernunft, genießt [er] einer uneingeschränkten Freiheit,[136] sich seiner eigenen Vernunft zu bedienen und in seiner eigenen Person zu sprechen. Denn daß die Vormünder des Volks (in geistlichen Dingen) selbst wieder unmündig sein sollen, ist eine Ungereimtheit, die auf Verewigung der Ungereimtheiten hinausläuft.[137]

---

117. Verb *jemandem etwas zur Last legen* "to accuse somebody of something"; here the accused is the conscience (*das Gewissen*).

118. Preposition; usually after the referent noun, here in front of it (*seines Amts*); translate as "according to."

119. Usually *Geschäftsträger* "representative."

120. Refers back to *was.*

121. Should be *in dessen* (referring back to *etwas*) *Ansehung* "in whose consideration."

122. Translate as "at one's own discretion."

123. Refers back to *Kirche.*

124. Refers back to *Satzungen.*

125. Translate as "all the same."

126. Outdated for *sich verpflichten* "to commit oneself."

127. Translate as "after all."

128. *Konjunktiv II*; translate with "would + verb."

129. Subject of the subclause, *Widersprechendes* is a nominalized adjective derived from a participle I.

130. If-clause without *wenn.*

131. *Konjunktiv II*; translate with "would + verb."

132. Modal particle; translate as "simply."

133. Translate together as "though however."

134. Translate here as "considering this."

135. Translate as "at times."

136. Translate as direct object of the sentence.

137. Translate *herauslaufen aus* as "to lead to."

Aber sollte nicht eine Gesellschaft von Geistlichen, etwa[138] eine Kirchenversammlung oder eine ehrwürdige Classis[139] (wie sie sich unter den Holländern selbst nennt) berechtigt sein, sich eidlich[140] untereinander auf ein gewisses unveränderliches Symbol zu verpflichten, um so eine unaufhörliche Obervormundschaft über jedes ihrer[141] Glieder und vermittelst ihrer[142] über das Volk zu führen und diese so gar[143] zu verewigen? Ich sage: das ist ganz unmöglich. Ein solcher Kontrakt, der auf immer alle weitere Aufklärung vom Menschengeschlechte abzuhalten geschlossen würde,[144] ist schlechterdings null und nichtig; und sollte er auch durch die oberste Gewalt, durch Reichstage und die feierlichsten Friedensschlüsse bestätigt sein. Ein Zeitalter kann sich nicht verbünden und darauf[145] verschwören, das folgende [Zeitalter] in einen Zustand zu setzen, darin[146] es ihm[147] unmöglich werden muß, seine (vornehmlich so sehr angelegentliche) Erkenntnisse zu erweitern, von Irrtümern zu reinigen und überhaupt in der Aufklärung weiterzuschreiten. Das wäre[148] ein Verbrechen wider[149] die menschliche Natur, deren ursprüngliche Bestimmung gerade in diesem Fortschreiten besteht; und die Nachkommen sind also[150] vollkommen dazu[151] berechtigt, jene Beschlüsse, als [in] unbefugter und frevelhafter Weise genommen, zu verwerfen. Der Probierstein alles dessen, was[152] über ein Volk als Gesetz beschlossen werden kann, liegt in der Frage: ob ein Volk sich selbst wohl[153] ein solches Gesetz auferlegen könnte? Nun wäre[154] dieses wohl,[155] gleichsam in der Erwartung eines bessern, auf eine bestimmte kurze Zeit möglich, um eine gewisse Ordnung einzuführen; indem[156] man es zugleich jedem der Bürger, vornehmlich dem Geistlichen, frei ließe,[157] in der

---

138. Translate here as "for example."

139. Latin for *Klasse* "class."

140. Translate here as "by oath."

141. Refers back to *Gesellschaft*.

142. Refers back to *Gesellschaft*.

143. Translate as "in this manner even."

144. *einen Vertrag* (here: *Kontrakt*) *auf etwas* (*ab*)*schließen* "conclude a contract"; here the relative pronoun refers to *Kontrakt* in the previous sentence.

145. Points toward the infinitive with *zu* construction.

146. Refers back to *Zustand* and functions here as a relative pronoun; translate here as "in which."

147. Refers back to *das folgende*.

148. *Konjunktiv II*; translate with "would + verb."

149. Preposition meaning "against."

150. Modal particle; translate here as "thus."

151. Points toward the infinitive with *zu* construction.

152. Translate as "of everything that."

153. Modal particle emphasizing the improbability of the question already expressed by the use of *Konjunktiv II*; can be omitted in the translation.

154. *Konjunktiv II*; translate with "would + verb."

155. Modal particle emphasizing the improbability of the question already expressed by the use of *Konjunktiv II*; can be omitted in the translation.

156. Conjunction; best translated with "by + ing form."

157. Not to be confused with the verb *freilassen* "to release," *etwas jemanden frei lassen* means "to leave somebody the choice or freedom to do something."

Qualität eines Gelehrten öffentlich, d. i.[158] durch Schriften, über das Fehlerhafte der dermaligen[159] Einrichtung seine Anmerkungen zu machen, indessen[160] die eingeführte Ordnung noch immer[161] fortdauerte, bis die Einsicht in die Beschaffenheit dieser Sachen öffentlich so weit gekommen und bewährt worden [ist], daß sie durch Vereinigung ihrer Stimmen (wenngleich nicht aller) einen Vorschlag vor den Thron bringen könnte[n], um diejenigen Gemeinden in Schutz zu nehmen, die sich etwa nach ihren Begriffen der besseren Einsicht zu einer veränderten Religionseinrichtung geeinigt hätten, ohne doch diejenigen zu hindern, die es beim alten wollten bewenden lassen.[162] Aber auf eine beharrliche, von niemanden öffentlich zu bezweifelnde[163] Religionsverfassung auch nur binnen der Lebensdauer eines Menschen sich zu einigen, und dadurch einen Zeitraum in dem Fortgange der Menschheit zur Verbesserung gleichsam zu vernichten und fruchtlos, dadurch aber wohl gar der Nachkommenschaft nachteilig zu machen, ist schlechterdings unerlaubt.[164] Ein Mensch kann zwar[165] für seine Person und auch alsdann[166] nur auf einige Zeit in dem, was ihm zu wissen obliegt,[167] die Aufklärung aufschieben; aber auf sie Verzicht zu tun, es sei für seine Person,[168] mehr aber noch[169] für die Nachkommenschaft, heißt die heiligen Rechte der Menschheit [zu] verletzen und mit Füßen [zu] treten. Was aber nicht einmal ein Volk über sich selbst beschließen darf, das darf noch weniger[170] ein Monarch über das Volk beschließen; denn sein gesetzgebendes Ansehen beruht eben[171] darauf,[172] daß er den gesamten Volkswillen in dem seinigen[173] vereinigt. Wenn er nur darauf[174] sieht, daß alle wahre oder vermeinte[175] Verbesserung mit der bürgerlichen Ordnung zusammenbestehe,[176] so[177] kann er seine Untertanen übrigens[178] nur selbst

---

158. Abbreviation for *das ist.*
159. Usually *damaligen* "current."
160. Translate as "while."
161. Modal particle + *immer*; translate as "still."
162. Verb *bei etwas bewenden lassen*; translate as "to maintain."
163. Participle I used as adjective with *zu*; translate with a relative clause specifying *Religionsverfassung.*
164. Underlined clause is the main clause with three preceding infinitive with *zu* constructions (see markings).
165. Followed by *aber* after the colon, *zwar . . . aber* is translated by introducing the first clause with "although" and omitting *aber* in the second clause.
166. Modal particle + adverb; translate as "even then."
167. *Obliegen* outdated for *zufallen* "to fall to"; here "what falls to him to know."
168. Translate whole clause as "be it for his person."
169. Modal particles; translate as "but even more."
170. Modal particle + quantifier; translate as "even less."
171. Modal particle; translate here as "precisely."
172. Verb *beruhen auf* "to be based on"; *da*-compound points toward *dass*-sentence.
173. Refers back to *Wille* in *Volkswillen*; translate as "in his will."
174. Verb *sehen auf* "to see to"; *da*-compound points toward *dass*-sentence.
175. Usually *vermeintlich* "alleged."
176. Translate in the following order: *zusammen mit der bürgerlichen Ordnung bestehe*; the verb *bestehen* here means "exist," here in *Konjunktiv I*, translate with indicative.
177. Omit in the translation.
178. Modal particle; translate as "incidentally."

machen lassen, was sie um ihres Seelenheils willen zu tun nötig finden; das geht ihn nichts an,[179] wohl aber[180] zu verhüten, daß nicht einer den andern gewalttätig hindere,[181] an der Bestimmung und Beförderung desselben[182] nach allem seinen Vermögen[183] zu arbeiten. Es tut selbst seiner Majestät Abbruch, wenn er sich hierin mischt,[184] indem er die Schriften, wodurch seine Untertanen ihre Einsichten ins reine zu bringen[185] suchen, seiner Regierungsaufsicht würdigt, sowohl[186] wenn er dieses aus eigener höchsten Einsicht tut, wo er sich dem Vorwurfe aussetzt:[187] Caesar non est supra grammaticos,[188] als auch und noch weit mehr, wenn er seine oberste Gewalt so weit erniedrigt,[189] den geistlichen Despotism[190] einiger Tyrannen in seinem Staate gegen seine übrigen Untertanen zu unterstützen.

Wenn denn nun gefragt wird: leben wir jetzt in einem aufgeklärten Zeitalter? so ist die Antwort: Nein, aber wohl in einem Zeitalter der Aufklärung. Daß die Menschen, wie die Sachen jetzt stehen, im ganzen[191] genommen, schon imstande wären[192] oder darin[193] auch nur gesetzt werden könnten,[194] in Religionsdingen sich ihres eigenen Verstandes ohne Leitung eines andern sicher und gut zu bedienen, daran[195] fehlt noch sehr viel. Allein,[196] daß jetzt ihnen doch das Feld geöffnet wird, sich dahin frei zu bearbeiten[197] und [daß] die Hindernisse der allgemeinen Aufklärung oder des Ausganges aus ihrer selbstverschuldeten Unmündigkeit allmählich weniger werden, davon haben wir doch deutliche Anzeigen.[198] In diesem Betracht[199] ist dieses Zeitalter das Zeitalter der Aufklärung oder das Jahrhundert Friedrichs. (. . .)[200]

---

179. Verb *jemanden etwas angehen* "to concern."

180. Modal particles; translate as "but nevertheless."

181. *Konjunktiv I*; translate with indicative.

182. Refers back to *Seelenheil*.

183. Translate as "with all his capabilities."

184. Usually *hier einmischt*, verb *einmischen* "to interfere."

185. Verb *etwas ins Reine bringen* "to sort something out."

186. Coordinating conjunction *sowohl. . . als auch*, here connects two *wenn*-sentences; translate with "as well as."

187. Verb *aussetzen* with direct object in the dative case; translate as "expose."

188. Latin for *Der Herrscher steht nicht über den Grammatikern* (the emperor does not stand above the grammarians).

189. Translate construction as follows: "degrades his outmost power so far as to" + infinitive construction.

190. Usually *Despotismus*.

191. Translate as "as a whole."

192. Verb *imstande sein* "to be able to," here in *Konjunktiv II*; translate with "would + verb."

193. Refers back to *imstande*; translate here together with *setzen* in the passive voice as "to be put in a state."

194. *Konjunktiv II*; translate as "could."

195. *Da*-compound refers back to what has been said in the previous clauses; verb *fehlen an* "to lack."

196. *allein* followed by *doch* in the second part of the clause; translate as "even" and omit *doch*.

197. Translate as "to freely alter themselves in this way" (referring to the previous sentence).

198. Main clause is underlined.

199. Translate as "in this view."

200. We left out one paragraph, as it is less important and very hard to read and translate, but you can find it in the English translation included in the back of the book.

Ich habe den Hauptpunkt der Aufklärung, die[201] des Ausganges der Menschen aus ihrer selbstverschuldeten Unmündigkeit, vorzüglich[202] in Religionssachen gesetzt, weil in Ansehung der Künste und Wissenschaften unsere Beherrscher kein Interesse haben, den Vormund über ihre Untertanen zu spielen, [weil] überdem[203] auch jene[204] Unmündigkeit, so wie[205] die schädlichste, also auch die entehrendste unter allen ist. Aber die Denkungsart[206] eines Staatsoberhaupts, der die erstere begünstigt, geht noch weiter und sieht ein: daß selbst in Ansehung seiner Gesetzgebung es ohne Gefahr sei, seinen Untertanen zu erlauben, von ihrer eigenen Vernunft öffentlichen Gebrauch zu machen und ihre Gedanken über eine bessere Abfassung derselben,[207] sogar mit einer freimütigen Kritik der schon gegebenen,[208] der Welt öffentlich vorzulegen; davon wir ein glänzendes Beispiel haben, wodurch noch kein Monarch demjenigen[209] vorging, welchen wir verehren.

Aber auch nur derjenige,[210] der, selbst aufgeklärt, sich nicht vor Schatten fürchtet, zugleich aber ein wohldiszipliniertes zahlreiches Heer zum Bürgen[211] der öffentlichen Ruhe zur Hand hat,[212] kann das sagen, was ein Freistaat nicht wagen darf: räsonniert, so viel ihr wollt, und worüber ihr wollt; nur gehorcht! So zeigt sich hier ein befremdlicher, nicht erwarteter Gang[213] menschlicher Dinge; so wie auch sonst, wenn man ihn[214] im großen[215] betrachtet, darin fast alles paradox ist. Ein größerer Grad bürgerlicher Freiheit scheint der Freiheit des Geistes des Volks vorteilhaft und setzt ihr doch unübersteigliche[216] Schranken[217]; ein Grad weniger von jener[218] verschafft hingegen diesem[219] Raum,[220] sich nach allem seinen Vermögen[221] auszubreiten. Wenn denn die Natur unter dieser harten Hülle den Keim, für den sie[222] am zärtlichsten sorgt, nämlich den Hang und Beruf

---

201. The whole phrase is an explanation to *Aufklärung*; *die* functions as demonstrative pronoun but should be translated here as a relative pronoun introducing a relative clause.
202. Translate here as "mainly."
203. Usually *außerdem*; translate here as "additionally."
204. Refers back to *Unmündigkeit in Religionssachen*.
205. Usually *sowohl . . . als auch* "as well as."
206. Usually *Denkart* "mindset" or "way of thinking."
207. Refers back to *Gesetzgebung*.
208. Refers back to *Abfassung*.
209. Specified in the relative clause.
210. Translate as "but only that person."
211. Translate as "as guarantee."
212. Verb *zur Hand haben* "have at hand."
213. Translate here as "way."
214. Refers back to *Gang*.
215. Translate as "on a large scale."
216. Usually *unüberwindlich* "insurmountable."
217. Verb *Schranken setzen* "to set barriers."
218. Refers back to *bürgerlicher Freiheit*.
219. Refers back to *der Freiheit des Geistes des Volkes*.
220. Verb *Raum verschaffen* "to make space."
221. Translate as "with all his capabilities."
222. Refers back to *Natur*.

zum freien Denken,[223] ausgewickelt hat: so <u>wirkt</u> dieser[224] allmählich <u>zurück auf</u>[225] die Sinnesart des Volks (wodurch dieses[226] der Freiheit zu handeln <u>nach und nach</u>[227] fähiger wird), und endlich auch sogar <u>auf</u> die Grundsätze der Regierung, die[228] es[229] ihr[230] selbst zuträglich findet, <u>den Menschen, der nun mehr als Maschine ist, seiner Würde gemäß zu behandeln.</u>[231]

Königsberg in Preußen, den 30. September 1784

---

223. Specifies *Keim*.

224. Refers back to *Keim*.

225. Verb *zurückwirken auf* "to have an effect on"; be aware that there is a second prepositional complement with *auf* in the clause (see markings).

226. Refers back to *Volk*.

227. Translate as "little by little."

228. Refers back to *Grundsätze*; relative pronoun *die* is not the subject but is the direct object of the relative clause.

229. Refers back to *Volk*.

230. Refers back to *Regierung*.

231. Specifies *Grundsätze*.

Moses Mendelssohn
The Jewish Socrates

7

The Enlightenment philosophies of the eighteenth century touched many areas of social, cultural, and religious life throughout Europe; Judaism was not immune from the influences of the Enlightenment period. In fact, the prevalent ideologies during the time ushered in a movement known as *Haskalah*, also known as the Jewish Enlightenment.[1] The primary voice of the movement was Moses Mendelssohn. On September 6, 1729, Moses Heymann was born. He would later change his last name to Mendelssohn in order to sound less Jewish, while still attempting to honor his father Menache Mendel Heymann.

Considered a brilliant scholar, Mendelssohn was committed to the prevalent thoughts of the Enlightenment period, and his reputation was even recognized by Christians.[2] He often corresponded with the most prominent thinkers of his time, including Immanuel Kant, though the two frequently disagreed. Despite this, some consider his demonstration of the possibility of cordial Jewish-Christian social relations one of his greatest legacies.[3]

Mendelssohn strived to present Judaism as a belief system with an intelligent and acceptable worldview.[4] One of his most notable achievements was his translation of the Hebrew Bible into German.[5] Out of necessity, the translation used Hebrew letters for the German words, since most Jews at the time were only able to read and study Hebrew texts.[6] This translation was considered very significant at the time as it allowed Jews to begin to integrate into the German society. Mendelssohn also produced a commentary that changed the way biblical exegesis was conducted in Judaism by introducing more philosophical approaches that had become popular in Christianity.[7]

His famous 1783 book *Jerusalem oder über religiöse Macht und Judentum* is recognized as a "landmark defense of Judaism."[8] Within the book, Mendelssohn explores topics

1. Karin Hedner Zetterholm, *Jewish Interpretation of the Bible: Ancient and Contemporary* (Minneapolis: Fortress, 2012), 147.

2. Jackson, ed., *New Schaff-Herzog Encyclopedia of Religious Knowledge*, 62.

3. Alan T. Levenson, *The Making of the Modern Jewish Bible: How Scholars in Germany, Israel, and America Transformed an Ancient Text* (Lanham, MD: Rowan & Littlefield, 2011), 29.

4. Sharon Rusten and E. Michael Rusten, *The Complete Book of When & Where in the Bible and throughout History* (Wheaton, IL: Tyndale, 2005), 312.

5. Rusten and Rusten, 312.

6. Jackson, *New Schaff-Herzog Encyclopedia of Religious Knowledge*, 62.

7. Michael V. Fox, *Ecclesiastes*, JPS Bible Commentary (Philadelphia: Jewish Publication Society, 2004), xxvii.

8. Elias Sacks, *Moses Mendelssohn's Living Script: Philosophy, Practice, History, Judaism* (Bloomington, IN: Indiana University Press, 2017), 1.

such as authority, belief, politics, and how religion should be practiced as he seamlessly merges exegetical, historical, and philosophical questions.[9] From such writings, it is clear that he believed it was possible to live as a Jew while being involved in the cultural, social, and civic duties of the nation in which he lived.[10] While we discussed the significant impact that Geiger, Hirsch, and Frankel had on modern Judaism, it was Mendelssohn and his fellow Enlightenment thinkers who set the stage for such developments.[11]

On a cold winter morning on January 4, 1786, Mendelssohn died at his home on 68 Spandau Street in Berlin.[12] He had contracted a cold a few days prior while carrying a manuscript to his publisher titled *An die Freunde Lessings*. He was only fifty-six years of age. Some of Mendelssohn's critics argue that he did more harm than good to Jewish life. Though Mendelssohn publicly defended Judaism on multiple occasions, his critics cite the fact that some of his family members and followers converted to Christianity, including his grandson, composer Felix Mendelssohn, after his death.[13]

Introduction to Mendelssohn's Writing Style

As a contemporary to Immanuel Kant, both authors show similarities in their use of vocabulary, due to their time. Mendelssohn's sentence structure is, however, much less complex and therefore easier to follow. His frequent use of various fixed phrases or *Funktionsverbgefüge* (see chapter 4, section 4.3) nonetheless make his text a challenge for non-native readers. We will provide translations of these kinds of verbs as well as explanations of outdated spellings or unusual uses of words.

Exercises

 MITTEL

1. You will encounter many reflexive pronouns, most of which do not need to be translated into English (see chapter 4 section 4.1.2).

    Find all sixteen instances of *sich* in the text and mark them. Look at the corresponding verb and possible footnotes to decide whether it should be translated or not. If it is used with a preposition, it has to be translated most of the time. Cross out all instances where it has to be omitted in the translation to support your reading process.

---

9. Sacks, 2.

10. Rusten and Rusten, 312.

11. Leonard Greenspoon, "Judaism," ed. John D. Barry et al., *The Lexham Bible Dictionary* (Bellingham, WA: Lexham, 2016).

12. Shmuel Feiner, *Moses Mendelssohn: Sage of Modernity* (New Haven, CT: Yale University Press, 2010), 3.

13. Levenson, 29.

┤├ **LEICHT**

2. Mendelssohn favors relative clauses over all other subclause constructions. Find all relative pronouns in the sentence below (taken from the text) and identify gender, number, and case. Finally, locate the referent noun of each relative pronoun. Be sure to continue this process throughout the text, as suggested in our checklist.

Beide wirken auf Gesinnung und Handlung der Menschen, auf Grundsätze und Anwendung: der Staat, vermittelst[14] solcher Gründe, die <u>auf</u> Verhältnissen zwischen Mensch und Mensch, oder Mensch und Natur, und die Kirche, die Religion des Staats, vermittelst solcher Gründe, die <u>auf</u> Verhältnissen zwischen Mensch und Gott <u>beruhen</u>.[15]

Excerpt from Jerusalem oder über religiöse Macht und Judentum (1783)

(. . .)

Hier zeigt sich also[16] schon ein wesentlicher Unterschied zwischen Staat und Religion. Der Staat gebietet und zwing[e]t; die Religion belehrt und überredet; der Staat erteilt Gesetze, die Religion Gebote. Der Staat hat physische Gewalt und bedient[17] sich derselben,[18] wo es nötig ist; die Macht der Religion ist Liebe und Wohltun. Jener[19] gibt den Ungehorsamen[20] auf, und stößt ihn aus; diese[21] nimmt ihn in ihren Schoß, und sucht[22] ihn noch in dem letzten Augenblicke seines gegenwärtigen Lebens, nicht ganz ohne Nutzen, zu belehren, oder doch wenigstens zu trösten. Mit einem Worte: die bürgerliche Gesellschaft kann, als moralische Person, Zwangsrechte haben, und hat diese[23] auch durch den gesellschaftlichen Vertrag würklich[24] erhalten. Die religiöse Gesellschaft macht keinen Anspruch auf Zwangsrecht und kann durch alle Verträge in der Welt kein Zwangsrecht erhalten. Der Staat besitz[e]t vollkommene, die Kirche bloß unvollkommene Rechte.

(. . .)

---

14. Outdated for *mittels* "by means of."
15. Verb *beruhen auf* "to be based on."
16. Translate as "so" and place at the beginning of the sentence.
17. Verb *sich bedienen*; translate as "to employ"; omit the reflexive pronoun.
18. Refers back to *Gewalt*.
19. Refers back to *Staat*.
20. Nominalized adjective *ungehorsam* "disobedient."
21. Refers back to *Religion*.
22. *suchen* + infinitive with *zu*; translate as "to seek to."
23. Refers back to *Zwangsrechte*.
24. Outdated for *wirklich*.

Zum Beschlusse[25] dieses Abschnitts will ich das Resultat wiederholen, auf das mich meine Betrachtungen geführt haben. Staat und Kirche haben zur Absicht, die menschliche Glückseligkeit in diesem und jenem Leben, durch öffentliche Vorkehrungen, zu befördern.[26] Beide wirken auf Gesinnung und Handlung der Menschen, auf Grundsätze und Anwendung: der Staat, vermittelst[27] solcher Gründe, die <u>auf</u> Verhältnissen zwischen Mensch und Mensch, oder Mensch und Natur, und die Kirche, die Religion des Staats, vermittelst solcher Gründe, die <u>auf</u> Verhältnissen zwischen Mensch und Gott <u>beruhen</u>.[28] Der Staat behandelt den Menschen als unsterblichen Sohn der Erde; die Religion als Ebenbild seines Schöpfers. Grundsätze sind frei. Gesinnungen leiden ihrer Natur nach[29] keinen Zwang, keine Bestechung. Sie gehören[30] für das Erkenntnisvermögen des Menschen, und müssen nach dem Richtmaß von Wahrheit und Unwahrheit entschieden werden. Gutes und Böses wirkt auf sein[31] Billigungs- und Mißbilligungsvermögen. Furcht und Hoffnung lenken seine Triebe. Belohnung und Strafe richten seinen Willen, spornen seine Tatkraft, ermuntern, locken, schrecken ab. Aber wenn Grundsätze glückselig machen sollen; so müssen sie weder eingeschreckt,[32] noch eingeschmeichelt [werden], so muß bloß[33] das Urteil der Verstandeskräfte für gültig angenommen werden. Ideen vom Guten und Bösen mit ein[zu]mischen,[34] heißt die Sachen von einem unbefugten Richter entscheiden [zu] lassen. Weder Kirche noch Staat haben also[35] ein Recht die Grundsätze und Gesinnungen der Menschen irgend einem[36] Zwange zu unterwerfen.

<u>Weder Kirche noch Staat (NOM) sind berechtiget[37] (verb), mit Grundsätzen und Gesinnungen Vorzüge, Rechte und Ansprüche auf Personen und Dinge (all AKK) zu verbinden (infinitive), und den</u> Einfluß (AKK), den (AKK) die Wahrheitskraft (NOM) auf das Erkenntnisvermögen hat[38](verb), <u>durch fremde Einmischung zu schwächen (infinitive).</u>

---

25. Outdated for *zum Abschluss* "in closing."
26. Translate as "promote."
27. Outdated for *mittels* "by means of."
28. Verb *beruhen auf* "to be based on."
29. Preposition *nach* used after the referent noun; translate as "according to."
30. Verb *gehören* is usually used with the preposition *zu* instead of *für*; translate as "to belong to."
31. Refers back to *des Menschen*; the same holds for the possessive pronouns in the next sentence.
32. Outdated for *eingeschüchtert* "intimidated."
33. Modal particle; translate as "merely."
34. Translate as "admix."
35. Modal particle; translate as "therefore."
36. Outdated for *irgendeinem* "any."
37. Verb *zu etwas berechtigt sein*; translate as "to be authorized to" + infinitive.
38. Verb *Einfluss auf etwas haben* "to have influence on something."

Selbst der gesellschaftliche Vertrag hat weder dem Staate noch der Kirche ein solches Recht einräumen können. Denn ein Vertrag über Dinge, die ihrer Natur nach[39] unveräußerlich sind, ist <u>an und für sich</u>[40] ungültig, hebt sich von selbst auf.[41] Auch die heiligsten Eidschwüre können hier die Natur der Sachen nicht verändern. Eidschwüre erzeugen keine neuen Pflichten, sind bloß feierliche Bekräftigungen desjenigen,[42] wozu wir ohnehin, von Natur oder durch Vertrag, verpflichtet sind.[43] Ohne Pflicht ist der Eidschwur eine leere Anrufung Gottes, die lästerlich sein kann, aber <u>an und für sich</u>[44] zu nichts verbindet. Zudem können die Menschen nur dasjenige[45] beeidigen, was die Evidenz der äußer[e]n Sinne hat, was sie gesehen, gehört, betastet haben. Wahrnehmungen des inner[e]n Sinnes sind keine Gegenstände der Eidesbekräftigung. Alles <u>Beschwören</u> und <u>Abschwören</u>[46] in Absicht auf Grundsätze und Lehrmeinungen sind diesemnach[47] unzulässig, und wenn sie geleistet worden [sind], so verbinden[48] sie zu nichts, als zur Reue, über den sträflich begangenen Leichtsinn. Wenn ich itzt[49] eine Meinung beschwöre; so bin ich <u>Augenblicks darauf</u>[50] <u>nichts desto weniger</u>[51] frei, sie zu verwerfen. Die Untat eines vergeblichen Eides ist begangen,[52] wenn ich sie[53] auch beibehalte; und Meineid ist nicht geschehen, wenn ich sie[54] verwerfe. Man vergesse[55] nicht, daß nach meinen Grundsätzen der Staat nicht befugt sei,[56] mit gewissen bestimmten Lehrmeinungen Besoldung, Ehrenamt und Vorzug zu verbinden. Was das Lehramt betrifft; so ist es seine Pflicht, Lehrer zu bestellen,[57] die Fähigkeit haben, Weisheit und Tugend zu lehren, und solche nützliche Wahrheiten zu verbreiten, auf denen die Glückseligkeit der menschlichen Gesellschaft unmittelbar beruh[e]t. Alle nähere Bestimmungen müssen ihrem besten Wissen und Gewissen überlassen werden, wo nicht unendliche Verwirrungen und Kollisionen der Pflichten entstehen sollen,

---

39. Preposition *nach* used after the referent noun; translate as "according to."
40. Fixed phrase; translate as "actually."
41. Verb *sich aufheben*; translate as "to cancel out."
42. Specified in the relative clause introduced by *wozu*.
43. Verb *zu etwas verpflichtet sein* "to be obligated to something."
44. Fixed phrase; translate as "actually."
45. Specified in the relative clause introduced by *was*.
46. Both are nominalized verbs referring to things.
47. Outdated for *demnach*; translate here as "according to this."
48. Translate here as "oblige."
49. Outdated for *jetzt*.
50. Translate as "a moment later."
51. Usually *nichtsdestotrotz* "nonetheless."
52. Translate as "commit."
53. Refers back to *eine Meinung*.
54. Refers back to *eine Meinung*.
55. *Konjunktiv I*; translate with indicative.
56. *Konjunktiv I*; translate with indicative.
57. Translate as "appoint."

die am Ende den Tugendhaften[58] selbst oft zur Heuchelei oder Gewissenlosigkeit führen. Jede Vergehung[59] wider die Vorschrift der Vernunft bleibet nicht ungerochen.[60] Wie aber? Wenn das Übel nun einmal geschehen ist: der Staat bestellt und besoldet einen Lehrer auf gewisse bestimmte Lehrmeinungen. Der Mann findet nachher diese Lehrmeinungen ohne Grund; was hat er zu tun? Wie [hat er] sich zu verhalten, um den Fuß aus der Schlinge herauszuwinden,[61] in welche ihn ein irriges Gewissen verwickelt[62] hat? Drei verschiedene Wege stehen hier vor ihm offen. Er verschließt die Wahrheit in seinem Herzen, und fähr[e]t fort, wider[63] sein besseres Wissen, die Unwahrheit zu lehren; oder er legt sein Amt nieder[64], ohne die Ursachen anzugeben, warum dieses geschehe; oder endlich[65] gibt er der Wahrheit ein lautes Zeugnis,[66] und <u>läßt es auf den Staat ankommen</u>,[67] was mit seinem Amte und mit der ihm ausgesetzten[68] Besoldung werden, oder was er sonst für seine unüberwindliche Wahrheitsliebe leiden soll. Mich dünkt,[69] keiner von diesen Wegen sei[70] unter allen Umständen schlechterdings[71] zu verwerfen. Ich kann mir eine Verfassung denken, in welcher es vor dem Richterstuhle des allgerechten Richters zu entschuldigen ist, wenn man fortfährt, seinem sonst heilsamen Vortrage gemeinnütziger Wahrheiten, eine Unwahrheit mit einzumischen,[72] die[73] der Staat, vielleicht aus irrigem Gewissen geheilig[e]t hat. Wenigstens würde ich mich hüten,[74] einen übrigens rechtschaffenen Lehrer dieserhalb[75] der Heuchelei, oder des Jesuitismus zu beschuldigen, wenn mir nicht die Umstände und die Verfassung des Mannes sehr genau bekannt[76] sind; so genau, als vielleicht die Verfassung eines Menschen niemals seinem Nächsten bekannt sein kann. Wer sich rühmt, nie in solchen Dingen anders gesprochen, als gedacht zu haben, hat entweder überall nie gedacht,

---

58. Nominalized adjective referring to a person.

59. Outdated for *das Vergehen* "wrongdoing."

60. Outdated for *ungerächt* "unavenged."

61. Usually *den Kopf aus der Schlinge ziehen*; literally "pull the head out of the noose" and means "get out of a tight spot."

62. Literally "entangle," and carries on the idea of *aus der Schlinge ziehen*; should be translated here as "put."

63. Preposition meaning "against."

64. Verb *das Amt niederlegen* "to resign."

65. Translate here as "finally."

66. Literally "a loud testimony"; *laut* is here meant in the sense of *unüberhörbar* "unmistakable."

67. Translate as "leaves it to the state."

68. Translate here as "suspended."

69. Outdated fixed phrase "it seems to me."

70. *Konjunktiv I*; translate with indicative.

71. Translate as "utterly."

72. Translate as "admix."

73. Refers back to *Unwahrheit*.

74. Verb *sich hüten* "to take care not to do something" or "to guard against doing something."

75. Translate here as "therefore."

76. *jemandem* (dative here: *mir*) *ist etwas* (nominative here: *die Umstände und die Verfassung*) *bekannt*; translate as "someone knows something."

oder findet vielleicht [für] gut, in diesem Augenblicke selbst, mit einer Unwahrheit zu prahlen, der sein Herz widerspricht.[77]

Also[78] <u>in Absicht auf</u>[79] Gesinnungen und Grundsätze kommen Religion und Staat überein,[80] müssen beide[81] allen Schein des Zwanges und der Bestechung vermeiden, und sich auf Lehren, Vermahnen, Bereden und Zurechtweisen einschränken.[82] Nicht also[83] in Absicht auf[84] Handlung. Die Verhältnisse von Mensch zu Menschen erfordern Handlung, als Handlung; die Verhältnisse zwischen Gott und Menschen, bloß insoweit[85] sie zu Gesinnungen führen. Eine gemeinnützige Handlung hört nicht auf, gemeinnützig zu sein, wenn sie auch erzwungen wird; eine religiöse Handlung hingegen ist nur <u>in dem Maße</u>[86] religiös, in welchem sie aus freier Willkür und in gehöriger[87] Absicht geschieh[e]t. Daher kann der Staat zu gemeinnützigen Handlungen zwingen; belohnen, bestrafen; Amt und Ehren, Schande und Verweisung austeilen, um die Menschen zu Handlungen zu bewegen, deren innere Güte nicht kräftig genug auf ihre Gemüter wirken will. Daher <u>hat</u> dem Staate, durch den gesellschaftlichen Vertrag, auch das vollkommenste Recht und das Vermögen, dieses zu tun, <u>eingeräumt werden können und müssen</u>.[88] Daher ist der Staat eine moralische Person,[89] die ihre eigenen Güter und Gerechtsame[90] hat, und damit nach Gutfinden schalten[91] kann. Fern von allem diesen ist die göttliche Religion. Sie verhält sich[92] gegen[über] Handlung nicht anders, als gegen[über] Gesinnung; weil sie Handlung bloß als Zeichen der Gesinnung befiehlt. Sie ist eine moralische Person; aber ihre Rechte kennen keinen Zwang; sie treib[e]t nicht mit eisernem Stabe; sondern leitet am Seile der Liebe. Sie zückt kein Rachschwert,[93] spendet kein zeitliches Gut [aus]; maß[e]t sich auf kein irdisches Gut[94] ein Recht, auf kein Gemüt[95] äußerliche Gewalt an.[96] Ihre Waffen sind Gründe und Überführung; ihre Macht die göttliche Kraft der

---

77. Verb with direct object in the dative case, here the relative pronoun *der*, which refers back to *Unwahrheit*.
78. Translate here as "in conclusion."
79. Outdated for *in Bezug auf* "with regard to."
80. Verb *übereinkommen* "to agree."
81. Subject of the clause, which refers back to *Religion und Staat*.
82. Here in the sense of *beschränken* "to limit."
83. Translate here as "but."
84. Outdated for *in Bezug auf* "with regard to."
85. Translate as "insofar."
86. Fixed phrase meaning "to the extent."
87. Translate here as "appropriate" or "adequate."
88. Complex verb form; present perfect in the passive voice with modal verbs, "could and must have been granted."
89. All pronouns with feminine gender in the following sentences refer back to *moralische Person*.
90. Outdated for *Privileg* "privilege," here in the plural.
91. Here used in the sense of *verfahren* "to act."
92. Verb *sich gegenüber etwas verhalten* "to behave toward something."
93. Verb *das Schwert zücken* "to draw the sword", here "the sword of revenge."
94. Specifies *ein Recht*.
95. Specifies *äußerliche Gewalt*.
96. Verb *sich etwas* (accusative) *anmaßen* "to claim something for oneself."

Wahrheit; die Strafen, die sie androh[e]t[97] sind, so wie die Belohnungen, Wirkungen der Liebe; heilsam und wohltätig für die Person selbst, die sie leidet. An diesen Merkmalen erkenne ich dich, Tochter der Gottheit! Religion! die du in Wahrheit allein die selig-machende[98] bist, auf der Erde, so wie im Himmel. Bann und Verweisungsrecht, das sich der Staat zuweilen erlauben darf, sind dem Geiste der Religion schnurstracks[99] zuwider.[100] Verbannen, ausschließen, den Bruder abweisen, der an meiner Erbauung Teil nehmen,[101] und sein Herz in wohltätiger Mitteilung, mit dem Meinigen[102] zugleich zu Gott erheben will!–Wenn sich die Religion keine willkürlichen Strafen erlaubt, am wenigsten diese Seelenqual, die ach![103] nur dem[104] empfindlich ist, der wirklich Religion hat. Gehet die Unglücklichen alle durch,[105] die von je her[106] durch Bann und Verdammnis haben gebessert werden sollen;[107]

> Leser (NOM)! welcher[108] äußerlichen Kirche, Synagoge oder Moschee (DAT) du (NOM) auch anhäng[e]st[109] (verb)! (indirect question) untersuche[110] (verb), ob du (NOM) nicht in dem Haufen der Verbannten mehr wahre Religion (AKK) antreffen (v2) wirst (v1, future tense), als (than) in dem ungleich größer[e]n Haufen ihrer Verbanner (indirect question)?

Nun hat die Verbannung entweder bürgerliche Folgen, oder sie hat keine. Zieh[e]t sie bürgerliches Elend nach sich;[111] so fällt sie nur dem Edelmütigen[112] zur Last,[113] der dieses Opfer der göttlichen Wahrheit schuldig zu sein[114] glaubt. Wer keine Religion hat,

---

97. Relative clause; comma after *androhet* is missing.
98. Adjective derived from the participle I of the verb *selig machen*; translate the whole clause here as follows: "who is in truth the only one who can make us blissful."
99. Translate here as "immediately."
100. Verb *zuwider sein* + dative "to be repugnant to."
101. Verb *Teil nehmen an* "to take part in."
102. Translate as "with mine" (meaning "with my heart").
103. Exclamation; translate as "alas."
104. Specified in the relative clause that follows.
105. Imperative, verb *etwas durchgehen*; translate here as "to review" or "to examine."
106. Usually *von jeher* "always."
107. Complex verb form, present perfect in the passive voice with modal verbs, "should have been improved."
108. Translate here as "whichever."
109. Verb with direct object in the dative case.
110. Underlined part is the main clause, verb in the imperative form.
111. If-sentence without *wenn*; verb *nach sich ziehen* "to entail."
112. Nominalized adjective referring to a person.
113. Verb *jemandem* (dative) *zur Last fallen* "to be a burden to someone."
114. Verb *jemandem* (dative) *etwas* (accusative) *schuldig sein* "to owe someone something."

ist ein Wahnwitziger,[115] wenn er sich [um] einer vermeinten[116] Wahrheit zu gefallen, der mindesten Gefahr aussetz[e]t.[117] Soll sie[118] aber, wie man sich bereden will, bloß geistige Folgen haben; so drücken sie abermals nur denjenigen, der für diese Art von Empfindnis[119] noch Gefühl hat. Der Irreligiose[120] lacht ihrer und bleibt verstockt. Und wo ist die Möglichkeit sie von allen bürgerlichen Folgen zu trennen? Kirchenzucht einführen, habe ich an einem andern Orte, wie <u>mich dünkt</u>,[121] <u>mit Recht</u>[122] gesagt, Kirchenzucht einführen, und die bürgerliche Glückseligkeit ungekränkt[123] erhalten, gleich[e]t dem Bescheide des allerhöchsten Richters an den Ankläger: Er sei[124] in deiner Hand, doch[125] schone[126] seines Lebens! Zerbrich das Faß, wie die Ausleger[127] hinzuset-zen;[128] doch laß[129] den Wein nicht auslaufen! Welche kirchliche Ausschließung, welcher Bann ist ohne alle bürgerliche Folgen, ohne allen Einfluß auf die bürgerliche Achtung wenigstens, auf den guten Leumund[130] des Ausgestoßenen[131] und auf das Zutrauen bei seinen Mitbürgern, ohne welches doch niemand seines Berufs warten,[132] und seinen Mitmenschen nützlich, <u>das ist, bürgerlich glückselig</u>[133] sein kann?[134] Man beruft[135] sich immer noch auf das Naturgesetz. Jede Gesellschaft, spricht man,[136] hat das Recht auszu-schließen: Warum nicht auch die religiose?[137] Allein ich erwidere: gerade hier macht die religiose Gesellschaft eine Ausnahme; vermöge[138] eines höher[e]n Gesetzes kann keine Gesellschaft ein Recht ausüben, das der ersten Absicht der Gesellschaft selbst <u>schnurstracks entgegengesetzt</u>[139] ist. Einen Dissidenten ausschließen, sagt ein würdiger

---

115. Nominalized adjective referring to a person.
116. Usually *vermeintlich* "alleged" or "supposed."
117. Verb *sich etwas* (dative) *aussetzen* "to expose oneself to something."
118. Refers back to *Verbannung* and also applies to the following feminine pronouns.
119. Usually *Empfindung* "sensation."
120. Usually *Irreligiöse*, nominalized adjective referring to a person, *irreligiös* "irreligious."
121. Outdated fixed phrase "it seems to me."
122. Fixed phrase *mit Recht* "rightly."
123. Negated form of the adjective *gekränkt* "offended" → "unoffended."
124. *Konjunktiv I*; translate with indicative.
125. Modal particle; translate here as "but."
126. Imperative form of the verb *schonen* "to spare," here with a genitive object, usually with accusative.
127. Nominalized verb *auslegen* referring to people (plural); translate as "interpreters."
128. Here in the sense of *hinzufügen* "to add."
129. Imperative form of the verb *lassen*.
130. Translate as "reputation."
131. Nominalized adjective derived from the participle II of *ausstoßen* "to expel," here referring to a person.
132. Here in the sense of *ausüben* "to exercise."
133. Specification to *nützlich*.
134. *ohne welches . . . kann* is one relative clause.
135. Verb *sich auf etwas berufen* "to invoke."
136. Usually *sagt man* "people say."
137. Usually *religiöse* "religious"; occurs several times in the text.
138. Outdated preposition with the genitive case; translate as "by means of."
139. Translate here as "diametrically opposed," in German with direct object in the genitive case.

Geistlicher aus dieser Stadt, einen Dissidenten aus der Kirche verweisen, heißt einem Kranken die Apotheke verbieten. In der Tat,[140] die wesentlichste[141] Absicht religioser Gesellschaften ist gemeinschaftliche Erbauung. Man will durch die Zauberkraft der Sympathie, die Wahrheit aus dem Geiste in das Herz übertragen, [man will] die zuweilen tote Vernunfterkenntnis durch Teilnehmung zu[142] hohen Empfindnissen[143] beleben.

(. . .)

---

140. Fixed phrase meaning "indeed" or "in fact."
141. Superlative form of *wesentlich*, translate as "the most essential."
142. Usually *durch Teilnahme an* "by participating in."
143. Usually *Empfindung* "sensation," here in the plural.

Friedrich Schleiermacher 8

Father of Modern Theology

The history of modern Christian theology begins with Friedrich Daniel Ernst Schleiermacher.[1] He was born on November 21, 1768 in Breslau and was the son of a Reformed army chaplain named Gottlieb Schleiermacher. At some point after his birth, his parents converted and became a part of the Herrnhuter Brüdergemeine, one of the oldest Protestant denominations in the world and known outside of Germany as the Moravian Church. For his formal education, he would attend the Moravian college at Niesky in Upper Lusatia, as well as their seminary at Barby, located near Magdeburg. Schleiermacher, however, was a very independent thinker and felt the teachings at Barby were much too narrow. He eventually persuaded his father, in 1787, to let him enter the University of Halle.[2]

While at Halle, Schleiermacher became extremely interested in the writings of Aristotle and Immanuel Kant, the latter of which would have a major influence on his life and work.[3] Much like Kant, he believed God was transcendent and rejected the notion that God is clearly revealed in the world.[4] In Schleiermacher's famous *Reden über die Religion* (1799), considered by some to represent one of the first modern studies on religion, Kant's influence can clearly be observed.[5] While he rejects the "sterile and purely cognitive approach of the Enlightenment,"[6] he also attempts to persuade the educated classes to return to religion, which he defines as "a sense and taste for the infinite."[7] The objective of the book was to defend religion against the idea that it was nothing more than dead orthodoxy.

Schleiermacher opposed the view that dogma and ethics were the focus of religion.[8] He likewise objected to the idea that the Bible was the foundation of theology. Instead, he believed that religion was a matter of feeling (*Gefühl*), particularly the feeling of absolute dependence on God, and believed that the Bible was simply a record of that

1. Olsen, *Journey of Modern Theology*, 73.

2. F. L. Cross and Elizabeth A. Livingstone, eds., *The Oxford Dictionary of the Christian Church* (Oxford; New York: Oxford University Press, 2005), 1474.

3. Millard J. Erickson, *Christian Theology*, 3rd ed. (Grand Rapids: Baker Academic, 2013), 5.

4. Cornelius Van Til, *A Christian Theory of Knowledge* (Phillipsburg, NJ: Presbyterian and Reformed, 1969).

5. Cross and Livingstone, 1474.

6. Alan J. Hauser, "Schleiermacher," ed. John D. Barry et al., *The Lexham Bible Dictionary* (Bellingham, WA: Lexham Press, 2016).

7. Cross and Livingstone, 1474.

8. Erickson, 5.

experience.[9] Therefore, instead of studying the Bible with a focus on grammar, linguistics, and historical background, Schleiermacher believed hermeneutics should focus on understanding the way in which the biblical authors thought and felt.[10] Likewise, he also believed it was important to "focus on the deeper, personal meaning of each passage."[11]

Although *Reden über die Religion* earned Schleiermacher the title of youthful genius, it is not the work he is known for. His book *Der christliche Glaube* is considered to be one of the most influential theological volumes ever produced. Using a systematic approach, the title presents Christian doctrine to the modern person. Schleiermacher was also a gifted orator. Upon arriving in Berlin, he was appointed preacher of the Dreifaltigkeitskirche in 1809, from whose pulpit he is said to have delivered extremely elegant sermons.[12]

One cannot underestimate or ignore the influence of Friedrich Schleiermacher. He is without a doubt the most influential theologian of the nineteenth century.[13] He has been labeled one of the few giants of Christian thought and has been referred to as the "prince of the church."[14] He became a professor at the University of Halle in 1804, though he left for Berlin three years later. In 1810, he became dean of the Theology Faculty for the newly founded Humboldt University of Berlin.[15] He stayed in Berlin until his death on February 12, 1834. Never wavering in popularity, it is said that tens of thousands of mourners lined the streets of Berlin to watch his funeral cortege pass by.[16]

Introduction to Schleiermacher's Writing Style

Schleiermacher addresses his audience directly and argues very passionately for his definition of religion. This results in many imperative forms, rhetorical questions, and much expressive language. He also tends to use infinitive with *zu* constructions—often in series, which makes their translation difficult. Furthermore, Schleiermacher's punctuation does not always correspond to modern German; we added commas to clarify the sentence structure when necessary. In addition, the author's use of words is often unique to the context, and we have provided translations best suitable to the context.

---

9. C. Stephen Evans, *Pocket Dictionary of Apologetics & Philosophy of Religion* (Downers Grove, IL: InterVarsity Press, 2002), 104–5.

10. Hauser, "Schleiermacher."

11. Hauser, "Schleiermacher."

12. Cross and Livingstone, 1474.

13. Olsen, 73.

14. Brian Gerrish, *A Prince of the Church: Schleiermacher and the Beginning of Modern Theology* (Philadelphia: Fortress, 1984), 20.

15. Cross and Livingstone, 1474.

16. Olsen, 131.

Exercises

 **LEICHT**

1. Find all infinitive with *zu* constructions (sentences taken from the text) and practice translating them.

> *In dieses Gebiet darf sich also die Religion nicht versteigen, sie darf nicht die Tendenz haben Wesen zu setzen und Naturen zu bestimmen, sich in ein Unendliches von Gründen und Deduktionen zu verlieren, letzte Ursachen aufzusuchen und ewige Wahrheiten auszusprechen*
>
> *Sie begehrt nicht das Universum seiner Natur nach zu bestimmen und zu erklären wie die Metaphysik, sie begehrt nicht aus Kraft der Freiheit und der göttlichen Willkür des Menschen es fortzubilden und fertig zu machen wie die Moral.*

 **MITTEL**

2. To be completed while translating: Find five examples of Schleiermacher's expressive language in the text and list them below with their corresponding translations (often to be found in the footnotes).

    1. _____

    2. _____

    3. _____

    4. _____

    5. _____

Excerpt from Über die Religion: Reden an die Gebildeten unter ihren Verächtern (1799)

Stell[e]t Euch[17] auf den höchsten Standpunkt der Metaphysik und der Moral, so werdet Ihr finden, daß beide mit der Religion denselben[18] Gegenstand haben, nämlich das Universum und das Verhältnis des Menschen zu ihm. Diese Gleichheit ist <u>von lange her</u>[19] ein Grund zu mancherlei Verirrungen gewesen; daher ist Metaphysik und Moral

---

17. Schleiermacher addresses his readers directly and therefore uses capital letters for the pronouns in the second-person plural.

18. Referent noun is *Gegenstand*; translate here simply as "the same."

19. Translate together as "for a long time."

in Menge[20] in die Religion eingedrungen, und manches[,] was der Religion angehört, hat sich unter einer unschicklichen Form[21] in die Metaphysik oder die Moral versteckt. Werdet Ihr aber deswegen glauben, daß sie[22] mit einer von beiden einerlei[23] sei? Ich weiß, daß Euer Instinkt Euch das Gegenteil sagt, und es geht auch aus Euren Meinungen hervor;[24] denn Ihr gebt nie zu, daß sie mit dem festen Tritte[25] einhergeht, dessen[26] die Metaphysik fähig ist, und Ihr vergess[e]t nicht fleißig zu bemerken, daß es in ihrer Geschichte eine Menge garstiger unmoralischer[27] Flecken gibt. Soll sie sich also unterscheiden, so muß sie ihnen ungeachtet[28] des gleichen Stoffs auf irgendeine Art entgegengesetzt sein; sie muß diesen Stoff ganz anders behandeln, ein anderes Verhältnis der Menschen zu demselben[29] ausdrücken oder bearbeiten, eine andere Verfahrungsart[30] oder ein anderes Ziel haben: denn nur dadurch kann dasjenige, was[31] dem Stoff nach[32] einem andern gleich ist, eine besondere Natur und ein eigentümliches[33] Dasein bekommen. Ich frage Euch also: was tut Euere[34] Metaphysik–oder wenn Ihr von dem veralteten Namen, der Euch zu historisch ist, nichts wissen wollt–Euere Transzendentalphilosophie? sie klassifiziert das Universum und teilt es ab[35] in solche Wesen und solche [Wesen], sie geht den Gründen dessen[,] was da ist[,] nach,[36] und deduziert die Notwendigkeit des Wirklichen, sie entspinn[e]t[37] aus sich selbst[38] die Realität der Welt und ihre Gesetze. In dieses Gebiet darf sich also die Religion nicht versteigen,[39] sie darf nicht die Tendenz haben[40] Wesen zu setzen[41] und Naturen zu bestimmen, sich in ein Unendliches von Gründen und Deduktionen zu verlieren, letzte Ursachen aufzusuchen und ewige Wahrheiten auszusprechen. Und was tut Euere Moral? Sie entwickelt aus der Natur des

---

20. Translate as "galore."
21. Translate as "in an improper fashion."
22. Refers back to *Religion*.
23. Translate as "the same."
24. Verb *hervorgehen aus* "to arise out of."
25. Here in the sense of *Schritt* "step"; translate as "with the firm step."
26. Refers back to *Tritte*.
27. Be aware that the adjectives are not in the comparative form, but carry the article endings (see zero article in chapter 3.6.1).
28. Preposition with the genitive case, translate as "notwithstanding."
29. Refers back to *Stoff*.
30. Usually *Verfahrensweise*; translate here as "approach."
31. Translate here as "that what."
32. Preposition *nach* may be used after the referent noun; translate here as "regarding."
33. Translate here as "distinctive."
34. Outdated for *Eure* "your"; occurs several times in the text.
35. Verb *abteilen* "to partition."
36. Verb *etwas* (dative) *nachgehen*; translate here as "to explore something."
37. Outdated verb; translate here as "to generate."
38. Translate as "from itself."
39. Outdated for *verirren* "to go astray" or "to stray."
40. Followed by a series of infinitive with *zu* constructions.
41. Translate here as "to state."

Menschen und seines Verhältnisses[42] gegen das Universum ein System von Pflichten, sie gebietet und untersagt Handlungen mit unumschränkter Gewalt. Auch das darf also[43] die Religion nicht wagen, sie darf das Universum nicht brauchen um Pflichten abzuleiten, sie darf keinen Kodex von Gesetzen enthalten. »Und doch[44] scheint das, was man Religion nennt, nur aus Bruchstücken dieser verschiedenen Gebiete zu bestehen.« Dies ist freilich der gemeine[45] Begriff. Ich habe Euch letzthin Zweifel gegen ihn beigebracht; es ist jetzt Zeit ihn völlig zu vernichten. Die Theoretiker in der Religion, die aufs Wissen über die Natur des Universums und eines höchsten Wesens, dessen Werk es ist, ausgehen,[46] sind Metaphysiker; aber artig genug, auch etwas Moral nicht zu verschmähen. Die Praktiker, denen der Wille Gottes Hauptsache ist, sind Moralisten; aber ein wenig im Stile der Metaphysik. Die Idee des Guten nehmt Ihr und tragt sie in die Metaphysik als Naturgesetz eines unbeschränkten und unbedürftigen Wesens, und die Idee eines Urwesens[47] nehmt Ihr aus der Metaphysik und tragt sie in die Moral, damit dieses große Werk nicht anonym bleibe, sondern vor einem so herrlichen Kodex das Bild des Gesetzgebers könne gestochen werden.[48] Mengt aber und rührt[49] wie Ihr wollt, dies geht nie zusammen. Ihr treibt ein leeres Spiel mit Materien, die sich einander nicht aneignen.[50] Ihr behaltet immer nur Metaphysik und Moral. Dieses Gemisch von Meinungen über das höchste Wesen oder die Welt, und von Geboten für ein menschliches Leben (oder gar[51] für zwei) nennt Ihr Religion! und den Instinkt[,] der jene Meinungen sucht, nebst[52] den dunklen Ahndungen, welche die eigentliche letzte Sanktion dieser Gebote sind, nennt Ihr Religiosität! Aber wie kommt Ihr denn dazu,[53] eine bloße Kompilation,[54] eine Chrestomathie[55] für Anfänger für ein eignes Werk zu halten,[56] für ein Individuum eignen Ursprunges und eigener Kraft? Wie kommt Ihr dazu,[57] seiner[58] zu erwähnen, wenn es

---

42. Be aware that this is also a genitive attribute to *Natur*.

43. Modal particle; translate here as "thus."

44. Modal particle; translate here as "still."

45. Translate here as "common."

46. Translate here as "aim at."

47. The prefix *Ur-* means "original"; *Urwesen* should be translated as "original being."

48. The verb *stechen (gestochen)* in combination with *Bild* refers to the method of engraving pictures.

49. The verbs *mengen* and *rühren* convey the idea of cooking or baking, bringing ingredients together and blending them into something new.

50. Literally "which do not acquire each other"; translate as "which do not become a unity."

51. Modal particle; translate as "even."

52. Preposition + dative; translate as "along with."

53. Common phrase meaning "how dare you" when accusing someone of something.

54. Same as in English "compilation."

55. Same as in English "chrestomathy."

56. Verb *etwas für etwas halten* "to take something for something (else)."

57. See above.

58. The referent noun for this is difficult to determine; it is most likely referring to *Gemisch* at the beginning of the paragraph because it is referred to several times in the following sentences with neuter pronouns.

auch nur geschieht um es zu widerlegen? Warum habt Ihr es nicht längst[59] aufgelös[e]t in seine Teile und das schändliche Plagiat entdeckt? Ich <u>hätte Lust,</u>[60] Euch durch einige sokratische Fragen zu ängstigen, und Euch zu dem Geständnisse zu bringen, daß Ihr in den gemeinsten[61] Dingen die Prinzipien <u>gar wohl</u>[62] kennt,[63] nach denen[64] das Ähnliche zusammengestellt und das Besondere dem Allgemeinen untergeordnet werden muß, und daß Ihr sie hier mir[65] nicht anwenden wollet, um mit der Welt über einen ernsten Gegenstand scherzen zu können. Wo ist denn die Einheit in diesem Ganzen? wo liegt das verbindende Prinzip für diesen ungleichartigen Stoff! Ist es eine eigne anziehende Kraft,[66] so müßt Ihr gestehen, daß Religion das Höchste ist in der Philosophie, und daß Metaphysik und Moral nur untergeordnete Abteilungen von ihr sind; <u>denn das</u>[,] worin zwei verschiedene aber entgegengesetzte Begriffe eins werden,[67] <u>kann nichts anders sein</u>, <u>als das Höhere,</u>[68] unter welches sie beide gehören. Liegt dies bindende Prinzip in der Metaphysik, habt Ihr aus Gründen,[69] die ihr[70] angehören, ein höchstes Wesen als moralischen Gesetzgeber erkannt, so vernichtet doch die praktische Philosophie, und gesteht[,] daß sie, und mit ihr die Religion, nur ein kleines Kapitel der theoretischen [Philosophie] ist.

> Wollt (v1) Ihr (NOM) das umgekehrte (AKK) behaupten[71] (v2); <u>so müssen (v1) Metaphysik und Religion (NOM) von der Moral verschlungen (v2) werden (v2, passive)</u>, *der (DAT) freilich*, nachdem sie (NOM) glauben (infinitive) gelernt[72] (v2) [hat] (v1) und sich in ihren alten Tagen[73] <u>bequemt (v2) hat (v1)</u> in ihrem innersten Heiligtume den geheimen Umarmungen zweier sich liebender[74] Welten ein stilles Plätzchen[75] zu bereiten (infinitive), *nichts mehr unmöglich sein* (v2, passive-like construction) *mag* (v1) (relative clause specifying Moral).

59. Modal particle; translate here as "by now."
60. Verb *Lust haben etwas zu tun* here in *Konjunktiv II*; translate here as "I would like to."
61. Superlative form of *gemein*; translate here as "most common."
62. Modal particles; translate here as "probably even."
63. Here in the sense of *erkennen* "to recognize."
64. Refers back to *Prinzipien*.
65. Omit in translation; outdated wording.
66. If-sentence without *wenn*.
67. Verb *eins werden* "to become one."
68. Main clause is underlined.
69. Two if-sentences without *wenn* in series.
70. Refers back to *Metaphysik*.
71. If-sentence without *wenn*.
72. Translate as "learned to believe"; *lernen* can be used with infinitive without *zu*.
73. Literally "in its old days," meaning "in its old age."
74. Adjective derived from participle I of the verb *lieben*.
75. Translate as "little place"; the suffix *-chen* is a diminutive.

Oder wollt Ihr etwa sagen,[76] das Metaphysische in der Religion hänge nicht vom Moralischen ab,[77] und dieses[78] nicht von jenem;[79][80] es gebe[81] einen wunderbaren Parallelismus zwischen dem Theoretischen und Praktischen, und eben diesen wahrnehmen und darstellen,[82] sei[83] Religion?[84]

Freilich zu diesem kann (v1) die Auflösung (NOM) weder in der praktischen Philosophie (PREP COMP) liegen (v2), denn diese (NOM) kümmert (verb) sich nichts um ihn (PREP COMP),[85] noch in der theoretischen (PREP COMP), denn diese (NOM) strebt (verb) aufs eifrigste,[86] ihn (AKK) so weit als möglich zu verfolgen (infinitive) und zu vernichten (infinitive), wie es denn auch ihres Amts[87] ist (verb).

Aber ich denke, ihr sucht von diesem Bedürfnisse getrieben[88] schon seit einiger Zeit nach einer höchsten Philosophie, in der sich diese beiden Gattungen vereinigen, und seid[89] immer auf dem Sprunge sie zu finden; und so nahe läge[90] dieser[91] die Religion! und die Philosophie müßte[92] wirklich zu ihr flüchten, wie die Gegner derselben so gern behaupten? Gebt wohl Achtung[,][93] was Ihr da sag[e]t. Mit allem dem bekommt[94] Ihr entweder eine Religion[,] die weit über der Philosophie steht, so wie diese sich gegenwärtig befindet,[95] oder Ihr müßt so ehrlich sein, den beiden Teilen derselben wiederzugeben[,] was ihnen gehört, und zu bekennen, daß, was die Religion betrifft.[96, 97] Ihr noch nichts

---

76. Main clause with modal particle *etwa*, followed by series of clauses that depend on it, translate as "or do you have the audacity to say."

77. Verb *abhängen von* "to depend on," here in *Konjunktiv I*, translate with indicative.

78. Refers back to *Moralischen*.

79. Refers back to *das Metaphysische*.

80. Translate with that-sentence despite the missing *dass*.

81. *Konjunktiv I*, translate with indicative.

82. Translate with that-sentence despite the missing *dass*.

83. *Konjunktiv I*, translate with indicative.

84. Translate with that-sentence despite the missing *dass*.

85. Verb sich *um jemanden* (accusative) *kümmern* "to take care of someone."

86. Translate as "eagerly."

87. Translate here as "duty."

88. Fixed phrase, usually *getrieben von* "driven by."

89. Usually *auf dem Sprung sein* "to be about to do something."

90. *jemandem/etwas* (dative) *nahelegen* "to suggest something to someone"; here in *Konjunktiv II*, translate with "would suggest itself."

91. Refers back to *Philosophie*.

92. *Konjunktiv II*; translate here as "should."

93. Verb *Achtung geben* "to be careful."

94. Verb *bekommen* "to get" or "to gain"; not to be mixed up with the English verb "become."

95. Verb *sich befinden* "to be situated."

96. Translate whole clause as "regarding religion."

97. Treat this period as a comma while translating; the *daß*-sentence continues after it.

von ihr wißt. Ich will Euch zu dem ersten nicht anhalten,[98] denn ich will keinen Platz besetzen, den ich nicht behaupten könnte, aber zu dem letzten werdet Ihr Euch wohl verstehen.[99] Laßt uns aufrichtig <u>miteinander umgehen</u>.[100] Ihr mögt die Religion nicht, davon sind wir schon neulich ausgegangen; aber indem[101] Ihr einen ehrlichen Krieg gegen sie führt, der doch[102] nicht ganz ohne Anstrengung ist, wollt Ihr doch[103] nicht gegen einen Schatten gefochten haben, wie dieser, mit dem wir uns herumgeschlagen haben;[104] sie muß doch[105] etwas eigenes[106] sein, was in der Menschen[107] Herz hat kommen können, etwas denkbares, wovon sich ein Begriff aufstellen läßt, über den man reden und streiten kann, und ich finde es sehr unrecht, wenn Ihr selbst aus so disparaten Dingen etwas Unhaltbares zusammennäh{e}t, das Religion nennt, und dann so viel unnütze Umstände damit macht. Ihr werdet leugnen, daß Ihr hinterlistig zu Werke gegangen seid. Ihr werdet mich auffordern, alle Urkunden der Religion – weil ich doch die Systeme, die Kommentare und die Apologien schon verworfen habe – alle aufzurollen[108] von den schönen Dichtungen der Griechen bis zu den heiligen Schriften der Christen, ob ich nicht überall die Natur der Götter finden werde, und ihren Willen, und überall den[109] heilig und selig gepriesen, der die erstere[110] erkennt und den letztern[111] vollbringt. Aber das ist es <u>ja eben</u>,[112] was ich Euch gesagt habe, daß die Religion nie rein erscheint, das alles sind nur die fremden Teile, die ihr anhängen, und es soll ja unser Geschäft sein, sie von diesen zu befreien. Liefert Euch doch die Körperwelt[113] keinen Urstoff[114] als reines Naturprodukt[115] Ihr müßtet[116] dann, wie es Euch hier in der intellektuellen [Welt] ergangen ist, sehr grobe Dinge für etwas Einfaches halten, sondern es ist nur das unendliche Ziel der analytischen Kunst, einen solchen[117] darstellen zu können; und in geistigen

---

98. Verb *jemanden zu etwas anhalten*; translate here as "to encourage someone to do something."

99. Verb *zu etwas verstehen* "to be able to do something," here in the future tense.

100. Translate here as "treat each other."

101. Conjunction; translate with "by" + the verb with an "ing"-form.

102. Modal particle; translate here as "supposedly."

103. Modal particle; translate here as "still."

104. Verb *sich mit etwas herumschlagen* "to grapple with something."

105. Modal particle, translate here as "surely."

106. Very difficult to find a literal translation; best translated as "characteristic."

107. Genitive attribute to *Herz*, here in an unusual but still grammatically correct position.

108. Schleiermacher uses *aufrollen* to convey the notion of a scroll-like document that he is unwrapping.

109. Specified in the relative clause.

110. Refers back to *Natur*.

111. Refers back to *Willen*.

112. The word *ja* signals that the reader knows the content of the statement already; translate *eben* as "exactly" and add "already" to the relative clause.

113. Translate as "bodily world."

114. See comment to *Urwesen*; translate here as "original matter."

115. If-sentence without *wenn*.

116. *Konjunktiv II*; translate here as "should."

117. Refers back to *Naturstoff*.

Dingen ist Euch[118] das Ursprüngliche nicht anders zu schaffen, als wenn Ihr es durch eine ursprüngliche Schöpfung in Euch erzeugt, und auch dann nur auf den Moment[,] wo Ihr es erzeugt. Ich bitte Euch, versteh[e]t[119] Euch selbst hierüber,[120] Ihr werdet unaufhörlich daran erinnert werden. Was aber die Urkunden und die Autographa[121] der Religion betrifft[122], so ist in ihnen diese Einmischung von Metaphysik und Moral nicht bloß ein unvermeidliches Schicksal, sie ist vielmehr künstliche Anlage[123] und hohe Absicht. Was als das erste und letzte gegeben wird, ist nicht immer das wahre und höchste. Wüßtet[124] Ihr doch nur zwischen den Zeilen zu lesen![125] Alle heilige Schriften sind wie die bescheidenen Bücher, welche vor einiger Zeit in unserem bescheidenen Vaterlande gebräuchlich waren, die unter einem dürftigen Titel wichtige Dinge abhandelten. Sie kündigen freilich nur Metaphysik und Moral an, und gehen gern am Ende in das zurück, was sie angekündigt haben, aber Euch wird zugemutet diese Schale[126] zu spalten. So liegt auch der Diamant in einer schlechten Masse gänzlich verschlossen, aber wahrlich nicht um verborgen zu bleiben, sondern um <u>desto sicherer</u>[127] gefunden zu werden. Proselyten[128] zu machen aus den Ungläubigen, das[129] liegt sehr tief im Charakter der Religion; wer die seinige[130] mitteilt, kann gar keinen andern Zweck haben, und so ist es <u>in der Tat</u>[131] kaum ein frommer Betrug, sondern eine schickliche Methode bei dem[132] anzufangen und um das[133] besorgt[134] zu scheinen, wofür der Sinn schon da ist, damit gelegentlich und unbemerkt sich das[135] einschleiche, wofür er erst[136] aufgeregt werden soll.[137] Es[138] ist, da alle Mitteilung der Religion nicht anders als rhetorisch sein kann, eine schlaue Gewinnung

---

118. Due to the verb being a passive-like construction, *Euch* has to be in the dative case; translate as "for you" or translate the whole clause in the active voice and use *Euch* as subject.

119. Translate here as "make sense of something."

120. Translate with that-sentence.

121. Plural to *Autograph*, which has the same meaning as the English word "autograph."

122. Translate the relative clause with an "ing"-form "but concerning . . ." and omit the *so* in the following main clause.

123. Translate as "artificial disposition."

124. Translate here as "could"; *wissen etwas zu tun* in *Konjunktiv II* expresses the incapacity for doing something.

125. Verb *zwischen den Zeilen lesen* as in English "to read between the lines."

126. Translate here as "shell."

127. Translate *desto* here as "all the"; *sicherer* is the comparative form of *sicher*; translate together as "all the more reliably."

128. Same as in English, here referring to people.

129. Refers back to the infinitive with *zu* construction.

130. Refers back to *Religion*.

131. Translate here as "indeed."

132. Specified in the following *wofür*-clause.

133. Specified in the following *wofür*-clause.

134. Verb *um etwas besorgt sein* "to be concerned about something," here with *scheinen* "seem to"; translate as "to be supposedly concerned about."

135. Specified in the following *wofür*-clause.

136. Modal particle; translate here as "only."

137. Present tense in passive voice with a modal verb; translate as "ought to be made excited."

138. Specified in the infinitive with *zu* construction at the end of the sentence.

der Hörenden, sie in so guter Gesellschaft einzuführen. Aber dieses Hilfsmittel hat seinen[139] Zweck nicht nur erreicht, sondern überholt, indem[140] selbst Euch unter dieser Hülle ihr eigentliches Wesen verborgen geblieben ist. Darum[141] ist es Zeit die Sache einmal beim andern Ende zu ergreifen, und mit dem schneidenden Gegensatz anzuheben,[142] in welchen sich die Religion gegen Moral und Metaphysik befindet. Das war es[,] was ich wollte. Ihr habt mich mit Euerem gemeinen Begriff gestört; er ist abgetan, hoffe ich, unterbrecht[143] mich nun nicht weiter. Sie entsagt hiermit, um den Besitz ihres Eigentums anzutreten, allen Ansprüchen auf irgend etwas, was jenen[144] angehört, und gibt alles zurück, was man ihr aufgedrungen[145] hat. Sie begehrt nicht das Universum seiner Natur nach[146] zu bestimmen und zu erklären wie die Metaphysik, sie begehrt nicht aus Kraft der Freiheit und der göttlichen Willkür des Menschen es[147] fortzubilden und fertig zu machen wie die Moral. Ihr Wesen ist weder Denken noch Handeln, sondern Anschauung *intuition* und Gefühl. *Feeling* ← Anschauen will sie das Universum, in seinen eigenen Darstellungen und Handlungen will sie es andächtig belauschen, von seinen unmittelbaren Einflüssen will sie sich in kindlicher Passivität ergreifen und erfüllen lassen. So ist sie beiden[148] in allem entgegengesetzt[,] was ihr Wesen ausmacht, und in allem[,] was ihre Wirkungen charakterisiert, Jene[149] sehen im ganzen Universum nur den Menschen als Mittelpunkt aller[150] Beziehungen, als Bedingung alles Seins und Ursach[e] alles Werdens; sie will im Menschen nicht weniger als[151] in allen andern Einzelnen und Endlichen das Unendliche sehen, dessen[152] Abdruck, dessen Darstellung.

1) Erregung = emotion
2) Urbildung = logic, empiricism.
3) Ausbildung = gefühl

---

139. Refers back to *Hilfsmittel*.
140. Conjunction, translate with a by + "ing"-form construction.
141. Translate here as "therefore."
142. Verb *anheben* "to pick up" is used here to continue the idea of *ergreifen* in the previous clause.
143. Imperative form.
144. Refers back to *Moral und Metaphysik*.
145. Outdated participle II of *aufdrängen* (*jemandem* [dative] *etwas* [accusative] *aufdrängen*) "to force something on someone."
146. Preposition *nach* follows here the referent noun *Natur*.
147. Refers back to *Universum*.
148. Refers back to *Moral und Metaphysik*.
149. Grammatically speaking there should be a period instead of a comma, which would explain the capital letter here; treat it as such while translating.
150. Genitive; translate with "of all + noun." The same holds for all further "all-" expressions in the sentence.
151. Translate as "as much as."
152. Refers back to *das Unendliche*.

Karl Barth

The Red Pastor of Safenwil

9

onsidered one the greatest Protestant theologians of the twentieth century,[1] Karl Barth was born in Basel, Switzerland on May 10, 1886 to Johann Friedrich (Fritz) Barth and Anna Katharina Sartorius. Fritz was Professor of New Testament Theology at the University of Bern.[2] The ministry was an intricate part of the Barth household, since his father and both of his grandfathers pastored at some point in their lives.[3] After studying at the Universities of Bern, Berlin, Tübingen, and Marburg, Barth continued the family tradition by assuming the position of pastor.[4]

The first three years of Karl Barth's ministry were spent in Geneva, Switzerland. He then pastored in Safenwil, where he spent a total of ten years.[5] It was while serving as pastor in Safenwil that Barth began to be disillusioned by the liberal theology he had once embraced.[6] He began to reject the feelings-focus of Schleiermacher's theological approach and embraced a more God-focused approach to theology.[7] Barth developed what would be known as "dialectical theology" which states that the "only proper object of theology is God."[8] In other words, Barth believed that one should not try to explain God in human terms, but instead focus solely on God.

While still serving as pastor, Barth became what Olsen calls "the world's foremost theologian without a doctoral degree."[9] He wrote what would become perhaps his most instrumental text, *Der Römerbrief*. The text marked a departure from the liberal and social ideologies that became prevalent in the Protestant Church after World War I. It is said that the commentary fell like a bomb on the theologian's playground.[10]

The original 1919 publication of *Der Römerbrief* was highly influential in the theological world and led to his invitation to teach at the University of Göttingen. The book was influential in that Barth emphasized his most common theme, God's saving grace

1. Alister E. McGrath, *Christian Theology: An Introduction*, 5th ed. (West Sussex: John Wiley, 2011), 76.
2. Cross and Livingstone, *Oxford Dictionary of the Christian Church*, 163.
3. Clifford Green, ed., *Karl Barth: Theologian of Freedom* (Minneapolis: Fortress, 1991), 13.
4. Daniel G. Reid et al., eds., *Dictionary of Christianity in America* (Downers Grove, IL: InterVarsity Press, 1990).
5. Cross and Livingstone, 163.
6. Reid et al., *Dictionary of Christianity in America*.
7. Cross and Livingstone, 1474.
8. Stuart Brown, Diané Collinson, and Robert Wilkinson, *Biographical Dictionary of Twentieth-Century Philosophers* (New York: Routledge, 1996), 51.
9. Olsen, 303.
10. Olsen, 301–3.

and humanity's inability to know God apart from the revelation of Jesus Christ. In 1921, a second edition of the book was published, which had been rewritten and revised by Barth over an eleven-month period. While the book was very influential and well received by pastors and teachers, many of Barth's former professors were confused over the unhistorical and uncritical approach featured in the book.[11]

His position in Göttingen lasted only a short time. Barth had serious disagreements with some of the scholars who held close the theological presuppositions of Ritschl. Ritschl had taught in Göttingen from 1864 until his death,[12] and his teachings had remained very influential. After leaving Göttingen, Barth took a position at the University of Münster in 1925, although he only stayed there for a short period of time, as well. In 1930, he accepted a position at the University of Bonn.[13] However, after five years he would lose his position in Bonn and was forced to leave Germany because he refused to swear an oath of unconditional loyalty to Hitler.[14]

It is said that Pope Pius XII considered Barth the greatest theologian of the twentieth century and, according to Thomas F. Torrance, stated that he was "the greatest theologian since Thomas Aquinas."[15] Perhaps Barth's greatest contribution to modern theology is his role in changing the reputation of biblical theology, which before had been viewed as primarily academic and conducted from naturalistic presuppositions.[16] Barth is also known for his unfinished five-volume series, *Church Dogmatics* (1932–1967). Within it, Barth's theology is showcased as he expresses the idea that God, through Jesus Christ, acts in love toward humanity by setting it free in all areas of life.[17]

Introduction to Barth's Writing Style

A series of noun phrases is a typical feature of Barth's writing style. He strings together noun phrases of the same case and therefore with the same role in the sentence—be it subject, object, or even prepositional complement or adverbial. They are separated by commas and should simply be translated consecutively. Barth also tends to give genitive attributes another genitive attribute in turn which leads to a chain of genitives, each specifying the previous noun, as in *im Munde des Gottes der Wahrheit*. Another feature

---

11. Olsen, 304–5.

12. William Baird, *History of New Testament Research: From Jonathan Edwards to Rudolf Bultmann*, vol. 2 (Minneapolis: Fortress, 2003), 71.

13. Baird, 305.

14. Brown, Collinson, and Wilkinson, 51.

15. Fergus Kerr, "Book Notes: Barthiana," *New Blackfriars* 79.934 (1998): 550–54.

16. P. Chase Sears, "Theology, New Testament," ed. John D. Barry et al., *The Lexham Bible Dictionary* (Bellingham, WA: Lexham, 2016).

17. Clifford Green, 11.

of Barth's is compound words, and we provide footnotes to the more obscure ones. In addition, he frequently uses participles as adjectives, often with attributes which should be translated with a relative clause following the head noun of the noun phrase (see exercise below). Furthermore, you will encounter several nominalized adjectives and verbs, a typical feature of modern academic writing, as well (see exercise below).

Exercises

⫘ MITTEL

1. Complex noun phrases with participles: Translate the following examples. If the participle has an attribute as in the first example *in ihm wieder enthüllte*, it should be translated with a relative clause following the head of the noun phrase (here: *Gerechtigkeit*). Some participles used as adjectives are very common and can be found in the dictionary. It is, therefore, worth looking up the adjectives.
   - die in ihm wieder enthüllte Gerechtigkeit Gottes

   _____
   - auf der schöpferischen, erlösenden, die Welt umfassenden Kraft Gottes

   _____
   - unsre im Christus realisierte Erkenntnis Gottes

   _____
   - das jetzt anhebende Werk der Kraft Gottes

   _____

⊣├ LEICHT

2. Nominalizations: The following examples are taken from the text. Identify the source of the noun and translate it. Note that the nouns can refer to a person or a thing (also a general notion) and that even superlative forms can be nominalized.
   - nichts Neues, sondern das Älteste: nichts Besonderes, sondern das Allgemeinste; nichts Geschichtliches

   _____
   - in den vom Christus Berufenen

   _____
   - die Glaubenden

   _____
   - der Getreue

   _____

Excerpt from Der Römerbrief (1919)

Denn ich schäme mich des Evangeliums nicht.[18] Ist es doch die Kraft Gottes zur Errettung für jeden, der glaubt, für den Juden zuerst und auch für den Griechen.[19] Denn die Gerechtigkeit Gottes offenbart[20] sich in ihm:[21] aus (seiner) Treue dem Glauben (der Menschen), wie geschrieben steht: Der aus Treue gerecht Gemachte[22] wird leben!

Eine Sache, die in der Welthauptstadt schüchtern verschwiegen werden müßte,[23] ist das Evangelium jedenfalls nicht. Die Leser brauchen sich damit[24] inmitten der Konkurrenz der Religionen und Philosophien nicht befangen und verlegen zu fühlen,[25] Paulus wird es auch nicht tun. Es[26] erträgt und es schlägt diese Konkurrenz. Es ist nicht eine Wahrheit, sondern die Wahrheit. Wer sie[27] erkennt, soll sich keinen Augenblick Sorge machen um[28] ihren Sieg, sondern er soll vor allem stolz darauf[29] sein,[30] daß er sie erkennen darf. Er braucht sie nicht zu vertreten[31] und zu tragen, wie die andern, die menschlichen Geistesbewegungen und Religionsunternehmungen vertreten[,][32] getragen sein wollen, sondern sie vertritt und trägt ihn. Berufene des Christus (1,6), die sich mit Gott genieren,[33] die sich ängstigen um[34] den Gang ihrer Sache – eine Unmöglichkeit! Gott müßte[35] sich unser schämen,[36] wenn er nicht Gott wäre, aber nicht umgekehrt.[37] Gott geht, nicht wir gehen.

Es ist Kraft ausgegangen von[38] Gott in der Auferstehung des Christus von den Toten. Das ist's,[39] was hinter uns steht, ganz abgesehen von[40] allem, was wir sind,

---

18. Outdated wording, verb *sich etwas* (genitive) *schämen* "to be ashamed of something."

19. If-sentence without *wenn*, unusual construction because main clause is the previous sentence, separated by a period.

20. Verb *sich offenbaren* "to manifest," translate the reflexive pronoun here.

21. Refers back to *Evangelium*.

22. Nominalized adjective derived from the participle II of *machen*, translate as "the one made just by loyalty."

23. *Konjunktiv II*, translate here as "should."

24. Refers back to *Evangelium*.

25. Complex verb construction, translate as "do not need to feel inhibited and shy."

26. Refers back to *Evangelium*.

27. Refers back to *Wahrheit* and applies to the following feminine pronouns as well.

28. Verb *sich Sorge machen um etwas* "to worry about something."

29. Specified in the *dass*-sentence.

30. Verb *stolz sein auf etwas* "to be proud of something."

31. Translate here and in the following instances as "advocate."

32. Relative clause.

33. Verb *sich genieren* "to be embarrassed."

34. Verb *sich ängstigen um etwas* "to be afraid for."

35. *Konjunktiv II*; translate here with "would have to."

36. Verb *sich schämen* + genitive "to be ashamed of."

37. Translate phrase as "but not the other way around."

38. Verb *ausgehen von* "to emanate from."

39. Abbreviation for *es ist* (here: *ist es*); mainly used in spoken German.

40. Fixed phrase *abgesehen von* "apart from."

denken und treiben.[41] Keine Theorie wird hier aufgerichtet, keine abstrakte Moral gepredigt, kein neuer Kultus empfohlen. Alles derartige,[42] was auch unter uns auftauchen mag, ist menschliches Beiwerk,[43] gefährlicher religiöser Rest, bedauerliches Mißverständnis, nicht die Sache selbst. Würde es sich nur darum handeln,[44] dann müßten[45] wir uns allerdings bald „schämen", dann ständen[46] wir nicht konkurrenzlos da, dann müßten wir der Welt erliegen, sobald ihre[47] Kräfte gegen uns ins Spiel träten. Denn in der Welt sind auch Kräfte (8,38), und die[48] sind stärker[49] als unsre Ideen. Aber wir haben nicht Ideen hinter uns, sondern die Kraft aller Kräfte,[50] die darum[51] auch die Idee aller Ideen ist: die Kraft Gottes. Unsre Sache ist <u>unsre im Christus realisierte Erkenntnis Gottes</u>,[52] in der[53] uns Gott nicht gegenständlich, sondern unmittelbar und schöpferisch nahetritt,[54] in der wir nicht nur schauen, sondern geschaut werden, nicht nur verstehen, sondern verstanden sind, nicht nur begreifen, sondern ergriffen sind.[55] Unser Gottesgedanke ist der lebendige Arm Gottes, unter den die Natur, die Geschichte, die Menschheit, wir selbst (wir selbst als im Besitz[56] der „Erstlinge des Geistes",[57] 8,23, zuerst!) wieder gestellt sind. Der Ursprung, der immer behauptete, gewußte, vermißte und unter Schmerzen gesuchte,[58] hat seinen Mund wieder aufgetan.[59] Das göttliche Wort, „Es werde!",[60] ist wieder erschollen,[61] gehört, in Erfüllung gegangen.[62] Also nichts Neues, sondern das Älteste: nichts Besonderes, sondern das Allgemeinste;[63] nichts Geschichtliches,[64] sondern die Voraussetzung aller Geschichte!

---

41. Translate here as "do."
42. Demonstrative pronoun specified in the following relative clause; translate with "all such things."
43. Translate as "accessories."
44. If-sentence without *wenn*.
45. *Konjunktiv II*; translate here with "should."
46. *Konjunktiv II*; translate with "would + verb," applies to *träten* as well.
47. Refers back to *Welt*.
48. Here used as a demonstrative pronoun referring back to *Kräfte*.
49. Comparative form to *stark* followed by *als*.
50. Genitive attribute to *Kraft*.
51. Translate here as "therefore."
52. One complex noun phrase with an adjective derived from the participle II of *realisieren*.
53. Refers back to *Erkenntnis*.
54. Verb *jemandem* (dative) *nahetreten* "to approach someone."
55. Barth puts active and passive voice in opposition to each other.
56. Fixed phrase with genitive "in possession of."
57. Translate as "firstfruits of the Spirit."
58. No relative clause but a series of adjectives derived from participle II.
59. Verb *sich auftun* "to open up."
60. Translate as "let there be."
61. *Sein*-passive, verb *erschallen* "to sound."
62. Verb *in Erfüllung gehen* "to come true."
63. Nominalized superlative form of *allgemein*.
64. Nominalized adjectives referring to things or a general notion.

> <u>Das (NOM)</u> (incomplete main clause), was (NOM) immer verhüllt war (verb) in den unverstandenen[65] Naturerscheinungen (1,20) und verschlossen (here: adjective used as a predicative) [war] (verb) in den nicht gehörten[66] Prophetenworten (16, 25–26), aber jetzt erst offenbart [war] (verb), so daß es (NOM) nun wieder im Anfang in den Augen und Ohren der Menschen (PREP COMP) ist (verb) und damit in der Welt (PREP COMP), deren Haupt und Zentrum (NOM) Mensch (predicative) ist (verb).

Und insofern nicht das alte Bekannte, sondern ein Neues, nicht das Allgemeine, sondern das Besonderste,[67] keine bloße Voraussetzung, sondern selber Geschichte: die Eröffnung eines neuen Äons, die Erschaffung der Welt,[68] in der Gott wieder Gewalt hat (relative clause). Diese Kraft Gottes steht hinter uns. Sie[69] ist das Evangelium, das wir verkündigen. Sie ist unsre Sache.

Das jetzt anhebende[70] Werk der Kraft Gottes ist die Errettung. Denn mit der ganzen gegenwärtigen Welt befindet sich der Mensch in einer Gefangenschaft. Eine Abkehr[71] des Menschen von Gott (1,18; 5,12) hat ihn seinem Ursprung[72] entfremdet,[73] [hat] Gott zu seinem Feind gemacht; [hat] die einst in Gott <u>gebundenen und spielenden</u>[74] natürlichen und geschichtlichen Weltkräfte herrenlos[75] gemacht, [hat] ihn und alle Kreaturen unter das Gericht der eigenen Verworfenheit[76] (1,24) und des Todes (5,12) gebracht. Den Knoten dieser hoffnungslos verwirrten Lage, die durch keine Sittlichkeit zu überwinden und durch keine Religiosität zu beschönigen war,[77] hat Gott nun zerhauen[78] durch die reale Tat der Eröffnung einer messianischen, göttlich-irdischen[79] Geschichte. Im Christus ist die Menschheit Gott wieder zugekehrt[80] und damit der Grund gelegt worden[81]

---

65. Translate as "not understood"; "misunderstood" would be *missverstanden*.

66. Adjective derived from the participle II of *hören*.

67. Series of nominalized adjectives referring to things or a general notion; note that *Besonderste* is a nominalized superlative form.

68. Elliptic sentence without verb.

69. Refers back to *Kraft*.

70. Adjective derived from the participle I of *anheben* "to arise."

71. Translate here as "turning away."

72. Translate here as "origin."

73. Outdated wording with passive meaning, usually *jemanden* (accusative) *von etwas entfremden* "to alienate someone from something."

74. Both adjectives derived from the participle I.

75. Translate here as "masterless."

76. Translate here as "depravity."

77. Passive-like construction; translate with passive voice.

78. Participle II of the verb *zerhauen* "to chop something up."

79. Translate as "messianic and god-earthly."

80. Verb *zukehren* + dative "to turn to," here as a *sein*-passive.

81. Present perfect in the passive voice.

zur Wiederbringung[82] alles dessen,[83] was verloren ist. Wir stehen schon in den Anfängen[84] dieses Geschehens, und eine weite Perspektive eröffnet sich[85] auf einen Zustand in der Freiheit Gottes (5,2; 8,18). Nicht mehr unter dem Gericht, sondern unter der Gnade, nicht mehr in der Sünde, sondern in der Gerechtigkeit, nicht mehr im Tode, sondern im Leben, das[86] ist der Weg der Errettung, den[87] die Kraft Gottes jetzt mit uns und einst mit der ganzen Welt gehen will und wird.

Jetzt mit uns! Es handelt sich darum,[88] an die Kraft Gottes zu glauben. Das „Centrum Paulinum"! (Bengel) Die kommende Welt kommt nicht mechanisch, sondern organisch! Und das schöpferische Organ,[89] das dazu in Wirksamkeit treten[90] muß, ist eine Vorausnahme des Zieles, das erreicht werden soll: die freie Vereinigung des Menschen mit Gott, wie sie[91] im Christus vollzogen war und wie sie in den vom Christus Berufenen[92] möglich und wirklich wird. Wenn der Mensch Ja sagt zu dem göttlichen Ja, das[93] im Christus zu ihm gesprochen hat, wenn er Gebrauch macht von den neuen Augen und Ohren, die ihm durch die Kraft Gottes geschenkt werden, wenn die Treue Gottes, der von der Welt und vom Menschen nicht lassen kann,[94] einer neuerwachten[95] Gegentreue[96] begegnet, das ist „Glaube". Da hebt die Errettung an.[97] Da setzt sich die im Christus begründete[98] Weltenwende[99] fort. Das ist das Gebot und die Einladung, die jetzt mit dem Evangelium allen Völkern verkündigt[100] wird, damit sie ihr[101] gehorchen sollen (1,5). [Es ist] Wohlzuverstehen,[102] daß die Wärme der Empfindung, die Wucht der Entscheidung und Überzeugung, die Tüchtigkeit der persönlichen Gesinnung keine wichtigen Merkmale des Glaubensvorgangs sind. Es handelt sich wesentlich um das, was auf der geistigen [Seite], nicht nur um[103] das, was auf der seelischen Seite des Menschen vorgeht.

---

82. Translate as "return."
83. Genitive attribute to *Wiederbringung*, specified in the following relative clause.
84. Here in plural but translate simply as "beginning."
85. Verb *sich eröffnen* "to open up."
86. Here used as a demonstrative pronoun.
87. Refers back to *Weg*.
88. Verb *sich handeln um* "to deal with" or "to concern."
89. Here used as reference to the adjective *organisch* in the previous sentence; translate as "agent."
90. Verb *in Wirksamkeit treten* "to come into effect."
91. Refers back to *Vereinigung*.
92. Nominalized verb referring to people; translate with a relative clause "those who . . ."
93. Refers back to *Ja*.
94. Verb *von jemandem nicht lassen können* "to not be able to stop interacting with."
95. Compound of *neu* and the participle II of *erwachen* used as an adjective; translate as "newly awoken."
96. Translate as "reciprocal loyalty."
97. Translate as "arise."
98. Fixed phrase *begründet in* "founded in" or "based upon."
99. Compound of *Welt* and *Wende*; translate as "world changing."
100. Outdated for *verkündet* "announced."
101. Refers back to *Einladung*.
102. Usually *wohl zu verstehen*; translate whole phrase as "it is well understood."
103. Verb *sich handeln um* "to deal with," here two times *um* + noun phrase, both complements of the verb.

Die Glaubenden[104] bilden das neue internationale Gottesvolk, das sich jetzt um die Auferstehungskraft[105] schart als um seine Sache.[106] Jedermann kann und soll dabei sein.[107] Der Glaube ist die Weltfrage[108] geworden. Als die Erben[109] der Verheißung und der verschlossenen[110] Prophetenworte hatten die Juden einen Vorsprung. In ihrer Mitte ist der Messias geboren; sie zuerst haben seine Botschaft gehört (10, 14–15). Dann aber brach sie heraus zu den Heiden.[111] Die Frage „kirchlich" oder „weltlich", ist keine Frage mehr. Die kommende[112] Welt kennt diese Schranken nicht. Nur eins entscheidet jetzt: ob[113] die wieder offenbar gewordene Kraft Gottes nun Glauben oder Unglauben findet.

So beruht das Bewußtsein und die Zuversicht, mit der[114] der Christ sich zu seiner Sache stellt,[115] selbst auf der schöpferischen, erlösenden, die Welt umfassenden Kraft Gottes.[116] Kraft Gottes ist die,[117] darüber soll es keine Zweideutigkeit geben[118] keine von den Weltkräften, die nichts Neues schaffen, sondern uns letzten Endes[119] immer im Kreise herumführen.[120] Denn das, was uns den Christus hat zur Kraft werden lassen,[121] das ist keine menschliche Größe, weder im Bösen noch im Guten, sondern die in ihm wieder enthüllte Gerechtigkeit Gottes. Gott handelt in Übereinstimmung mit sich selber, wenn er der Welt in diesem Einen[122] die Retterhand[123] reicht. Denn es[124] ist in diesem Einen auf der Erde wieder erschienen das ursprüngliche, unmittelbare, normale Verhältnis des Menschen zu Gott, das Verhältnis;[125] das Gott selbst recht ist, das[126] seinem Sinne[127] entspricht. In ihm[128] kann sich Gott[,] wie er ist[,] wieder zum Menschen

---

104. Nominalized verb referring to people.
105. Compound of *Auferstehung* and *Kraft*; translate as power of resurrection.
106. Verb *sich scharen um* "to rally around."
107. Verb *dabei sein*; translate here as "to take part (in)."
108. Compound; translate as "question of the world."
109. *das Erbe* "inheritance" vs. *der Erbe* "heir"; *das Erbe* exists only in singular; *die Erben* "heirs."
110. Adjective derived from the participle II of *verschließen* "to seal."
111. *der Heide* "heathen," here plural.
112. Adjective derived from the participle I of *kommen*.
113. Indirect question; translate with "if."
114. Relative pronoun + preposition; refers back to *Zuversicht*.
115. Verb *sich zu etwas stellen*, translate here as "to position oneself toward something."
116. Verb *beruhen auf* "to be based on."
117. Translate here as "this."
118. *geben* + *es* "there is," here with modal verb.
119. Fixed phrase *letzten Endes* "ultimately."
120. Unusual wording, *im Kreise herumführen* "to lead around in a circle."
121. Verb *sich lassen* + infinitive: passive-like construction, here in the past tense; translate phrase as "which transformed Christ into power for us."
122. Refers back to *Christus*.
123. Compound; translate as "saving hand."
124. Refers to das *Verhältnis*.
125. This should be a comma; the following sentences are relative clauses.
126. Refers back to *das Verhältnis*.
127. Translate here as "will."
128. Refers back to *das Verhältnis*.

bekennen[129] und im Bilde des Menschen sich selber wiedererkennen. Diese Gerechtigkeit Gottes, die im Christus war, ist das Geheimnis der Kraft seiner Auferstehung, sie ist auch die Voraussetzung der Errettung der Welt vom Verderben, die[130] durch diese Kraft begonnen hat. Denn allein die wiedergewonnene[131] Unmittelbarkeit des Menschen zu Gott im Gehorsam des Christus vermochte[132] des Grabes Türe zu sprengen, sie allein macht die Errettung real, zu einer entscheidend neuen Bewegung, schützt sie vor dem Rücklauf aller menschlichen Bewegungen in neue Sünde und neuen Tod. <u>Es ist also die Liebe</u>, mit der[133] sich jetzt Gott der Welt wieder zuwendet,[134] <u>keine Sentimentalität</u>, durch die[135] er im Widerspruch mit sich selbst und mit dem Tatbestand der menschlichen Verfassung geraten würde,[136] <u>sondern</u> (indem er dem menschlichen Wesen im Christus seine „gerechte" Verfassung wiedergibt) <u>vielmehr die Verkündigung und Aufrichtung seiner eigenen innersten Wahrheit auf Erden</u>,[137] Gott erträgt die Ungerechtigkeit unter den Menschen nicht mehr; er will, daß seine Gerechtigkeit wieder gelte.[138] Darum und in diesem Sinne spricht er im Christus das erlösende[139] Wort, durch das der Mensch aus der Fremde wieder in die Heimat gerufen wird. Es ist also[140] auch menschlicherseits[141] kein eigenmächtig tumultuarisches[142] Ansichreißen[143] des Göttlichen, durch das wir der Heiligkeit Gottes zu nah träten,[144] wenn wir der Auferstehungskraft des Christus Glauben schenken[145] und uns der kommenden Errettung freuen,[146] sondern es ist Erkenntnis Gottes im strengsten Sinn, was uns dazu führt; es ist (im Gegensatz zu aller menschlichen Willkür, aber auch zu aller menschlichen Moralität und Religiosität) „Erkenntnis der Klarheit Gottes <u>in dem Angesichte</u>[147] Jesu Christi" (II.Kor. 4,6), Beugung[148] vor dem innersten Wesen Gottes, Gehorsam, wie der Christus gehorsam war. Und darum,

---

129. Verb sich *zu jemandem/etwas* (dative) *bekennen* "to acknowledge someone/something."

130. Refers back to *die Errettung.*

131. Adjective derived from the participle II of *wiedergewinnen* "to regain."

132. Outdated, verb *vermögen* "to be able to."

133. Refers back to *Liebe.*

134. Verb *zuwenden* + dative "to turn to."

135. Refers back to *Sentimentalität.*

136. Phrase in *Widerspruch geraten* "to fall into contradiction."

137. Main clause underlined.

138. *Konjuntiv I*; translate with indicative.

139. Adjective derived from the participle I of *erlösen.*

140. Modal particle; translate here as "therefore."

141. The adjective *menschlich* with the suffix *-seits*; translate as "from humans."

142. More common is the adjective *tumultartig* "riot like."

143. Nominalized verb *an sich reißen* "to take over."

144. Verb *jemandem* (dative) *zu nahe treten* "to offend someone" (dative object here: die Heiligkeit Gottes); note that the verb is in *Konjunktiv II.*

145. Verb *jemandem/etwas* (dative) *Glauben schenken* "to believe in."

146. Outdated wording, usually *sich freuen auf* here instead of *auf* with a dative object; translate as "to look forward to."

147. Fixed phrase, often used in religious contexts; translate as "in the face of."

148. Translate as "bending."

weil[149] es sich nicht um irgend etwas,[150] sondern um die Gerechtigkeit Gottes handelt,[151] täuschen wir uns nicht in der Zuversicht,[152] daß Gott selbst unsre Sache führt. Es ist aber eine Offenbarung, durch die Gott dies lösende Wort spricht und der wir diese Erkenntnis verdanken.[153] Es versteht sich nicht von selbst,[154] daß das Verhältnis[155] des „Zorns“, der „Frevelhaftigkeit und Ungerechtigkeit“ (1,18) zwischen ihm und uns aufgehoben, der tragisch unfruchtbare Ernst der Moral und der Religion zerbrochen, die Kraft Gottes zur Errettung in der Welt wirksam wird.[156] Es ist ein Wunder, daß der sündige und todgeweihte[157] Mensch, so wie er ist, im Christus das Urteil hören darf, daß er Gott recht ist,[158] und daß er durch dieses Urteil (das im Munde des Gottes der Wahrheit[159] ein Schöpfungswort ist[160]), wenn er es hören will, gerecht und lebendig gemacht wird. Wir stehen also[161] gerade[162] in Bezug auf das innerste Wesen der Kraft Gottes vor einer tatsächlichen Wende der Zeiten,[163] vor der Enthüllung eines Mysteriums, „das durch Weltalter hindurch[164]verschwiegen war“ (16,26). Denn auch die Propheten konnten nur wie vor verschlossenen Türen die Gerechtigkeit, aus der[165] das Leben kommt, bezeugen und ihre[166] Enthüllungen weissagen. Nun aber erschließt sie sich selbst, indem das Urteil und die Erkenntnis, durch die der Mensch wieder in das ursprüngliche und positive Verhältnis zu Gott versetzt wird, in dem geschichtlichen Ereignis der Erscheinung des Christus[167] zur Aussprache kommt. So[168] ist uns gerade der Inhalt des Evangeliums eine Entdeckung, nicht eine allgemeine Wahrheit, und von Gott aus betrachtet:[169] der

---

149. Translate as "because."

150. Usually one word; translate as "something."

151. Verb *sich handeln um* "to deal with."

152. Verb *sich täuschen in* "to be mistaken in."

153. Verb *jemandem/etwas* (dative) *etwas* (accusative) *verdanken* "to owe someone something," here the dative object is the relative pronoun *der* referring to *Offenbarung*.

154. Fixed phrase, usually without negation *nicht:* "it goes without saying," here: "it does not go without saying."

155. Followed by three genitive attributes.

156. Verb part 1, goes to all the two previous participles in the sentence as well and forms in these instances the passive voice, but in the last part of the sentence it is used as a full verb "become" + adjective (here: *wirksam* "effective").

157. Translate as "moribund."

158. Usually *etwas* (nominative) *jemandem* (dative) *recht sein* "to be acceptable to someone," here a person (*er*) is acceptable to someone (*Gott*).

159. Genitive attribute to *des Gottes*.

160. Relative clause specifying *Urteil*.

161. Modal particle; translate as "therefore."

162. Modal particle; translate as "especially."

163. Translate simply as "times."

164. Translate as "throughout the ages."

165. Refers back to *Gerechtigkeit*.

166. Refers back to *Gerechtigkeit*.

167. Genitive attribute to *Erscheinung*.

168. Modal particle; translate as "therefore."

169. Translate phrase as "seen from God's perspective."

Gegenstand einer Tat, nicht einer ruhenden Eigenschaft so sicher menschlicherseits[170] die Möglichkeit dieser Entdeckung und götterlicherseits[171] die Bereitschaft zu dieser Tat immer vorhanden war. Die Wirklichkeit der Gerechtigkeit Gottes im Christus ist das Neue[172] im Evangelium.

Und das[173] nun eben in der freien Vereinigung mit Gott, in der[174] die Treue Gottes beim Menschen Glauben findet, oder in der[175] Gott dem Menschen wieder glaubt und einer Treue begegnet.[176] Vom Himmel her[177] kommt dieses Neue, und auf der Erde schlägt es Wurzel.[178] Gottes Handeln in einer Gehorsamstat[179] des Menschen, ein Anerkennen und Annehmen, ein Ergriffenwerden und Begreifen[180]– das ist das gläubige Verhalten gegenüber der Offenbarung. Was, „durch Weltalter hindurch verschwiegen", nur in Gott und nicht im Menschen war, das bricht nun durch[181] von Gott zum Menschen, geschieht am Menschen als freieste Gottestat[182] und entspringt doch in ihm als die Entdeckung seines eigensten[183] Wesens. So schafft sich Gott selber[184] das Organ seiner Kraft auf Erden.[185] Er, der Getreue,[186] ist im Glauben der Gläubigen wieder in ein dynamisches, schöpferisches Verhältnis zu seiner Welt eingetreten.

So[187] erfüllt sich in[188] unsrer Sache die prophetische Weissagung: „Der aus Treue gerecht Gemachte[189] wird leben". Man könnte[190] auch sagen: „Der durch den Glauben gerecht Gewordene";[191] es ist dasselbe; denn es handelt sich um ein Machen[192] Gottes und um ein Werden[193] des Menschen in Einem.[194] Gottes Gerechtigkeit ist nun wieder aufgerichtet auf Erden durch das lösende Wort, das im Christus gesprochen [wurde,] und

---

170. See above; translate here as "for men."
171. Translate here as "for God."
172. Nominalized adjective; translate as "newness."
173. Here used as a demonstrative pronoun referring back to *das Neue* or *Evangelium*.
174. Relative pronoun referring back to *Vereinigung*.
175. Relative pronoun referring back to *Vereinigung*.
176. The verbs *glauben* and *begegnen* both take dative objects.
177. Preposition *von . . . her* "from."
178. Usually *Wurzeln schlagen*; translate as "to put down roots."
179. Compound of *Gehorsam* and *Tat* "deed of obedience."
180. Series of nominalized verbs; translate *Ergriffenwerden* as "being seized."
181. Verb *durchbrechen* "to break through."
182. Compound of *Gott* and *Tat* "God's deed."
183. Superlative form of *eigen*; translate here as "very own."
184. Verb *sich selbst* (here: *selber*) *etwas schaffen* "to create something by/for yourself."
185. Fixed phrase often used in religious contexts "on earth."
186. Nominalized adjective *getreu* "faithful" referring to a person.
187. Modal particle; translate here as "with that."
188. Verb *sich erfüllen in* "to come true in."
189. Nominalized participle II of *machen* referring to a person.
190. *Konjunktiv II*; translate with "could."
191. Nominalized participle II of *werden* referring to a person.
192. Nominalized verb; translate as "making."
193. Nominalized verb; translate as "becoming."
194. Fixed phrase; translate as "in one."

durch die Erkenntnis, die in den Christen zustande gekommen ist.[195] Und wie unter dem herrschenden[196] göttlichen „Zorn" und im Gebiet der menschlichen „Frevelhaftigkeit und Ungerechtigkeit" der Tod die höchste Gewalt haben mußte[197] auf Eden, so[198] ist durch jene Aufrichtung der göttlichen Gerechtigkeit die Keimzelle[199] des Lebens wieder in die Geschichte und in die Natur gegeben. Nun wächst in die menschliche Weltgeschichte hinein[200] die göttliche [Weltgeschichte]. Nun hat die neue Schöpfung angefangen, in der[201] der Tod nicht mehr sein wird.[202]

---

195. Verb *zustande kommen* "to come about."
196. Adjective derived from the participle I of *herrschen* "to rule."
197. Past tense of *müssen* "had to."
198. Modal particle; translate here as "so."
199. Translate as "nucleus" or "seed."
200. Preposition *in . . . hinein* "into."
201. Refers back to *Schöpfung.*
202. *Futur I*; translate with will-future.

Dietrich Bonhoeffer

A Modern Martyr

10

Dietrich Bonhoeffer was born into a large family on February 4, 1906 in Breslau, Silesia.[1] He had seven siblings, including his twin sister Sabine. When he was six, his family moved from Breslau to Berlin.[2] His father Karl Bonhoeffer was a well-known professor, psychiatrist, and neurologist who was a vocal critic of Sigmund Freud. His mother Paula was the granddaughter of Karl August von Hase, respected church historian and theologian. Dietrich showed incredible intellect very early in life.[3] By the age of fourteen, he had already announced to his family that he was going to become a theologian, though they were not particularly fond of the idea.[4]

Bonhoeffer, like his father and brothers, studied at the University of Tübingen.[5] It was there that he completed his *Staatsexamen* before moving to Berlin to complete his doctorate. In 1927, at the age of twenty-one, Bonhoeffer completed his dissertation titled, *Sanctorum Communio* at Berlin University. His dissertation would later be referred to as a "theological miracle" by the greatest theologian of the twentieth century.[6]

Such compliments were most meaningful to Bonhoeffer, since he had been drawn to the writings of Karl Barth during his studies. In the winter semester of 1924–1925 in Berlin, he encountered Karl Barth's doctrine of revelation.[7] Barth's teachings were of great influence to Bonhoeffer. Though he would criticize Barth "for interpreting God's freedom as more a freedom from the world than a freedom for the world,"[8] Bonhoeffer, like Barth, opposed the teachings of liberal theology that were so prevalent in the nineteenth century.[9]

After completing his dissertation in 1927, he served for some time as an assistant pastor to a German-speaking congregation in Spain.[10] He later returned to Berlin, where

1. Before World War II, Breslau was part of Germany. However, after the war, territorial changes took place, and Breslau is now part of Poland. The cities name has changed to Wrocław.

2. Ferdinand Schlingensiepen, *Dietrich Bonhoeffer, 1906–1945: Martyr, Thinker, Man of Resistance* (New York: T&T Clark, 2010), 1.

3. John G. Stackhouse Jr., "Following Jesus in the Dark," *Christian History* 94 (2007).

4. Mark Galli and Ted Olsen, *131 Christians Everyone Should Know* (Nashville: Broadman & Holman, 2000), 379.

5. Schlingensiepen, 18.

6. John D. Godsey, "Barth and Bonhoeffer," *Christian History* 32 (1991).

7. Schlingensiepen, 25.

8. Godsey, "Barth and Bonhoeffer."

9. Godsey, "Barth and Bonhoeffer."

10. Galli and Olsen, 379.

he completed his postdoctoral fellowship in 1930. When he finished his "second book"[11] at Berlin University, Bonhoeffer made his first trip to the United States, working out of Union Theological Seminary in New York.[12]

America provided Bonhoeffer with a unique perspective for his theological development. While he felt America lacked any theoretical theologial interest, his encounter with African American Christianity left a lasting impression upon him. He would often visit black congregations, particularly the Abyssinian Baptist Church in Harlem, where he would sometimes teach Sunday school. This experience proved to be very formative and possibly influenced what many considered Bonhoeffer's most significant contribution to modern theology: the understanding of how cultural situations influence the way in which Jesus is preached and how the Christian must respond within that framework.[13] This theology can be observed in his book *Nachfolge* (1937).

Due to his stance against Nazism, he was eventually no longer allowed to teach and was banned from Berlin. While he did make a second trip to the United States to lecture, he felt it was his responsibility to return to Germany. In 1942, Bonhoeffer tried to help the German opposition to Hitler by mediating with the British government; however, he was arrested in 1943 and imprisoned in Buchenwald. On April 9, 1945, he was hanged at the Flossenbürg concentration camp, when the Allied armies were just a few miles away.[14]

Introduction to Bonhoeffer's Writing Style

As an author of the twentieth century, Bonhoeffer's German is much closer to the authors you will encounter in part III of this book. The frequent use of participles used as adjectives is a typical characteristic of academic writing in modern German and therefore also typical for Bonhoeffer's text. In addition, the text contains several sentences with verbs in the *Konjunktiv I*. So far, we recommended that you translate *Konjunktiv I* as indicative in English because it usually signals simply that the sentence reports indirect speech. However, it can express a suggestion or recommendation, as well. Please refer to exercise 2 below for translation advice. Furthermore, Bonhoeffer uses a number of compound words that are difficult to translate without interpretation. Here, your creativity is needed, though we have provided suggestions for their translation in the footnotes.

---

11. Academic institutions within German-speaking countries require indivdiuals to write a second book know as *habilitation* in order to be eligible for a professorship. Habilitation is done after the completion of a doctoral degree and is similar to a postdoc.

12. Cross and Livingstone, *Oxford Dictionary of the Christian Church*, 224.

13. McGrath, *Christian Theology*, 433.

14. Daniel G. Reid et al., *Dictionary of Christianity in America*.

Exercises

 **SCHWER**

1. Identify the following for each participle used as an adjective: infinitive of the verb, type of participle, case,[15] number and gender of the noun phrase (see table below).

   Translate the noun phrase! Keep in mind that the participle II should be translated with the past tense and the participle I with an "-ing" form.

noun phrase	infinitive	participle I/II	case	number	gender	translation
verschleudertes Sakrament						
die gezahlte Rechnung						
den menschgewordenen Jesus						
der verborgene Schatz						
vergebendes Wort						
die aufgebrachten Kosten						
der zunehmenden Verweltlichung						

 **MITTEL**

2. *Konjunktiv I* vs. imperative form:

   As mentioned before, you will encounter verbs in *Konjunktiv I*, expressing a suggestion or recommendation. It is best to translate these as "should" plus the infinitive of the verb. If the verb is *sei* (*Konjunktiv I* of the verb *sein*), then it should be translated as "be." However, please note the similarity to the imperative form. The examples below are taken from the text.

---

15. Sometimes more than one case is possible because the words are taken out of context. If so, write both options in the column.

Locate the verb and identify person and number. Translate the sentences and find the grammatical difference between *Konjunktiv I* and the imperative form.

Konjunktiv I:
  Es lebe also auch der Christ wie die Welt

  _____

  Der Christ aber sei in seiner Weltlichkeit . . . getrost und sicher.

  _____

imperative form:
  bleibe nur weiter, wo du warst, und tröste dich der Vergebung.

  _____

Excerpt from Nachfolge (1937)

Billige Gnade ist der Todfeind unserer Kirche. Unser Kampf heute geht um[16] die teure Gnade. Billige Gnade heißt Gnade als Schleuderware, verschleuderte[17] Vergebung, verschleuderter Trost, verschleudertes Sakrament; Gnade als unerschöpfliche Vorratskammer der Kirche, aus der mit leichtfertigen Händen bedenkenlos und grenzenlos ausgeschüttet wird; Gnade ohne Preis, ohne Kosten. Das sei[18] ja[19] gerade das Wesen der Gnade, daß die Rechnung im voraus[20] für alle Zeit beglichen ist. Auf die gezahlte Rechnung hin[21] ist alles umsonst zu haben. Unendlich groß sind die aufgebrachten[22] Kosten, unendlich groß daher auch die Möglichkeiten des Gebrauchs und der Verschwendung. Was wäre auch Gnade, die nicht billige Gnade ist?

Billige Gnade heißt Gnade als Lehre, als Prinzip, als System; heißt Sündenvergebung als allgemeine Wahrheit, heißt Liebe Gottes als christliche Gottesidee. Wer sie bejaht, der[23] hat schon Vergebung seiner Sünden. Die Kirche dieser Gnadenlehre ist durch sie schon der Gnade teilhaftig.[24] In dieser Kirche findet die Welt billige Bedeckung ihrer Sünden, die sie nicht bereut und von denen frei zu werden sie erst recht nicht[25] wünscht.[26]

---

16. Verb *um etwas gehen* "to concern" or "to deal with."
17. Adjective derived from the participle II of the verb *verschleudern* "to squander."
18. *Konjunktiv I*; translate with indicative.
19. Modal particle; expresses that the sentence states something the reader already knows.
20. Translate as "in advance."
21. *auf etwas hin* "as a result of."
22. Adjective derived from the participle II of the verb *aufbringen* "to raise."
23. Here in the function of a demonstrative pronoun.
24. Verb *etwas* (dative) *teilhaftig sein*; translate as "to share in something."
25. Translate *erst recht nicht* together as "certainly not."
26. Two relative clauses connected by *und*; the relative pronouns are underlined.

Billige Gnade ist darum Leugnung des lebendigen Wortes Gottes,[27] Leugnung der Menschwerdung[28] des Wortes Gottes.

Billige Gnade heißt Rechtfertigung der Sünde und nicht des Sünders.[29] Weil Gnade doch alles allein tut, darum kann alles beim alten bleiben.[30] „Es ist doch unser Tun umsonst".[31] Welt bleibt Welt, und wir bleiben Sünder „auch in dem besten Leben". Es lebe[32] also auch der Christ wie die Welt, er stelle[33] sich der Welt in allen Dingen gleich und unterfange sich[34] ja[35] nicht – bei der Ketzerei des Schwärmertums![36] – unter der Gnade[37] ein anderes Leben zu führen als unter der Sünde![38] Er hüte sich[39] gegen die Gnade zu wüten,[40] die große, billige Gnade zu schänden und neuen Buchstabendienst[41] aufzurichten durch den Versuch eines gehorsamen Lebens unter den Geboten Jesu Christi! Die Welt ist durch Gnade gerechtfertigt, darum – um des Ernstes dieser Gnade willen!,[42] um dieser unersetzlichen Gnade nicht zu widerstreben![43] – lebe[44] der Christ wie die übrige Welt! Gewiß, er würde gern ein[45] Außerordentliches tun, es[46] ist für ihn unzweifelhaft der schwerste Verzicht, dies nicht zu tun, sondern weltlich leben zu müssen. Aber er muß den Verzicht leisten,[47] die Selbstverleugnung üben, sich von der Welt mit seinem Leben nicht zu unterscheiden. Soweit muß er die Gnade wirklich Gnade sein lassen, daß er der Welt den Glauben an diese billige Gnade nicht zerstört. Der Christ aber sei[48] in seiner Weltlichkeit, in diesem notwendigen Verzicht, den er um der Welt [willen] – nein, um der Gnade willen! – leisten muß, getrost und sicher (securus)

---

27. Here genitive attribute to a genitive attribute; translate as "God's word"; the same holds for all further uses of *Wort Gottes.*

28. Translate as "incarnation"; literally "becoming human."

29. Not to be confused: *die Sünde* "sin" but *der Sünder* "sinner."

30. Fixed phrase *beim alten bleiben* "to stay the same."

31. Quotes from Luther.

32. All verbs in the sentence in *Konjunktiv I*, which expresses here the notion of a suggestion; translate with "should + verb."

33. Verb *sich etwas (dative) gleichstellen* "to equate yourself to something."

34. Verb *sich unterfangen* "to venture."

35. Emphasizes the meaning of "not"; translate together as "by no means."

36. Term arose during the Reformation, and refers to enthusiasts, the Anabaptists, and similarly minded people.

37. Translate as "in grace."

38. Translate as "in sin."

39. Verb *sich hüten etwas zu tun* "to beware of doing something," here followed by a series of infinitive with *zu* constructions, which in this context are best translated with "ing"-forms.

40. Verb *gegen etwas wüten* "to rage against something."

41. Compound; translate as "religion of the letter."

42. Preposition *um . . . willen* "for the sake of."

43. Verb *etwas* (dative) *widerstreben* "to oppose something."

44. *Konjunktiv I*, expresses here the notion of a suggestion; translate with "should + verb."

45. Here in the sense of *etwas* "something."

46. Specified by the infinitive with *zu* construction.

47. Translate here as "do."

48. *Konjunktiv I*; expresses here the notion of a suggestion; translate with "be."

im Besitz dieser Gnade, die alles allein tut. Also, der Christ folge nicht nach, aber er tröste sich der Gnade![49] Das ist billige Gnade als Rechtfertigung der Sünde, aber nicht als Rechtfertigung des bußfertigen Sünders, der von seiner Sünde läßt[50] und umkehrt; nicht Vergebung der Sünde, die von der Sünde trennt. Billige Gnade ist die Gnade, die wir mit uns selbst haben. Billige Gnade ist Predigt der Vergebung ohne Buße, ist Taufe ohne Gemeindezucht,[51] ist Abendmahl ohne Bekenntnis der Sünden, ist Absolution ohne persönliche Beichte. Billige Gnade ist Gnade ohne Nachfolge, Gnade ohne Kreuz, Gnade ohne den lebendigen, menschgewordenen[52] Jesus Christus.

Teure Gnade ist der verborgene Schatz im Acker, um dessentwillen der Mensch hingeht und mit Freuden alles verkauft, was er hatte; die köstliche[53] Perle, für deren Preis der Kaufmann alle seine Güter hingibt; die Königsherrschaft Christi, um derentwillen sich der Mensch das Auge ausreißt, das ihn ärgert, der Ruf Jesu Christi, auf den hin[54] der Jünger seine Netze verläßt und nachfolgt. Teure Gnade ist das Evangelium, das immer wieder gesucht, die Gabe, um die gebeten, die Tür, an die angeklopft <u>werden muß</u>.[55] Teuer ist sie, weil sie in die Nachfolge ruft, Gnade ist sie, weil sie in die Nachfolge Jesu Christi ruft; teuer ist sie, weil sie dem Menschen das Leben kostet, Gnade ist sie, weil sie ihm so[56] das Leben erst[57] schenkt; teuer ist sie, weil sie die Sünde verdammt, Gnade, weil sie den Sünder rechtfertigt. Teuer ist die Gnade vor allem <u>darum, weil</u>[58] sie Gott teuer gewesen ist, weil sie Gott das Leben seines Sohnes gekostet hat – „ihr seid teuer erkauft" – , und weil uns nicht billig sein kann, was Gott teuer ist. Gnade ist sie vor allem <u>darum, weil</u>[59] Gott sein Sohn nicht zu teuer war für unser Leben, sondern ihn für uns hingab.[60] Teure Gnade ist Menschwerdung[61] Gottes.

Teure Gnade ist Gnade als das Heiligtum Gottes, das vor der Welt behütet werden muß, das nicht vor die Hunde geworfen werden darf, sie ist darum Gnade als lebendiges Wort, Wort Gottes, das er selbst spricht, wie es ihm gefällt. Es[62] trifft uns als gnädiger Ruf in die Nachfolge Jesu, es kommt als vergebendes Wort zu dem geängsteten[63] Geist und dem zerschlagenen[64] Herzen. Teuer ist die Gnade, weil sie den Menschen unter das

---

49. Use of dative with *trösten* outdated; conveys a passive meaning; translate as "he is comforted by grace."
50. Verb *von etwas lassen* "to stay away from (doing) something."
51. Translate as "church discipline."
52. Adjective derived from the participle II of *menschwerden* "to incarnate."
53. Here in the sense of *kostbar* "precious."
54. Translate as "for which."
55. Relates to all verb forms in the sentence.
56. Modal particle; translate here as "that way."
57. Modal particle; translate here as "in the first place."
58. Translate simply as "because."
59. See above.
60. Translate as "sacrifice."
61. Translate as "incarnation," literally "becoming human."
62. All neuter pronouns in the sentence refer back to *Wort*.
63. Adjective derived from the participle II of *ängstigen*, here in the sense of *verängstigt* "scared" or "terrified."
64. Adjective derived from the participle II of *zerschlagen* "to crush" or "to shatter."

Joch der Nachfolge Jesu Christi zwingt, Gnade ist es, daß Jesus sagt: „Mein Joch ist sanft und meine Last ist leicht."

Zweimal ist an Petrus der Ruf ergangen: Folge mir nach! Es war das erste und das letzte Wort Jesu an seinen Jünger[65] (Markus 1,17; Joh. 21,22). Sein ganzes Leben liegt zwischen diesen beiden Rufen. Das erstemal[66] hatte Petrus am See Genezareth auf Jesu[67] Ruf hin[68] seine Netze, seinen Beruf verlassen und war ihm aufs Wort nachgefolgt. Das letztemal[69] trifft ihn der Auferstandene[70] in seinem alten Beruf, wiederum am See Genezareth, und noch einmal heißt es: Folge mir nach! Dazwischen lag ein ganzes Jüngerleben in der Nachfolge Christi. In seiner[71] Mitte stand das Bekenntnis zu Jesus als dem Christus Gottes. Es ist dem Petrus dreimal <u>ein und dasselbe</u>[72] verkündigt, am Anfang, am Ende und in Cäsarea Philippi, nämlich daß Christus sein Herr und Gott sei.[73] Es ist dieselbe Gnade Christi, die ihn ruft: Folge mir nach! und die sich ihm offenbart im Bekenntnis zum Sohne Gottes.

Es war ein dreifaches Anhalten[74] der Gnade auf dem Wege des Petrus, die Eine[75] Gnade dreimal verschieden verkündigt; so war sie Christi[76] eigene Gnade, und gewiß nicht Gnade, die der Jünger sich selbst zusprach. Es war dieselbe[77] Gnade Christi, die den Jünger überwand,[78] alles zu verlassen um der Nachfolge willen, die in ihm das Bekenntnis wirkte,[79] das aller Welt eine Lästerung scheinen[80] mußte, die den untreuen Petrus in die letzte Gemeinschaft des Martyriums rief und ihm damit alle Sünden vergab. Gnade und Nachfolge gehören für das Leben des Petrus unauflöslich zusammen. Er hatte die teure Gnade empfangen. Mit der Ausbreitung des Christentums und der zunehmenden Verweltlichung der Kirche ging die Erkenntnis der teuren Gnade allmählich verloren.[81] Die Welt war christianisiert, die Gnade war Allgemeingut einer christlichen Welt geworden.[82] Sie war billig zu haben. Doch bewahrte die römische Kirche einen Rest

---

65. Translate as "disciple." Be aware that the singular and plural of *Jünger* look identical. However, the article indicates the number.

66. Usually *das erste Mal* "the first time."

67. Specific genitive form used for *Jesus*.

68. Preposition *auf . . . hin*; translate here as "following."

69. Usually *das letzte Mal* "the last time."

70. Nominalized adjective derived from the participle II of *auferstehen* "to rise" or "to resurrect," referring to a person.

71. Refers back to *Jüngerleben*.

72. Fixed phrase; translate as "one and the same."

73. *Konjunktiv I*; translate here with "be."

74. Nominalized verb *anhalten*, translate as verb of the sentence, "to continue."

75. Here with a capital letter to emphasize its uniqueness.

76. Specific genitive form used for *Christus*.

77. Specified in the following relative clauses introduced by *die*.

78. Verb *überwinden*; translate here as "to lead (someone) to do something."

79. Here in the sense of *bewirken* "to cause" or "to bring about."

80. Usually jemandem/etwas (dative) als etwas erscheinen "to appear to someone as something."

81. Verb *verloren gehen* "to get lost."

82. Pluperfect of *werden* "to become."

der ersten Erkenntnis. Es war von entscheidender[83] Bedeutung, daß das Mönchtum sich nicht von der Kirche trennte und daß die Klugheit der Kirche das Mönchtum ertrug. Hier war am Rande[84] der Kirche der Ort, an dem die Erkenntnis wachgehalten wurde, daß Gnade teuer ist, daß Gnade die Nachfolge einschließt. Menschen verließen um Christi willen alles, was sie hatten, und versuchten, den strengen Geboten Jesu zu folgen in täglicher Übung. So[85] wurde das mönchische[86] Leben ein lebendiger Protest gegen die Verweltlichung des Christentums, gegen die Verbilligung[87] der Gnade. Indem[88] aber die Kirche diesen Protest ertrug und nicht zum letzten Ausbruch kommen ließ,[89] relativierte sie ihn, ja sie gewann nun aus ihm sogar die Rechtfertigung ihres eigenen verweltlichten[90] Lebens; denn jetzt wurde das mönchische Leben zu der Sonderleistung Einzelner, zu der die Masse des Kirchenvolkes nicht verpflichtet werden konnte. Die verhängnisvolle Begrenzung der Gebote Jesu in ihrer Geltung auf eine bestimmte Gruppe besonders qualifizierter Menschen führte zu der Unterscheidung einer Höchstleistung und einer Mindestleistung des christlichen Gehorsams. Damit war es gelungen, bei jedem weiteren Angriff auf die Verweltlichung der Kirche hinzuweisen [und] auf die Möglichkeit des mönchischen Weges innerhalb der Kirche, neben dem dann die andere Möglichkeit des leichteren Weges durchaus gerechtfertigt war.

> So[91] mußte (v1) der Hinweis (NOM) auf das urchristliche[92] Verständnis der teuren Gnade, wie er (NOM) in der Kirche Roms[93] durch das Mönchtum erhalten (infinitive) bleiben (v2) sollte (v1), in paradoxer Weise selbst wieder der Verweltlichung der Kirche (DAT) die letzte Rechtfertigung (AKK) geben (v2).

Bei dem allen lag der entscheidende Fehler des Mönchtums nicht darin,[94] daß es–bei allen inhaltlichen Missverständnissen des Willens Jesu–den Gnadenweg der strengen Nachfolge ging. Vielmehr entfernte sich das Mönchtum wesentlich darin[95] vom

---

83. Adjective derived from the participle I of *entscheiden* "to decide," which has become part of the lexicon; translate as "significant."

84. Translate as "at the edge of."

85. Modal particle; translate here as "that way."

86. Adjective to *Mönch* "monk"; translate as "monastic."

87. Noun formed with the verb *verbilligen* "to cheapen" and the suffix *-ung*, translate as "cheapening."

88. Conjunction; translate with "by + ing-form."

89. Verb *nicht zu etwas kommen lassen* "to prevent something from happening."

90. Adjective derived from the participle I of *verweltlichen* "to secularize."

91. Modal particle; translate here as "thus."

92. The prefix *ur-* is used with nouns and adjectives and should be translated as "genuine" or "original."

93. Genitive attribute to *Kirche*; translate as "Roman Church."

94. Specified in the *dass*-sentence, verb *liegen in*.

95. Specified in the *dass*-sentence.

Christlichen, daß es seinen Weg zu einer freien Sonderleistung einiger Weniger[96] werden ließ[97] und damit für ihn eine besondere Verdienstlichkeit[98] in Anspruch nahm.[99] Als Gott durch seinen Knecht Martin Luther in der Reformation das Evangelium von der reinen, teuren Gnade wieder erweckte, führte er Luther durch das Kloster. Luther war Mönch. Er hatte alles verlassen und wollte Christus in vollkommenem Gehorsam nachfolgen. Er entsagte[100] der Welt und ging[101] an das christliche Werk. Er lernte den Gehorsam gegen[102] Christus und seine Kirche, weil er wußte, daß nur der Gehorsame[103] glauben kann. Der Ruf ins Kloster kostete Luther den vollen Einsatz seines Lebens. Luther scheiterte[104] mit seinem Weg an Gott selbst. Gott zeigte ihm durch die Schrift, daß die Nachfolge Jesu nicht verdienstliche[105] Sonderleistung Einzelner, sondern göttliches Gebot an alle Christen ist. Das demütige Werk der Nachfolge war im Mönchtum zum verdienstlichen Tun der Heiligen geworden. Die Selbstverleugnung des Nachfolgenden[106] enthüllte sich hier als die letzte geistliche Selbstbehauptung der Frommen.[107] Damit[108] war die Welt mitten in[109] das Mönchsleben hineingebrochen und in gefährlichster Weise wieder am Werk.[110] Die Weltflucht des Mönches war als feinste Weltliebe durchschaut. In diesem Scheitern der letzten Möglichkeit eines frommen Lebens ergriff Luther die Gnade. Er sah im Zusammenbruch der mönchischen Welt die rettende Hand Gottes in Christus ausgestreckt. Er ergriff sie im Glauben daran,[111] daß „doch unser Tun umsonst ist, auch in dem besten Leben“. Es war eine teure Gnade, die sich ihm schenkte, sie zerbrach ihm seine ganze Existenz. Er mußte seine Netze abermals zurücklassen und folgen. Das erstemal, als er ins Kloster ging, hatte er alles zurückgelassen, nur sich selbst, sein frommes Ich, nicht. Diesmal war ihm auch dieses genommen. Er folgte nicht auf[112] eigenes Verdienst, sondern auf Gottes Gnade hin.[113] Es wurde ihm nicht gesagt: du hast zwar gesündigt, aber[114] das ist

---

96. Genitive attribute to *Sonderleistung.*
97. Verb *etwas* (accusative) *zu etwas werden lassen* "to let something become something."
98. Translate as "merit."
99. Verb *etwas in Anspruch nehmen* "to use."
100. Translate as "forsake."
101. Translate here as "begin."
102. Translate here as "to."
103. Nominalized adjective referring to a person.
104. Verb *an etwas scheitern* "to fail (because of)."
105. Adjective to *Verdienst* "merit"; translate as "meritorious."
106. Nominalized adjective derived from the participle I of the verb *nachfolgen*, here referring to a person.
107. Nominalized adjective referring to people.
108. *Da*-compound; translate as "with that."
109. Preposition *mitten in* "in the middle of."
110. Verb *am Werk sein* "to be at work."
111. Specified in the *dass*-sentence, necessary because of the construction *Glaube an etwas.*
112. Translate here as "for."
113. *auf . . . hin* translate here as "because of."
114. Conjunction *zwar . . . aber*, omit *zwar* and translate simply with "but" in the second clause.

nun alles vergeben, bleibe[115] nur weiter, wo du warst, und tröste[116] dich der Vergebung! Luther mußte das Kloster verlassen und zurück in die Welt, nicht weil die Welt an sich gut und heilig wäre, sondern weil auch das Kloster nichts anderes war als Welt. Luthers Weg aus dem Kloster zurück in die Welt bedeutete den schärfsten Angriff, der seit dem Urchristentum[117] auf die Welt geführt worden war. Die Absage, die der Mönch der Welt gegeben hatte, war ein Kinderspiel[118] gegenüber der Absage, die die Welt durch den in sie Zurückgekehrten[119] erfuhr. Nun kam der Angriff frontal. Nachfolge Jesu mußte nun mitten in[120] der Welt gelebt werden. Was unter den besonderen Umständen und Erleichterungen des klösterlichen Lebens als Sonderleistung geübt wurde, war nun das Notwendige und Gebotene für jeden Christen in der Welt geworden.[121] Der vollkommene Gehorsam gegen das Gebot Jesu mußte im täglichen Berufsleben geleistet werden. Damit vertiefte sich der Konflikt zwischen dem Leben des Christen und dem Leben der Welt in unabsehbarer Weise. Der Christ war der Welt auf den Leib gerückt.[122] Es war Nahkampf.[123]

> Man (NOM) kann (v1) die Tat Luthers (AKK)[124] nicht verhängnisvoller[125] mißverstehen (v2) als mit der Meinung, Luther (NOM) habe[126](v1) mit der Entdeckung (DAT) des Evangeliums der reinen Gnade[127] einen Dispens (AKK)[128] für den Gehorsam gegen das Gebot Jesu in der Welt proklamiert (v2);[129] die reformatorische[130] Entdeckung (NOM) sei[131] (v1) die Heiligsprechung (AKK), die Rechtfertigung der Welt (AKK) durch die vergebende[132] Gnade gewesen (v2).[133]

---

115. Imperative form.
116. Imperative form.
117. See footnote above on prefix *ur-*.
118. Fixed phrase *ein Kinderspiel sein* "be a walk in the park."
119. Nominalized adjective derived from the participle II of the verb *zurückkehren*, here referring to a person.
120. Preposition *mitten in* "in the middle of."
121. Pluperfect of *werden* "to become."
122. Fixed phrase *jemandem/etwas* (dative) *auf den Leib rücken* "to get close to someone/something."
123. Translate as "close combat."
124. Genitive attribute to *Tat*.
125. Comparative form followed by *als*.
126. *Konjunktiv I*; translate with indicative.
127. Complex word group with two genitive attributes specifying the noun they follow.
128. Translate as "dispensation."
129. Translate with that-sentence.
130. Adjective to *Reformation*.
131. *Konjunktiv I*; translate with indicative.
132. Adjective derived from the participle I of the verb *vergeben*, translate as "forgiving."
133. Translate with that-sentence.

Der weltliche Beruf des Christen erfährt vielmehr seine Rechtfertigung für[134] Luther allein <u>dadurch, daß</u>[135] in ihm[136] der Protest gegen die Welt in letzter Schärfe angemeldet wird. Nur sofern[137] der weltliche Beruf des Christen in der Nachfolge Jesu ausgeübt wird, hat er vom Evangelium her[138] neues Recht empfangen. Nicht Rechtfertigung der Sünde, sondern Rechtfertigung des Sünders war der Grund für Luthers Rückkehr aus dem Kloster. Teure Gnade war Luther geschenkt worden.[139] Gnade war es, weil sie[140] Wasser auf das durstige Land, Trost für die Angst, Befreiung von der Knechtschaft des selbstgewählten Weges, Vergebung aller Sünden war. Teuer war die Gnade, weil sie nicht dispensierte vom Werk, sondern den Ruf in die Nachfolge unendlich verschärfte. Aber gerade worin[141] sie teuer war, darin[142] war sie Gnade, und worin[143] sie Gnade war, darin[144] war sie teuer. Das war das Geheimnis des reformatorischen Evangeliums, das Geheimnis der Rechtfertigung des Sünders.

---

134. Translate here as "according to."
135. Translate simply as "because."
136. Refers back to *Beruf*.
137. Translate here as "only so far as."
138. Preposition *von . . . her*, translate here as "from."
139. Pluperfect passive of the verb *schenken*.
140. Refers back to *Gnade*.
141. *Wo*-compound; translate as "in what" or simply as "where."
142. *Da*-compound; translate here as "there."
143. See above.
144. See above.

PART III

A Semi-Modern German Reader

Overview

In order to help you advance in your reading and translation skills, we have selected eight texts for you, based on their focus on various areas of research. To accommodate the interests of all learners, we have selected two texts within each field, including Hebrew Bible/biblical archaeology, New Testament studies, Jewish studies, and church history/theology. Many of the authors in this section represent modern scholarship, with the exception of Geiger and Frankel; however, due to their influence on modern Judaism, they have been included here, as well.

An introduction to the writing styles of each author is not presented in this part of the book, as they are similar to each other and represent typical elements of modern academic writing. You will notice that these authors try to fit a lot of information into one sentence. They like to use the passive in order to avoid mentioning the subject, thereby making the sentence sound more objective. Fewer footnotes are provided than in part II in order to challenge your skills and boost your confidence when encountering German language texts in your own research.

Lesson Bulletpoints

- Review grammatical concepts for:
  - Participles used as adjectives
  - Compound words
  - Passive/passive-like constructions
  - Zero article declension

Learning Objectives

- Learners will become comfortable using the Mainz Method Checklist.
- Learners will be introduced to modern German scholars.
- Learners will recognize the differences in writing styles throughout the centuries.
- Learners will develop confidence in translating texts selected for their own research.

Othmar Keel & Christoph Uehlinger 11

Excerpt from Göttinnen, Götter und Gottessymbole (2010)

§ 112. Die sogenannte „Vereinigte Monarchie", in der weitgehend[1] aus judäischer Perspektive redigierten[2] religiösen Überlieferung zuweilen geradezu als Idealzeit Israels gefeiert und beschworen, ist bekanntlich mit dem Tode Salomos (um 925) zu einem abrupten Ende gekommen. Kulturgeschichtlich gesehen stellt die EZ 11 A deshalb eine relativ kurze Episode in der Geschichte der Region dar.[3] Die folgende EZ 11 B, die von ca. 925 bis ins letzte Drittel des 8. Jhs. reicht, umfaßt die rund zwei Jahrhunderte dauernde Zeitspanne, in der Israel und Juda als getrennte Staaten nebeneinander existierten, umgeben von den nunmehr wieder unabhängigen Nationalstaaten Moab, Ammon, Aram-Damaskus, den südphönizischen Stadtstaaten Tyrus und Sidon und dem philistäischen Städteverbund.

Neben zahlreichen Elementen der Kontinuität in Wohnhausarchitektur, Bestattungswesen, Handwerk u.ä. dokumentiert die Archäologie der EZ 11 B als besonders nennenswerte Neuerung und Eigenheit eine klare Tendenz zur monumentalen Stadtarchitektur. Die lokalen Königtümer[4] bemühten sich v.a. in den Landes- und Distriktshauptstädten um demonstrativen Prunk. Zu den vorwiegend Verwaltungs- und Repräsentationszwecke erfüllenden[5] Palastbauten traten[6] nun vermehrt auch militärische Befestigungen. In den größeren Zentren fanden sich[7] Garnisonen und Kasernen für stationär gehaltene Truppen. Umfangreiche Befestigungen und Maßnahmen zur Sicherung der Wasserversorgung im Belagerungsfall (z.B. in Hazor, Megiddo, Geser und el-Gib) lassen deutlich das Bedürfnis nach defensiver Sicherung erkennen. Vor dem Hintergrund der zahlreichen Erzählungen der Königsbücher, die von Kriegen mit Aram und Moab, aber auch von Feindseligkeiten zwischen Israel und Juda berichten, läßt sich mühelos nachvollziehen, daß defensive Maßnahmen besonders zu Beginn der EZ II B eine Priorität darstellen mußten.

---

1. Translate as "largely."
2. Participle II of the verb *redigieren*; translate as "redacted."
3. Verb *darstellen* is often used in contemporary academic writing; translate simply with the verb "be."
4. Translate as "monarchies."
5. Complex noun phrase with participle I of the verb *erfüllen* used as adjective; translate with a relative clause.
6. Past tense of the verb *treten*; translate here as "came."
7. Verb *sich finden* expresses a passive meaning; translate as "are to be found."

194

Die Gründe für den schon zu Salomos Lebzeiten eingetretenen Verlust der von David unterworfenen Vasallengebiete und für das Auseinanderbrechen[8] Groß-Israels in zwei Teilstaaten sind zu komplex, um an dieser Stelle im einzelnen diskutiert zu werden. Nach 1 Kön 12 spielte die ungleiche Verteilung von Abgaben und Frondienstleistungen an die in Jerusalem residierenden Davididen eine entscheidende Rolle. Daß die Nordstämme trotz ihrer archaisch anmutenden Parole „Zu deinen Zelten, Israel!" (1 Kön 12,16; vgl. 2 Sam 20,1) das Prinzip der Monarchie nicht in Frage stellten und ihren Staat sogleich als Königtum konstituierten, ist vor dem Hintergrund der seit dem Ende des 11. Jhs. weit fortgeschrittenen Reurbanisierung des ganzen Landes zu verstehen und weist auf die führende Rolle städtischer Eliten in der israelitischen Unabhängigkeitsbewegung. Trifft die Darstellung von 1 Kön 11–12 das Richtige, dann hat auch Ägypten bei den Ereignissen, die schließlich zur Trennung von Nord- und Südreich führten, eine wichtige Rolle gespielt.

Die Siegelgruppe des „eckig Stilisierten" (s.o. § 83), die fortlaufenden Amun-Skarabäen (§ 84) und die Präsenz des „schlagenden Gottes" in Geser (Anm. 92) zeigen deutlich, daß der kulturelle Einfluß Ägyptens mindestens im Bereich der südpalästinischen Küstenebene auch während der EZ II A noch beträchtlich geblieben war. Der erste Pharao der 22. Dynastie, Scheschonq I. (944–923), hat sich in der zweiten Hälfte des 10. Jhs. dann offensichtlich darum bemüht, die Machtkonzentration in Jerusalem zu untergraben und in Palästina auch politisch wieder Fuß zu fassen.[9]

Von Salomo verfolgte Rebellen wie der „Edomiter" (bzw. Aramäer?) Hadad (1 Kön 11,14–25) oder der Efraimiter[10] Jerobeam fanden zunächst am Hofe Scheschonqs politisches Asyl (1 Kön 11, 40; 12,2). Nur wenige Jahre nach Salomos Tod unternahm Scheschonq dann einen Feldzug nicht nur gegen Juda (1 Kön 14,25t), sondern auch gegen Jerobeam, und zwar – wenn auch nur kurzfristig – mit Erfolg, wie das in Megiddo gefundene, ursprünglich aus Str. IV A stammende Bruchstück einer Siegesstele mit den Kartuschen des Pharaos zeigt (Abb. 194; Lamon/Shipton 1939: 60f; vgl. Ussishkin 1990: 71–74). [Footnote 126][11]

Man kann sich fragen, ob es sich bei diesem Feldzug nicht geradezu um eine Strafaktion gegen den einstigen Schützling handelte. Die Vermutung liegt nahe, wenn

---

8. Nominalized verb referring to a general notion.
9. Fixed phrase *Fuß fassen* "to take root."
10. A person belonging to the tribe of Ephraim.
11. You will find all footnotes provided by the author at the end of this chapter.

man bedenkt, daß Jerobeam sein vor den Jungstierbildern von Bet-El und Dan (s.u. § 119) proklamiertes Autonomieprogramm nach 1 Kön 12,28 mit der ägyptenkritischen Exodustradition verband. Wie immer dem sei:[12] Scheschonq starb bald darauf, und die Nachfolger führten seine offensive Politik nicht weiter, so daß sich in Palästina nun für rund zwei Jahrhunderte ein relativ stabiles System von Kleinstaaten etablieren konnte.[13]

§ 113. Der folgende Blick auf religionsgeschichtlich relevante Dokumente wird nicht nur das Problem der Kontinuität bisheriger Entwicklungen verfolgen müßen (bes. § 114ft), sondern auch die Frage zu diskutieren haben, ob Ikonographie und Epigraphik angesichts des neuen Nebeneinanders unabhängiger Kleinstaaten auch Hinweise auf je spezifische religiöse Eigenheiten zu liefern vermögen. Zwar blieb Ägypten <u>nach wie vor</u>[14] der kulturelle Hauptanziehungspunkt der ganzen Region und [zwar] finden sich allenthalben deutliche Spuren der Faszination durch die Großmacht am Nil. Doch[15] pflegten die beiden uns primär interessierenden Staaten Israel und Juda ein je eigenes Verhältnis zu Ägypten. Durch die Reichstrennung zu einem relativ bedeutungslosen Rumpfstaat[16] abseits der großen Handelsrouten relegiert, erlebte Juda, zeitweilig – etwa unter Joasch ben Joachas und Jerobeam II. – deutlich von Israel dominiert (vgl. 2 Kön 13f und unten § 146), zunächst bis in die Mitte des 8. Jhs. eine Zeit kultureller Stagnation. Israel behielt dagegen durch seine engen politischen und ökonomischen Beziehungen zu den nördlichen Nachbarn, besonders zu den südphönizischen Städten Tyrus und Sidon, stets die Kontrolle über die durch sein Gebiet führenden großen Handelsrouten. Ab der Mitte des 9. Jhs. beteiligte es sich[17] mit den phönizischen Städten und den Aramäern regelmäßig an anti-assyrischen Bündnissen, ein eindeutiges Indiz gemeinsamer politischer wie ökonomischer Interessen.

Es kann nicht überraschen, daß sich die unterschiedliche geopolitische Einbindung der beiden Staaten auch im Bereich der Ikonographie äußert: In Juda beschränkt sich diese zunächst weitgehend auf fortlebende autochthone Motive (s.u. § 114ft) und provinzielle Adaptationen ägyptischer Königssymbolik (§ 156ft); erst gegen Ende des 8. Jhs. wurden, vielleicht durch Kunsthandwerker aus dem Norden angestoßen, auch in Juda spezifisch „religiöse" Motive rezipiert (§ 160t). Im äußerst produktiven israelitisch-phönizischen Kunsthandwerk des Nordens lassen sich dagegen ab dem 9. Jh. viel größere Eigenständigkeit und größeres Selbstbewußtsein bei der Beerbung ägyptischer religiöser Symbole feststellen (§ 148ft). Gleichzeitig sind im Norden aber auch syrisch „kanaanäische" Traditionen und Motive belegt, die in Juda weitgehend fehlen (§ 122ft).

---

12. Fixed phrase *wie immer dem sei* "be that as it may."
13. Verb construction *sich etablieren können* conveys a passive meaning; translate here as "could be established."
14. Fixed phrase; translate as "still."
15. Here instead of *aber* as the second part of the conjunction *zwar . . . aber*, omit *zwar* in the previous sentence and translate *doch* simply as "but."
16. Translate as "rump state."
17. Verb *sich beteiligen an etwas* "to join something."

Ägyptisierende[18] ebenso wie syrisch-„kanaanäische" Motive finden in der EZ II B besonders markanten und charakteristischen Ausdruck in der Glyptik (anepigraphische und Namenssiegel) und in Elfenbeinschnitzereien. Letztere hatten sich schon im sbzeitlichen Kanaan großer Beliebtheit erfreut (s.o. § 37f), doch war ihre Produktion mit dem Niedergang der Stadtkultur und der Krise des internationalen Handels unterbrochen worden. In der EZ II B erlebten sie mit dem phönizisch-israelitischen Kunsthandwerk neuen Aufschwung. Dieses wird gern nur als „phönizisch" qualifiziert. In der Tat war Phönizien in der ersten Hälfte des 1. Jts. eines der aktivsten Zentren der Produktion und Vermittlung von stark ägyptisierenden[19] Luxusgütern wie Metallschalen, Elfenbeinschnitzereien u.ä. Pretiosen, und ein Teil der in Israel gefundenen Produkte dieses Kunsthandwerks, etwa eine dekorierte Bronzeschale aus Megiddo Str. IV A (Lamon/Shipton 1939: PI. 115,12), dürfte aus Phönizien importiert worden sein. Aber es scheint auch auf dem Boden des Nordreiches Israel Werkstätten gegeben zu haben, in denen Produkte dieses Kunsthandwerks, besonders Elfenbeine und Siegel, hergestellt worden sind. [Footnote 127] Es ist deshalb wohl richtiger, eher als von einem „Einfluß" Phöniziens auf das Nordreich Israel von einer „parenté de culture entre les deux regions"[20] zu sprechen (Parayre 1990: 289). Diese Verwandtschaft kommt auch im linguistisch-epigraphischen Bereich recht deutlich zum Ausdruck.[21] Das Israelitische stand dem Phönizischen (beides zentrale „Dialekte" des Kanaanäischen) näher als dem Iudäischen (einem „peripheren", konservativeren Dialekt des Kanaanäischen, dem Ammonitischen und Moabitischen vergleichbar[22]). Allerdings sollte die Betonung dieser Verwandtschaft umgekehrt nicht dazu verleiten, zwischen der phönizischen und der israelitischen Kultur keine Unterschiede mehr erkennen zu wollen. [Footnote 128]

Hinsichtlich der Datierung des phönizisch-israelitischen Kunsthandwerks steht zur Diskussion, ob die Elfenbeinkunst bereits im 9. Jh. eine neue Blüte erreichte (Barnett 1982: 46–55) oder erst nach dem Aussterben des syrischen Elefanten im 8. Jh. aufkam, als die binnensyrische Elfenbeinschnitzerei (z.B. in Damaskus) nur noch schwer Zugang zum Rohmaterial fand,[23] während die Küste ihr Rohmaterial aus Ägypten beziehen konnte (I. Winter 1976: 15f). Die einzige größere Gruppe von Elfenbein- und Knochenschnitzereien der EZ II B aus Palästina ist in Samaria gefunden worden. Ihr stratigraphischer Kontext erlaubt keine klare Datierung ins 9. oder 8. Jh. Auch literarische

---

18. Adjective formed with the participle I of the verb *ägyptisieren*, which is formed by using the noun *Ägypten* + *-isieren* and expresses "to make something Egyptian."

19. See above.

20. French for "kinship of culture between the two regions."

21. Fixed phrase *zum Ausdruck kommen in etwas* "to be reflected in something."

22. Appositional phrase to *Kanaanäischen*.

23. Fixed phrase *Zugang finden zu etwas* "to gain access to something."

Erwähnungen des Elfenbeinluxus Samarias helfen nicht weiter; einschlägige biblische Texte beziehen sich auf das 9. Jh. (1 Kön 22,39, wahrscheinlich ein Annalenauszug für die Zeit Achabs, der mit einer tyrischen Königstochter vermählt war) ebenso wie auf das 8. Jh. (Am 3,12–15; 6,4, um 750; zum Ganzen vgl. I. Winter 1981: 109–115;123–127; H. Weippert 1988: 652–660).

Die phönizisch-israelitischen *anepigraphischen Siegelamulette*, meist Skaraboide, setzen jedenfalls schon im 9. Jh. ein. Sie sind sehr flach geschnitten und mit Innenzeichnungen versehen,[24] die durch schematische parallele Striche charakterisiert sind. Von wenigen Ausnahmen abgesehen sind die Basisdekorationen vertikal organisiert, wobei mehrere durch horizontale Linien abgetrennte Register übereinander liegen oder der Eindruck solcher Register ohne die horizontalen Linien einfach durch übereinander angebrachte horizontale Motive hervorgerufen wird. Inhaltlich dominieren auf diesen Siegeln solar determinierte ägyptische Motive (§ 148ff).

Die Namenssiegel stellen eine Denkmälergattung[25] dar, die in der Levante ebenfalls am Ende des 9. und zu Beginn des 8. Jhs. neu auftaucht. Es handelt sich um Siegelamulette, die dadurch charakterisiert sind, daß sie neben dem ikonographischen Motiv den Namen des Besitzers oder der Besitzerin tragen, meist mit dem *lamed* der Zugehörigkeit davor. Häufig ist ihnen der Name des Vaters beigesellt,[26] meist, aber nicht immer mit *bn* „Sohn des" oder *bt* „Tochter des" verbunden. Manchmal steht auch ein Titel oder eine Berufsbezeichnung dabei (vgl. überblickshalber[27] Lemaire 1988; Sass 1993). [Footnote 129]

Das Material wird im Folgenden nach ikonographischen Gesichtspunkten gruppiert. Zwar kann die religionsgeschichtliche Diskussion nun verschiedentlich mit epigraphischen Quellen angereichert werden, die ab der 2. Hälfte des 9. Jhs. Reichlicher zu fließen beginnen (§ 125ff). Da aber die inschriftlichen Quellen in der Regel[28] sehr viel besser bekannt und – in der Regel unter völliger Vernachlässigung der nicht literarischen Dokumentation – auch immer wieder Gegenstand wissenschaftlicher Diskussion gewesen sind, werden wir die Ikonographie, der besonderen Eigenart dieses Bandes entsprechend,[29] weiterhin in den Vordergrund stellen. Nach einem Blick auf wesentliche Gemeinsamkeiten der ikonographisch dokumentierten religiösen Vorstellungswelten Israels und Judas (§ 114–118) sollen auch ihre je spezifischen Eigenheiten skizziert werden.

---

24. Verb *versehen sein mit etwas* "to be equipped with something."

25. Compound word formed with the plural of *das Denkmal* "monument" and *die Gattung* "class" or "type."

26. Outdated verb *beigesellen*, translate as "to add."

27. Adjective formation with noun and suffix *-halber* should be translated with "for + noun," here "for a review."

28. Fixed phrase *in der Regel* "as a rule" or "usually."

29. Appositional phrase to *Ikonographie*.

Footnotes by the Author

126 Eine Liste eroberter Orte am Amun-Tempel von Karnak nennt Siedlungen im Negev und in Zentralpalästina, dagegen keine Namen von Orten im judäischen Bergland oder in der judäischen Schefela. Vgl. Aharoni 1984: 332–340.

127 In Juda scheint das Elfenbeinhandwerk dagegen bis ans Ende der EZ 11 B nur marginal vertreten gewesen zu sein. Vgl. etwa die spärlichen Funde aus Lachisch, der zweitwichtigsten Stadt Judas (Tufnell 1953: PI. 63; Ussishkin 1978: PI. 16,2), mit den im folgenden diskutierten aus Samaria, Hazor, Megiddo oder Geser. Wenig bekannte Elfenbeinschnitzereien aus Juda, die frühestens ans Ende der EZ 11 B bzw. in die EZ II C datieren dürften, sind eine Plakette mit Flötenspieler und Schafen von ijirbet Kirmil (genauer Fundkontext unbekannt, heute im Archäologischen Museum in Amman ausgestellt, unseres Wissens unpubliziert) sowie ein rundplastischer Frauenkopf „aus der Gegend von Hebron" (Bet Aula?; Chouraqui 1983: 111475), der heute im R. Hecht Museum in Haifa aufbewahrt wird (Hachlili/Meshorer 1986: 35).

128 Zwischen Verwandtschaft, die produktive autochthone Kräfte voraussetzt, und von außen kommendem Einfluß zu unterscheiden, ist naturgemäß äusserst schwierig. Hätte die hier genannte „parenté de culture" nicht auch schon in der EZ 11 A registriert werden müssen, wo wir im Hinblick gerade auf nordisraelitische Befunde wiederholt von einem „phönizischem Einfluß" gesprochen haben (vgl. bes. § 87 und 111 zur ‚Herrin der Löwen')? Die zugegebenermaßen unscharfe Grenzlinie kann nur ziehen, wer Traditionsgeschichte (von Motiven und Konstellationen) und Belegbreite (Quantität und Verteilung auf verschiedene Bildträgergattungen) berücksichtigt und die Frage nach den Produktionszentren stellt. Dies ließ uns z.B. oben in § 111 die Befunde von ‚Herrin der Muttertiere' und ‚Herrin der Löwen' differenzieren.

129 Wir werden auch im Bereich der Namenssiegel in der Regel von Objekten mit archäologisch gesichertem Fundkontext ausgehen. Höchstens 10 % der bekannten nordwestsemitischen Namenssiegel stammen von wissenschaftlichen Ausgrabungen, alle anderen sind über den Antikenhandel bekannt geworden, wobei die hebräischen (d.h. israelitischen oder judäischen) Siegel weit mehr als die Hälfte aller bekannten nordwestsemitischen Siegel ausmachen. Die schwierige Frage der Authentizität kann im Rahmen dieser Skizze jeweils nicht im Einzelnen diskutiert werden (vgl. zur Problematik schon Garbini 1982: 163f, neuerdings Hübner 1993; Sass 1993).

Wolfgang Zwickel

Excerpt from Der salomonische
Tempel *(1999)*

12

Die Geschichte des salomonischen Tempels erstreckt sich von seiner Errichtung im 10. Jh. bis zur seiner Zerstörung 587 v.Chr. In diesem langen Zeitraum blieb[1] die Theologie, wie sie von den Priestern in Jerusalem vertreten wurde, nicht völlig konstant. Die vergangenen Kapitel haben gezeigt, dass man z.B. bei der Einführung des Brandopferkults[2] kultischen Neuerungen durchaus aufgeschlossen war. Andererseits gab es im 8. Jh. auch zunehmend Überlegungen, inwieweit das Bilderverbot aufrechterhalten werden kann, wenn YHWH mit tierischen Symbolen dargestellt wird. Aber auch die politischen Verhältnisse hatten sich im Verlauf der Geschichte erheblich geändert. Im 10. Jh. v.Chr. war Jerusalem noch eine Stadt, die abseits der großen Handelswege und damit auch im Schatten machtpolitischen Interesses stand.[3] Seit dem 8. Jh. v.Chr. stand Juda dagegen in politischer Abhängigkeit von den Assyrern und musste regelmäßig Tribute zahlen. Spätestens zu dieser Zeit lässt sich[4] auch ein Aufschwung des Handels in Juda mit Ägypten, Mesopotamien und Saudi-Arabien feststellen. Die intensiver werdenden Handelsbeziehungen ließen den Wohlstand in Juda und Jerusalem ansteigen. Andererseits ergaben sich damit auch vielfältige kulturelle Kontakte. Schon im 10. Jh. war der Jerusalemer Tempel ein Bau gewesen, der gewissermaßen multikulturell war: in wesentlichen Teilen von einem Phönizier erbaut, mit starken phönizischen, ägyptischen, aber auch kanaanäischen Einflüssen versehen. Seit dem 8. Jh. v.Chr. dürften[5] die fremden Strömungen, vor allem aus dem mesopotamischen Raum, noch nachhaltiger gewesen sein. Die politische Abhängigkeit von den Assyrern führte sicherlich dazu, dass man deren Kultur und damit auch deren Religion durchaus attraktiv fand. Auch wenn große Teile der Bevölkerung sicherlich weiterhin YHWH-Anhänger waren, schlichen sich allmählich auch fremde Einflüsse in den YHWH-Glauben ein. Für die YHWH-Anhänger der damaligen Zeit stellte dies auch eine intellektuelle Herausforderung dar. Mit dem Eindringen fremder Einflüsse in den YHWH-Glauben waren sie aufgefordert, nach dem Proprium[6] des eigenen Glaubens zu fragen. Was war mit dem YHWH-Glauben vereinbar, was musste dagegen abgelehnt werden? Nicht zufällig treten gerade in der

---

1. Past tense; you will encounter many verbs in the past tense in this text; keep in mind what we discussed in 2.2.2.
2. Compound word of *das Brandopfer* "burned" offering and *der Kult* "cult," translate as "cultic burned offering."
3. Fixed phrase *in jemandes/etwas* (dative) *Schatten stehen* "to be in someone's (here: *machtpolitischen Interesses*) shadow."
4. Passive-like construction *sich lassen* + infinitive.
5. *Konjunktiv II* of the modal verb *dürfen*, expresses a high probability; translate with "would surely."
6. Nominalized adjective, borrowed from Latin *proprius* "characteristic" or "essential."

zweiten Hälfte des 8. Jh.s mit den Propheten Amos, Hosea, Jesaja und Micha einige Gestalten auf, die zu einer religiösen Abgrenzung von Fremdkulten aufrufen. Im 7. und 6. Jh. v.Chr. sind es dann vor allem dtr Kreise, die zunehmend die Frage nach einem reinen YHWH-Glauben stellen.[7] Mit der damals herrschenden Realität konnten sie nicht einverstanden sein. Zu sehr verbanden weite Kreise der Bevölkerung fremde Einflüsse mit traditionellem YHWH-Glauben. Die Theologie der Deuteronomisten dürfte aber auch vielen Zeitgenossen nicht einsichtig gewesen sein. Bei der Suche nach dem reinen YHWH-Glauben wurden nun auch Elemente als heidnisch angesehen, die über die Jahrhunderte hinweg als legitimes Element der YHWH-Religion angesehen wurden. So wurden beispielsweise in der dtr Kritik die Masseben[8] verurteilt (Dtn 7,5; 12,3; 2 Kön 3,2 u.ö.), obwohl etwa in der Jakobsüberlieferung ein derartiger Stein noch als Ursprung des Heiligtums von Bet-El verstanden worden war (Gen 28,18f.22). Auch in dem Heiligtum in Arad, das sich in einer staatlichen Festung befand und das deshalb mit großer Sicherheit YHWH geweiht war, fanden sich derartige Masseben (Taf. 424). Als unverzierter[9] Stein eignete sich eine Massebe offenbar in vor-dtr Zeit hervorragend, den bildlos[10] verehrten YHWH darzustellen.

424: Kultnische des Heiligtums in Arad mit zwei dort aufgestellten Masseben und zwei Räucheraltären am Eingang.

In den alttestamentlichen Texten finden sich zahlreiche Belege für einen Fremdkult, der den Israeliten und Judäern offenbar nicht aufgezwungen wurde, sondern freiwillig von ihnen im Rahmen des Kulturkontaktes übernommen wurde. Vielfach stammen die biblischen Notizen allerdings aus dtr Hand und schildern daher einen religiösen Sachverhalt recht einseitig und unter historischen Gesichtspunkten oft auch falsch. Betroffen von Überfremdungen des YHWH-Kults war vornehmlich der Bereich der privaten Frömmigkeit. Aber auch für den Tempelkult lassen sich einige Texte zusammenstellen, die einen Hinweis auf fremde Einflüsse enthalten.

Eine große Beliebtheit genoss in Palästina die Fruchtbarkeitsgöttin Aschera (vgl. z.B. 1 Kön 15,13a). Das hebräische Wort Aschera kann gleichzeitig die Göttin,

424: Kultnische des Heiligtums in Arad mit zwei dort aufgestellten Masseben und zwei Räucheraltären am Eingang.

---

7. Fixed phrase *eine/die Frage stellen* "to pose a/the question."

8. Translate as "massebah."

9. Negated adjective *verziert* "decorated"; translate as "undecorated."

10. Adjective formation with *-los* "-less"; translate as "pictureless."

aber auch einen Kultpfahl meinen, wobei der Kultpfahl wahrscheinlich die Göttin repräsentieren sollte. Die Göttin Aschera war in der Volksfrömmigkeit eng mit YHWH verbunden. In einer Grabinschrift in *Ḫirbet el-Kōm* (etwa 35 km südwestlich von Jerusalem in der Schefela gelegen), die aus dem letzten Viertel des 8. Jh. v.Chr. stammt, kann man lesen:

> *Uriyahu, der Reiche, hat es schreiben lassen. Gesegnet war Uriyahu vor YHWH.*
> *Und von seinen Feinden hat er ihn durch seine Aschera errettet. Durch Oniyahu*
> *(geschrieben).*

YHWH und Aschera werden auch noch in zwei Inschriften genannt, die in der Festung *Kuntilet Aǧrūd* im Negev entdeckt wurden und aus dem Ende des 9. Jh.s v.Chr. stammen. Die eine, z.T. nur fragmentarisch erhaltene Inschrift lautet:

> *Gesagt hat [. . .]: Sprich zu [. . .] und zu Joasa und zu [. . .]: Ich segne euch*
> *gegenüber YHWH von Samaria und seiner Aschera.*

In der anderen Inschrift ist zu lesen:

> *Amarjo: Sprich zu meinem Herrn: Geht es dir gut? Ich segne dich gegenüber YHWH*
> *von Teman und durch seine Aschera. Er segne dich und behüte dich und sei mit*
> *meinem Herrn.*

Umstritten ist, was in den Inschriften jeweils mit Aschera gemeint ist. Am ehesten wird man unter der Aschera jedoch das Kultsymbol zu verstehen haben, das YHWH zugeordnet ist und den Segen und die Hilfe YHWHs ausdrücken soll. Der ursprünglich als Symbol einer Göttin verstandene Kultpfahl wurde somit in den YHWH-Glauben integriert und konnte nun für YHWHs Hilfe stehen. Auf diesem Hintergrund kann es nicht verwundern, wenn König Manasse (696–642 v.Chr.) im Jerusalemer Tempel einen derartigen Kultpfahl aufstellte (2 Kön 21,7). Dieser Sachverhalt wird zwar in einem typisch dtr gefärbten Zusammenhang berichtet, dürfte[11] aber trotzdem historisch zuverlässig sein. Hierfür spricht das Verbot Dtn 16,21, neben dem Altar einen Kultpfahl aufzustellen. Verbote werden nur dann schriftlich fixiert, wenn sie eine existierende Situation verändern wollen. Daher wird sich Dtn 16,21 eben auf jenen Kultpfahl des Manasse beziehen, der offenbar vor dem Tempel aufgestellt war. Tatsächlich hat König Josia im Rahmen seiner Reformmaßnahmen, die sich auf das Buch Deuteronomium gründeten,[12] den anrüchigen Kultpfahl wieder beseitigen lassen (2 Kön 23,6).

---

11. *Konjunktiv II* of the modal verb *dürfen*, expresses a high probability; translate with "would surely."
12. Verb *sich gründen auf* "to be based upon."

In 2 Kön 18,4 wird eine Reformmaßnahme des Königs Hiskia (728–700 v.Chr.) beschrieben:

> *Er war es, der die Kulthöhen abschaffte und die Masseben zertrümmerte und die Aschera zerschlug und die eherne Schlange zerschlug, die Mose gemacht hatte, denn bis in jene Tage hatten die Israeliten ihr geräuchert[13] und sie Nechuschtan genannt.*

Die Formulierungen dieses Satzes sind typisch dtr. Bei jedem König stellten die Deuteronomisten an den Anfang des jeweiligen Abschnittes in den Königebüchern[14] neben historischen Angaben eine Wertung, die relativ differenziert ausfallen[15] konnte und sich an der Durchsetzung des Monotheismus und der Abschaffung als heidnisch empfundener Kultstätten orientierte. Durchweg positiv beurteilt werden dabei Hiskia und Josia, die eine Kultreform durchgeführt haben sollen. Gesicherte Nachweise für eine Reform des Hiskia gibt es bislang allerdings nicht. Es ist durchaus möglich, dass sich die positive Einschätzung des Hiskia in den Augen der Deuteronomisten allein oder vornehmlich an der Abschaffung der ehernen Schlange orientierte. Die entsprechende Notiz in 2 Kön 18,4 dürfte[16] auf jeden Fall historisch zuverlässig sein. Die Herstellung der Schlange wird in Num 21,4–9 berichtet. Wurde ein Israelit von einer Schlange gebissen, so sollte er zu der auf einem Stab aufgerichteten ehernen Schlange (vgl. Abb. 83) aufblicken, und das Schlangengift würde ihn nicht töten können.

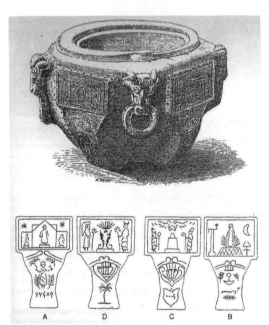

Abb. 83: Marmorvase aus Sidon (4. Jh. v.Chr.), die ursprünglich auf einem Metallständer aufgestellt wurde (vgl. die Bohrlöcher).

Am oberen Rand ist eine Schlange sichtbar. Auf Seitenfläche B ist auf der Ritzzeichnung links eine auf einem Gestell aufgerichtete Schlange erkennbar, die der Gestalt nach der ehernen Schlange in Jerusalem entsprochen haben könnte.

Diese Erzählung verdeutlicht anschaulich, welche Gefahr Schlangen für die damalige Menschheit darstellten. Aus der Umwelt des Alten Testaments gibt es mehrere

---

13. Translate as "to burn incense."
14. Translate "Book of Kings."
15. Verb *ausfallen* + adjective; translate as "to turn out to be" + adjective.
16. *Konjunktiv II* of the modal verb *dürfen*, expresses a high probability; translate with "would surely."

Beschwörungstexte, deren Rezitation bei einem Schlangenbiss helfen sollte. Aller Wahrscheinlichkeit nach war die eherne Schlange im Jerusalemer Tempel aufgestellt, auch wenn dies nicht ausdrücklich gesagt wird. Von den Reformmaßnahmen des Königs Ahas (s.o. zum ehernen Meer Kap. 5.4. und zu den Kesselwagen Kap. 5.5.) blieb sie offenbar verschont, weil die Schlange nicht als Symbol für YHWH verstanden wurde. Sie anzublicken bedeutete lediglich, dass YHWH dem Hilfesuchenden Heil zukommen lassen[17] wird. Trotzdem scheint sie im Verlauf der zunehmenden Entwicklung des Bilderverbotes Anstoß erregt zu haben, so dass sie nun unter König Hiskia ebenfalls beseitigt wurde.

Die lange Regierungszeit des Königs Manasse (696–642 v.Chr.) bedeutete für Juda eine Zeitspanne außenpolitischer Ruhe. Die Ruhe wurde freilich mit einem friedvollen Einverständnis mit den Assyrern erkauft. Manasse vermied es offenbar, jeglichen Konflikt mit den Herrschern aus dem Zweistromland aufkommen zu lassen.[18] Ein Ansteigen der in Mesopotamien gebräuchlichen Rollsiegel im Palästina dieser Zeit macht deutlich, dass es nun auch eine stärkere personelle Präsenz von Assyrern gab. Auf den Stempelsiegeln dieser Zeit lässt sich eine zunehmende Astralisierung mit der Abbildung der Himmelskörper beobachten (Abb. 84). Offenbar war es eine Zeitströmung, sich Astralgottheiten aufgeschlossen zu zeigen. Wenn die dtr Angabe, Manasse habe Altäre für das ganze Himmelsheer im Tempelbereich aufstellen lassen (2 Kön 21,5), historisch wirklich zutreffend ist, dann spiegelte diese kultische Änderung sicherlich das Verständnis der damaligen Menschen. Im Rahmen der josianischen Reform wird schließlich die Zerstörung dieser Altäre erwähnt (2 Kön 23,12).

Abb. 84: Siegel aus Tell Kçsân (spätes 8. Jh. v.Chr.). Links ist der muðhuððu-Drache abgebildet, auf dessen Rücken die Symbole der babylonischen Götter Marduk und Nabu zu sehen sind. Rechts ist die Sichelstandarte des Mondgottes Sin von Haran, die von zwei Zweigen flankiert wird, zu sehen. Auf der Basis ist ein Beter vor einem Räucherständer

---

17. Fixed phrase *jemandem* (dative) *etwas zukommen lassen* "to provide somebody with something."
18. Fixed phrase *etwas aufkommen lassen* "to raise something."

dargestellt; offenbar betet er die Götter Sin (Mondsichel) und Venus (Stern) sowie das Siebengestirn (ausgedrückt durch zwei Punkte) an. Der Zweig hinter dem Beter könnte anzeigen, dass die Götter für das Gedeihen der Vegetation angerufen werden.

Ein vieldiskutiertes Problem ist, was man sich unter den Pferden und Sonnenwagen vorzustellen habe, die gleichfalls im Rahmen der josianischen Reform beseitigt wurden (2 Kön 23,11). Man hat an Pferdefigurinen gedacht, die mit einer Sonnenscheibe auf der Stirn versehen waren und in Jerusalem, aber auch an anderen Orten[,] gefunden wurden. Andere Forscher vertreten die Meinung, es habe sich um lebendige Tiere gehandelt, die einen Prozessionswagen des assyrischen Gottes Schamasch gezogen haben. Auf jeden Fall[19] stellt die Verbindung von Pferden und Sonnengott keine palästinische Tradition dar, sondern stammt aus Assyrien. Die 622 v.Chr. durchgeführte josianische Reform (2 Kön 22f.) war nicht nur eine Reinigung des YHWH-Glaubens von als heidnisch verstandenen Elementen, sondern auch eine politische Loslösung von der assyrischen Obermacht, die zu jener Zeit ihre Oberherrschaft über Palästina nicht mehr aufrecht erhalten konnte.[20] Josia nutzte die Gunst der Stunde[21] und verband die politische Emanzipation mit den religiösen Bestrebungen einer Führungsschicht in seinem Lande. Hierbei wurden alle assyrischen Elemente, und dazu gehörten eben auch die Pferde und Sonnenwagen, beseitigt.

Letztendlich hatte die josianische Reform aber nur zu einer teilweisen Reinigung des YHWH-Glaubens von fremden Elementen geführt. In der Volksfrömmigkeit blieben noch manche Elemente verwurzelt. In einer Vision des Propheten Ezechiel, die auf den 28. September 593 v.Chr. datiert wird (vgl. Ez 8,1), wird der im babylonischen Exil weilende[22] Prophet nach Jerusalem geführt und sieht dort am Eingang des Tempelhofes Frauen, die den Tammuz beweinten (Ez 8,14)[,] sowie unmittelbar vor dem Tempel Männer, die die Sonne anbeteten (Ez 8,16). Tammuz war ein mesopotamischer Gott, der als Vegetationsgott verehrt wurde; alljährlich wurde sein Weggehen, das mit dem Verdorren der Landschaft im Sommer gleichgesetzt wurde, betrauert. Das Territorium des Tempels war somit auch nach der josianischen Reform noch immer ein Platz, an dem Fremdkulte betrieben wurden. Angesichts der inzwischen aufgekommenen politischen Dominanz Babylons ist es auch nicht verwunderlich, dass sich Menschen der damaligen Zeit wieder an den offensichtlich starken mesopotamischen Göttern orientierten. Der Tempelplatz wurde als Ort des Staatskultes verstanden, und von daher[23] lag es nahe, dort eben auch diejenigen Götter anzubeten, die für die Staatsgeschicke zur jeweiligen Zeit von Belang waren.

---

19. Fixed phrase *auf jeden Fall* "in any case."
20. Fixed phrase *etwas* (accusative) *aufrechterhalten* "to maintain."
21. Fixed phrase *die Gunst der Stunde nutzen* "to seize the opportunity."
22. Participle I of the verb *weilen* "to reside" used as adjective.
23. Translate simply as "therefore."

Gerd Theißen
Excerpt from Texttranszendenz *(2019)*

13

Eine theologische Lektüre der Bibel ist von der Erwartung motiviert, verborgen im Gestrüpp der Worte, Sätze und Texte einen „Schatz im Acker" zu finden, um des-sentwillen[1] es sich lohnt,[2] alles dahinzugeben. Dieser Schatz ist das Wort Gottes. Es ermöglicht Dialogaufnahme mit Gott. Wenn das geschieht, werden Texte transparent für Gott. Das ist die erste Bedeutung von Texttranszendenz.[3] Die hier vorgelegten Beiträge zu einer *polyphonen Bibelhermeneutik* vertreten die These einer *doppelten Texttranszendenz*: Wie in einem Sonatensatz[4] das erste Thema nur zusammen mit einem Gegenthema der Musik eine innere Dynamik gibt und sie zum Klingen bringt,[5] so wird die Bibel nur lebendig, wenn wir zugleich ihren Kontext im menschlichen Leben erfassen. Zur theologischen Texttranszendenz tritt eine *menschliche Lebenstranszendenz*. Um sie zu erfassen, müssen wir alle uns zur Verfügung stehenden[6] humanwissenschaftlichen Kenntnisse aktivieren: Literaturwissenschaft, Soziologie, Psychologie, Ethnologie, Religionswissenschaft und Religionsphilosophie. Unsere These ist, dass beides untrennbar verbunden ist. Das ist keineswegs selbstverständlich. Beide Ansätze erleben sich oft als Konflikt.

Die Erforschung der menschlichen Texttranszendenz wurde[7] von der überlegenen Warte[8] einer Offenbarungstheologie manchmal dezidiert abgelehnt, Psychologie sogar als Götzendienst verdammt, Soziologie als Irrweg erkannt, der den gesuchten Schatz nicht findet, sondern zerstört. Mit dem Pathos des Unbedingten wurde abgelehnt, was in der Wissenschaft selbstverständlich ist: Dass wir alle uns zur Verfügung stehenden Theorien und Methoden ausschöpfen, um uns über die Religion zu verständigen. Worauf Menschen ihr Leben bauen, ist es wert, intensiv erforscht zu werden. Wir sind dazu verpflichtet. Aber lange gehörte ein konfessorischer Antipsychologismus und Antisoziologismus zur Identität vieler Theologen. Es herrschte in der Theologie eine

---

1. Preposition *um . . . willen* combined with a relative pronoun in the dative case, translate as "for the sake of which."

2. Verb *sich lohnen* "to be worth."

3. Compound word of *der Text* and *die Transzendenz*; you will encounter several compound words in this text. Keep in mind what has been discussed in section 4.3.

4. Technical term from the field of music, "movement of a sonata."

5. Fixed phrase *etwas zum Klingen bringen* literally "to make something sound"; conveys the same meaning as "to make something shine."

6. Fixed phrase *zur Verfügung stehen* "to be available," here in the form of a participle I used as an adjective; translate simply as "available."

7. Followed by several participles.

8. Translate as "superior position."

innere Unfreiheit, sich auf diese neuen Fragestellungen einzulassen. Sie ist heute in der Regel[9] überwunden, freilich nicht überall.

Umgekehrt waren die Urteile der Religionskritik nicht weniger schroff: Aus der Perspektive einer religionskritischen Psychologie und Soziologie gelten oft alle Versuche, in der Religion einen Zugang zu einer letzten Wirklichkeit zu finden, als Illusion oder Neurose, Repression oder Ressentiment. Für viele Zeitgenossen steht das negative Urteil über Religion fest. Ihnen gegenüber muss man geduldig darum werben,[10] als intellektuell und moralisch integer anerkannt zu werden, wenn man für die Religion eintritt. Gerade jene sympathischen modernen Zeitgenossen, die sich eingestehen, dass sie dabei gescheitert sind, die Gesellschaft von kapitalistischer Profitsucht zu befreien, reagieren manchmal auf Religion mit starken Abwehrreflexen. Es scheint so, als sei ihnen als einziger Trost geblieben, dass sie sich wenigstens konsequent von der Religion getrennt haben. Eine konfessorische Religionskritik ist Teil ihrer Identität und wird oft mit dem Pathos des Unbedingten vertreten.

Zwischen dem, was in diesen Beiträgen als Suche nach einer doppelten Texttranszendenz vereint wurde, herrscht also ein tiefgehender „*hermeneutischer Konflikt*" (P. Ricœur). Dieser Konflikt ist Kennzeichen der Verständigung über Religion in unserer modernen Gesellschaft. Religionskritik wurde zum Medium des modernen Religionsdiskurses in- und außerhalb der Kirche. Gerade deshalb bemühen sich[11] die hier vorgelegten Beiträge um eine Verständigung, bei der man darauf angewiesen ist,[12] dass sie von beiden Seiten angebahnt wird. Ziel wäre es, den hermeneutischen Konflikt in eine „*hermeneutische Polyphonie*" zu verwandeln – nicht in die harmonische Musik alter Zeiten, sondern in moderne Musik, die sich jenseits von Tonalität entfaltet und dadurch unserer Zeit gerecht wird.

Von theologischer Seite her kann man sich für die hermeneutische Suche nach einer doppelten Texttranszendenz auf das Doppelgebot der Liebe berufen. In ihm wird im Zentrum der Bibel die Beziehung zu Gott mit der zu anderen Menschen gleichgestellt. Die Beziehung zu Gott umfasst den ganzen Menschen. Ausdrücklich heißt es, dass diese Liebe das ganze Herz, die ganze Seele (*psyché*) und alle Kräfte umfassen soll. Wenn man ethisch beide Beziehungen gleich hoch bewerten soll, spricht alles dafür, dass man auch hermeneutisch beide Beziehungen zusammensieht. Der ganze Mensch wird durch Psychologie erforscht, seine Beziehungen zu anderen Menschen durch Soziologie. Wer diese Fragestellungen mit theologischem Pathos ablehnt, urteilt nicht im Geist der Bibel.

Von religionskritischer Seite her kann man sich auf große Religionskritiker berufen. Sie haben ihrer Intention nach die Beseitigung der Religion angestrebt, aber ihre Kritik kann auch dazu dienen, die Religion besser zu verstehen. Ich habe zu zeigen versucht,

---

9. Fixed phrase *in der Regel*; translate as "usually" or "as a general rule."
10. Verb *um etwas werben* "to solicit," the *etwas* is described by the infinitive with *zu* construction.
11. Verb *sich bemühen um* "to strive to."
12. Verb *angewiesen sein auf etwas* "to rely on."

dass sich ihre religionskritischen Thesen gegenseitig relativieren. Einerseits heißt es, Religion widerspreche[13] empirischer Erkenntnis, andererseits wirft man ihr vor, dass sie empirisch nicht widerlegbar sei. Einerseits beruhe sie auf Projektionen in eine nicht-existierende Wirklichkeit hinein, andererseits soll sie Reaktion auf die Übermacht der Wirklichkeit sein. Sie setze sich als wunschbedingte[14] Illusion über alle Grenzen hinweg, arbeite sich aber in Ritualen an einschneidenden Grenzen des Lebens ab. Sie diene den Herrschenden zur Repression der Beherrschten, den kleinen Leuten aber als Ressentiment zur Domestizierung der Herrschenden. Sie sei Brandbeschleuniger menschlichen Fanatismus, aber zugleich Motor eines Gutmenschentums,[15] das unfähig macht, sich gegen Fremde und Feinde zu wehren. Religionskritik ist wertvoll, weil sie mit diesen Thesen einem differenzierten Verstehen der Religion dient. Religion ist eine komplexe Realität. Wer das Gespräch mit der Religion verweigert, handelt nicht im Geist[16] der Religionskritik, aber auch nicht im Geist der Bibel. Denn Religionskritik ist auch in der Bibel verwurzelt. Religionskritik beginnt in der Antike mit den Propheten in Israel und den Philosophen in Griechenland.

Konflikte sind Antrieb für Entwicklungen, aber nur, wenn sie nach Regeln geführt werden und im Rahmen[17] gegenseitiger Anerkennung. Das ist das Prinzip der Demokratie. Ähnliches gilt auch für den hermeneutischen Konflikt zwischen Religionskritik und Religionsbewahrung. Sich ihm zu entziehen, wäre Zeichen einer Vitalitätsschwäche. Eine große Hilfe ist es, wenn man erkennt: Religionen und unter ihnen besonders die biblische Religion haben Religionskritik motiviert. Die „mosaische Unterscheidung" (J. Assmann) interpretiere ich als Verpflichtung, nicht alles in der Religion zu akzeptieren. Kriterium dessen, was[18] man akzeptieren kann, ist die Ethik. Daher steht im Zentrum des Alten Testaments ein „ethischer Monotheismus" und im Zentrum des Neuen Testaments das Doppelgebot der Liebe. Deswegen können wir antireligiöse Kritik von außen in innerreligiöse Kritik verwandeln und so fruchtbar machen. Auch hat schon die Bibel Visionen einer reformierten und veränderten Religion entworfen – wie die Vision vom „Neuen Bund" bei Jeremia. Umgekehrt ist es eine Hilfe, wenn man zugibt: Selbst scharfe Religionskritiker waren oft durch den Traum motiviert, auf Erden zu verwirklichen, was sie an Wertvollem in der Religion erkannt hatten – auch wenn sie dabei den Himmel gleich[19] mitabschaffen wollten.

Die Theologie kann sich auf die Bibel als Inspiration für diesen Weg berufen. Eine moderne Theologie, die sich kritisch zu ihren Traditionen verhält, sollte daher eine

---

13. *Konjunktiv I*; translate with indicative. The same holds for the verbs in the following sentences.

14. Suffix *-bedingt* means "caused by" or "motivated by."

15. Complex compound word, *Gutmensch* means "do-gooder" and has a negative connotation; the suffix *-tum* forms nouns denoting collectives.

16. Fixed phrase *im Geist(e) von* or with genitive case "in the spirit of."

17. Fixed phrase *im Rahmen von* or with genitive case "within" or "in the course of."

18. Translate as "of what."

19. Translate *gleich mit* + verb as "at the same time" + verb.

„*schriftinspirierte Theologie*" sein. Sie ist nicht an den Buchstaben der Schrift gebunden, <u>wohl aber</u>[20] an ihren Geist. Dieser Geist wirkt konzentriert in den beiden wichtigsten Kriterien, an denen wir alles messen müssen, was in der Bibel steht: Das ist erstens die mosaische Unterscheidung, die jede Gottesverehrung an das Tun des Guten bindet, und zweitens das jesuanische Doppelgebot der Liebe, das diese mosaische Unterscheidung zusammenfasst und die Liebe ausweitet auf Fremde, Sünder und Feinde. Dieser Geist enthält jedoch noch sehr viel konkretere Impulse. Er wird erkennbar, wenn wir die Schrift als Grundlage einer *Zeichensprache* erkennen. Denn Religionen sind Zeichensprachen mit einer eigenen Grammatik. Die Regeln dieser Grammatik, ihre *Axiome und Grundmotive*, sind ihr Geist, der durch den Buchstaben hindurch wirkt, aber nicht mit dem Buchstaben identisch ist. Diese Motive seien[21] abschließend noch einmal genannt: Das Motiv der Schöpfung, der Weisheit, des Wunders, der Distanz zwischen Gott und Mensch, das Hoffnungs- und Erneuerungsmotiv, das Umkehrmotiv, das Exodusmotiv, das Motiv[22] des Glaubens, der Inkarnation, der Stellvertretung, des Positionswechsels, der Liebe, des Gerichts und der Rechtfertigung. Wer diese (und andere biblische) Motive internalisiert hat und sich von ihnen inspirieren lässt, kann im Geiste der Bibel neue Texte schaffen, neue Erfahrungen machen und zu neuen Einsichten kommen. All das ist „schriftgemäß".[23] Das Schriftprinzip muss dabei freilich neu verstanden werden. In diesem Schriftprinzip ist angelegt,[24] dass wir uns nicht nur an der Schrift, sondern an Schrift *und* Tradition, Erfahrung *und* Vernunft (entsprechend dem methodistischen *Quadrilateral*) orientieren. Schon in der Schrift selbst begegnen wir nämlich Texten, die als Traditionen weiter geschrieben wurden, schon in der Schrift finden wir den Ausdruck reicher Erfahrungen in den Psalmen und vernünftige Reflexionen in der Weisheit. Wenn der Geist der Schrift von den Propheten bis hin zu Jesus und Paulus in Theologie und Kirche lebendig bleibt, können wir mit Vernunft den „Schatz im Acker" finden. Denn das Doppelgebot der Liebe wurde im Neuen Testament um einen kleinen Zusatz ergänzt. Es sagt: Wir sollen Gott lieben mit ganzem Herzen, ganzer Seele, *mit ganzem Verstand* und allen Kräften (Mk 12,30). [Footnote 23]

Footnote by the Author

23 Diese Beiträge wollen nur zeigen, dass sich die hermeneutische Suche nach einem Schatz im Acker lohnt. Hin und wieder wurde inhaltlich umrissen, worin dieser Schatz besteht. Ich habe versucht, das in meditativen Texten zusammenzufassen und zu entfalten in G. Theißen, Glaubenssätze. Ein kritischer Katechismus, 2012 ⁴2018.

---

20. Translate together as "but nonetheless."
21. *Konjunktiv I*; translate as "are."
22. Followed by a series of genitive attributes.
23. Suffix -*gemäß* is used to form an adjective and means "according to."
24. Fixed phrase *angelegt sein in etwas* "to be integrated in" or "to be part of."

Ruben Zimmermann
Die Fiktion Des Faktischen (2015)

14

Wie schön war doch das Studium des Neuen Testaments als man noch mit klaren Kriterien echte von unechten Jesusworten schied,[1] präzise die Entstehung des 1. Petrusbriefs datierte, oder sich von Josephus sagen lassen konnte, wie der historische Johannes der Täufer wirklich war. Inzwischen ist alles komplizierter geworden. Josephus gilt keineswegs mehr als faktenorientierter Geschichtsschreiber, dessen Informationen man als objektiven Maßstab gegen die tendenziellen neutestamentlichen[2] Texte setzen könnte. Datierungs- und Einleitungsfragen sind zweifelhaft geworden und die Gültigkeit von Echtheitskriterien ist nicht nur in der Jesusforschung radikal bestritten worden. Bei diesen Veränderungen handelt es sich allerdings nicht nur um den üblichen Wandel der Wissenschaft, vielmehr sind grundlegende frühere Überzeugungen wie die Möglichkeit oder theologische Notwendigkeit der Suche nach Ursprüngen und Fakten ins Wanken geraten.[3]

Nirgends deutlicher als in der Frage nach Jesus, gewissermaßen bei der Kernfrage neutestamentlicher Wissenschaft, kann man diesen Umbruch erkennen. Noch ist hier und da der Abgesang[4] des so genannten „third quest", der dritten Fragerunde nach dem historischen Jesus, zu vernehmen. Da wurde politisch korrekt das Judesein Jesu betont und mit ausgefeilter Kriteriologie[5] die Jesustradition historisch plausibilisiert oder im Jesus-Seminar des amerikanischen Westar-Instituts authentische Jesusworte sogar mittels demokratischer Wahl bestimmt. Allein, die differenzierte Methodologie, breitere Kontextwahrnehmung und selbst die Einbeziehung von außerkanonischen Quellen wie des Thomasevangeliums haben keineswegs zu konsensfähigen Ergebnissen geführt. Stattdessen überraschte die Variationsbreite der wissenschaftlichen Jesusbilder: Neben dem jüdischen Restaurationspropheten (Sanders) stand der Sozialrevolutionär (Horsley) und der kynische Weisheitslehrer (Crossan) oder Wandercharismatiker (Theißen) reihte sich an den Wunderheiler (Borg) und Exorzisten (Twelftree), um nur wenige Beispiele zu nennen. Am Ende des ‚Third Quest' musste man nüchtern zugestehen, dass die Vielzahl der Jesusbilder am ehesten die Vielzahl der Jesusforscher spiegelte, aber keineswegs

---

1. Past tense of *scheiden von* "to separate."
2. The adjective *tendenziell* has no equivalent in English; translate as "trending toward New Testament."
3. Fixed phrase *ins Wanken geraten* has a passive-like meaning; translate as "to shake" but in the passive voice.
4. Translate as "farewell."
5. Translate as "set of criteria" or "framework."

die historische Wahrheit zu Tage fördern konnte.[6] Kein Wunder, dass sich manche an die Bilanz von Albert Schweitzer nach der liberalen Leben-Jesu-Forschung erinnert fühlten–100 Jahre zuvor.

Mit Recht wurde nun kritisch gefragt, ob die Suche nach dem historischen Jesus jenseits der neutestamentlichen Texte nicht im Kern verfehlt sei und sich die Kriterien der Authentizität nicht notwendigerweise im hermeneutischen Zirkel verfangen mussten. Unterstützt wurde diese Skepsis durch Einsichten der Geschichtswissenschaft, die im Zuge des ‚linguistic turn' zu mehr Selbstkritik[7] ihres eigenen Tuns herausforderte. Geschichtstheoretiker wie White überführten ausgerechnet Werke des Historismus (z.B. Ranke) eines ‚narrativen Plots', d.h. einer Erzählstruktur, obwohl diese doch eigentlich nur sagen wollten, wie es wirklich gewesen war. Seither gilt es als Gemeinplatz, was die Sprache immer schon bewahrt hatte: ‚Geschichte' wird nur in ‚Geschichten' greifbar, ‚History' gibt es nicht ohne ‚Story'. Mehr noch: Fakten sind, wie das lateinische ‚factum' (= gemacht) nüchtern offenbart, keineswegs gegeben, sondern gemacht. Eine objektive Re-konstruktion von Ereignissen ist unmöglich. Und nicht nur, weil diese nicht mehr unsprachlich zugänglich sind, sondern weil Ereignisse bereits im Moment des Geschehens immer schon gedeutet und interpretiert werden, sogar von den Erlebenden und Augenzeugen selbst. Deshalb gibt es auch nur die „Fiktion des Faktischen". Damit war der Ideologie der Faktenrekonstruktion als Maxime neutestamentlicher Wissenschaft der Boden entzogen.[8] Dies hatte auch gravierende methodische Konsequenzen: Die klassischen Regeln der historisch-kritischen Suche nach den Ursprüngen mussten revidiert werden. Oder muss die geschichtliche Rückfrage sogar gänzlich aufgegeben werden?

Ein Ausweg bot sich durch die Gedächtnisforschung an. Die frühchristliche Geschichte wurde hierbei als eine Erinnerungsgeschichte gedeutet, die Evangelien entsprechend als Erinnerungsmedien, in denen Vergangenheit bewahrt und zugleich für die Gegenwart relevant ausgelegt wurde. Um ein Beispiel zu nennen: Die Evangelien erinnern den Tod Jesu an einem Passa-Fest, allerdings mit unterschiedlichen chronologischen Details, sei es am Vortag zum Passa, dem 14. Nisan (so Johannes), sei es am 15. Nisan (so die Synoptiker). Die historische Jesusforschung versuchte nun eine eindeutige Klärung, die allerdings nicht zu erreichen war. Jede Erzählung ist zwar faktual auf Passa bezogen, aber zugleich zeigt sie auch einen theologischen Gestaltungswillen, der die Ereignisse in einen größeren Erzählzusammenhang einordnet (Passamahl bei den Synoptikern; Schlachtung des Passalamms bei Johannes). Ein gedächtnisorientierter Ansatz ist gerade an dieser fruchtbaren Verbindung zwischen historischer Referenz und literarischer Erzählung interessiert. Innerhalb der Jesusforschung wird dieser

---

6. Fixed phrase *zu Tage bringen* "to bring to light."

7. For readability translate as "to engage in more self-criticism."

8. Fixed phrase *den Boden entziehen*, here in the passive voice; translate with active voice "has lost its footing."

„Memory-Approach" schon als neues Leitparadigma gepriesen, bei dem die Frage nach dem ‚historischen Jesus' derjenigen [Frage] nach dem „Jesus remembered" (Dunn) weichen musste.

Während die geschichtliche Gedächtnisforschung für die Analyse von Texten wenig konkretes Handwerkszeug bot, hat nun die literaturwissenschaftliche Gedächtnisforschung Texte als Erinnerungsmedien eigens gewürdigt. Dies kommt einem ‚narrative turn' des Memory-Approach gleich. *Der erinnerte Jesus ist zugleich der erzählte Jesus.* Weil die Texte des Neuen Testaments Anfangs- und Endpunkt der Analyse sind, ist man gut beraten sie auch in ihrer sprachlichen Gestalt eigens zu würdigen. Die Erzählforschung bot hierbei eine ausdifferenzierte Theorie der Textinterpretation. Einige Beispielskizzen[9] sollen zeigen, wie dieser Perspektivenwechsel Einfluss auf klassische Felder der Jesus- bzw. Evangelienforschung hat:

Bei *Gleichnissen* interessiert nicht mehr die „ipsissima vox" der Gleichnisrede Jesu (Jülicher, Jeremias), vielmehr können sie literarisch als metaphorische Texte analysiert werden, die als typisierte Erinnerungsmedien einen Gedächtnisprozess einfangen, bei dem der Gleichniserzähler selbst als „Gleichnis Gottes" inszeniert wird und die Leser/innen in einen dynamischen Prozess aktueller theologischer Sinnfindung hineinzieht.

Hatte sich die ntl. Forschung zu *Wundern* lange an der Frage abgearbeitet,[10] was wirklich passiert sein kann, so wird nun der Blick auf die Erzählweise gelenkt, in der eine charakteristische Spannung zwischen geschichtlichem Referenzanspruch und realitätsdurchbrechendem Inhalt aufgebaut wird. Es ist gerade diese paradoxe Zuordnung zwischen Vergangenheitsbezug und der Irritation gewohnter Erfahrungswelt,[11] das die Wundererzählungen als „fantastische Tatsachenberichte" zu einem provokanten Medium der Jesuserinnerung und Gottesoffenbarung macht.[12]

Schließlich wird auch die Frage der *Christologie* nicht mehr auf die historische Rekonstruktion einer Selbstidentifikation Jesu mit einem traditionellen Hoheitstitel (Messias, Menschensohn etc.) reduziert, vielmehr wird untersucht, wie die Erzählung selbst oder die Übertragung von Metaphern (z.B. Sohn) eine „narrative Christologie" oder „Christopoetik" erzeugt.

Die neue Wahrnehmung der Texte hinsichtlich ihres sprachlichen Eigenwerts hat auch in anderen Bereichen neutestamentlicher Wissenschaft ein Umdenken erwirkt: Der Verfasser des *lukanischen Doppelwerks* muss nicht mehr zwischen den Polen „Historiker" oder „Poet" hin- und hergezerrt[13] werden, denn sein Werk hat sowohl historiographischen als auch poetisch-theologischen Anspruch.

---

9. Translate simply as "examples."
10. If-sentence without *wenn*.
11. Translate as "experiential world."
12. Verb *machen zu* "to turn into."
13. Translate as "pull to-and-fro."

Waren Personen der erzählten Welt vielfach nur auf historische Gestalten und Gemeinden bezogen worden,[14] so kann jetzt die Figurenwelt etwa des *Johannesevangeliums* wie z.B. der „Lieblingsjünger" in ihrem literarisch-theologischen Eigenwert gewürdigt werden ohne einen geschichtlichen Anspruch negieren zu müssen. Johannes der Täufer z.B. wird bereits im Prolog des vierten Evangeliums als geschichtliche Gestalt erinnert, aber zugleich im Konzept des idealen Zeugen inszeniert, das wiederum den Adressaten zum Modell werden kann.

Bei *Paulus* geht es nicht mehr primär um die Frage, ob Jesus nun tatsächlich ein „sühnendes Opferlamm" war oder „losgekauft" wurde , sondern wie z.B. traditionelle Kult-oder Sklavenerfahrung innerhalb metaphorischer Aussagen genutzt wurde, um das geschichtliche Ereignis des Kreuzes zu deuten und zu verstehen.

Oder hatte sich die Frage nach der Pseudepigraphie der *Deuteropaulinen oder Pastoralbriefe* zu einem Bekenntnisakt der Wahrheit hochstilisiert, so wird bei einer literarischen Betrachtung das Stilmittel der „Verfasserfiktion" gewürdigt, das genutzt werden konnte, um der Wahrheit des Evangeliums ohne jede Betrugsabsichten im gegenwärtigen Kommunikationsvorgang zu dienen.[15]

Die Beispiele ließen sich reichlich vermehren. Nun drängt sich aber die Frage auf, ob mit dem „narrative turn" nicht umgekehrt die geschichtliche Dimension der Texte verloren geht? Wird mit der sprachlichen Würdigung der Texte nicht einer geschichtlichen Rückfrage ausgewichen, die doch zum Grundbekenntnis der Inkarnationstheologie gehört, dass Jesus konkret in Raum und Zeit gelebt hat?

Obgleich die historische Rückfrage reflektierter und hinsichtlich der Rekonstruierbarkeit von Vergangenheit bescheidener ausfallen[16] muss als in früheren Zeiten, bleibt sie doch für die neutestamentliche Wissenschaft unverzichtbar. Die Texte des Neuen Testaments sind keine zeitlosen Mythen, sondern müssen in ihrem Selbstanspruch faktuale, d.h. geschichtlich referenzielle Texte zu sein, ernst genommen werden. Um sie zu verstehen, sind Kenntnisse über ihre Entstehungskontexte und -zeiten nicht nur hilfreich, sondern geradezu notwendig.

Und auch hier wird gegenwärtig intensiv geforscht. Nicht nur die inzwischen stärker ausgewerteten Textfunde des 20. Jh. von Qumran und Nag Hammadi, <u>sondern auch die Arbeit am Corpus Hellenisticum, d.h. den jüdischen wie auch philosophischen griechischen Schriften um die Zeitenwende</u>[17] haben ein facettenreiches Bild der antiken mediterranen Kultur entstehen lassen. Das Finden von Motiv- und Begriffsparallelen ist dabei durch den Einsatz von Computerkonkordanzen (TLG) entscheidend erleichtert worden. Besonderer Erwähnung bedarf auch die biblische Archäologie, die inzwischen

---

14. If-sentence without *wenn*.

15. Translate here as "support."

16. Translate here simply with the verb "to be."

17. Put this part at the end of the sentence in your translation.

als multidisziplinäres Unternehmen die Entstehungskontexte der frühchristlichen Texte entscheidend erhellt. Es ist nicht übertrieben, wenn man gelegentlich von einer neuen „religionsgeschichtlichen Schule" spricht, bei der das Neue Testament als ein (kleiner) Teil der antiken Kultur und Textwelt begriffen wird.

Die Hochspezialisierung der unterschiedlichen Methoden, sei es des narratologischen oder auch des kulturgeschichtlichen Zugangs, lässt bisweilen den Eindruck entstehen, dass diese unverbunden neben einander stehen. Beide Arbeitsweisen bergen ihre Chancen, aber haben ebenso auch ihre Grenzen: Der Religionsgeschichtler steht in der Gefahr in seiner Verliebtheit in fremde Texte und Kulturen die neutestamentlichen Texte zunehmend aus dem Blick zu verlieren. Der Literaturwissenschaftler wagt sich als terminologischer und methodologischer Hochseilartist kaum noch bis in die Niederungen konkreter Textauslegung vor. Dabei bietet gerade der ‚narrative turn' der Geschichtswissenschaft, wie auch der ‚realistic turn' der Literaturwissenschaft Chancen der gemeinsamen Wahrnehmung von Geschichte und Text, wie oben am Beispiel der Jesusforschung skizziert wurden. Die Texte des Neuen Testaments sind historisch-literarische „Wirklichkeitserzählungen", die nur in der Integration beider Zugänge angemessen zu interpretieren sind. Die erzählende Vergegenwärtigung schafft zugleich eine Brücke zwischen den ersten Adressaten und gegenwärtigen Rezipienten und bringt die neutestamentliche Wissenschaft somit wieder stärker zu ihrem Kerngeschäft zurück: Das ist die sinnstiftende Auslegung neutestamentlicher Texte. Die Texte des Neuen Testaments sind (gemeinsam mit denen des Alten Testaments) gewordener[18] Kanon, d.h. Maßstab des Christentums. Die Interpretation des Neuen Testaments kann sich deshalb weder mit geschichtlicher Archivierung noch mit narratologischer Deskription zufrieden geben, sondern zielt auf gegenwärtiges Verstehen und theologische Sinnstiftung. Dies bedarf einer Wiederbelebung hermeneutischer Reflexion einschließlich ihrer theologischen Prämissen. In einer sich ausdifferenzierten Methodik transformierte die neutestamentliche Wissenschaft immer mehr zu einem Spezialistenfach, das sich in die Verästelungen philologischer oder religionsgeschichtlicher Detailbeobachtungen verirrte. Kein Wunder, dass umgekehrt auch die Rückbeziehung[19] der gegenwärtigen Dogmatik oder Ethik auf das Neue Testament auf homöopathische Dosen reduziert wurde.

Der Blick in die Geschichte der Bibelauslegung macht allerdings deutlich, dass gegenwärtige Sinnstiftung immer schon mittels ganz unterschiedlicher Zugänge zur Entfaltung gekommen[20] ist, man denke an den vierfachen Schriftsinn oder die Sehepunkte des Chladenius. Der aktuelle Methodenpluralismus kann somit an eine bewährte Tradition anknüpfen, bei der Schriftauslegung noch als ‚Auslegungskunst'

---

18. Participle II of *werden*; translate here as "developed."
19. Translate as "reference."
20. Fixed phrase *zur Entfaltung kommen* "to develop."

verstanden wurde. Mehr Ehrlichkeit hinsichtlich der Konstruktivität ihres Tuns, ja sogar Mut zur Kreativität und Ästhetik würden die neutestamentliche Wissenschaft nicht nur farbenfroher und freudiger ins 21. Jahrhundert bringen, sondern auch interessanter machen als Gesprächspartnerin für andere theologische Disziplinen und darüber hinaus.

Zacharias Frankel

Excerpt from Die Eidesleistung der Juden in Theologischer und Historischer Beziehung *(1840)*

15

Zu den Problemen, deren Lösung selten auf dem Gebiet[e][1] der freien Forschung versucht wurde, gehört <u>die seit undenklicher Zeit angeregte Frage[2]</u> über den Judeneid. Schon der Begriff, den man mit dem Worte Judeneid verband[3] und noch heute gewöhnlich verbindet, zeigt, daß man von einem untergeordneten Standpunkte ausging und auf eine freie, absolute Forschung verzichtete; denn statt[4] die Untersuchung zu beginnen von dem Eid[e] des Juden nach seinen Glaubensdogmen, statt[5] zu fragen, auf welcher Basis die Heiligkeit und Unverletzbarkeit des Eides nach jüdischen Religionsbegriffen ruhe, begnügte man sich <u>über den von einem Juden vor christlicher Obrigkeit abzulegenden Eid[6]</u> zu argumentieren, zog den Kreis noch enger und behielt den Eid des Juden gegen einen Christen im Auge.[7] Nun führte man <u>einige von einem Autor zum andern übergegangene und oft mißverstandene hebräische Stellen[8]</u> an, und nicht wurde etwa gelehrt, wie der Eid des Juden bindend sei, sondern wie die Obrigkeit sich gegen den Meineid – denn solcher Frevel wurde beim Juden ohne Bedenken vorausgesetzt – vorzusehen habe. Man konnte daher, da man über jede rationale Theorie wegschritt,[9] nicht zur unparteiischen Würdigung der Frage gelangen: Und wenn auch der Philolog[e] den Eid, wie er in der Schrift sich findet, zum Gegenstand[e] seiner Untersuchung machte, so begnügte er sich, ihn von der antiquarischen Seite betrachtet zu haben, ohne das Resultat in nähere Beziehung zur Gegenwart zu bringen, ohne es so zu gestalten, daß praktischer Nutzen, Anwendung auf Fälle des Lebens daraus hervorgehe, und die Rechtslehre das Ergebniß als Unterlage benütze. Um so unsicherer mußte nun die Rechtslehre selbst werden: Die Forschung begann aus einem durch Vorurt[h]eile getrübten Standpunkte, daher fiel das Resultat je nach der Subjektivität der Forscher verschieden aus, und es zeigte sich die Ungewißheit, das Hin- und Herschwanken, das überall sich kund t[h]ut, wo nicht von der Idee zum Realen, vom Allgemeinen

---

1. Outdated spelling, we indicated the letters that are redundant for modern German to simplify the reading process.
2. One complex noun phrase with *Frage* as head noun.
3. Past tense of *verbinden*; look out for verbs in past tense in this text!
4. Preposition *statt* "instead of" combined with infinitive with *zu* construction, translate here with "-ing" form to accommodate for the preposition.
5. See above.
6. One complex noun phrase with *Eid* as head noun.
7. Fixed phrase *etwas im Auge behalten* "to keep an eye on something."
8. One complex noun phrase with *Stellen* as head noun.
9. Past tense of *wegschreiten*, usually *hinwegschreiten*, outdated verb; translate here as "to pass over."

zum Concreten[10] übergegangen wird. Der Ausgangspunkt war mit dem Beginn[e] der Forschung verkannt, da mußte man sich also <u>von vorn herein</u>[11] der Hoffnung begeben, je[mals] zu einem positiven Resultate zu gelangen.

Und wer mußte die verkehrte Forschung entgelten? Der Jude! Denn da man in Vorurt[h]eilen befangen die Meinung zur Basis nahm, der Jude scheue sich nicht vor christlicher Obrigkeit, und vorzüglich wenn es gegen Christen gilt, falsch zu schwören, so handelte es sich bloß um Häufung der Vorsichtsmaßregeln <u>gegen den mit dem Verdachte des Meineides Behafteten</u>:[12] man faßte mit Beseitigung der Theorie allen Aberglauben und alles Gehässige auf, um Bollwerk auf Bollwerk, Veste[13] auf Veste gegen den Feind zu häufen und ihm das Geständniß der Wahrheit abzubringen.

Daß man noch weiter ging, nicht bei der vermeinten Not[h]wehr stehen blieb, sondern auch dem Mut[h]willen, und der vorsätzlichen in Religionshaß gewurzelten Verhöhnung ein weites Feld einräumte, zeigen die meisten in dieser Abhandlung zu erwähnenden Formen der Judeneide; es spricht sich in ihnen der roheste,[14] ungezügelte Fanatismus aus, sie tragen an sich das Denkmal der Barbarei ihrer Zeit: und man irrt nicht, wenn man annimmt, daß Religionshaß selbst den Gedanken an eine Not[h]wehr eingegeben [habe[15]], daß die erste Veranlassung zu der verletzenden Form des Judeneides nicht Mißtrauen gewesen sei, sondern die kleinliche Lust, den Andersglaubenden zu verhöhnen, ihn in seiner Religion zu kränken. Und ließ zuweilen eine bessere Regung das Unwürdige eines solchen Verfahrens erkennen,[16] so wollte doch der Fanatismus sich von seiner Beute nicht lossagen und nahm die Schlechtigkeit des Juden zum Vorwande[17] solcher Maßregeln. Die Handhabung des Judeneides zeigte sich daher in der empörendsten, die Menschheit entwürdigenden Gestalt: der freventlichste Mut[h]wille wurde geübt, der Eid vor christlichen Behörden galt als eine erwünschte Gelegenheit den Juden zu kränken, ihn moralisch mit Füßen zu treten:[18] der Judeneid artete aus in ein freches Spiel, das mit dem Heiligsten getrieben wurde, denn diese Formen entbehren jeder Würde, jedes solchem hohen Akte geziemenden Ernstes. <u>Man wurde es zwar inne,</u>[19] daß der Eid auf solche Weise zum verächtlichen Spielzeuge herabgewürdigt sei, und man wurde mißtrauisch gegen ihn; aber statt sich freiem Geiste über die Vorurt[h]eile zu erheben

---

10. Usually *Konkreten*; in older texts you will often find a "c" instead of a "k" in words that are derived from Latin.

11. Fixed phrase, usually *von vorneherein* "from the start" or "a priori."

12. One complex noun phrase with *Behafteten* (nominalized verb referring to a person) as head noun.

13. Usually *Feste*, outdated word for *Festung* "fortress" or "castle."

14. Superlative form of *roh* "rough."

15. *habe* and *sei* are *Konjunktiv I* forms; translate with indicative.

16. If-sentence without *wenn*.

17. Fixed phrase *etwas zum/als Vorwand nehmen* "to use something as an excuse for," usually with a prepositional phrase with *für* but here with genitive attribute *solcher Maßregeln*.

18. Fixed phrase *jemanden mit Füßen treten* literally "to trample all over someone," but here used with *moralisch* so translate with "scorn someone morally."

19. Outdated wording with a passive meaning, translate as "one came to realize."

und der Quelle des Übels nachzuforschen, glaubte man in unglücklicher Verblendung, die abermals der Jude entgelten mußte, durch weitläufigere und ausgesuchtere Maßregeln sich zu sichern: man überbot an T[h]orheiten das vorhergehende Zeitalter, es wurden die lächerlichsten Versuche gemacht, Unwesentliches auf Unwesentliches abermals gehäuft, und noch[20] fühlte man sich nicht beruhigt: denn die Unwahrheit hat ihre Strafe in sich, und wo nach bestimmten Zwecken – denen noch[21] dazu Menschenfeindliches zu Grunde liegt[22] – geforscht wird, da kann nur Entehrendes erzielt werden: nichts kann dem in Absichten und Haß befangenen Geiste die Wahrheit je aufgeben![23]

Denn wenden wir uns ab von der Unwürdigkeit des Judeneides in seiner gewöhnlichen Form und fragen, ob er überhaupt den mit dem Eide beabsichtigten Zweck: „die Wahrheit an den Tag zu bringen und die Lüge zurückzuweisen," erfülle, so zeigt sich abermals die Verkehrtheit der grundlosen, einseitigen Forschung: es beurkundet sich,[24] daß der Judeneid seinem Wesen nach in demselben Maße ungeeignet sei, der an ihn gestellten Aufgabe zu entsprechen, als er durch seine äußere Form das Gefühl verletzt.

Betrachtet man überhaupt den Eid und[,] welche Gewißheit jede Eidesleistung zu geben vermag, so bringt sich der Gedanke auf, daß der Eid dem Göttlichen, dem Unsichtbaren angehöre; er müßte daher im Grunde ein unstatthaftes Mittel der Vergewisserung für den irdischen Richter sein, wenn nicht die Voraussetzung geltend gemacht werden dürfte,[25] daß die in der höhern Idealität, in dem Gefühle unserer Göttlichkeit gegründete Ehrfurcht vor dem Urprincipe[26] der Wahrheit – vor Gott – in der Brust eines jeden Menschen lebe. Der Eid ist das Band, das Irdisches mit Ueberirdischem[27] in unmittelbare Verbindung bringt: er ist dem Richter nicht erkennbar; denn das menschliche Auge vermag nicht das Unsichtbare zu durchschauen: und doch soll er Aufschluß geben über Zweifelhaftes; welche Ueberzeugung[28] liegt vor, daß nicht zu noch Zweifelhafterem[29] die Zuflucht genommen werden? Die Androhung, daß im Falle ein Meineid geleistet wird und [dass, wenn] er an den Tag komme, strenge richterliche Ahndung folge, kann nicht als Basis des Vertrauens, das man dem Eide schenkt, genommen werden: denn Drohung verrät[h] Ungewißheit, und Drohung vollends für einen eintretenden Fall – wenn der Meineid an den Tag komme – vermag

---

20. Modal particle; translate here as "still."

21. Modal particle; translate here as "even."

22. Fixed phrase *etwas zu Grunde liegen*; translate here as "to be based upon."

23. Verb *aufgeben* here used with an additional dative object conveying a passive-like meaning; *nichts* is the subject of the sentence but *dem (. . .) Geiste* would be the subject if it were a sentence in the active voice.

24. Outdated wording with a passive meaning; translate as "it is confirmed."

25. Verb *etwas geltend machen* "to assert" here in *Konjunktiv II* in the passive voice with modal verb; translate verb form here as "would not be allowed to be asserted."

26. Usually *Urprinzip*; the prefix *Ur-* should be translated as "original."

27. Usually *Überirdischem* "celestial," here a nominalized adjective.

28. Usually *Überzeugung* "belief."

29. Nominalized adjective in the comparative form.

selten eine abschreckende Wirkung hervorzubringen. Zudem muß der Drohung selbst schon ein Princip des Eides und seiner Heiligkeit vorangehen; denn was sollte sonst die strenge Ahndung rechtfertigen? Welches daher das Princip des Eides sei, ob es von Erhebung oder von Furcht ausgehe, (wie weiter besprochen werden wird) stets muß die Annahme stattfinden, der Schwörende teile mit uns den Glauben an einen höhern Richter, der das Geistige durchschauet und der zur Wahrheit allein angerufen werden darf. Aber daß selbst unter dieser Voraussetzung noch Manches gefährdet sei, daß noch Manches der Besorgniß eingeräumt werden müsse, ob Jener nicht in anderer Absicht, in anderer Meinung Gott zum Zeugen der Wahrheit anrufe, beurkunden die getroffenen Vorkehrungen gegen die sogenannten Reservationen, durch die jeder hinterlistigen Umgehung vorgebeugt werden soll. Und auch diesen Vorkehrungen muß die Annahme, das Princip des Eides habe allgemeine Geltung,[30] vorausgehen. Einmal, weil, wenn der Eid dem Schwörenden nicht heilig ist, es nichts nützen würde, ihn durch Umgränzungen[31] so zu beengen, daß er auf den Punkt beschränkt werde, den der Richter beschworen haben will; denn der Meineidige erkennt die Heiligkeit des Eides nicht an, und schwört also auf Unwahrheit, wenn sich ihm auch kein Vorwand dafür darbietet. Und noch aus einem andern Gesichtspunkt[e] zeigen sich diese Vorbeugungen an sich betrachtet als fruchtlos. Reservationen sind nicht Gegenstand der sinnlichen Anschauung, es sind Auswege, die der Geist mit List ersinnt; und wer will den Ausflüchten nachspüren, die er aufzufinden weiß, wer kann ihn aus allen Schlupfwinkeln verdrängen? Darum muß auch hier auf die Idee zurückgegangen [werden] und der Schwörende dahin gebracht werden, daß in dem Augenblicke, wo er den Eid ablegt, er die Gottheit, in deren Namen die Obrigkeit den Eid abnimmt, vor Augen habe und der Gottheit gleichsam schwöre. So gewinnt der Eid eine höhere Bedeutung, die desto[32] heiliger bewahrt werden muß, als man sonst den Eid ganz aus der Rechtslehre verbannen, oder ihn wenigstens nie als religiösen Akt betrachten dürfte.[33] Der Eid werde göttlich gemacht, und je[34] mehr es durch Entfernung menschlicher Zut[h]at dahin gebracht werden kann, daß mit der Eidesleistung der Gedanke sich verbinde, <u>nicht vor Menschen, sondern vor Gott werde die Bet[h]euerung abgelegt</u>,[35] desto heiliger wird der Eid, desto mehr wird er an Zulässigkeit gewinnen.

Wie erfüllt der sogenannte Judeneid diese Aufgabe? Ist es bei ihm abgesehen auf Erhebung des Gefühls? Erinnert er, der durch und durch mit Menschenhaß und Entwürdigung gefärbt ist, an Wahrheit, an Heiliges? Läßt er den Richter als Stellvertreter

---

30. Explanatory phrase to *Annahme*, translate with a that-sentence.
31. Outdated spelling, usually *Umgrenzungen* "boundaries."
32. Translate as "all the more."
33. *Konjunktiv II*; translate here with "ought not."
34. Two-part conjunction *je . . . desto*; translate with "the more . . . the more."
35. Explanatory phrase to *Gedanke*; translate with a that-sentence.

der Gottheit erscheinen, und mahn[e]t daran, daß vor dem, der Herz und Nieren prüft und der Urquell der Wahrheit und Heiligkeit ist, geschworen werde? Er zeigt nur den feindlichen, mißtrauischen Richter, der trotz der menschlichen Begränztheit[36] in das Innere eindringen will, und dieses mit gehässigem Blicke, und dieses auf solche Art, daß der Schwörende sich erinnere,[37] er schwöre[38] vor Menschen, denn der Gottheit ist solcher Eid unwürdig! Welchen Wert[h] nun ein solcher Eid habe, läßt sich leicht berechnen; weder bei dem Gewissenhaften, noch bei dem minder Gewissenhaften kann er zur Erörterung der Wahrheit beitragen: er zeigt sich vielmehr als Bundesgenosse der Lüge, als Mittel zur Beförderung des Triumphes der Unwahrheit. Bei dem minder Gewissenhaften kann der sogenannte Judeneid nur Spott erregen: das unwürdige Spiel, das mit dem Eide getrieben wird, dient nur dazu, bei ihm den Wunsch zu erwecken, das Raffinement des Religionshasses und der Verhöhnung durch größeres Raffinement zu übertreffen: es wird ihm nur zu deutlich gezeigt, daß man den Eid als Menschliches betrachte, und er hält gern diese Ansicht fest, um sich mit seinem Gewissen auszusöhnen, um den Vorwand zu finden, das ihm anget[h]ane Unrecht mit gleichem Unrechte zu vergelten. Und der Gewissenhafte? Er scheu[e]t sich, solchen Eid auch zur Wahrheit abzulegen; er fühlt seinen Wert[h] als Mensch, und er kann sich der Würde, die der Persönlichkeit des Menschen zukommt, nicht begeben; denn welche Kränkung des Ehrgefühls, welche Verletzung zeigt nicht der Judeneid! Er ist eine Brandmarkung, die der Ehrliebende nur mit dem tiefsten Widerwillen ertragen kann, der er selbst mit Verlust eines T[h]eiles seines Rechts zu entgehen sucht: er zieh[e]t es vor, Manches aufzuopfern, als solche Verhöhnung zu ertragen, und die Früchte dieser Aufopferung genießt der Betrüger; der falsche Kläger oder der mit Recht Angeklagte; und der Gewinn des Eides ist Beförderung des Unrechts und der Unwahrheit!§ Dieses über den Judeneid, wie er gewöhnlich gang und gäbe war:[39] und es ist schmerzlich, bemerken zu müssen, daß auch der im Coder Augusteus vorgeschriebene Eid mit den dazu gehörigen Formalitäten meist an den oben gerügten Mängeln leidet; daß er sogar Manches enthält, das t[h]eils in sich ein falscher Schwur ist, t[h]eils zum Meineide auffordert. Der Eid des Coder Augusteus verfehlt also ganz seine Aufgabe, und das Residuum bleibt nur Verletzung der Menschlichkeit und Herabwürdigung der Gerichtsstätte. Aber auch in manchem andern deutschen Staate zeigt der Judeneid sich noch auf solcher niedern Stufe, und man ist nur in wenigen Staaten dahin gelangt, alles Unwürdige bei der Eidesleistung des Juden zu entfernen. Das Bedürfniß den Judeneid zu verbessern, t[h]ut sich daher allgemein

---

36. Outdated spelling, usually *Begrenztheit* "limitation."

37. *Konjunktiv I*; translate with indicative.

38. *Konjunktiv I*; translate with indicative; occurs frequently in this text and will therefore not be footnoted each time, so be aware of it when translating verb forms.

39. Fixed phrase *gang und gäbe sein* "to be common practice."

kund,[40] doch wird mit Recht die Vorlage verlangt, nach der man erkenne, was statt des Abzuschaffenden zu geben sei, und welche Form des Eides dem Staate hinlängliche Garantie sowohl in politischer als bürgerlicher Hinsicht darbiete. Auf diese Frage würde genügen anzugeben, auf welchem Grundsatz[e] bei den Juden der Eid beruhe und was in der jüdischen Rechtslehre dieser Name umfasse. Aber auch die Geschichte hat ihre Forderung; sie macht mit Recht geltend,[41] daß berücksichtigt werde, wie es entstanden sei. Und so wird es zur unabweisbaren Pflicht, nachzuweisen, daß nur verworrene Begriffe Schreckbilder vorspiegelten, wenn man nicht überhaupt den Schrecken zum Vorwande nahm und noch nimmt. Und diese Forderung ist umso dringender, da der Judeneid noch nicht der Geschichte anheim gefallen ist,[42] sondern noch in der Gegenwart wuchernd Früchte treibt: es zeigt sich daher die Not[h]wendigkeit, ihn durch seine verschiedenen Phasen zu begleiten, sein Entstehen, Fortschreiten und heutige Ausbildung zu beobachten, um ihn nach seinem Wert[h]e ganz zu würdigen.

Es muss daher die Forschung über folgende Punkte sich erstrecken:

I. Ueber[43] das Princip des Eides bei den Juden und die Art, wie er nach der jüdischen Rechtslehre zu leisten sei.

II. Ueber das Gebiet, welches die jüdische Rechtslehre dem Eide anweis[e]t, und das Verhältniß zwischen ihm und dem Gelübde.

III. Ueber die Veranlassung der verschiedenen Formen des Judeneides, und wie sie ihrem Zwecke entsprochen [haben], wobei der noch in manchen Staaten herrschende Judeneid zu vergleichen kommt.[44]

Und aus diesen Untersuchungen soll sich als Resultat ergeben:

Welches die sowohl der jüdischen und allgemeinen Rechtslehre als dem Geiste unserer Zeit angemessenste Fassung des assertorischen und promissorischen Eides für Juden sei, und welches die dazu gehörigen Formen.

---

40. Fixed phrase *etwas kundtun* "to make known."
41. Verb *etwas geltend machen* "to assert."
42. Verb *etwas anheimfallen* "to fall victim to" or "to become subject to."
43. Outdated spelling, usually *über*.
44. Translate as *ist* "is."

Abraham Geiger

Excerpt from Unser Gottesdienst, eine Frage, die dringend Lösung verlangt *(1868)*

16

Die Wiederherstellung der alten Zustände – das war die sehnsüchtige Erwartung für die Zukunft, das ist sie nicht mehr. Wir verlangen nicht wieder nach Palästina zurück, wollen nicht eine besondere Volkst[h]ümlichkeit darstellen, nicht einen eigenen Staat gründen, wir erkennen vielmehr in allen Gauen[1] der Erde die große Heimath, lieben das uns zuertheilte Vaterland mit aller Seeleninnigkeit, blicken vertrauend der großen Verheißung entgegen, daß voll die Erde werde der Erkenntniß Gottes, ein großes Heiligt[h]um, und daß an jedem Orte[,] wo wir Gott preisen, Er zu uns kommen und uns segnen werde. Keine lügnerische Bitte um Wiederherstellung eines jüdischen Staates, um Sammlung der Zerstreuten nach dem fernen Winkel des Ostens überschreite die Pforten unserer Lippen, auch die Klage um die dahingeschwundene alte Herrlichkeit schweige! Diese Aenderung[2] ist auch meistens in den erneuten Gebetordnungen vorgenommen worden, und mit vollem Rechte. Der Zwiespalt zwischen der Wirklichkeit, nicht bloß der Zustände, sondern auch der Empfindung, und <u>den zu flacher Sentimentalität herabgesunkenen ehedem[3] romantisch genährten phantastischen Gebilden</u>[4] muß getilgt werden. Jerusalem bleibt uns der heilige Quell, aus dem in der Vergangenheit die Lehre der Wahrheit entsprang, der Quell ist nun zum mächtigen Strome geworden, welcher befruchtend sich über die ganze Erde ergießt. Der gegenwärtige Trümmerhaufe Jerusalem ist für uns höchstens eine poetische wehmüt[h]ige Erinnerung, keine Geistesnahrung; keine Erhebung, keine Hoffnung knüpft sich an ihn. „Von Zion ist die Lehre ausgegangen, und das Wort Gottes von Jerusalem" mag[5] froh von uns verkündet werden, und bei dem wandelbaren Ausdruck[e], welchen die Zeitvorstellungen im Hebräischen ertragen, bedeutet das Schriftwort für uns nicht buchstäblich, die Lehre werde von dort ausgehen,[6] sondern sie gehe aus, sei von dort ausgegangen.[7] Jerusalem ist uns ein Gedanke, keine räumlich begränzte[8] Stätte. Wo der Wortsinn der Gebete jedoch das Mißverständniß aufkommen läßt, daß dem Orte unsere Huldigung dargebracht wird, da muß ein solches beseitigt werden.

---

1. Outdated word, plural of *der Gau* "district."
2. Outdated spelling, usually *Änderung.*
3. Translate as "formerly."
4. One complex noun phrase with *Gebilden* as the head noun.
5. Here used as a modal verb; translate as "may."
6. Translate with that-sentence.
7. Translate with that-sentence.
8. Outdated spelling, usually *begrenzte.*

Anders verhält es sich mit Israels Stellung und Beruf. Wir müßten aufhören Juden zu sein, wenn wir glauben sollten, unsere weltgeschichtliche Mission sei zu Ende, wenn wir dem Gedanken Raum gäben,[9] die uns gestellte Aufgabe sei längst vollzogen, unsere Sonderstellung als Glaubensgenossenschaft sei bloß ein Erbe aus der Vergangenheit, nicht ein noch fortdauerndes Zusammenhalten zu eigent[h]ümlichem gemeinsamen Heilswirken in Gegenwart und Zukunft. Nein, unsere Aufgabe ist noch nicht erfüllt, unsere Tage sind nicht abgelaufen; noch sind wir die Zeugen der Gotteseinheit, der aus sich heraus zur Reinheit emporstrebenden Menschennatur, der Völkerverbrüderung[10] in Wahrheit, Gerechtigkeit und Liebe, Zeugen für die ganze Menschheit, die bald[11] durch das eigne treue Festhalten in Stille belehren, bald auch durch das mut[h]ige Wort die Lehre weithin verkünden. Israel ist als geistige Lebensmacht noch nicht erloschen, seine weltgeschichtliche Bedeutung nicht geschwunden, aber es erfüllt seinen Beruf[12] nur dann in Wahrheit, wenn es für die ganze Menschheit, in ihr und mit ihr zu wirken das Bewußtsein hat. Jede Absperrung, sei es phantastisch volkst[h]ümliche oder religiöse, jede Ueberhebung[13] und Selbstbespiegelung[14] trübt diese Aufgabe, zerstört seinen Beruf. Es mag verzeihlich, ja not[h]wendig und heilsam gewesen sein in Tagen schweren Druckes, tiefer Seelenleiden, wo sich der Jude in sich zurückziehen, aus seinen Wunden Trost und Erhebung schöpfen mußte; nun aber gilt[15] es, mit freiem Blicke, in liebendem Anschluss[e] der Gesammtheit zu spenden wie von ihr zu empfangen. Ausdrücke des Dankes, daß Gott abgesondert Israel von den Völkern, daß er – wie es in der üblichen Form des „Alenu" lautet[16] – „uns nicht gemacht wie die Völker der Länder, nicht gesetzt wie die Stämme des Erdbodens, nicht unsern Ant[h]eil gesetzt wie den jener, unser Loos wie das ihrer Menge", diese und ähnliche Ausdrücke widerstreben unserer ganzen Empfindung, geben zur Verkennung unserer ganzen Aufgabe Veranlassung.[17] Im etwaigen Hinblick[e] auf die Vergangenheit sind sie überflüssig, auf die Gegenwart bezogen, zu welcher Deutung sie dem ganzen Zusammenhange nach verleiten, werden sie zu dünkelhafter Selbstgefälligkeit. Wir wollen wahrlich unsere Eigent[h]ümlichkeit nicht verläugnen,[18] wir wollen den trefflichen Geistesboden,[19] auf dem wir wurzeln, festhalten und sorgsam pflegen, aber wir dürfen ebensowenig[20] verkennen, daß es dieser

---

9. *Konjunktiv II*; translate as "would give."
10. Compound word; translate as "fraternization of peoples."
11. Two-part conjunction *bald . . . bald*; translate with "first . . . then."
12. Here in the sense of *Berufung* "vocation."
13. Outdated spelling, usually *Überhebung*.
14. Translate as "introspection."
15. Fixed phrase *es gilt etwas zu* + *infinitive* "it is important to" or "it is needed to."
16. Translate simply with "is."
17. Fixed phrase *Veranlassung geben zu etwas* "to give cause for."
18. Outdated spelling, usually *verleugnen*.
19. Translate as "spiritual ground."
20. Translate as "nonetheless."

Pflege ernstlich bedarf, daß der Boden von den wuchernden Schlingpflanzen gereinigt werden muß, wie andererseits daß auch die übrige Menschheit nicht umsonst gerungen [haben], ihr Mühen nicht ein eitles[21] gewesen [ist]. Vereint mit ihr, ein jeder T[ħ]eil nach seinem Erbe, nach seiner Begabung, wollen wir die Wahrheit fördern, lehren und lernen, freudig geben und empfänglich annehmen, aber nicht abseiten[22] stehn in geringschätzendem Hochmut[ħ]e, und sei dieser auch nicht beabsichtigt, so doch sich unwillkürlich einschleichend. Wozu jene immerwährende Wiederholung der Phrase: „der uns erwählt hat aus allen Völkern" oder gar „uns erhoben über all Sprachen", was soll dieses eitle Selbstrühmen, und gälte[23] es blos als einleitend zum dafür schuldigen Danke? Sprechen wir immerhin es aus: der uns erwählt hat, erkennen wir den Beruf,[24] den die Weltgeschichte uns aufgetragen und dem wir treu bleiben sollen, werden wir der Pflichten inne,[25] die er uns auferlegt: wozu aber der Seitenblick, der im Vergleiche liegt und dem unberechtigten Stolz[e] so leicht Nahrung gi[e]bt? Wer seiner Kraft und Tüchtigkeit sicher ist, prunkt nicht damit; nur der Kleinliche führt sie im Munde,[26] und sein T[ħ]un straft seine Worte dann Lügen.[27] Es ist keine Gottesverehrung, die Saat der Trennung, wo sie unnöt[ħ]ig ist, in die Gemüt[ħ]er Tag für Tag aus[zu]streuen; die Folge davon ist entweder, daß auch der Keim wirklicher Entfremdung genährt wird oder – was gegenwärtig mehr der Fall ist – daß die Worte gedankenlos hergesprochen[28] werden, hie und da[29] mit einem inneren Proteste oder mit einem überlegenen Lächeln über solche kindische Ausdrucksweise. Das ist nicht Andacht, nicht Seelenreinigung, solche Anstöße müssen weggeräumt werden.

---

21. Translate as "for nothing."
22. Outdated wording, usually *abseits* "apart."
23. *Konjunktiv II*; translate as "would count."
24. Here in the sense of *Berufung* "vocation."
25. Fixed phrase *etwas* (dative) *inne werden* "to become aware of."
26. Fixed phrase *etwas im Munde führen* "to voice something."
27. Fixed phrase *etwas Lügen strafen* "to belie."
28. In the sense of *aussprechen* "to utter."
29. Outdated wording, usually *hier und da* "here and there."

Ulrich Volp

17

Thesen zur patristischen Ethik und ihrem Verhältnis zu den biblischen Texten (2019)

Einleitende Thesen

1. Angesichts der Tatsache, dass ein großer Teil der erhaltenen Literatur der Kirchenväter Exegese ist, kann von einer prägenden Bedeutung der biblischen Narrative und der anthropologischen Grundannahmen der biblischen Texte auf die Entwicklung der christlichen Ethik in der Antike ausgegangen werden.[1]

2. Damit ist die Frage aber noch nicht annähernd beantwortet, in welcher Form diese Prägung Einfluss genommen hat – ob etwa die patristischen Ethiken „auf dem Boden des Evangeliums" entstanden sind, ob sie eher „ein Produkt des griechischen Geistes" sind, oder ob die Ethik der Kirchenväter das Ergebnis ganz anderer Herausforderungen[2] war.

Thesen zur Entstehung patristischer Ethik

3. Deutungsversuche[3] der patristischen Ethik sind in der Vergangenheit im Wesentlichen drei unterschiedliche Wege gegangen: Zum einen[4] wurde versucht, Abhängigkeiten von bestimmten philosophischen Tugendlehren zu rekonstruieren (Epikur, Stoa, Aristoteles, Platon). Ein zweites Vorgehen bestand darin, die Ethik von einem oder mehreren Grundbegriffen her zu verstehen, die als für die patristische Ethik bestimmend analysiert wurden (der menschliche Wille, Gerechtigkeit, Jüngerschaft, Glaube und Liebe usw.). Der dritte Ansatz profilierte die Originalität patristischer Ethik[5] gegenüber der philosophischen Ethik oder gegenüber den antiken Vulgärethiken. Alle drei Ansätze sind nicht unangemessen und haben unserem Verständnis der patristischen Ethik erheblich genutzt.

4. Gleichzeitig haben sich diese drei Ansätze auch als unzureichend erwiesen,[6] denn sie nehmen die (theologische, soziale, rituelle usw.) Kontextbedingtheit der antiken ethischen Überlegungen oft nicht ausreichend auf. Jede Erforschung patristischer Ethik muss versuchen, die Fragen und Herausforderungen zu benennen, die hinter ethischen Äußerungen der Kirchenväter liegen.

---

1. Verb *von etwas ausgehen* "to presume," here in passive voice with modal verb.
2. Genitive attribute to *Ergebnis.*
3. Compound word; translate as "efforts of interpretation."
4. Translate here as "firstly."
5. Genitive attribute to *Originalität*, zero article declension; occurs frequently in this text.
6. Fixed phrase *sich als unzureichend erweisen* "to prove to be insufficient."

Zum Verhältnis von Bibel
und patristischer Ethik

5. In der bisherigen Erforschung der patristischen Ethik wurde mit Recht auf große Differenzen zwischen „biblischer Ethik" und „philosophischer Ethik", aber auch auf manche Übereinstimmungen z.B. zwischen paganer[7] Popularethik, neutestamentlicher Gemeindeethik und deren Rezeption bei den Kirchenvätern hingewiesen.

6. Genauso bedeutend ist allerdings auch die historische Entwicklung zentraler Muster christlicher Lebensführung, die weder unmittelbar in der philosophischen Tradition noch[8] in der Bibel bereits ausgebildet vorliegen: Märtyrertum, Virginität, Demut als monastische Lebensform usw.

7. Auch die oft in Anschlag gebrachten Kategorien „Intellektualismus" und „Gemeindeethik" erklären die zu beobachtenden Differenzen und Entwicklungen alleine nicht.

8. Als Konsequenz daraus verbietet es sich, unbedarft von einem unmittelbaren oder mittelbaren Prozess der Applikation biblischer oder philosophischer Ethik auf die Lebensführung der antiken Christen auszugehen.

9. Dies bedeutet positiv formuliert: Um das Verhältnis zwischen biblischer und patristischer Ethik bestimmen zu können, müssen zunächst die Fragen rekonstruiert werden, auf die ethische Konzepte und Vorstellungen Antworten zu geben versuchten.[9]

10. Zu einem solchen kontextorientierten Ansatz gehört die Einbettung der ethischen Konzepte in die sehr unterschiedlichen exegetischen Traditionen der Alten Kirche.

11. Schließlich ist im Auge zu behalten,[10] welche Art von „Bibel" jeweils das Verhältnis patristischer Ethik zur Schrift determiniert. In vielen Fällen ist es etwa die Septuaginta, die für Kirchenväter die heilige Schrift konstituiert. Im Prozess der Kanonbildung verändert sich das, worauf man sich bezieht, jedoch fortlaufend. Auch für die Entwicklung eines ausdifferenzierten Verhältnisses zum Judentum, zur Heilsgeschichte, zu Gesetz und Evangelium usw. hat <u>der sich in den ersten Jahrhunderten immer wieder wandelnde Bezugstext</u>[11] enorme Konsequenzen. Diese Situation bedeutet auch eine grundlegende Differenz zu einer theologischen Ethik heute und ihr Verhältnis zur Bibel.

---

7. Translate as "pagan."
8. Two-part connector *weder . . . noch* "neither . . . nor."
9. Past tense.
10. Fixed phrase *etwas* (accusative) *im Auge behalten* "to keep an eye on something."
11. One complex noun phrase as subject, head noun is *Bezugstext*.

Die Bedeutung der patristischen Ethik für heutige[12] „Ethik"

12. Die Erforschung der patristischen Ethik verspricht ein großes Potenzial für ein besseres Verständnis der ethischen und anthropologischen Parameter, von denen alle ethischen Überlegungen in christlich geprägten Kulturen geprägt sind.[13]

13. Einer Betrachtung jener christlichen (Väter-)Texte, die erstmals auf systematische Art theologische Ethik formulierten, sollte nicht weniger Bedeutung zugemessen werden wie die jener klassischen ethischen Texte der antiken Philosophie, in denen viele ethische Grundfragen ebenfalls zum ersten Mal philosophisch durchdrungen wurden.

14. In manchen christlichen Kirchen besitzen die Kirchenväter eine eigene Autorität als doctores ecclesiae oder als Garanten der Orthodoxie. Ein ethischer Dialog kann mit diesen Kirchen nicht an den antiken Texten vorbei geführt werden. Auch die Reformatoren waren nicht ohne Ehrfurcht vor der patristischen Ethik. Deshalb gehört sie auch für die reformatorischen Theologien zur Geschichte und Gegenwart der Ethik.

---

12. Zero article adjective declension.
13. Verb *von etwas geprägt sein* "to be influenced by."

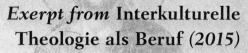

Volker Küster
Exerpt from Interkulturelle Theologie als Beruf *(2015)*

18

Summary: Intercultural theology explores the interreligious, intercultural, and interconfessional dimensions of Christian faith. Volker Küster (1) sketches the vocational profile of an intercultural theologian, (2) demarcates the vocational field, and (3) opens the methodological and terminological toolbox of the vocational practice. In the encounter with other religions, other theologies, and other churches, the three dimensions of intercultural theology become concrete. Aesthetics, hermeneutics, and ethics serve in equal measure its re / construction. (p. 447)

(. . .)

2 Das Berufsfeld (p. 451–454)

Entsprechend der drei eingangs genannten Dimensionen lässt sich das Berufsfeld zunächst einmal grob einteilen[1] in die Begegnung mit fremden Religionen, fremden Theologien und fremden Kirchen.

2.1 Fremden Religionen begegnen

Das Christentum teilt in Europa eine lange Geschichte mit Judentum und Islam. Es breitete[2] sich anfangs im Umfeld der Diasporasynagogen aus und wurde im Rahmen der Religionspolitik des römischen Reiches zunächst als jüdische Sekte eingestuft, was ihm den Status einer „erlaubten Religion" (religio licitas) verlieh.[3] Nach der endgültigen Zerstörung des Jerusalemer Tempels im Jahre 70 n.Chr. und der Vertreibung der Juden aus der Heiligen Stadt verstärkte sich die jüdische Präsenz auf europäischem Boden allmählich durch Migration. Um die Jahrtausendwende hatte sich der Schwerpunkt jüdischen Lebens in den Westen verlagert.

Der Islam breitete sich ab dem 7. Jahrhundert[,] unmittelbar nach seiner Entstehung auf der arabischen Halbinsel,[4] aggressiv aus. Er nahm Europa gewissermaßen in die Zange.[5] Im Süden überquerten muslimische Truppenverbände die Meerenge von Gibraltar. Für mehr als 700 Jahre setzen sich die Mauren auf der iberischen Halbinsel

---

1. *sich lassen* + infinitive (passive-like construction); translate here as "can be divided into."
2. Past tense; verb *sich ausbreiten in* "to spread out in."
3. Past tense of *jemandem* (dative) *etwas* (accusative) *verleihen* "to give someone something."
4. Phrase in apposition.
5. Past tense of fixed phrase *in die Zange nehmen*, literally "to take in the tongs"; translate here as "took in its grip."

fest (711–1492). Im Osten drangen sie bis auf das Territorium des byzantinischen Reiches vor und bestürmten wiederholt Konstantinopel, das 1453 schließlich fiel. Nicht zu vergessen ist auch die muslimische Herrschaft über Sizilien (827–1091). Obwohl Karl Martell ihnen in der Schlacht bei Poitiers im Süden Einhalt gebot,[6] sollte es noch 500 Jahre dauern, bis Ferdinand II. von Aragon und Isabella von Kastilien den endgültigen Sieg davon trugen[7] und die Muslime über das Mittelmeer zurückdrängten. Die Juden wurden bei dieser Gelegenheit gleich[8] mit[9] vertrieben. Der Reconquista sollte die Conquista folgen, der territorialen Rückeroberung [sollte] die Eroberung von Territorien in der neuen Welt [folgen]. Christoph Kolumbus (ca. 1451–1506), in dessen Namen sich die Verquickung von christlichem Glauben und kolonialem Projekt auf mysteriöse Weise abbildet – nomen est omen – [10] nutzte den Siegestaumel, um bei Hofe zu antichambrieren[11] und [um,] indem er der Krone Gewinn in Aussicht stellte, die Finanzierung seiner Entdeckungsreisen zu sichern.

Die Herrscher Mitteleuropas hatten sich auf Drängen des römischen Papsttums unterdessen zu mehreren Kreuzzügen (1096–1291) in Richtung Osten aufgemacht. Das Ziel der Befreiung Jerusalems und des Heiligen Landes war trotz aller Anstrengungen schon allein aufgrund der schwierigen Nachschubsituation zum Scheitern verurteilt.[12] Den Muslimen gelang es demgegenüber ihrerseits, sich im Osten Europas festzusetzen. Die langwierigen Türkenkriege (1423–1878) gegen die weitere Ausbreitung des Osmanischen Reiches (ca. 1299–1923) und die „Türken vor Wien" (1529 und 1683) sind geradezu sprichwörtlich geworden für europäische Islamophobie. Was bei der Schilderung dieser Konfliktgeschichte oft vergessen wird, ist die relative Toleranz, die die muslimischen Herrscher den „Leuten des Buches", [Footnote 6] Juden und Christen,[13] entgegenbrachten[,] und der fruchtbare Kulturaustausch, dessen Spuren noch heute in Andalusien oder auf Sizilien zu besichtigen sind. Die Ambiguitäten der Religionen treten deutlich zu Tage. Ihre lebensfördernden Lehren stehen oft in krassem Gegensatz zu der brutalen Gewalt[,] an der sie beteiligt sind.

Bei den Gegenschlägen im Osten kam es ebenfalls zu Ausschreitungen gegen die Juden, wo immer die mordenden Horden auf sie trafen. Solche Progrome[14] und Vertreibungen der Juden – den „Ungläubigen" im eigenen Lande, den „Mördern des Messias", wie sie geschmäht wurden – haben auch das geistige Zentrum jüdischen

---

6. Past tense of fixed phrase *jemandem/etwas* (dative) *Einhalt gebieten* "to stop someone/something."

7. Past tense of fixed phrase *den Sieg davon tragen* "to triumph"; here "finally triumphed."

8. Translate here as "at the same time."

9. Translate here as "as well."

10. End of relative clause.

11. Translate as "to ingratiate oneself with."

12. Fixed phrase *etwas ist zum Scheitern verurteilt* "something is doomed to failure."

13. Explanation to *Leuten des Buches*.

14. Usually *Pogrome* "pogroms."

Lebens am Rhein in Mainz, Worms und Speyer erschüttert. Noch bei Luther finden sich böse Worte über die Juden. [Footnote 7] Der Jahrhunderte alte christliche Antijudaismus endete schließlich in den Gaskammern des Dritten Reiches. Durch die industriell organisierte Ermordung von sechs Millionen europäischer Juden und die Flucht von noch einmal ca. 280.000 Juden allein aus Deutschland beraubten die Nazis und ihre Kollaborateure Europa nicht zuletzt eines Großteiles seines intellektuellen und kreativen Potentials.

Das koloniale Projekt und in desse[m]n Gefolge die christliche Mission hatte die Europäer unterdessen auch mit den primalen[15] Religionen Afrikas oder des Pazifik sowie den asiatischen Religionen, allen voran Hinduismus und Buddhismus[,] in Kontakt gebracht. Die oft strikte Ablehnung der fremden Religionen und Kulturen wurde durch die Notwendigkeit konterkariert,[16] die christliche Botschaft zu übersetzen. Ohne Kenntnis des fremden kulturell-religiösen Kontextes war das nicht zu machen. Dass es dabei auch zu Aufzeichnung und Übersetzung der fremden heiligen Texte kam und Missionare gelegentlich zu Forschern wurden, ist wiederum ein Indiz für die Ambiguität dieser interkulturell-religiösen Austauschprozesse. Die ersten Übersetzungen der heiligen Texte Asiens im 19. Jahrhundert erweckten das intellektuelle Interesse von Philosophen wie Arthur Schopenhauer (1788–1860). Letztendlich manifestieren Hinduismus und Buddhismus sich in Europa heute außerhalb der Migrantengemeinschaften aber vor allem im Bereich von wellness und interieur design. Nennenswerte Übertritte sind nicht zu verzeichnen. [Footnote 8] Die christliche Mitschuld am Holocaust führte nach dem Ende des Zweiten Weltkrieges zu einer Neubesinnung über das Verhältnis der christlichen Kirchen zum Judentum. Katholischerseits sollte das während des Zweiten Vatikanischen Konzils (1962–65) geschehen. Politische Intervention aus der arabischen Welt sorgte jedoch dafür, dass es schließlich zu einer Erklärung über das Verhältnis der Kirche zu den nichtchristlichen Religionen (Nostra Aetate) allgemein kam. Dies war die Geburtsstunde der modernen Theologie der Religionen.

Im Weltrat der Kirchen, der protestantische und orthodoxe Kirchen repräsentiert,[17] wurde die Frage des Verhältnisses von „Kirche und Israel" zunächst bei der Abteilung für Glauben und Kirchenverfassung angesiedelt,[18] einer Art innerchristliches „Eichamt". Erst im Zuge der Gründung eines Sekretariats für den interreligiösen Dialog (1971) wurde auch das Verhältnis zum Judentum zu einer Frage des Dialogs erklärt, ja ist gewissermaßen zum Nukleus der modernen Dialogbewegung geworden. [Footnote 9]

Während die Theologie der Religionen nach dem Ort der anderen Religionen im eigenen Denksystem fragt, überschreitet die Theologie des Dialogs die Grenzen des

---

15. Same meaning as the English adjective "primal."
16. Participle II of the verb *konterkarieren* "to thwart."
17. Relative clause!
18. Participle II of the verb *ansiedeln*; translate here as "to allocate."

eigenen Glaubens und macht sich dabei für den anderen „verwundbar" – um einen Begriff des Hamburger Missiologen Hans-Jochen Margull aufzugreifen. [Footnote 10] Die Theologie der Religionen steht letztendlich vor einem Exklusivismus-Inklusivismus-Dilemma: Fällt der religiös Fremde der ewigen Verdammnis anheim,[19] wenn er sich nicht zum Christentum bekehrt, oder ist er immer schon in den Heilsplan Gottes eingeschlossen? Die postmoderne pluralistische Theologie der Religionen wollte diesen Rubikon überschreiten[20] und vom Ekklesio- bzw. Christozentrismus des Exklusivismus über die theozentrisch-inklusivistische [Position] zu einer Position jenseits von Theismus / Non-Theismus fortschreiten. [Footnote 11] Sie endete damit jedoch in einer Art Meta-Inklusivismus. Die Theologie des Dialogs beschreitet demgegenüber einen anderen Weg, ihr Doppelgebot lautet: Zeugnis ablegen[21] vom je eigenen Glauben und den anderen so verstehen zu lernen, das[s] er / sie sich darin selbst wiedererkennen kann. Das Exklusivismus-Inklusivismus Dilemma jedweder Religion ist damit verdiskontiert.[22]

Die Frage[,] wer mit wem über was einen Dialog führt[,] kann letztendlich nur so beantwortet werden, dass der Dialog ein Geschehen zwischen Anhängerinnen und Anhängern der verschiedenen Religionen ist. Sie können lediglich für sich selbst sprechen, nehmen aber gleichzeitig die Funktion von Grenzgängern zwischen den religiösen Gemeinschaften wahr. Der Dialog kennt unterschiedliche Typen: Der Dialog des Lebens ist präkonzeptuell, er richtet sich auf das gute Zusammenleben der Menschen vor Ort.[23] Er hat sich in der interreligiösen Zusammenarbeit etwa in der Katastrophenhilfe immer wieder bewährt. Der Dialog des Verstandes hingegen wird getragen von den Gelehrten der verschiedenen Traditionen. Hier stehen Loyalitäten zu den Konzepten der jeweiligen Lehre auf dem Spiel. Ein „we agree to disagree" ist daher oft unvermeidlich. Dennoch ist diese gemeinsame Suche nach Wahrheit unabdingbar für das gegenseitige Verständnis. Im Dialog der Herzen treffen sich die Mystiker der verschiedenen Traditionen. Dieses Teilen spiritueller Erfahrungen in Meditation und Gebet ist post-konzeptuell.

Sowohl die Theologie als auch der Dialog der Religionen setzen Kenntnis der fremden Religionen voraus. Hier kommt die Religionswissenschaft ins Spiel,[24] die heute selbstverständlich zum Curriculum des Theologiestudiums gehören sollte. Ich würde aber noch einen Schritt weiter gehen: Da wir religiöse Professionals ausbilden und nicht Leute, die sich professionell mit Religion beschäftigen, sollten Gastvorlesungen von gelehrten Vertreterinnen und Vertretern der anderen Religionen und interreligöse[25] Begegnungen zum Normalfall an theologischen Fakultäten werden.

---

19. Fixed phrase *etwas* (dative) *anheimfallen* "to fall victim to."
20. Fixed phrase *den Rubikon überschreiten* "to cross the Rubicon."
21. Fixed phrase *Zeugnis ablegen von* "to bear witness to."
22. Translate as "discounted."
23. Fixed phrase, translate as "on site."
24. Fixed phrase *ins Spiel kommen* "to come into play."
25. Usually *interreligiös* "interreligious."

Footnotes by Küster

6 Sure 2,105.145; 5,15.19.

7 Vgl. Luthers Schrift „Von den Juden und ihren Lügen" von 1543; aus aktuellem Anlass hat die EKD zu diesem Themenkomplex eine Broschüre für die Gemeinden aufgelegt: Schatten der Reformation. Der lange Weg zur Toleranz. Das Magazin zum Themenjahr 2013 Reformation und Toleranz, Hannover 2012.

8 Die einschlägigen Wikipedia-Artikel etwa verbuchen für Deutschland ca. 97.500 Hindus und 250.000 Buddhisten. Der Religionswissenschaftliche Medien und Informationsdienst e. V., Marburg (REMID) zählt 100.000 Hindus (Stand 2012) und 270.000 Buddhisten (Stand 2012) (www.remid.de am 2.09.2015).

9 Ähnlich wurde auf katholischer Seite die 1974 von Papst Paul VI gegründete Kommission für die religiösen Beziehungen zum Judentum dem Sekretariat zur Förderung der Einheit der Christen zugeordnet. Dieses 1960 von Johannes XXIII gegründete Organ war wiederum federführend bei Nostra Aetate.

10 Vgl. Hans Jochen Margull, Verwundbarkeit. Bemerkungen zum Dialog, in: ders.: Zeugnis und Dialog. Ausgewählte Schriften, Ammersbeck bei Hamburg 1992, 330–342.

11 Vgl. John Hick / Paul Knitter (Hg.), The Myth of Christian Uniqueness. Toward a Pluralistic Theology of Religions, Maryknoll, NY 1989; Küster (s. o. Anm. 1), 132–153.

Appendices

Appendix 1
Common Grammatical Terms

Nouns are words that name people, creatures, places, things, activities, conditions, or ideas. In German, nouns can be easily recognized by the capitalization of the first letter. They are declined according to the four **cases:** nominative, genitive, dative, and accusative. The case of a noun is determined by its role in the sentence or by a preposition. They also are declined according to their **number** (singular or plural) and their **gender** (masculine, feminine, or neuter). Nouns are used with **determiners** (articles, demonstrative and possessive pronouns). Other parts of speech, such as adjectives and verbs, can be turned into nouns, a process called **nominalization**. When a noun is specified by attributes such as adjectives, it forms a **noun phrase**, beginning usually with some kind of determiner and ending with the noun which is then called the **head noun**.

    Verbs are words naming an action done by or to someone or something, a state of being experienced by someone or something or an occurrence. They are **conjugated** according to the person that is doing the action. We differentiate between first, second, and third person and between singular and plural. Verbs have no gender and do not display cases. The basic form is called the **infinitive form** and is composed of the **stem** of the verb and the ending *-en* as in *tragen* (to carry). A verb displays different forms depending on the **tense** (present, past, future), the **voice** (active or passive), and **the mood** (indicative or subjunctive). We call forms that do not conjugate according to the person **infinite or non-finite verb forms** and all forms that do conjugate **finite verb forms**. In German, the infinitive form and the two types of participles belong to the infinite forms. Most tenses and the passive voice are formed by using a finite form of an **auxiliary verb** and an infinite form of a full verb. Auxiliary verbs such as *sein* (be) or *haben* (have) therefore help (Latin: *auxiliare*) to form new verb forms, whereas all other verbs are called **full verbs**. As active is the opposite to passive, indicative is the opposite to subjunctive. The indicative is basically the default version of all tenses.

    Adjectives modify nouns by ascribing qualities. In German, they decline in **agreement** with the noun they are modifying. We call the noun they are agreeing with a

referent noun, following the German term *Bezugsnomen*. Adjectives display endings according to case, number, and gender unless they are used as complements to a verb as in *Das Buch ist gut.* (The book is good.)

Adverbs qualify a whole sentence or a verb. They typically express time, place, reason, and so on. For example, *heute* (today), *dort* (there), *deswegen* (therefore). Adjectives can be used as adverbs and do not decline in these instances. In German, **adjectives used as adverbs** do not have a special ending like "-ly" in English. You can only identify them by their role in the sentence. For example, *Er spricht lange* (adverb). (He talks for a long time.) *Er hat lange* (adjective) *Haare.* (He has long hair.)

Pronouns are substitutes for nouns and decline according to case, number, and gender. They always refer to a noun and agree with the so-called referent noun in number and gender. There are **different types of pronouns** such as personal, possessive, demonstrative, and relative pronouns.

Sentences are often comprised of more than one **clause**. A clause consists of at least a subject and a finite verb form. We differentiate between **coordination** (two or more main clauses in one sentence) and **subordination** (a main clause and one or more subclauses in one sentence). A **subclause** is not independent and can therefore never occur without a main clause. There are two types of **conjunctions**, depending on the type of clause they connect. Coordinating conjunctions such as *und* (and) or *oder* (or) connect clauses or phrases of the same type, whereas subordinating conjunctions introduce a subclause such as *weil* (because) or *dass* (that).

Prepositions introduce a noun phrase or are followed by a pronoun and usually provide information such as position, time, or direction (*an* [at], *auf* [on], *in* [in]). In German, they determine the case of the noun or pronoun that follows. Prepositions are often preset by the verb (see list of verbs with prepositions; see table in appendix 3).

Appendix 2
List of Irregular Verbs
with Their Stem Forms
(Past Tense and Participle II)

H ow to use this list: the first column presents the infinitive form and information
on the complements the verb takes (see verb valency in section 3.6.4). As most
verbs take a direct object in the accusative case, we assume this as the default
option and do not specify the complement.

- If the verb takes a direct object in the dative case, we indicate it with the
  abbreviation DAT.
- If the verb takes a direct object in the genitive case, we indicate it with the
  abbreviation GEN.
- If the verb takes a direct object in the accusative case and an object in the
  dative case, we indicate it with DAT AKK.
- If the verb takes a complement with a locative meaning (location), we indicate
  it with LOK.
- If the verb takes a direct object in the nominative case, we indicate it
  with NOM.

The second column displays the basic English translation of the verb. In the third
and fourth columns, we provide you with the present tense and the past tense in the
third-person singular because it is the most common form in the texts you will wish to
read and translate. If a verb has a separable prefix, you can see it in the third person,
as well (*eindringen/dringt . . . ein*). The last column shows the participle II used to form
several tenses or the adjective form.

The list only includes verbs that are likely to be used in theological texts and is
therefore not a complete list of all irregular verbs in German.

Infinitive	Translation	Present Tense	Past Tense	Participle II
befehlen DAT AKK	to command	befiehlt	befahl	befohlen
beginnen	to begin	beginnt	begann	begonnen
betrügen	to betray	betrügt	betrog	betrogen
bieten DAT AKK	to offer	bietet	bot	geboten
binden	to bind	bindet	band	gebunden
bitten	to request	bittet	bat	gebeten
bleiben LOK	to stay	bleibt	blieb	geblieben
bringen DAT AKK	to bring	bringt	brachte	gebracht
denken	to think	denkt	dachte	gedacht
eindringen in	to penetrate	dringt . . . ein	drang . . . ein	eingedrungen
empfangen DAT AKK	to receive	empfing	empfang	empfangen
empfehlen DAT AKK	to recommend	empfiehlt	empfahl	empfohlen
finden	to find	findet	fand	gefunden
geben DAT AKK	to give	gibt	gab	gegeben
gehen LOK	to go	geht	ging	gegangen
gelingen DAT	to succeed	gelingt	gelang	gelungen
gelten	to apply	gilt	galt	gegolten
geraten in	to get into	gerät in	geriet in	in . . . geraten
geschehen DAT AKK	to happen	geschieht	geschah	geschehen
gewinnen	to win	gewinnt	gewann	gewonnen
gleichen DAT	to equal	gleicht	glich	geglichen
greifen	to grasp	greift	griff	gegriffen
haben	to have	hat	hatte	gehabt
heißen NOM	to be named	heißt	hieß	geheißen
helfen DAT	to help	hilft	half	geholfen
kennen	to know	kennt	kannte	gekannt
kommen LOK	to come	kommt	kam	gekommen
lassen	to let	lässt	ließ	gelassen

Infinitive	Translation	Present Tense	Past Tense	Participle II
leiden an/unter	to suffer from	leidet	litt	gelitten
lesen	to read	liest	las	gelesen
liegen LOK	to lay	liegt	lag	gelegen
lügen	to lie	lügt	log	gelogen
meiden	to avoid	meidet	mied	gemieden
nehmen	to take	nimmt	nahm	genommen
nennen	to name	nennt	nannte	genannt
preisen	to praise	preist	pries	gepriesen
raten DAT AKK	to advise	rät	riet	geraten
rufen	to call	ruft	rief	gerufen
schaffen	to achieve	schafft	schuf	geschaffen
scheinen	to seem	scheint	schien	geschienen
schreiben	to write	schreibt	schrieb	geschrieben
schreien	to yell	schreit	schrie	geschrien
schweigen	to keep quiet	schweigt	schwieg	geschwiegen
schwinden	to fade, to disappear	schwindet	schwand	geschwunden
schwören DAT AKK	to vow	schwört	schwor	geschworen
sehen	to see	sieht	sah	gesehen
sein NOM	to be	ist	war	gewesen
senden DAT AKK	to send	sendet	sandte	gesandt
singen	to sing	singt	sang	gesungen
sprechen	to speak	spricht	sprach	gesprochen
stehen LOK	to stand	steht	stand	gestanden
stehlen	to steal	stiehlt	stahl	gestohlen
sterben	to die	stirbt	starb	gestorben
sich streiten mit	to argue with	streitet sich	stritt sich	sich gestritten
tragen	to carry	trägt	trug	getragen
treffen	to meet	trifft	traf	getroffen

(cont.)

Infinitive	Translation	Present Tense	Past Tense	Participle II
trinken	to drink	trinkt	trank	getrunken
tun	to do	tut	tat	getan
vergessen	to forget	vergisst	vergaß	vergessen
verlieren	to lose	verliert	verlor	verloren
werden NOM	to become	wird	wurde	geworden
wissen	to know	weiß	wusste	gewusst
ziehen	to pull	zieht	zog	gezogen
zwingen AKK + zu	to force	zwingt	zwang	gezwungen

Appendix 3
List of Verbs with Prepositions

Ⅎ ow to use this list: Verbs with prepositions are verbs that have a prepositional complement (see verb valency in section 3.6.4). The preposition is fixed, but a few verbs can take different prepositions, often resulting in a different meaning. For example, *sich freuen auf* (to look forward to) or *sich freuen über* (to be happy about). The case of the complement, which is determined by the preposition, is not relevant for reading and translating, as you can identify the complement easily by its preposition. If you, for example, come across a sentence with the verb *sich freuen*, you should look for a prepositional phrase with *auf* or *über* to find the complement. The case of the complement is therefore irrelevant and will not be included in the list to avoid information overload.

The first column shows the verb with its preposition; the second column provides you with a translation. In the third column we give you additional information about the verb. If the verb is irregular, we give you the stem forms (for an explanation, see appendix 2, "List of Irregular Verbs with Their Stem Forms"). If the verb has a separable prefix, we have provided the third-person singular.

The list only includes verbs that are likely to be used in theological texts and is therefore not a complete list of all verbs with prepositions in German.

Infinitive	Translation	Notes
abhängen von	to depend on	hängt . . . ab/ hing . . . ab/ abgehangen
achten auf	to pay attention to	
anfangen mit	to begin	fängt . . . an/ fing . . . an/ angefangen
ankommen auf	to depend on	kommt . . . an/ kam . . . an/ angekommen
antworten auf	to answer	
sich ärgern über	to get annoyed at	

(cont.)

Infinitive	Translation	Notes
aufhören mit	to stop	hört . . . auf
ausgeben für	to spend on	gibt . . . aus/ gab . . . aus/ ausgegeben
beginnen mit	to begin	beginnt/ begann/ begonnen
sich bemühen um	to strive after	
berichten über/von	to report	
sich beschäftigen mit	to be concerned with	
bestehen auf	to insist on	besteht/ bestand/ bestanden
bestehen aus	to be comprised of	besteht/ bestand/ bestanden
sich beteiligen an	to take part in	
sich beziehen auf	to refer to	bezieht/ bezog/ bezogen
denken an	to think of/about	denkt/ dachte/ gedacht
erfahren von	to hear about	erfährt/ erfuhr/ erfahren
sich erinnern an	to remember	
erkennen an	to recognize by	erkennt/ erkannte/ erkannt
fragen nach	to ask for/after	
sich freuen auf	to look forward to	
sich freuen über	to be happy about	
gehen um	to concern	geht/ ging/ gegangen
gehören zu	to belong to	
glauben an	to believe in	
halten für	to take for	halt/ hielt/ gehalten
sich handeln um	to be about	used in academic contexts
handeln von	to deal with	
hindern an	to prevent	
hoffen auf	to hope for	
hören von	to hear about	
sich interessieren für	to be interested in	
sterben an	to die of	stirbt/ starb/ gestorben
streiten mit/über	to argue with/about	streitet/ stritt/ gestritten

Infinitive	Translation	Notes
teilnehmen an	to participate in	nimmt . . . teil/ nahm . . . teil/ teilgenommen
sich unterhalten mit/ über	to talk with/about	unterhält / unterhielt / unterhalten
sich verabschieden von	to say goodbye to	
vergleichen mit	to compare to	vergleicht/ verglich/ verglichen
sich verlassen auf	to rely on	verlässt/ verließ/ verlassen
sich vorbereiten auf	to prepare for	
warnen vor	to warn against	
warten auf	to wait fort	
sich wenden an	to address	wendet/ wandte or wendete/ gewandt or gewendet
werden zu	to turn into	wird/ wurde/ geworden
wissen von	to know about	weiß/ wusste/ gewusst
sich wundern über	to be surprised about	
zweifeln an	to doubt	

Appendix 4
Alphabetical List of Conjunctions

How to use this list: In section 3.2 we discussed the different types of conjunctions and their role in the sentence structure. The list below is alphabetically organized and provides information on specific conjunctions that you will come across while reading and translating the texts in part II and part III of this book. The last column identifies the type of clause the conjunctions connect as well as their frequency.

Conjunction	Translation	Notes
aber	but	coordinating with comma
als	when/like	subordinating
auf dass	so that	subordinating, less frequent
bevor	before	subordinating
da	because, since, as	subordinating
damit[1]	so that	subordinating
dadurch, dass	translated with a construction of "by" and "-ing"	subordinating
derart, dass	so that	subordinating, less frequent
denn	because	coordinating
ehe	before	subordinating, less frequent
entweder . . . oder	either . . . or	coordinating
indem	translated with a construction of "by" and "-ing"	subordinating
insofern (als)	(in) so far as	subordinating, less frequent
insoweit (als)	inasmuch as	subordinating, less frequent

[1]not to be confused with the *da*-compound with the preposition *mit*

(cont.)

Conjunction	Translation	Notes
jedoch	but	coordinating, less frequent
nachdem	after	subordinating
ob	if	subordinating
obgleich	(al)though	subordinating, less frequent
obschon	(al)though	subordinating, less frequent
obwohl	(al)though	subordinating
obzwar	(al)though	subordinating, less frequent
oder	or	coordinating
seit(dem)	since	subordinating
sobald	as soon as	subordinating
sodass, so dass	so that	subordinating
solange	as long as	subordinating
sondern	but	coordinating with comma
sooft	as often as, whenever	subordinating
soweit	(in) so/as far as	subordinating
sowie	and	coordinating
sowie	as soon as	subordinating
sowohl . . . als auch	as well as	coordinating
teils . . . teils	partly . . . partly	coordinating, less frequent
und	and	coordinating
weder . . . noch	neither . . . nor	coordinating
weil	because	subordinating
wenn	if	subordinating
wenngleich	(al)though	subordinating
wie	like, as	subordinating and coordinating
wiewohl	(al)though	subordinating
zumal	especially as	subordinating, less frequent
zwar . . . , aber	(al)though	subordinating

Appendix 5
Solutions to Exercises

Part I

Step One

Underline all verb forms in the following paragraphs from Luther's *Von der Freiheit eines Christenmenschen*. Fill in the table below with the missing information. The number of lines indicates the number of verb forms in the paragraph.

Paragraph 1:

> *Und um dieses Unterschieds willen* <u>werden</u> *von ihm in der Schrift Dinge* <u>gesagt</u>, *die sich vollständig* <u>widersprechen</u> *wie das, was ich jetzt von der Freiheit und Dienstbarkeit* <u>gesagt</u> <u>habe</u>.

Verb form	Infinitive	Verb type	Person	Tense	Subjunctive or Indicative	Passive or Active
werden . . . gesagt	sagen	regular	3. Pers. Pl.	present tense	indicative	passive
widersprechen	widersprechen	irregular	3. Pers. Pl.	present tense	indicative	active
habe . . . gesagt	sagen	regular	1. Pers. Sg.	present perfect	indicative	active

Paragraph 2:

> *Hier* <u>beginnt</u> *nun der fröhliche Tausch und Streit: weil Christus Gott und Mensch* <u>ist</u>, *der noch nie* <u>gesündigt hat</u>, *und seine Rechtschaffenheit unüberwindlich, ewig und allmächtig* <u>ist</u>, *so müssen die Sünden in ihm* <u>verschlungen</u> *und* <u>ersäuft</u> <u>werden</u>, *wenn er die Sünden der gläubigen Seele durch ihren Brautring, d. h. den Glauben, sich selbst zu eigen* <u>macht</u> *und so* <u>handelt</u>, *wie er* <u>gehandelt</u> <u>hat</u>.

Verb form	Infinitive	Verb type (regular/irregular)	Person	Tense	Subjunctive or Indicative	Passive or Active
beginnt	beginnen	irregular	3. Pers. Sg.	present tense	indicative	active
ist	sein	irregular	3. Pers. Sg.	present tense	indicative	active
hat . . . gesündigt	sündigen	regular	3. Pers. Sg.	present perfect	indicative	active
ist	sein	irregular	3. Pers. Sg.	present tense	indicative	active
werden . . . verschlungen	verschlingen	irregular	3. Pers. Pl.	present tense	indicative	passive
werden . . . ersäuft	ersaufen	irregular	3. Pers. Pl.	present tense	indicative	passive
macht	machen	regular	3. Pers. Sg.	present tense	indicative	active
handelt	handeln	regular	3. Pers. Sg.	present tense	indicative	active
hat . . . gehandelt	handeln	regular	3. Pers. Sg.	present perfect	indicative	active

Paragraph 3:

Aber damit er nicht müßig ginge, gab ihm Gott etwas zu schaffen, das Paradies zu bepflanzen, zu bebauen und zu bewahren. Und dies wären lauter freie Werke gewesen, die sonst nichts zuliebe getan worden wären als nur Gott zu gefallen und nicht, um die Rechtschaffenheit zu erlangen, die er schon vorher besaß, und die auch uns allen von Natur angeboren[1] gewesen wäre.

Verb form	Infinitive	Verb type (regular/irregular)	Person	Tense	Subjunctive or Indicative	Passive or Active
ginge	gehen	irregular	3. Pers. Sg.	past tense	subjunctive	active
gab	geben	irregular	3. Pers. Sg.	past tense	indicative	active
schaffen	schaffen	regular	infinitive	present tense	indicative	active

---

1. The word *angeboren* is an adjective although it looks like a participle. It was at some point in the history of German a participle but is now only used as an adjective.

Verb form	Infinitive	Verb type (regular/irregular)	Person	Tense	Subjunctive or Indicative	Passive or Active
bepflanzen	bepflanzen	regular	infinitive	present tense	indicative	active
bebauen	bebauen	regular	infinitive	present tense	indicative	active
bewahren	bewahren	regular	infinitive	present tense	indicative	active
wären . . . gewesen	sein	irregular	3. Pers. Pl.	present perfect	subjunctive	active
wären . . . getan worden	tun	irregular	3. Pers. Pl.	present perfect	subjunctive	passive
erlangen	erlangen	regular	infinitive	present tense	indicative	active
besaß	besitzen	irregular	3. Pers. Sg.	past tense	indicative	active
wäre . . . gewesen	sein	irregular	3. Pers. Sg.	present tense	subjunctive	active

Step Two

Find and mark all verb forms and all commas:

Umgekehrt <u>schadet</u> es der Seele nichts, wenn der Leib unheilige Kleider <u>trägt</u>, sich an unheiligen Orten <u>befindet</u>, wenn er <u>ißt</u> und <u>trinkt</u>, nicht <u>wallfahrtet</u> und <u>betet</u> und all die Werke <u>unterläßt</u>, die die genannten Gleißner <u>tun</u>.

Und wenn du das wirklich <u>glaubst</u>, wie du <u>verpflichtet</u> <u>bist</u>, so <u>mußt</u> du an dir selbst <u>verzweifeln</u> und <u>bekennen</u>, daß der Spruch Hoseas wahr <u>sei</u>.

Step Three

Find and translate all conjunctions:

Umgekehrt schadet es der Seele nichts, <u>wenn</u> (if) der Leib unheilige Kleider trägt, sich an unheiligen Orten befindet, <u>wenn</u> (if) er ißt und trinkt, nicht wallfahrtet <u>und</u> (and) betet <u>und</u> (and) all die Werke unterläßt, die die genannten Gleißner tun.

<u>Und</u> (and) <u>wenn</u> (if) du das wirklich glaubst, <u>wie</u> (as) du verpflichtet bist, so mußt du an dir selbst verzweifeln und (and) bekennen, <u>daß</u> (that) der Spruch Hoseas wahr sei.

Step Four

Mark the main clause:

> <u>Umgekehrt schadet es der Seele nichts,</u> wenn der Leib unheilige Kleider trägt, sich an unheiligen Orten befindet, wenn er ißt und trinkt, nicht wallfahrtet und betet und all die Werke unterläßt, die die genannten Gleißner tun.

> Und wenn du das wirklich glaubst, wie du verpflichtet bist, <u>so mußt du an dir selbst verzweifeln und bekennen,</u> daß der Spruch Hoseas wahr sei.

Step Five

Perform the following steps with all examples below:

1. Find all verbs.
2. Establish noun phrases and determine their case.
3. Identify the complements of all verbs.

> *Gott* (NOM, subject, complement) *wird* <*auf der Erde*> (adverbial, local)
> <*ein kurzes Fazit*> (AKK, direct object, complement) <u>ziehen,</u> *und* <*dem kurzen Fazit*>
> (DAT, direct object, complement) <u>wird</u> <*wie eine Sintflut*> (NOM, explanatory phrase
> to the subject) <*die Gerechtigkeit*> (NOM, subject, complement) <u>entströmen.</u>

> *Denn* <*kein gutes Werk*> (NOM, subject, complement) <u>hängt (verb with preposition)</u>
> <*an dem göttlichen Wort*> (prepositional complement) *so* <*wie der Glaube*>
> (NOM, explanatory phrase to the subject).

> *So* <u>wird</u> <*die Seele*> (NOM, subject, complement) <*von all ihren Sünden*>
> (DAT, prepositional complement[2]) *einzig* <*durch ihr Brautgeschenk*> (adverbial, modal),
> *d.h.* <*um des Glaubens willen*> (adverbial, reason), <*frei und los*> (predicative complement)
> *und* <*mit der ewigen Gerechtigkeit ihres Bräutigams Christus*> (adverbial, modal, with a
> genitive attribute) <u>beschenkt.</u>

---

2. Strictly speaking, this is a complement to the adjective *frei* which is here used as a predicative. We did not discuss adjective complements in this book because verb complements are more frequent and more important for reading and translating German texts.

Step Six

Find all pronouns and identify their case and the noun to which they refer.

Wenn Gott daher sieht, daß <u>ihm</u> (Gott, personal pronoun, dative singular) *die Seele Wahrhaftigkeit zugesteht und <u>ihn</u>* (Gott, personal pronoun, accusative singular) *so durch <u>ihren</u>* (Seele, personal pronoun, accusative singular) *Glauben ehrt, so ehrt <u>er</u>* (Gott, personal pronoun, nominative singular) *<u>sie</u>* (Seele, personal pronoun, accusative singular) *ebenfalls und hält <u>sie</u>* (Seele, personal pronoun, accusative singular) *auch für rechtschaffen und wahrhaftig, und durch so einen Glauben ist <u>sie</u>* (Seele, personal pronoun, nominative singular) *auch rechtschaffen und wahrhaftig.*

Damit <u>wir</u> (personal pronoun, nominative plural) *gründlich erkennen, <u>was</u>* (interrogative pronoun used a relative pronoun, accusative singular) *ein Christenmensch ist, und <u>wie</u>* (interrogative pronoun used as a relative pronoun) *<u>es</u>* (impersonal use, personal pronoun, nominative singular) *um die Freiheit stehe, <u>die</u>* (Freiheit, relative pronoun, nominative singular) *<u>ihm</u>* (Christenmensch, personal pronoun, dative singular) *Christus erworben und gegeben hat, <u>wovon</u>* (*wo*-compound used as interrogative pronoun) *Sankt Paulus viel schreibt, will <u>ich</u>* (personal pronoun, nominative singular) *<u>diese</u>* (demonstrative pronoun, accusative plural) *zwei Sätze aufstellen: (. . .)*

Step Seven

1. Mark the participles used as adjectives:
   Der <u>erinnerte</u> Jesus ist zugleich der <u>erzählte</u> Jesus.
2. Answer the following questions for each participle:
   What kind of participle is it? What is the infinitive of the verb?
   erinnerte (participle II of erinnern)
   erzählte (participle II of erzählen)
3. Translate the sentence!
   The remembered Jesus is at the same time the recounted[3] Jesus.
4. Fill in the comparative forms of the adjectives:

schlecht	schlechter	am schlechtesten
rechtschaffen	rechtschaffener	am rechtschaffensten
treu	treuer	am treu(e)sten
gläubig	gläubiger	am gläubigsten

---

3. "The told Jesus" is grammatically correct as well but does not sound very natural in English.

Step Eight

1. Find the modal particle in both examples!

> *Darum sollte das <u>wohl</u> für alle Christen das einzige Werk und die einzige Übung sein*

> *wenn der Glaube alles ist und allein <u>schon</u> als genügend gilt*

2. Translate the sentence in both examples! Remember that the definite article can be used as a demonstrative pronoun.

> Because of that, this should presumably be the only work and the only practice for all Christians

> if the faith is everything and is already considered to be ample by itself

Step Nine

Perform a rough translation of the sentence by applying steps 1 through 8 on the checklist!

> *Obwohl der Mensch innerlich der Seele nach durch den Glauben genügend gerechtfertigt ist und alles hat, was er haben soll, nur daß dieser Glaube und diese Genüge immer zunehmen müssen, bis in jenes Leben, bleibt er doch noch in diesem leiblichen Leben auf der Erde und muß seinen eigenen Leib regieren und mit Leuten umgehen.*

> Although man is inwardly according to the soul sufficiently justified through the faith and has everything that he should have, only that this faith and this sufficiency always has to grow, till that life, he stays nevertheless in this bodily life on earth and has to govern his own body and has to deal with people.

Step Ten

Revise your translation from the exercise to step 9.

> Although, according to the soul, man is inwardly, sufficiently justified through faith and has everything that he should have, only that this faith and this sufficiency always has to grow till that life, nevertheless, he remains in this bodily life on earth and has to govern his own body and deal with people.

Part II

Chapter 5

1. Before reading and translating the text: Find all sentences where Luther uses *so* and circle it! While reading and translating: When you get to a sentence with *so*, decide which of the following uses fits the context best.
   a. comparison, translate with "as" or "like"
   b. relative pronoun
   c. conditional, translate as "if"
   d. consecutive, translate as "then," "that," or "so that"
   e. concessive, translate as "although"

   1. <u>so</u> (as) *ein jeglicher Christ zur Not wissen soll*
   2. <u>so</u> (if) *in den Katechismus oder Kinderpredigt gehören*
   3. so (although) *doch, die zum Sakrament gehen, billig mehr wissen (. . .) sollen*
   4. so (as/like) *von alters her in der Christenheit geblieben sind*
   5. <u>so lange, bis</u> (so long until) *man sich in denselben wohl übe und geläufig werde*
   6. <u>so</u> (then) *merke*
   7. <u>so</u> (relative pronoun, die) *die ganze Woche ihrer Arbeit und Gewerbe gewartet*
   8. *doch das Feiern nicht <u>so</u> eng* (so tight) *gespannt*
   9. <u>so</u> (relative pronoun, die) *man nicht umgehen kann*
   10. <u>so</u> (then) *antworte*
   11. <u>so</u> (if) *du heiliges oder unheiliges Ding daran treibst*
   12. <u>so</u> (then) *soll es kein Christenfeiertag heißen*
   13. <u>so</u> (then) *wäre uns doch nichts damit geholfen*
   14. <u>so</u> (then) *wird dadurch Person, Tag und Werk geheiligt*
   15. <u>so</u> (so that) *[es] uns alle zu Heiligen macht*
   16. <u>so</u> (then) *geht dies Gebot in seiner Kraft und Erfüllung*
   17. *Weil nun <u>so</u> viel* (so much) *an Gottes Wort gelegen ist*
   18. so (relative pronoun, die) *dazu geordnet ist*
   19. so (relative pronoun, der) *Gottes Wort hören als einen andern Tand und nur aus Gewohnheit zur Predigt und wieder herausgehen*
   20. *können sie heuer <u>so</u> viel als fert* (today as much as before)
   21. <u>so</u> (relative pronoun, die) *man bisher unter die Todsünden gezählt hat und heißet Akidia*
   22. <u>so</u> (then) *bist du doch täglich unter des Teufels Reich*
   23. <u>so</u> (then) *bricht er ein und hat den Schaden getan*
   24. <u>so</u> (then) *sollte doch das jedermann dazu reizen*

2. Analyze the first paragraph labeled *Vorrede* by applying the checklist introduced in chapters 2–4. Note that v1 stands for verb part 1, v2 stands for verb part 2.

Diese Predigt (S) ist (v1₎*sein*-passive) dazu geordnet (v2) und angefangen (v2), dass es (S) sei (verb₎*Konjunktiv I*) ein Unterricht (S) für die Kinder und Einfältigen. Darum sie (S₎Predigt) auch von alters her auf griechisch heißt (verb) Katechismus (S₎das (S₎demonstrative pronoun) ist (verb) eine Kinderlehre (S₎so ein jeglicher Christ (S) zur Not wissen (v2) soll (v1₎also dass [,] wer (interrogative pronoun used as relative pronoun) solches (DO) nicht weiß (verb₎nicht könnte (v1) unter die Christen gezählt (v2) und zu keinem Sakrament (PC) zugelassen (v2) werden (v2₎passive with modal verb). Gleichwie man (S) einen Handwerksmann (DO₎der (S) seines Handwerks Recht und Gebrauch (DO) nicht weiß (verb₎ auswirft (verb) und für untüchtig hält (verb with preposition *für*). Derhalben soll (v1) man (S) junge Leute (DO) die Stücke (DO₎so in den Katechismus oder Kinderpredigt gehören₎wohl und fertig lernen (v2) lassen (v2₎passive-like construction) und mit Fleiß darin üben (v2) und treiben (v2₎still part of the passive-like construction). Darum auch ein jeglicher Hausvater (S) schuldig ist (verb₎dass er zum wenigstens die Woche einmal seine Kinder und Gesinde (DO) umfrage (verb) und verhöre (verb₎was (interrogative pronoun) sie (S) davon wissen (verb) oder lernen (verb₎und wo (interrogative pronoun) sie es nicht können (verb₎ mit Ernst dazu halte (verb).

Chapter 6

1. Kant uses very complex sentence structure. Steps 2 and 3 on our checklist are very important while reading Kant. Find all the commas, conjunctions, and relative pronouns in the following sentences taken out of the text:

Besonders ist hiebei: daß das Publikum₎welches zuvor von ihnen unter dieses Joch gebracht worden [ist₎sie hernach selbst zwingt₎darunter zu bleiben₎wenn es von einigen seiner Vormünder₎die selbst aller Aufklärung unfähig sind₎dazu aufgewiegelt worden [ist].

Faulheit und Feigheit sind die Ursachen₎warum ein so großer Teil der Menschen₎nachdem sie die Natur längst von fremder Leitung freigesprochen (naturaliter maiorennes) [hat], dennoch gerne zeitlebens unmündig bleiben; und warum es anderen so leicht wird₎sich zu deren Vormündern aufzuwerfen

2. While reading the text, fill out the table below, using tallies to mark how often the respective meaning is used in the text.

Modal particle	Meaning 1	Meaning 2	Meaning 3
bloß	simply II		
ja	implying previous knowledge I	in no case I	yes III
schon	surely I	already III	
wohl	probably II	presumably III	nevertheless I
sogar	even IIIII I	as a matter of fact I	

Chapter 7

1. Find all 16 instances of *sich* in the text and mark them. Look at the verb and possible footnotes to decide if it has to be translated or not. If it is used with a preposition, it has to be translated most of the time. Cross out all instances where it has to be omitted in the translation.

   1. *Hier zeigt sich also schon ein wesentlicher Unterschied zwischen Staat und Religion.*
   2. *Der Staat hat physische Gewalt und bedient sich derselben (. . .)*
   3. *Denn ein Vertrag über Dinge, die ihrer Natur nach⁴ unveräußerlich sind, ist an und für sich* (fixed phrase) *ungültig,*
   4. *hebt sich von selbst auf.*
   5. *(. . .) aber an und für sich* (fixed phrase) *zu nichts verbindet.*
   6. *Wie [hat er] sich zu verhalten* (*sich verhalten*, either "behave" or "conduct oneself," if you choose the latter, you need to translate *sich*)
   7. *Wer sich rühmt, (. . .)*
   8. *und sich auf Lehren, Vermahnen, Bereden und Zurechtweisen einschränken*
   9. *Sie verhält sich gegen[über] Handlung nicht anders (. . .)*
   10. *maß[e]t sich auf kein irdisches Gut ein Recht*
   11. *das sich der Staat zuweilen erlauben darf*
   12. *Wenn sich die Religion keine willkürlichen Strafen erlaubt*
   13. *Zieh[e]t sie bürgerliches Elend nach sich*
   14. *wenn er sich [um] einer vermeinten Wahrheit zu gefallen, der mindesten Gefahr aussetz[e]t*
   15. *wie man sich bereden will*
   16. *Man beruft sich immer noch auf das Naturgesetz.*

---

4. Preposition *nach* used after the referent noun; translate as "according to."

2. Mendelssohn favors relative clauses over all other subclause constructions. Find all relative pronouns in the sentence below (taken from the text), identify gender, number, and case. Finally, locate the referent noun of each relative pronoun.

> *Beide wirken auf Gesinnung und Handlung der Menschen, auf Grundsätze und Anwendung: der Staat, vermittelst solcher Gründe, die* (relative pronoun, referring back to *Gründe*, nominative plural) *auf Verhältnissen zwischen Mensch und Mensch, oder Mensch und Natur, und die Kirche, die Religion des Staats, vermittelst solcher Gründe, die* (relative pronoun, referring back to *Gründe*, nominative plural) *auf Verhältnissen zwischen Mensch und Gott beruhen.*

Chapter 8

1. Find all infinitive with *zu* constructions (sentences taken from the text) and practice translating them.

> *In dieses Gebiet darf sich also die Religion nicht versteigen, sie darf nicht die Tendenz haben Wesen <u>zu setzen</u> und Naturen <u>zu bestimmen,</u> sich in ein Unendliches von Gründen und Deduktionen <u>zu verlieren,</u> letzte Ursachen <u>aufzusuchen</u> und ewige Wahrheiten <u>auszusprechen</u>*
>
> In this area religion must therefore not enter, it must not have the tendency to state beings and to determine natures, to lose itself in an infinity of reasons and deductions, to seek out final causes and to voice eternal truths.

> *Sie begehrt nicht das Universum seiner Natur nach <u>zu bestimmen</u> und <u>zu erklären</u> wie die Metaphysik, sie begehrt nicht aus Kraft der Freiheit und der göttlichen Willkür des Menschen es <u>fortzubilden</u> und fertig <u>zu machen</u> wie die Moral.*
>
> It does not desire to determine the universe according to its nature and to explain it as metaphysics [does], it does not desire out of the power of freedom and the godly arbitrariness of men to educate it and to complete it, as ethics [does].

2. To be completed while translating: Find five examples of Schleiermacher's expressive language in the text and list them below with a suitable translation (often to be found in the footnotes). Note that the given solutions are simply examples. You might have found different ones that are nonetheless correct.

1. *eine Menge garstiger unmoralischer Flecken* (lots of nasty immoral stains)
2. *es ist jetzt Zeit ihn völlig zu vernichten* (it is now time to destroy it completely)
3. *aber artig genug, auch etwas Moral nicht zu verschmähen* (but well-behaved enough not to spurn some morale, as well)
4. *Aber wie kommt Ihr denn dazu* (But how dare you)
5. *Ich hätte Lust, Euch durch einige sokratische Fragen zu ängstigen* (I would like to scare you with a few Socratic questions)

Chapter 9

1. Complex noun phrases with participles: Translate the following examples.
   - *die in ihm wieder enthüllte Gerechtigkeit Gottes*
     God's justice that has been revealed again in him
   - *auf der schöpferischen, erlösenden, die Welt umfassenden Kraft Gottes*
     on the creative and redeeming power of God, which encompasses the world
   - *unsre im Christus realisierte Erkenntnis Gottes*
     our recognition of God realized in Christ
   - *das jetzt anhebende Werk der Kraft Gottes*
     the now arising work of the power of God

2. Nominalizations. The following examples are taken from the text. Identify the source of the noun and translate it. Note that the nouns can refer to a person or to a thing (also a general notion) and that even superlative forms can be nominalized.
   - *nichts Neues, sondern das Älteste: nichts Besonderes, sondern das Allgemeinste; nichts Geschichtliches*
     nothing new, but the oldest; nothing special but the most general, nothing historical
   - *in den vom Christus Berufenen*
     in those appointed by Christ
   - *die Glaubenden*
     the believers
   - *der Getreue*
     the faithful (singular)

Chapter 10

1. Identify for each participle used as adjective the following: infinitive of the verb, type of participle, case, number and gender of the noun phrase (see table below)

noun phrase	infinitve	participle I/II	case	number	gender	translation
verschleudertes Sakrament	verschleudern	II	nominative or accusative	sg.	neuter	squandered sacrament
die gezahlte Rechnung	zahlen	II	nominative or accusative	sg.	feminine	the paid bill
den menschge-wordenen Jesus	menschwerden	II	accusative	sg.	masculine	the incarnated Jesus
der verborgene Schatz	verbergen	II	nominative	sg.	masculine	the hidden treasure
vergebendes Wort	vergeben	I	nominative or accusative	sg.	neuter	forgiving word
die aufgebrachten Kosten	aufbringen	II	nominative or accusative	pl.	no gender, plural word	the raised costs
der zunehmenden Verweltlichung	zunehmen	I	dative or genitive	sg.	feminine	Of the rising secularization

2. *Konjunktiv I* vs. imperative form:

Locate the verb and identify person and number. Translate the sentences and find the grammatical difference between *Konjunktiv I* and the imperative form.

Konjunktiv I:

- *Es <u>lebe</u> (3. Pers. Sg.) also auch der Christ wie die Welt,*
  May the Christian therefore live also like the world,
- *Der Christ aber <u>sei</u> (3. Pers. Sg.) in seiner Weltlichkeit getrost und sicher.*
  But may the Christian be confident and safe in his secularity.

imperative form:

- *<u>bleibe</u> (1. Pers. Sg.) nur weiter, wo du warst, und <u>tröste</u> (1. Pers. Sg.) dich der Vergebung.*
  Just continue to stay where you were and be comforted by forgiveness.
  (*sich etwas* [dative] *trösten* has passive-like meaning)

Appendix 6
Translations of Texts

S ince our goal has been to help learners interact with original German sources and prepare for German comprehension examinations, the following translations are not intended to be polished English translations of the texts examined in this book. Instead, they are based off the footnotes used within this book and feedback given during the International Summer School, German (and) Theology. It is intended that these rough translations encourage the users of this book by providing translations that would be similar to their own initial attempts, while also encouraging individual preference in selecting translations of words with multiple meanings.

Martin Luther

Excerpt from The Large Catechism (1529)
Preface

This sermon is ordered and begun so that it is a lesson for the children and the simple-minded. Therefore it also has been called "catechism" in Greek from ancient times, that is, a children's teaching, as any Christian in need should know, so that whoever does not know it, could not be counted among Christians and not be admitted to any sacrament. Just as one removes a craftsman, who does not know the law and the use of his work, and deems him inefficient. For this reason, young people should be allowed to learn the pieces, which belong in the catechism or children's sermon, well and completely and with diligence therein practice and drive them. That's why any housefather is also guilty, that he at least once a week ask and consult his children and servants, what they know or learn from it, and where they cannot (answer), urge them with seriousness (to the task). For I think of the time, yes it still happens daily, that one finds crude, old, elderly people who have not known or still do not know anything of this, who still go to the same baptism and sacrament and need all that Christians have; though those, who go to sacrament should reasonably know more and have a more complete understanding than the children and new students; although we let it remain for common people with the three pieces, as they have remained in Christianity from long ago, but have little correctly learned and were driven so long, until one practices and becomes familiar with them, both young and old, who want to be called Christians and want to be (Christians); and are namely these:

[it follows List of Commandments, not part of our translation]

The Third Commandment
You Shall Sanctify the Holy Day

We have named "holiday" after the Hebrew word "Sabbath," which actually means "to celebrate," that is to stand idle from work. Therefore, we care to say "make an evening of celebration" or "give a holy evening." Now, God has, in the Old Testament, selected and set up the seventh day to celebrate and commanded to keep it holy from all others. And, according to this outward holiday, this commandment is given only to the Jews, that they should stand still and rest from gross works, so that both man and beast would recover and would not become weakened from constant work. Even though they afterward stretched it all too thin and grossly misused it, that they even blasphemed against Christ and could not tolerate such work, which they themselves still did—as one reads in the Gospels. Just as if the commandment should be fulfilled with that one does no outward work at all, which was not at all the opinion, but merely that they should sanctify the holiday or day of rest, as we will hear.

Therefore this commandment now according to rough understanding does not concern us Christians, because it is an entirely outward thing, as are other statutes of the Old Testament, bound to a special way, person, time, and place, which, now through Christ, are all set free. But to grasp a Christian understanding for all the simple-minded, what God demands in this commandment from us, then note that we do not hold the holiday for the sake of the understanding and learned Christians, because they do not need anything like this, but firstly even for the sake of bodily cause and need for help, which nature teaches and demands for the common people, servants, and maids, who have maintained their work and trade the whole week, that they themselves may also have a day to rest and refresh. Then mostly therefore, that on such a day of rest (because otherwise one has no time for it) one may take space and time to maintain church services; so that one may come together to hear God's Word and take action, therefore to praise, sing, and pray to God. But such things (I say) are not therefore bound by time as with the Jews, that it must be exactly this or that day; because no day is in itself better than any other: but it should probably happen daily, but because the common people cannot maintain it, one must each select at least one day in the week for it. But because from long ago Sunday has been selected, one should also thereby let it remain, so that it may go in a peaceful order, and nobody through unnecessary innovation creates chaos. So this is the simple-minded opinion of this commandment: because otherwise one holds a holiday, that one may create such a celebration, in order to learn God's word; so that the actual office of this day be the priesthood for the sake of the young people and the poor common people; yet, the celebration is not to be stretched so thin, that therefore other random work, if one cannot bypass it, would be forbidden. Therefore, if one asks, what has been said: You shall sanctify the holy day? Then answer: To sanctify the Sabbath means as much as to keep [it] holy. What then is to keep holy? Nothing else than to lead holy words, works, and lives; because the day requires no sanctifying for itself because it is created holy in itself; but God wants it to be holy to you. So it will be holy or unholy because of you, as you do holy or unholy things on it. Now how does such sanctifying come about? Not by one sitting behind the oven or doing no great work or putting on a wreath and dressing in his best clothes, but (as has been said) by acting on and practicing God's Word. And indeed, we Christians should always keep such a holiday, to do an idle holy thing, that is, to deal daily with God's Word, to carry it in heart and mouth. But because we (as has been said) do not all have the time and leisure, we must require quite a few hours of the week for the youth or at least a day for all the common people, that [or better here: on which] one takes alone care of it and even practices the Ten Commandments, the faith, and the Lord's Prayer and so (that) our whole life and way complies with God's Word. Now when this becomes customary, there [or: at this time] a proper holy day will be kept. Where it is not, then it should not be called a Christian holiday; because non-Christians can also very well celebrate and go idly, just like the whole ulcer [pejorative for a group of people] of our spiritual leaders daily in the church stands, sings, and sounds, but does not sanctify a holy day, for they do not preach nor practice God's Word, but even teach and live against it.

For the Word of God is the sanctuary over all sanctuaries, yes the only one, which we Christians know and have. For even if we had all holy bones or holy and consecrated clothes in a heap, then we would still not be helped; for all of it is a dead thing, which no one can sanctify. But God's Word is that treasure, which makes all things holy, by which they themselves, all the saints, have been sanctified. Whichever hour one acts, preaches, hears, reads, or considers God's Word, then by that a person, day, and work is sanctified, not because of external works, but because of the Word, which makes us all saints. Therefore, I say all the time that all of our lives and works must go about in the Word of God, should they be called pleasing or holy to God. Where this happens, then this commandment takes effect and comes true. On the other hand, what happens with a being and work outside of God's Word, which is unholy before God, shine and blaze as it may, as it wants, when one hangs on it an idle relic, as there are [meaning: comparable to] fictional spiritual classes/estates, which do not know God's Word and seek holiness in their works. Therefore, take note that the power and might of this commandment lay not in celebration, but in sanctification, so that this day has a special holy practice. For other works and businesses are not actually called holy practices, unless the person is already holy (beforehand). But here such a work must happen, thereby a person themself becomes holy, which alone happens (as we've heard) through God's Word; for this site, time, people, and the entire external order of worship are founded and ordered, that even such things become customary.

Because so much depends on God's Word that no holy day would be sanctified without the very same, we should know that God wants this commandment to be upheld strictly and punishes all who despise his Word, who do not want to hear or learn (it), especially in the time that is meant for it. Thus, not only do those sin against this commandment who grossly misuse and desecrate the holy day, as those who want to hear the Word of God lessened for the sake of their greed and frivolity, or who lie in taverns, mad and drunken as pigs; but also the other group of common people, who hear God's Word as another frill and go to (hear) the sermon only out of habit and leave again, and when the year is over, they know as much as before. Because until now one has thought that it probably would have been celebrated, if one on Sundays would hear read a Mass or the Gospel; but no one asked for God's Word, as no one taught it anyway.

Now, (just) because we have God's Word, we nevertheless do not dismiss the misuse (and do not) allow ourselves to be preached at and admonished. We hear it, but without seriousness and concern. Therefore, know that it is not only about hearing, but also about learning and keeping it, and do not think that it depends on your whims or that great might does not lie in it; but that it is God's commandment, who (God) will promote it, as you have heard, learned, and honored his Word.

Likewise, the foul spirits are also to be punished, who, when they have heard a sermon or two, are full and tired of it, as if they were now themselves able to do it and required no more teacher.

For that is just the sin, that until now has been called *akidia* and counted under the mortal sins, that is inertia or weariness, a hostile, harmful plague, with that the devil enchants and betrays many hearts so that he may overtake us and secretly withdraw God's Word again.

For let it be said to you: even if you could do your best and would be the master of all things, then you are still daily under the devil's kingdom, who rests neither day nor night to stalk you, that he may ignite unbelief and evil thoughts in your heart against the former and all commandments. Therefore, you must always have God's Word in your heart, mind, and ears. But where the heart stands idle and the Word does not sound, then he (the devil) breaks in and has done the damage, before one is even aware of it. Again, it (the Word) has the power, where one considers, hears, and acts upon it with seriousness, so that it never departs without fruit, but always awakens new understanding, desire, and devotion, and makes the heart and thoughts pure; for they are not lazy nor dead, but busy (and) lively words. And if no other use or need drove us, then everybody should still be excited by it, so that through this the devil is shooed and chased away, so that this commandment will be fulfilled, and [that] God is more pleasing than all other hypocritical works.

Immanuel Kant

Excerpt from An Answer to the Question: What Is Enlightenment? (1784)

Enlightenment is man's emergence from his self-imposed immaturity. Immaturity is the inability to use one's own understanding without the guidance of another. This immaturity is self-imposed if its cause is not lack of understanding, but lack of resolution and courage to use it without the guidance of another. Sapere aude! Have courage to use your own understanding! is therefore the motto of enlightenment.

Laziness and cowardice are the reasons why such a large proportion of people, even after nature has long absolved them from alien guidance (naturaliter maiorennes), nevertheless gladly remain immature for life; and why it is all too easy for others to set themselves up as their guardians. It is so convenient to be immature! If I have a book that has understanding in place of me, a spiritual adviser to have a conscience for me, a doctor to judge my diet for me, and so on, I need not make any effort at all. I do not need to think, if I can only pay; others will surely take over the tiresome job for me. The guardians who have kindly taken upon themselves the work of supervision will soon see to it that by far the largest part of mankind (including the entire fair sex) should consider the step forward to maturity besides it being laborious as highly dangerous. After they have made their domesticated animals dumb, and carefully prevented the docile creatures from daring to take a single step outside their cage in which they locked them up, they next show them the danger which threatens them if they try to walk unaided. Now this danger is not in fact so very great, for they would probably learn to walk eventually after falling a few times. Even an example of this kind is intimidating, and commonly frightens off from all further attempts.

Thus, it is difficult for each separate individual to work his way out of the immaturity which has become almost second nature to him. He has even grown fond of it and is really incapable for the time being to use his own understanding, because he was never allowed to make the attempt. Dogmas and formulas, those mechanical instruments for rational use (or rather misuse) of his natural endowments, are the shackles of his permanent immaturity. And whoever would throw them off would still merely dare an uncertain jump over even the narrowest of trenches, because he is not used to free movement of this kind. Thus there are only a few who have succeeded to free themselves from immaturity by cultivating their own minds and to still walk in a sure way.

That an audience enlightens itself is more likely. Yes, it is almost inevitable, if only it is left in freedom. For there will always be a few independent thinkers, even among those appointed as guardians of the common mass who, once they have themselves thrown off the yoke of immaturity, will disseminate the spirit of rational respect for personal value and for the vocation of all men to think for themselves. It is here exceptional that the public, which was previously put under this yoke by the guardians, may subsequently compel the guardians themselves to remain under the yoke if it is suitably stirred up by some of the latter who are incapable of enlightenment. For it is very harmful to plant prejudices, because they finally avenge themselves on the very people who or whose predecessors were their originators. Thus a public can only achieve enlightenment slowly. By a revolution, the abandonment of autocratic despotism and of rapacious or power-seeking oppression may possibly come about, but never a true reform in ways of thinking. Instead, new prejudices as well as the old ones will serve as a leash to control the great unthinking mass.

But for this enlightenment all that is needed is freedom. And the freedom in question is the most harmless form of all that may be called freedom, namely: to make public use of one's reason in all matters. But I hear on all sides the cry: Don't reason! The officer says: Don't reason, but drill! The tax-official: Don't reason, but pay! The clergyman: Don't reason, but believe! (Only one ruler in the world says: Reason as much as you like and about whatever you like, but obey!). There is restriction of freedom everywhere. But which restriction prevents enlightenment, and which does not, and can presumably even promote it? I reply: The public use of one's reason must always be free, and it alone can achieve enlightenment among people; the private use of the same may quite often be very tightly restricted though without particularly hindering by it the progress of enlightenment. But by the public use of one's own reason I mean this kind of use which anyone may make of it as a scholar addressing the entire reading public. What I term the private use of reason is this kind of use which a person may make of it in a particular civil post or office with which he is entrusted.

Now in some affairs which affect the interests of the commonwealth, we require a certain mechanism whereby some members of the commonwealth must behave simply passively, so that they may, by an artificial common agreement, be directed by the government to public ends or at least be deterred from the destruction of these ends. Here, it is, of course, not allowed to reason; but one has to obey. In so far as this part of the machine also considers itself as a member of a complete commonwealth, yes even of global society, at times in the quality of a scholar who addresses a public through his writings in the truest sense of the word, he can indeed reason without harming the affairs to which he is attached partly as a passive member. Thus it would be very harmful if an officer, receiving an order from his superiors, wanted to reason openly, while on duty, about the appropriateness or usefulness of this order. He must simply obey. But he cannot justly be banned from making observations as a scholar on the errors in the military service, and from submitting these to his public for judgment. The citizen cannot refuse to pay the taxes imposed upon him; even hasty criticisms of such taxes, where he is called upon to pay them, can be punished as a scandal which could lead to general uprisings. Notwithstanding, exactly the same person does not contravene his civil obligations if, as a scholar, he publicly voices his thoughts on the impropriety or even injustice of such announcements. In the same way, a clergyman is bound to preach his sermon to his pupils and his congregation in accordance with the doctrines of the church he serves, for he was employed by it on that condition. But as a scholar, he has a complete freedom, yes even the vocation to inform the public of all his carefully considered, well-intentioned thoughts on the mistaken aspects of those doctrines, and of his suggestions for a better arrangement of religious and ecclesiastical affairs. And there is anyway nothing in this which the conscience could be accused of. For what he teaches according to his office as a representative of the church is presented by him as something in whose consideration he is not empowered to teach at his own discretion, but which he is employed to expound in a prescribed manner and in someone else's name. He will say: Our church teaches this or that, and these are the arguments it uses. He then extracts as much practical value as possible for his congregation from precepts to which he would not himself subscribe with full conviction, but to whose sermon he can all the same commit himself, since it is not after all wholly impossible that they would contain truth, but in any case at least that nothing opposing to the essence of religion is present in such doctrines. For if he thought he could find anything of this sort in them, he would not be able to administer his office conscientiously and would have to resign. Thus, the use which someone employed as a teacher makes of his reason in the presence of his congregation is simply private, since a congregation, though however large it is, is never any more than a domestic gathering. And considering this, he is not and cannot be free as a priest, since he is acting on an alien order. Conversely, as a scholar addressing the real public, namely the world, through his writings, at times the clergyman making public use of his reason enjoys unlimited freedom to use his own reason and to speak in his own person. For to maintain that the guardians of the people (in spiritual matters) should themselves be immature, is an absurdity which amounts to a perpetuation of absurdities.

But should not a society of clergymen, for example an ecclesiastical synod or a venerable classis (as the Dutch call it), be entitled to commit itself by oath to a certain unalterable symbol, in order to lead and in this manner even to perpetuate a constant guardianship over each of its members, and by means of them over the people? I reply that this is quite impossible. Such a contract, concluded with a view to preventing all further enlightenment of mankind forever, is absolutely null and void, even if it were ratified by the supreme power, by Imperial Diets and the most solemn peace treaties. One age cannot enter into an alliance or oath to put the next age in a position where it would be impossible for it to extend its (primarily so pressing) knowledge and to clear it from errors and generally to make any progress in enlightenment. This would be a crime against human nature, whose original destiny lies precisely in such progressing. The descendants are thus perfectly entitled to dismiss these agreements as unauthorizedly and criminally taken. The touchstone of what can be decided as law for a people, lies in the question: whether a people could impose such a law upon itself? This might be possible, so to speak, in expectation of a better solution for a specified short period in order to introduce a certain order. By giving each citizen, particularly the clergyman, a free hand as a scholar to make publicly, i.e. in writings, comments on the inadequacies of current institutions, while the newly established order would still continue, until public insight into the nature of such matters had progressed and proved itself to the point where, by unification of their voices (if not of all), a proposal could be submitted to the throne, to protect the congregations who had, for instance, agreed to alter their religious establishment in accordance with their own notions of better insight, but without obstructing those who wanted to maintain the old ways. But it is absolutely impermissible to agree, even for a single lifetime, to a permanent religious constitution which no one might publicly question and by that to virtually nullify a phase in man's progress to improvement and to make it fruitless and with that even detrimental to subsequent generations. Although a man can for his own person, and even then only for a limited period, postpone enlightening himself in what falls to him to know, to renounce such enlightenment completely, be it for his person, but even more so for later generations, means violating and trampling underfoot the sacred rights of mankind. But something which a people may not even impose upon itself, a monarch can even less impose upon it; for his legislative authority depends precisely upon his uniting the collective will of the people in his own will. So long as he sees to it that all true or alleged improvements exist within the civil order, he can incidentally leave his subjects to do whatever they find necessary to do for the sake of their salvation, which does not concern him, but nevertheless it concerns him to stop someone from forcibly hindering another from working with all his capabilities on the definition and promotion of his salvation. It indeed detracts from his majesty if he interferes in these affairs by subjecting the writings in which his subjects attempt to sort out their ideas to governmental supervision, as well as if he does so acting upon his own exalted opinions, in which case he exposes himself to the reproach: Caesar non est supra grammaticos, but much more so if he degrades his utmost power so far as to support the spiritual despotism of a few tyrants within his state against the rest of his subjects.

If it is now asked whether we now live in an enlightened age, the answer is: No, but we do live in an age of enlightenment. There is still lacking a lot, as things are at present, that men as a whole would be in a state (or could ever be put in a state) to use their own understanding confidently and well in religious matters, without outside guidance. We simply have distinct indications that the way is now being cleared for them to work freely in this direction, and that the obstacles to universal enlightenment, to man's emergence from his self-incurred immaturity, are gradually becoming fewer. In this respect our age is the age of enlightenment, the century of Frederick.

[A prince who does not regard it as beneath him to say that he considers it his duty, in religious matters, not to prescribe anything to his people, but to allow them complete freedom, a prince who thus even declines to accept the presumptuous title of tolerant, is himself enlightened. He deserves to be praised by a grateful present and posterity as the man who first liberated mankind from immaturity (as far as government is concerned), and who left all men free to use their own reason in all matters of conscience. Under his rule, ecclesiastical dignitaries, notwithstanding their official duties, may in their capacity as scholars freely and publicly submit to the judgment of the world their verdicts and opinions, even if these deviate here and there from orthodox doctrine. This applies even more to all others who are not restricted by any official duties. This spirit of freedom is also spreading abroad, even where it has to struggle with outward obstacles imposed by governments which misunderstand their own function. For such governments can now witness a shining example of how freedom may exist without in the least jeopardizing public concord and the unity of the commonwealth. Men will of their own accord gradually work their way out of barbarism so long as artificial measures are not deliberately adopted to keep them in it.]

I have put the focal point of enlightenment, i.e. of man's emergence from his self-incurred immaturity, mainly into matters of religion, because our rulers have no interest in assuming the role of guardians over their subjects so far as the arts and sciences are concerned and additionally because this kind of immaturity is the most pernicious and dishonorable one of all. But the attitude of mind of a head of state who favors freedom in the arts and sciences extends even further and he realizes: that there is no danger, even considering his legislation, to allow his subjects to make public use of their own reason and to put before the public their thoughts on better ways of drawing up the very same, even with forthright criticism of the current legislation. We have before us a brilliant example of this kind, in which no monarch has yet surpassed the one who we worship.

But only that person who is himself enlightened and has no fear of phantoms, yet who likewise has at hand a well-disciplined and numerous army as a guarantee to public security, can say what no republic would dare to say: Reason as much as you like and about whatever you like, but obey! This reveals to us a strange and unexpected way of human affairs; as are most things, if we consider them in the widest sense, nearly everything is paradoxical in them. A higher degree of civil freedom seems advantageous to a people's intellectual freedom, yet it also sets up insurmountable barriers to it. Conversely, a single degree less of it makes more space for the latter to spread itself out with all its capabilities. If then nature has unwrapped the germ on which it has lavished its most tender care, namely the inclination and vocation to think freely, from this hard shell, it gradually has an effect upon the mentality of the people by which it little by little becomes more able to act freely; and even eventually upon the principles of government, which find it beneficial to treat man, who is now more than a machine, in a manner appropriate to his dignity.

Moses Mendelssohn

Excerpt from Jerusalem: Or on Power and Judaism (1783)

So, here is already demonstrated an essential difference between state and religion. The state gives orders and coerces, religion teaches and persuades. The state prescribes laws, religion commandments. The state has physical power and employs it where it is necessary; the power of religion is love and beneficence. The one abandons the disobedient and expels him; the other receives him in its bosom and seeks to instruct, and not entirely without benefit, or at least to console him, even during the last moments of his earthly life. In one word: civil society, viewed as a moral person, can have the right of coercion, and also has actually obtained this right through the social contract. Religious society lays no claim to the right of coercion, and cannot obtain it by any possible contract. The state possesses perfect, the church merely imperfect rights.

(...)

To conclude this section, I want to repeat the result to which my reflections have led me. State and church have the intention to promote, by means of public measures, human felicity in this life and in the future life. Both act upon man's conviction and action, on principles and application; the state, by means of reasons which are based on the relations between man and man, or between man and nature, and the church, the religion of the state, by means of reasons which are based on the relations between man and God. The state treats man as the immortal son of the earth; religion treats him as the image of his Creator. Principles are free. Convictions, according to their nature, permit no coercion or bribery. They belong to man's cognitive faculty and must be decided by the criterion [literal: standard gauge] of truth or untruth. Good and evil act upon his capability of approval and disapproval.

Fear and hope guide his impulses. Reward and punishment direct his will, spur his vigor, encourage, entice, or deter (him). But if principles are to make man blissful, then they must be neither intimidated nor ingratiate themselves, merely then the judgment by his powers of intellect can be accepted as valid. To admix ideas of good and evil with his deliberations is to permit the matter to be decided by an unauthorized judge. Therefore, neither church nor state has a right to subject men's principles and convictions to any coercion. Neither church nor state is authorized to connect privileges and rights, claims on persons and title to things, with principles and convictions, and to weaken through outside interference the influence that the power of truth has upon the cognitive faculty. Not even the social contract could grant such a right to either state or church. For a contract on things which, according to their nature, are inalienable, is inherently invalid, and cancels itself out. Not even the most sacred oaths can here change the nature of things. Oaths do not generate new duties, (they) are merely solemn confirmations of that to which we are in any case obligated by nature or through a contract. Without duty, an oath is an empty invocation of God, which can be blasphemous, but can in and of itself create no obligation. Moreover, men can swear only to what has the evidence of the external senses, to what they saw, heard, or touched. Perceptions of the internal senses are not objects of oath confirmation. All adjuring and abjuring in reference to principles and doctrines is according to this inadmissible, and if they (the oaths) have been taken, then they oblige to nothing but regret for acting in culpable thoughtlessness. If I swear now to an opinion, I am nonetheless free to disavow it a moment later. The misdeed of taking a vain oath has been committed, even if I retain the opinion; and perjury did not happen if I repudiate it. It must not be forgotten that, according to my principles, the state is not authorized to connect income, offices of honor, and privilege with certain specific doctrines. Regarding the teaching profession, it is its (the state's) duty to appoint teachers who are able to teach wisdom and virtue, and to pass on such useful truths upon which the felicity of human society directly rests. All closer definitions must be left to their (the teachers') best knowledge and conscience where (better: if) endless confusion and collisions of duties should not arise which, in the end, frequently lead even the virtuous into hypocrisy and unscrupulousness. No wrongdoing against the dictates of reason remains unavenged. But what? if the harm has already been done: Suppose the state appoints and pays a teacher for certain specific doctrines. The man later finds these doctrines unfounded. What is he to do? How must he act in order to get out of the tight spot into which an erroneous conscience has put him? Three different ways are open to him here. He locks up the truth in his heart and continues to teach untruth, against his better judgment; he resigns from his office without giving the reasons why this has happened; or, finally, he gives unmistakable witness to the truth, and leaves it to the state to determine what is to become of his office and his suspended salary, or what else he should suffer on account of his invincible love of truth. It seems to me, none of these ways is to be utterly rejected under all circumstances. I can imagine a state of mind in which it is pardonable before the bench of the all-righteous judge if one continues to admix into his otherwise salutary speech of truths beneficial to the public some untruth that, perhaps, on account of an erroneous conscience, has been sanctioned by the state. I would, at any rate, guard against accusing, on this account, an otherwise honest teacher of hypocrisy or Jesuitry, unless I were thoroughly acquainted with this man's circumstances and state of mind—so thoroughly as perhaps no man can ever be with his neighbor's state of mind. Who boasts of having never spoken on such matters differently from what he thought, has either never thought at all, or perhaps, at this very moment, finds it advantageous to brag with an untruth which his heart contradicts. In conclusion with regard to convictions and principles, religion and state agree, both must avoid any semblance of coercion or bribery, and limit themselves to teaching, admonishing, persuading, and reprimanding. But not with regard to actions. The relations between man and man require action as action; the relations between God and man require them only insofar as they lead to convictions. A charitable action does not cease to be charitable, even if it is being coerced. A religious action, however, is only to the extent religious to which it happens out of free will and with appropriate intention. The state can therefore compel charitable actions; it can reward and punish, distribute offices and honors, disgrace and banishment, in order to stir men to actions whose intrinsic goodness does not want to impress itself forcefully enough on their minds. Therefore, the most perfect right as well as the ability to do these things could and must have been granted to the state through the social contract. Therefore, the state is a moral person, which possesses its own goods and privileges, and can act toward them according to (its) pleasing [or: as it pleases]. Divine religion is far from all this. It behaves the same toward actions as toward convictions, for it commands actions merely as tokens of convictions. It is a moral person, but its rights know no coercion. It does not drive (men) with an iron rod; but rather it guides (them) with a rope of love. It draws no sword of revenge, bestows no temporal goods, claims right to no earthly possessions, and claims no external power over any mind for itself. Its weapons are reason and persuasion; its strength is the divine power of truth. The punishments it threatens, just like the rewards, are the effects of love—salutary and beneficial for the very person who suffers them. By these signs I recognize you, daughter of Divinity! Religion! who is in truth the only one who can make us blissful on earth even as in heaven. Excommunication and the right to banish, which the state may occasionally permit itself, are immediately repugnant to the spirit of religion. To banish, to exclude, to turn away the brother who wants to take part in my edification and lift up his heart to God in beneficial sharing together with mine! If religion permits itself no arbitrary punishments, it should least of all allow this torture of the soul which, alas, is perceptible only to a person who truly has religion. Review all the unfortunate ones who always should have been improved by excommunication and damnation. Reader! To whichever visible church, synagogue, or mosque you may belong! See if you will not find more true religion among the host of the excommunicated than among the far greater host of those who excommunicated them. Now, excommunication either has civil consequences or it does not. If it entails civil misery, then it is only a burden to the high-minded man who believes to owe this sacrifice to divine truth. He who has no religion must be a madman if he exposes himself to the least danger for the sake of pleasing a supposed truth. If, however, its consequences are merely of a spiritual nature, as one may wish to persuade himself, they, again, will afflict only the man who has still feelings for this kind of sensation. The irreligious man laughs at such things and remains impenitent. But where is the possibility to separate it from all civil consequences? To grant the church disciplinary power, as I have said elsewhere, it seems to me with justice, to grant the church disciplinary power and to keep civil felicity unoffended, is like the answer of the most supreme judge to the prosecutor: Let him be in your hands; but spare his life! Break the barrel, as the interpreters add, but do not let the wine run out! What ecclesiastical excommunication or ban is without any civil consequences, without any influence, at least, upon the civil reputation, upon the reputation of the expelled and upon the trust by his fellow citizens, without which no one can exercise his occupation and be useful, that is, be civilly happy, to his fellow men? One still invokes the law of nature. Every society, people say, has the right to exclude. Why not also the religious? But I reply: precisely here a religious society constitutes an exception. By means of a higher law, no society can exercise a right which is diametrically opposed to the primary purpose of the society itself. To exclude a dissident, says a worthy clergyman of this city, to expel a dissident from the church means to forbid a sick person a pharmacy. In fact, the most essential purpose of religious societies is mutual edification. By the magic power of sympathy, one wants to transfer truth from the mind to the heart; one wants to vivify, by participating in high sensations, the recognition of reason, which at times is lifeless.

(. . .)

Addition (left out in Chapter 7)

When the heart clings too strongly to sensual pleasures to listen to the voice of reason, when it is on the verge of ensnaring reason itself, then let it be seized here with a tremor of pious enthusiasm, kindled by the fire of devotion, and acquainted with joys of a higher order which outweigh even in this life the joys of the senses. And would you turn away from the door the sick man who is most in need of this medicine, who needs it all the more, the less he feels the necessity, and in his delirium imagines that he is healthy? Should it not rather be your first concern to restore to him this feeling and to call back to life that part of his soul which is, as it were, threatened with gangrene? But instead of doing this, you refuse him all assistance, and let the helpless fellow die a moral death, from which, perhaps, you might have rescued him? A certain Athenian philosopher acted in a much nobler manner and more in accordance with the purposes of his school. An Epicurean came away from his banquet, his senses clouded by the night's debauchery, and his head wreathed with roses. He stepped into the lecture hall of the Stoics, in order to indulge, at the hour of dawn, the last pleasure of an enervated voluptuary—the pleasure of scoffing. The philosopher left him undisturbed, redoubled the fire of his eloquence against the seductions of debauchery, and described with irresistible force the felicity of virtue. The disciple of Epicurus listened, grew attentive, cast down his eyes, tore the wreaths from his head, and became himself an adherent of the Stoa.

Friedrich Schleiermacher

Excerpt from On Religion: Speeches to the Educated Among Its Despisers (1799)

Place yourselves on the highest standpoint of metaphysics and morality, and you all will find that both have the same subject matter with religion, namely the universe and the relationship of people to it. This similarity has for a long time been the reason for some aberrations; as a result, metaphysics and morality has penetrated religion galore, and some of what belongs to religion hid in an improper fashion in metaphysics or morality. Would you really therefore believe that it (religion) would be the same to one of both? I know that your instinct tells you the contrary, and it also arises out of your opinions. For you never admit that it (religion) walks with the firm step of which metaphysics is capable, and you do not forget to observe diligently that there is a good deal of ugly immoral blemishes on its history. If religion is thus to be differentiated, then it must be set apart from those in some manner notwithstanding the common subject matter. It (religion) must treat this subject matter completely differently, express or work out another relationship of humanity to it, have another approach or another goal; for only in this way can that which is similar, according to the subject matter, to something else achieve a particular nature and a distinctive existence. I ask you, therefore, what does your metaphysics do or—if you want to have nothing to do with the outdated name that is too historical for you—your transcendental philosophy? It classifies the universe and partitions it into this being and that (being), explores the reasons for what exists and deduces the necessity of what is real, generates from itself the reality of the world and its laws. Into this area, therefore, religion must not stray too far, it must not have the tendency to state beings and to determine natures, to lose itself in an infinity of reasons and deductions, to seek out final causes and to proclaim eternal truths. And what does your morality do? It develops a system of duties out of the nature of man and (of) his relationship to the universe, it commands and forbids actions with unlimited authority. This also therefore religion must not presume to do, it must not use the universe in order to derive duties and is not permitted to contain a code of laws. "And still it seems that what one calls religion only consists of fragments of these different areas." This is, of course, the common term. I have recently provided you all with doubts about it; it is now time to completely destroy it. The theorists of religion, who aim at knowledge of the nature of the universe and its highest being, whose work it (the universe) is, are metaphysicians; but (they are) well-behaved enough at least not to spurn some morality. The practitioners whose main subject matter is the will of God are moralists, but a little in the manner of metaphysics. You take the idea of the good and bring it into metaphysics as natural law from a being without limits and without needs, and you all take the idea of an original being out of metaphysics and bring it into morality, so that the great work may not remain anonymous, but so that an image of the law-giver could be engraved in view of such a glorious code. But mix and stir as much as you want, this will never go together. You practice an empty game with matters which do not become a unity. You will always only have metaphysics and morality. This mixture of opinions about the highest being or the world, and of the commandments for a human life (or even for two), you call religion! And the instinct, which seeks these concepts, along with the shadowy intuitions, which are the real final penalty of these commandments, you call religiosity! But how then do you dare to take a mere compilation, a chrestomathy for beginners for an integral work, for an individual with its own origin and power? How do you dare to mention it even if it only happens in order to refute it? Why have you not by now long analyzed it into its parts and discovered the shameful plagiarism? I would like to alarm you with some Socratic questions and to bring you to confess that even in the most common things you probably even recognize the principles according to which the similar must be compiled and the particular subordinated to the universal, and that you only do not want to apply these principles here in order to be able to make fun of a serious subject with the world. Where then is the unity in all of this? Where does the unifying principle lie for this dissimilar material! If it is an attractive force on its own, then you must confess that religion is the highest in philosophy and that metaphysics and morality are only subordinate divisions of it; for that in which two varied but opposed concepts become one can only be the higher under which the other two belong. If this binding principle lies in metaphysics, if you have recognized for reasons that are related to it (metaphysics) a highest being as the moral lawgiver, then annihilate practical philosophy anyway, and admit that it and with it, religion is only a small chapter of the theoretical (philosophy). If you want to claim the opposite, then metaphysics and religion must be swallowed up by morality, for which indeed nothing may any longer be impossible after it has learned to believe, and in its old age has acquiesced in preparing a quiet little space in its innermost sanctuary for the secret embraces of two self-loving worlds. Or do you have the audacity to say that the metaphysical in religion does not depend on the moral, nor the latter on the former? (or that) there is a remarkable parallelism between the theoretical and the practical, and that to perceive and represent this is religion? To be sure, the solution to this (parallelism) can lie neither in practical philosophy, for it does not take care of it, nor in theoretical philosophy, for it strives eagerly to pursue and annihilate it (the parallelism) as far as possible, as this is anyway its duty. But I think that you, driven by this need, have already been seeking for some time a highest philosophy in which these two categories unite and are always about to find it; and religion would suggest itself here! And philosophy, should it really have to flee toward religion, as the opponents of philosophy like to maintain? Be careful what you say there. With all this either you will get a religion that stands far above philosophy as it is situated at present, or you must be honest enough to give back to both parts of it (philosophy) what belongs to them and (must) admit that you are still ignorant regarding religion. I do not want to encourage you to the former, for I want to take no position that I could not maintain, but you will very likely be able to do the latter. Let us treat each other honestly. You do not like religion; we assumed that already earlier. But in conducting an honest battle against it, which is supposedly not completely without effort, you still do not want to have fought against a shadow like the one which we have grappled with. It (religion) must surely be something characteristic that could have arisen in the human heart, something thinkable from which a term can be formulated about which one can speak and argue, and I find it very unjust if you yourselves stitch together something untenable out of such disparate things, call it religion, and then make so much needless trouble about it. You will deny that you went about it deceitfully. You will call upon me to roll out all the ancient sources of religion, since I have, after all, already rejected systems, commentaries and apologies, from the beautiful compositions of the Greeks to the holy writings of the Christians, whether I would not find the nature of the gods and their will everywhere, and (would not find) everywhere persons praised as holy and blessed who acknowledge the former and fulfill the latter. But that is exactly what I have already said to you, that religion never appears in a pure state, all these are only the foreign parts that cling to it, and it should be our business to free it from them. If the bodily world provides you with no original matter as pure product of nature, you would then, as has happened to you here in the intellectual (world), take very rough things for something simple, but it is only the infinite goal of the analytical art to depict such a (matter). And in spiritual things the original cannot be created any other way than if you create it by a genuine creation in yourself, and even then only for the moment in which you create it. I beg you that you make sense of it for yourself, you will be reminded of it continuously. But concerning the records and autographs of the religions, this admixture of metaphysics and morality is not only an inevitable fate for them, but rather an artificial disposition and a high intent. That which is given as the first and the last is not always the true and the highest. If you could only read between the lines! All holy writings are like the modest books which were common in our modest fatherland some time ago (and) which dealt under a meager title with important things. Of course, they only announce metaphysics and morality, and like to turn back at the end to that which they have announced, but you are expected to split this shell. Just as the diamond lies completely sealed in bad material, but truly not in order to stay hidden, but rather to be found all the more reliably. To make proselytes out of non-believers, that lies deeply in the character of religion. Whoever shares the one belonging to him can have no other purpose, and therefore it is indeed hardly a pious betrayal, but a proper method to start with that and to appear to be concerned about that for which the purpose is already there, so that it can creep in occasionally and unnoticed, for which he only ought to be made excited. It is, because all sharing of the religion cannot be anything else but rhetorical, a smart exploitation of the listeners to introduce them into such good company. But this tool has not only reached its purpose but has overtaken (it), by hiding its true being under this shell, even from you. Therefore, it is finally time to grasp the matter by the other end, and to pick (it) up by the sharp contrast, in which religion stands against morality and metaphysics. That is what I wanted. You have troubled me with your common term; it is dismissed, I hope, now do not interrupt me again. In order to take its property into possession, religion hereby renounces all claims on anything that belongs to them, and gives all back that one has forced on religion. It does not desire to determine and to explain the universe according to its nature as metaphysics, it does not desire to further form and to complete it from a power of freedom and of the godlike capriciousness of people, as (does) morality. Its essence is neither thoughts nor actions but rather intuition and sensation. It wants to examine the universe and devoutly listen to it in its own representations and actions, it wants to be in childlike passivity seized and filled from its immediate influences. Therefore, it is set against both in everything that constitutes its nature and in everything that characterizes its effects. The latter see in the whole universe only man as the center of all relations, as the condition of all being and as reason for all becoming; it wants to see the infinite in man as much as in all other individual and finite things, its impression, its depiction.

Karl Barth

Excerpt from The Epistle to the Romans (1919)

For I am not ashamed of the Gospel. For it is the power of God for salvation for everyone who believes, for the Jew first and also for the Greek. For the righteousness of God manifests itself in it: from (his) faith to the belief (of men), as has been written: the one made just by faith will live!

The gospel is not in any case a thing that must be timidly concealed in the world capital. The readers need not feel inhibited or shy with it amid the rivalry of religions and philosophies, just as Paul also will not. It endures and it beats this rivalry. It is not a truth, but the truth. Whoever recognizes it should not for a second be worried about its victory, but he should above all be proud that he is allowed to recognize it. He doesn't need to advocate and to support it, like the others who want to be supported, who advocate human spiritual movements and religious enterprises, but it (the gospel) advocates for and supports him. The ones called by Christ (Rom 1:6), who are embarrassed with God, who are afraid for the course of their cause—an impossibility! God would have to be ashamed of us, if He were not God, but not the other way around. God goes; we do not go.

Power emanated from God in the resurrection of Christ from the dead. That is what is behind us, totally apart from everything we are, think, and do. No theory is erected here, no abstract morality is preached, no new cult is recommended. All such things that may arise among us are human accessories, dangerous religious remnants, regrettable misunderstandings, not the matter itself. If it only concerned these things, then we should soon be "ashamed," then we would not be unrivaled, then we would have to succumb to the world as soon as its opposing forces would come into play. For in the world there are also forces (8:38), and they are stronger than our ideas. But we have not ideas behind us but the power of all powers, which is therefore also the idea of all ideas: the power of God. Our subject matter is our knowledge of God realized in Christ, in which God is approaching us not objectively, but directly and creatively, in which we are not merely looking, but are being looked upon, not merely understanding but being understood, not merely comprehending but being comprehended. Our idea of God is the living arm of God, under which nature, history, humanity, we ourselves (we ourselves, as those in possession of the firstfruits of the Spirit, Rom 8:23, first!) are restored. The origin, which was always asserted, known, missed, and painfully searched for, opened up his mouth again. The divine word, "Let there be," was again sounded, heard, and has come true. So nothing new, but rather the oldest: nothing particular, but rather the most common; nothing historical, but rather the requirement of all history! That which was always veiled in the not understood natural phenomena (Rom 1:20) and sealed in the unheard prophetic words (Rom 16:25–26) is now initially manifested, so that it is now again in the beginning in the eyes and ears of men and thereby in the world, of which the human is the head and center. And in this respect, not the old familiar, but rather a new, not the common, but rather the most particular, not a mere requirement, but rather history itself: the dawning of a new age, the creation of the world in which God again has power. This power of God stands behind us. It is the gospel that we preach. It is our cause.

The now arising power of God is salvation. For with the whole present world man finds himself in captivity. A turning away of man from God (Rom 1:18; 5:12) alienated him from his provenance and made God an adversary to him. The once bound in God playing natural and historical world powers were made masterless and brought him and all creatures under the law of its own turpitude (Rom 1:24) and of death (Rom 5:12). God had now chopped up the knot of this hopeless and disconcerted situation, which was to be overcome by no morality and to be whitewashed through no religiosity, through the real act of the inauguration of a messianic and godly-earthly (hi)story. In Christ, human beings are turned back to God, and through this the foundation is laid to the reconciliation of all that is lost. We are already standing in the beginning of this event, and a wide perspective opens itself up to a state in the freedom of God (Rom 5:2; 8:18). No longer under judgment, but under grace, no longer in sin, but in righteousness, no longer in death, but in life, that is the way of salvation that the power of God now wants to go with us and will one day go with the whole world.

Now with us! It is about believing in the power of God. The "Centrum Paulinum!" (Bengel). The coming world does not come mechanically but organically! And the creative agent which must therefore come into effect is an anticipation of the goal which should be achieved: the free union of man with God, as it was accomplished in Christ, and how it becomes possible and actualized in those who are called by Christ. When someone says "yes" to the divine "yes" which was spoken to him in Christ when he makes use of the new eyes and ears which are bestowed to him through the power of God, and when the loyalty of God who cannot stop interacting with the world and with people, meets a newly awoken reciprocal loyalty, that is "faith." There salvation arises. There the world-turn, based upon Christ, continues. This is the commandment and the invitation that is now being announced with the gospel to all peoples, so that they may obey it (Rom 1:5). It is well understood that the warmth of feeling, the force of decision and conviction, the efficiency of personal sentiment are not important features of the process of faith. It essentially concerns that which is spiritual, not just what goes on in the soul aspect of man.

The believers form the new international people of God that now rallies around the power of the resurrection as if around its (own) cause. Everyone can and should take part. Faith has become the question of the world. As the heirs of the promise and the sealed words of the prophets, the Jews had an advantage. The Messiah was born within their midst; they were the first to have heard his message (Rom 10; 14–15). But then it broke out to the heathens. The question of whether something is "of the church" or "of the world" is no longer the question. The coming world does not know these barriers. Only one thing determines the outcome now: if the again revealed power of God will now find faith or unfaith.

Thus, the conscious mind and the confidence, with which the Christian positions himself toward his matter, is based on the creative, redeeming, world-covering power of God. The power of God is this—of that there should be no ambiguity—not one of the powers of the world that create nothing new, but ultimately always lead us around in a circle. For that (thing), which transformed Christ into power for us, is not human greatness, neither in the good or bad sense, but the righteousness of God revealed again in him. God acts in accordance with himself, when he reaches out with his saving hand to the world in this One (Christ). For it has reappeared in this One on earth, the original, immediate, normal relationship of man to God, the relationship that God is in agreement with and that corresponds with his will. In him, God as he is can acknowledge himself to mankind and can once again recognize himself in the image of mankind. This righteousness of God that was in Christ is the mystery of the power of his resurrection, it is also the requirement for the salvation of the world from damnation, which has started by means of this power. For only the regained immediateness of man to God in the obedience of Christ was able to blow open the door of the grave, this alone makes salvation real, (makes it) to a distinctively new movement, protects it from the return of all human movements to new sin and new death. It is therefore the love, with which God now turns again to the world, not a sentimentality, through which he would fall into contradiction with himself and into contradiction with the fact of the human condition, but rather (by giving back to the human being in Christ its "just" condition), it is the proclamation and establishing of his own most inner truth on earth, God no longer endures the injustice that is among men; he wants his justice to apply again. Therefore, in this sense, he speaks in Christ the redeeming word by which man is called from abroad back into the homeland. It is therefore not a self-empowered, riot-like taking over of the Divine from men, by which we would offend the holiness of God, if we believe in the power of the resurrection of Christ and look forward to the coming salvation; but rather it is recognition of God in the strictest sense that leads us to this (as opposed to all human arbitrariness but also (opposed to) to all human morality and religiosity) "the recognition of the clarity of God in the face of Jesus Christ" (2 Cor 4:6), bending before the innermost being of God, obedience as Christ was obedient. And therefore, because it deals not with just anything but rather with the righteousness of God, we are not mistaken in the confidence that God himself is leading our cause. But it is a revelation through which God speaks this resolving word and to which we owe this recognition. It is not to be taken for granted that the relationship between the "wrath," the "wickedness and injustice" (Rom 1:18) between him and us is cancelled, that the tragically sterile seriousness of morality and religion is abolished, that the power of God for salvation becomes effective in the world. It is a miracle that the sinful and moribund man, just as he is, may hear the verdict in Christ, that he is acceptable to God, and that through this verdict (that in the mouth of the God of truth is a creative word), if he wants to hear it, he will be made righteous and alive. We stand therefore especially in reference to the innermost essence of the power of God before an actual turn of the times, before the revelation of a mystery, "that throughout the ages was kept secret" (Rom 16:26). For even the prophets could only witness before closed doors the justification from which life comes and prophesy its revelation. But now it reveals itself, by voicing the verdict and the recognition, through which the person is transposed again to the original and positive relationship with God, in the historical event of the appearance of Christ. Therefore, especially the content of the gospel is a discovery to us, not a general truth, and seen from God's perspective: the subject of a deed, not of a dormant attribute, so far as the possibility of this discovery was always available for man and the willingness to this deed (was always available) on the side of God. The reality of the justification of God in Christ is the newness of the gospel.

And that is now simply in the free unification with God, in which the faithfulness of God finds belief in man or in which God again believes man and encounters a faithfulness. This new thing comes from heaven, and on earth, it puts down roots. The acting of

God in a deed of obedience of man, an acknowledging and accepting, a being seized and understanding—that is the devout behavior toward revelation. What, "throughout ages has been kept a secret," was only in God and not in man, that now breaks through from God to man, happens to man as the freest deed of God, and still it arises from him as the discovery of his very own being. Thus, God himself creates the organ of his power on earth. He, the faithful one, has reentered in the faith of the believers into a dynamic and creative relationship to his world.

With that the prophetic prophecy comes true in our matter: "The one who is made just by faithfulness will live." One could also say: "The one who has become just by faith"; it is the same; for it deals with a making by God, and about a becoming of man in One. Now God's righteousness is again established on earth through the liberating Word, that in Christ has been spoken, and through the recognition, that has come about in the Christians. And as under the ruling divine "wrath" and in the sphere of human "wickedness and injustice" death had to have the highest authority in Eden, so is through this establishment of divine justice the nucleus/seed of life again given into history and into nature. Now, the divine course of history grows into the course of human history. Now the new creation has started, in which death will be no more.

Dietrich Bonhoeffer

Excerpt from Discipleship (1937)

Cheap grace is the mortal enemy of our church. Our struggle today deals with costly grace. Cheap grace means grace as cheap goods, squandered forgiveness, squandered comfort, squandered sacrament. Grace as inexhaustible repertory of the church out of which is poured out unhesitatingly and immeasurably with frivolous hands. Grace without price, without cost. For that is precisely the nature of grace, that the bill is paid in advance for all time. As a result of the paid bill, everything can be had for free. Infinitely large are the raised costs, infinitely great, therefore, the possibilities for their use and their waste. For what would grace be which is not cheap grace?

Cheap grace means grace as doctrine, as principle, as a system; (grace) means forgiveness of sin as common truth, means love of God as the Christian idea of God. The one who affirms it (grace), already has forgiveness of his sin. The church of this doctrine of grace shares already in this grace through it. In this church the world finds cheap coverage of its sins, from which it does not repent and from which it certainly does not even wish to be free. Therefore, cheap grace is a denial of God's living word, a denial of the incarnation of God's word.

Cheap grace means the justification of the sin and not the sinner. Because grace alone does everything, therefore all can stay the same. "So our doing is for nothing." World remains world, and we remain sinners, "even in the best life." It should also live thus, the Christian like the world, he should equate himself to the world in all things and should venture by no means, through the heresy of enthusiasts, the Anabaptists, and similar minded people, to lead another life in grace rather than in sin. He should beware of raging against the grace, of defiling the great and cheap grace and of establishing new religions of the letter through the attempt of an obedient life under the commandments of Jesus Christ! The world is justified through grace, therefore—for the sake of the seriousness of this grace!, in order to not oppose this irreplaceable grace—the Christian should live like the rest of the world! Surely, he would like to do something extraordinary, it is for him without any doubt the most difficult of sacrifices to not do this, but to have to live worldly. But he has to make the sacrifice, to practice the self-renunciation, to not differ with his life from the world. Insofar he has to let grace truly be grace, so that he does not destroy the faith of the world in this cheap grace. But the Christian be in his reality, in this necessary sacrifice, which he has to do for the sake of the world—no, for the sake of grace!—comforted and secure (securus) in the possession of this grace, which does everything by itself. Thus, the Christian should not follow, but he is comforted by grace! That is cheap grace as justification of the sin, but not as justification of the repentant sinner who renounces his sin and repents; not forgiveness of sin, which separates from the sin. Cheap grace is the kind of grace, which we have with ourselves. Cheap grace is the preaching of forgiveness without repentance, it is baptism without church discipline, it is the Lord's Supper without confession of sins, it is absolution without personal confession. Cheap grace is grace without discipleship, grace without the cross, grace without the living, incarnate Jesus Christ.

Costly grace is the hidden treasure in a field for the sake of which man goes and with joy sells everything that he had; the precious pearl for whose price the merchant sells all his goods. It is the kingship of Christ for the sake of which a man tears out the eye that offends him, the call of Christ for which the disciple abandons his nets and follows. Costly grace is the gospel that must always be sought after, the gift that must be asked for, the door that must be knocked on. It is costly, because it calls to discipleship, it is grace, because it calls to discipleship of Jesus Christ. It is costly, because it costs man his life, it is grace because that way it bestows life to him in the first place. It is costly, because it condemns sin, grace, because it justifies the sinner. Grace is costly above all, because it was costly for God, because it cost God the life of his Son, "You have been bought at a price," and because what is costly to God cannot be cheap to us. It is above all grace, because to God his Son was not too costly [in exchange] for our life, but he sacrificed him for us. Costly grace is the incarnation of God.

Costly grace is grace as the sanctuary of God that has to be sheltered from the world, which may not be thrown to the dogs, it is therefore grace as living word, God's word which he himself utters as it pleases him. It reaches us as a gracious call in the discipleship of Jesus, it comes as a forgiving word to the scared mind and to the crushed heart. Costly is the grace because it forces man under the yoke of the discipleship of Jesus Christ, it is grace that Jesus says: "My joke is easy and my burden is light."

Two times Peter received the call "Follow me!" It was the first and the last word of Jesus to his disciple (Mark 1:17; John 21:22). His whole life lies between these two calls. The first time Peter had left, following Jesus's call, at the Sea of Galilee his nets and his profession and had followed him at his word. The last time the resurrected one meets him in his old profession, again at the Sea of Galilee, and once again he says: "Follow me!" Between them lay a whole life as a disciple in the discipleship of Christ. At its center stood the acknowledgement of Jesus as the Christ of God. Three times one and the same was announced to Peter, at the beginning, at the end, and in Caesarea Philippi, namely that Christ is his Lord and God. It is the same grace of Christ which calls him: "Follow me!" and which reveals itself in the acknowledgement of the Son of God.

Three times grace continued on Peter's way, the One grace three times announced differently. Therefore, it was Christ's own grace and surely not grace which the disciple bestowed upon himself. It was the same grace of Christ that led the disciple to leave everything for the sake of discipleship, which brought about the acknowledgement in him which had to appear as blasphemy to the whole world, which called the unfaithful Peter into the last fellowship of martyrdom and thereby forgave him all his sins. Grace and discipleship belong for the life of Peter insolubly together. He received the costly grace. With the spread of Christianity and the increasing secularization of the church, the recognition of costly grace was gradually lost. The world had been Christianized, grace had become the common good of a Christian world. It could be obtained cheaply. But the Roman Church retained a remainder of the initial insight. It was significant that the monkhood did not separate itself from the church and that the wisdom of the church bore the monkhood. Here was at the edge of the church the place where the insight was kept awake that grace is costly, that grace includes discipleship. Men left everything that they had for the sake of Christ and tried to follow the strict commandment of Jesus in daily practice. That way the monastic life became a living protest against the secularization of Christianity, against the cheapening of grace. By enduring this protest and by not letting it come to a last uprising, the church relativized it, yes, it gained even from it the justification for its own secularized life; for now the monastic life became the special achievement of individuals to which the mass of church people could not be obligated. The fatal limitation of the commandments of Jesus in their application to a specific group of especially qualified men led to a differentiation between a highest performance and a lowest performance of Christian obedience. With that it had been achieved to point out the secularization of the church with every further attack and (point out) the possibility of the monastic way in the church next to which then the other possibility of the easier way appeared by all means justified. Thus, the reference to the original understanding of costly grace, as it should be maintained in the Roman Church by the monkhood, had in a paradoxical manner to be again the last justification for the secularization of the church. With all that, the significant error of the monkhood lay not in that it took—with all content-related misunderstandings of the will of Jesus—the way of grace by way of strict discipleship. Rather the monkhood distanced itself significantly from the Christian way by letting its way become a voluntary special achievement of a few and with that ascribed to it as a special merit (way). When God through his servant Martin Luther in the Reformation raised again the gospel of the pure, costly grace, he led Luther through the monastery. Luther was a monk. He had left everything and wanted to follow Christ in complete obedience.

He forsook the world and began doing Christian work. He learned obedience to Christ and his church because he knew that only the obedient can believe. The call into the monastery cost Luther the full commitment of his life. Luther failed in this because of God Himself. God showed him through the Scriptures that discipleship is not a meritorious extra performance of individuals but a divine commandment to all Christians. The humble work of discipleship had become a meritorious work of the saints in the monkhood. The self-renunciation of the disciple [literal: follower] unveiled itself here as the last spiritual self-assertion of the pious. With that the world had broken into the middle of the monastic life and was at work again in the most dangerous way. Monastic escapism had been exposed as great attachment to the world. He saw in the breakdown of the monastic world outstretched the saving hand of God in Christ. He took it with the faith that "our doing is in vain anyway, even in the best life." It was a costly grace that bestowed itself on him, it broke his whole existence. He had to leave his nets behind once again and follow. The first time, when he went into the monastery, he had left everything behind, except for himself, his pious Ego. This time even that was taken from him. He did not follow based on his own merit but because of God's grace. It had not been told to him: you have sinned but that is now all forgiven, continue to stay where you were and comfort yourself with forgiveness! Luther had to leave the monastery and (to go) back into the world, not because the world is in itself good or holy but because the monastery was itself nothing but the world. Luther's way from the monastery back into the world meant the sharpest attack which had been led against the world since original Christianity. The rejection that the monk had handed the world was "a walk in the park" compared to the rejection that the world underwent through the one who had returned to it. Now the attack came head-on. Now, discipleship of Jesus had to be lived in the midst of the world. What had been practiced under the special circumstances and simplifications of the monasterial life as an extra achievement had now become the necessary and commanded practice for every Christian in the world. Complete obedience to the commandment(s) of Jesus had to be performed in daily professional life. With that the conflict between the life of the Christian and the life of the world deepened in an unforeseeable way. The Christian got uncomfortably close to the world. It was close combat. One cannot misunderstand Luther's action more fatally than with the opinion that Luther had with the discovery of the gospel of the pure grace a dispensation for the obedience proclaimed to the commandment of Jesus in the world; that the reformatory discovery had been the canonization, the justification of the world through forgiving grace.

The worldly profession of the Christian rather receives its justification according to Luther only because in it the protest against the world is registered with final severeness. Only so far as the worldly profession of the Christian is practiced in the discipleship of Jesus, it has received from the gospel a new justification. Not justification of sin but justification of the sinner was the reason for Luther's return from the monastery. Costly grace had been bestowed upon Luther. It was grace because it was water for the thirsty land, comfort for the fear, liberation from the servitude of the self-imposed way, and forgiveness of all sins. The grace was costly because it did not dispense from the work but infinitely intensified the call into discipleship. But precisely where it was costly, there it was grace, and where it was grace, there it was costly. This was the secret of the gospel of the Reformation, the secret of the justification of the sinner.

Othmar Keel & Christoph Uehlinger

Excerpt from God, Goddesses, and God Symbols (2015)

§112. The so-called "United Monarchy," an era that was at times celebrated and held up as the ideal age for Israel in the redacted religious transmission written largely from the Judean perspective, came, as we know, to an abrupt end with the death of Solomon (ca. 925 BC). From the vantage point of cultural history, the Iron Age IIA thus is a relatively brief episode in the history of the region. The following Iron Age IIB, which lasts from about 925 BC until the last third of the eighth century, encompasses the duration that continues for about two centuries during which time Israel and Judah existed next to one another as separate states, surrounded by the other nation-states that were now again themselves independent: Moab, Ammon, Aram-Damascus, the southern Phoenician city-states of Tyre and Sidon, and the Philistine league of cities.

In addition to numerous points of continuity in residential architecture, burial customs, handicraft, etc., archaeological research of the Iron Age IIB documents as a particularly noteworthy innovation and unique contribution an obvious tendency to monumental architecture in the cities. The local monarchies took great pains to show off their wealth, especially in the regional and district capitals. In addition to the predominant palaces, which supported the necessary functions of administration and representation, military fortifications were built in greater numbers, as well. Garrisons and barracks were to be found for permanent military forces in the larger centers. Massive fortifications and measures taken to secure the water supply in case of siege (e.g., at Hazor, Megiddo,

Gezer, and el-Jib) clearly demonstrate a need for taking defensive measures to ensure security. Against the background of numerous narratives in the book of Kings that tell of wars with Aram and Moab, as well as about the animosity between Israel and Judah, it is not hard to imagine that defensive measures must have been a priority, especially at the beginning of the Iron Age IIB.

The reasons for the loss—which occurred already during Solomon's lifetime—of the vassal regions that had been subjugated by David and for the breakup of the larger state of Israel into two smaller states are too complex to be discussed here in detail. According to 1 Kings 12, the unequal distribution of taxes and the compulsory service for the Davidic kings who resided in Jerusalem played a decisive role. That the northern tribes, despite their seemingly archaic slogan, "To your tents, O Israel!" (1 Kgs 12:16; cf. 2 Sam 20:1), did not question the appropriateness of a monarchical form of government in principle and even constituted their own state as a monarchy, can be explained against the background of the well-advanced reurbanization of the entire country that had been taking place ever since the end of the eleventh century and it also points toward the leading role taken by the urban elite in the Israelite independence movement. If the description in 1 Kings 11–12 is correct, then even Egypt played an important role in the events that led to the ultimate separation of the Northern and Southern Kingdoms.

The "angularly stylized" group of seals (see above, § 83), the ongoing use of Amun scarabs (§ 84), and the presence of the "striking god" in Gezer (§84, note 92) all show clearly that the cultural influence of Egypt remained considerable during Iron Age IIA, at least along the southern Palestinian coastal plain. The first pharaoh of the twenty-second Dynasty, Sheshonq I (944–923 BC), apparently took great pains to undermine the concentration of power in Jerusalem and to establish himself in Palestine politically during the second half of the tenth century. Rebels pursued by Solomon, such as the "Edomite" (or Aramean?) Hadad (1 Kgs 11:14–25) or the Ephraimite Jeroboam, found political asylum initially in the court of Sheshonq (1 Kgs 11:40, 12:2). Just a few years after Solomon's death, Sheshonq undertook a military campaign, not only against Judah (1 Kgs 14:25f.) but against Jeroboam as well, and—even if only for a short time—with some success, as is demonstrated by a fragment of a victory stele with the cartouche of that pharaoh that was found at Megiddo and was originally from Str. IV A (illus. 194; Lamon/Shipton 1939, 60f.; see Ussishkin 1990, 71–74.[1]

One may wonder whether this campaign might have even been punitive action against a former protégé. The assumption suggests itself when one considers that, according to 1 Kings 12:28, Jeroboam tied his plan for autonomy announced before the young bull images in Bethel and Dan (see below, §119) to an exodus tradition that was critical of Egypt. Be that as it may: Sheshonq died shortly afterward, and his successors did not continue his aggressive policies, so that a relatively stable system of small states could establish itself in Palestine for about two hundred years.

§113. The following survey of documents that are relevant from a religio-historical perspective will need to pursue not only the question about continuity with previous developments (esp. §§114ff.) but will also have to discuss the question of whether the iconography and epigraphy can deliver clues of any specific religious peculiarities regarding the new parallel existence of small independent states. Egypt still remained the cultural center of the entire region and clear traces of a fascination with that great power situated on the Nile can be found everywhere, but the two states that are our primary focus, Israel and Judah, each fostered their own relationship with Egypt. After the kingdoms were split, Judah was relegated to a rather insignificant rump state situated off the main trade routes and was clearly dominated at times by Israel as under Jehoash ben Jehoahaz and Jeroboam II (see 2 Kgs 13f. and below, §146), Judah experienced a period of cultural stagnation that lasted at first into the middle of the eighth century. By contrast, because of its close political and economic ties with its northern neighbors, especially the southern Phoenician cities of Tyre and Sidon and Aramean Damascus, Israel maintained control of the major trade routes that passed through its country. From the middle of the ninth century, it regularly joined with the Phoenician cities and with the Arameans in anti-Assyrian coalitions, a clear indication of common political and economic interests.

It cannot be surprising that the differing geopolitical ties of the two states would show up in the area of iconography, as well. In Judah, iconography was generally limited at first to the continued use of indigenous motifs (see below, §§114 ff.) and to provincial adaptations of Egyptian royal symbols (§§156ff.). Specifically "religious" themes were received in Judah only late in the eighth century, influenced perhaps by craftsmen who had resettled there from the north (§§160ff.). By contrast, in the especially productive Israelite/Phoenician craft of the North, from the beginning of the ninth century on, much greater independence and a greater self-confidence can be seen in the use of the religious symbols inherited from Egypt (§§148ff.). At the same time, Syrian-"Canaanite" traditions and motifs were attested in the north that are generally absent in Judah (§§122ff.).

Adaptations of Egyptian motifs, as well as Syrian-"Canaanite" motifs, find very prominent and characteristic expression during Iron Age IIB in the glyptic art (both anepigraphic and on name seals) and on ivory carvings. The latter had enjoyed great popularity already during the Late Bronze Age in Canaan (see above, §§37f.). Their production had been interrupted, however, by the decline of urban culture and the crisis in international trade. Phoenician-Israelite craftsmanship gave it new impetus during Iron Age IIB. This is often qualified simply as "Phoenician." In fact, during the first half of the first millennium, Phoenicia was one of the most active centers for the production and trade of luxury goods using a clearly Egyptian style, such as metal bowls, ivory carvings, and similar precious goods and at least some of these products of craftsmanship that have been found in Israel, such as a decorated bronze bowl from Megiddo Str. IV A

(Lamon/Shipton 1939, pl. 115.12), may have been imported from Phoenicia. But there seem to also have been workshops in the Northern Kingdom of Israel in which these products of craftsmanship, especially ivories and seals, were produced[2]. For that reason, it is probably more correct, rather than speaking of a Phoenician "influence" on the Northern Kingdom of Israel, to refer to a "kinship between cultures of the two regions" (Parayre 1990, 289). This kinship is also clearly reflected in the realm of linguistics and epigraphy. The Israelite language was closer to Phoenician (both of them being major Canaanite "dialects") than the Judahite language (a "peripheral," more conservative dialect of Canaanite, comparable to Ammonite and Moabite dialects). Conversely, emphasis on this kinship should however not lead to no longer want to recognize any differences between the Phoenician and Israelite cultures[3].

With regard to the dating of the Phoenician/Israelite crafts, it is being discussed whether ivory carving began to flourish again already in the ninth century (Barnett 1982, 46–55) or came into existence only after the extinction of the Syrian elephant population in the eighth century, when the ivory carving in central Syria (e.g., in Damascus) had difficulties to gain access to the raw material, whereas the coastal regions would have still been able to get ivory from Egypt (I. Winter 1976, 15f.). The only fairly large collection of Iron Age IIB ivory and bone carvings from Palestine was found in Samaria. The stratigraphic context of its assemblage does not permit sure dating either to the ninth or to the eighth century. Even literary references to Samaria's luxurious ivories are of little help. Relevant biblical texts refer to the ninth century (1 Kgs 22:39 is probably a reference taken from annals for the time of Ahab, who was married to the daughter of a king of Tyre) as well as to the eighth century (Amos 3:12–15; 6:4, ca. 750 BC; on the whole topic, see I. Winter 1981, 109–115, 123–127; H. Weippert 1988, 652–660).

Phoenician/Israelite *anepigraphic seal amulets*, mostly scaraboids, start in fact already in the ninth century. The engraving is very shallow, and they are embellished with inner drawings, identifiable by their use of schematic parallel lines. Apart from a few exceptions, the decorations on their base are organized vertically whereby several registers are arranged one above the other, being separated by horizontal lines, or else the impression of registers is created by motifs that are placed one above the other without any line demarcations. Regarding the content, Egyptian solar motifs dominate these seals (§§148ff.).

Inscribed name seals represent a class of monuments that also appears again in the Levant at the end of the ninth century and at the beginning of the eighth century. It concerns seals which are characterized by carrying along with the iconographic motif the names of the male or female owner, usually preceded by the *lamed* that identifies ownership. The name of the owner's father is frequently added, generally but not always combined with *bn*, "son of" or *bt*, "daughter of." Sometimes a title or an indication of occupation is provided also (for a general overview, see Lemaire 1988; Sass 1993).[4]

The following material will be grouped according to iconographic aspects. The discussion of religio-historical issues can occasionally be supplemented from now on by epigraphic sources which start to flow more amply by the second half of the ninth century (§§125ff.). But since the inscriptional materials are usually much better known and are discussed in scholarly literature again and again, usually without any attention being paid to non-literary documentation, we will highlight what can be learned from the iconography, which is after all the primary reason for this book. After a glance at the essential similarities of the religious concepts based on Israel and Judah's iconographical records (§§114–118), their specific characteristics will be sketched out, as well.

Wolfgang Zwickel

Excerpt from The Temple of Solomon (1999)

The history of the Solomonic Temple stretches from its construction in the tenth century until its destruction 587 BC. During this long timeframe, theology, as it was represented by the priests in Jerusalem, was not completely constant. The previous chapters have demonstrated that there was quite an openness to cultic innovations, e.g., at the time of the introduction of the cult of burnt offerings. On the other hand, there were also considerations in the eighth century about how the picture prohibition could be maintained if YHWH was shown with animal symbols. But the political circumstances changed significantly in the course of history. In the tenth century BC, Jerusalem was still a city remote from major trade routes and therefore in the shadow of political interests. Since the 8th BC, Judah was politicaly dependent on the Assyrians and had to pay tributes regularly. At this time at the latest an increase of trade between Judah and Egypt, Mesopotamia and Saudi-Arabia can be observed. The intensifying trade relations caused an increase in wealth in Judah and Jerusalem. On the other hand, this provided more varied cultural contacts. The temple of Jerusalem had already been an almost multi-cultural building in the 10th century: for the most part built by a Phoenician with strong Phoenician, Egyptian, but also Canaaic influences.

Since the 8th century BC, the foreign influences would have been much more current, especially from the Mesopotamic area. The political dependency on the Assyrians surely led to not only finding their culture but also their religion attractive. Even though large parts of the population remained devoted YHWH followers, foreign influences also crept into the YHWH belief. For the YHWH followers of those times this was also an intellectual challenge. With the infiltration of foreign influences into the YHWH belief, they were challenged to question the *proprium* of their own belief system. What was compatible with the YHWH belief system and what had to be rejected? It is not a coincidence that during the second half of the eighth century prophets like

Amos, Hosea, Isaiah, and Micah emerged that called for a greater differenciation to foreign cultures. In the 7th and 6th century BC it is in particular dtr [i.e., Deuteronomic or Deuteronomistic] circles that increasingly pose the question of a pure YHWH belief. They could not agree with the dominant reality at that time. Wide circles of the population combined too many foreign influences with the traditional YHWH belief. The theology of the Deuteronomists was likely hard to comprehend by many other people at that time. In search of the pure YHWH belief, elements were now deemed to be heathen that had been seen as a legitimate part of the YHWH belief for centuries. For example, in dtr criticism the massebes were judged (Deut 7:5; 12:3; 2 Kings 3:2; etc.), even though a stone like this was understood to be the origin of the holiness of Beth-El in the tradition of Jacob (Gen 28:18–19, 22). The sanctuary of Arad, placed in a state-owned fortress and therefore surely dedicated to YHWH, housed such massebes as well (Table 424). As an undecorated stone a massebe can obviously be easily used to honour the pictureless YHWH during the pre-dtr era.

Table 424: Cult niche of the sanctuary in Arad with the two massebahs mounted there and two incense altars at the entrance.

In Old Testament texts you can find countless evidence for a foreign cult that was obviously not forced on the Israelites and Judeans, but that was voluntarily adopted by them as part of cultural contact. In many cases, the biblical notes are from dtr hand and show the religious reality only from one side and from a historical point of view are often incorrect as well. The area of private piety was especially impacted by the foreign takeover of the YHWH cult. But, for the temple cult as well, there are some text that will point out foreign influences.

The fertility godess Asherah enjoyed huge popularity in Palestine (cf. e.g., 1 Kings 15:13a). The Hebrew word Asherah can mean simultaneously the goddess but also a cult stake, even though it is likely that the stake represents the goddess. The goddess Asherah was closely linked with YHWH in polular piety. In an epitaph in *Ḥirbet el-Kōm* (approx. 35 km southwest of Jerusalem in the Shephelah) from the last quarter of the 8th century BC one can read:

> *Uriyahu, the rich, has let it be written. Blessed was Uriyahu by YHWH. And from his enemies he has rescued him through his Asherah. By Oniyahu (written).*

YHWH and Asherah are furthermore named in two more inscriptions that were discovered in the fortress *Kuntilet Aǧrūd* in Negev and stem from the end of the 9th century BC. Even though only fragments remain one inscription contains,:

> *Said has [. . .]: Speak to [. . .] and to Joasa and to [. . .]: I bless you opposite of YHWH of Samaria and his Asherah.*

In the other inscription one can read:

Amarjo: Speak to my Lord: Are you feeling good? I bless you opposite of YHWH of Teman and through his Asherah. He blesses you and protects you and be with my Lord.

It is debated what is meant by Asherah in the inscriptions. Most likely the Asherah was understood to be the cult symbol that was allocated to YHWH and expressed YHWH's blessing and the support. The cult stake was originally understood as a symbol of a goddess and was integrated in the YHWH belief and could now represent YHWH support. Based on this background, it is not surprising that King Manasseh (696–642 BC) erected such a cult stake in the temple of Jerusalem (2 Kings 21:7). This fact is reported in a typical dtr influenced context but should be historically reliable. The prohibition of Deut 16:21 to erect a cult stake next to the altar speaks to this. Prohibitions will now be set in writing when they are supposed to change an existing situation. Therefore, Deut 16:21 is likely linked to this cult stake from Manasseh that was obviously set up in front of the temple. King Josiah indeed had this disreputable stake removed as part of his reformatory measures that were based on the book Deuteronomy (2 Kings 23:6).

In 2 Kings 18:4 a reformatory measure by King Hezekiah (728–700 BC) is described:

It was he who removed the heights of worship and destroyed the Massebes and destroyed the Asherah and the iron snake that was made by Moses because until those days the Israelites had burned incense for her and named her Nechuschtan.

The wording of this sentence is typical for dtr. For each king, the Deuteronomists placed historical information at the beginning of the paragraph in the Book of Kings, which could be relatively differentiated and was based on the implementation of monotheism and the abolition of places of worship perceived as pagan. Hezekiah and Josiah, who completed cult reformations, are consistently, positively evaluated. Secure proof of a reformation of Hezekiah so far has not been found. It is possible that the positive evaluation of Hezekiah in the eyes of the Deuteronomists mostly stems from the removal of the iron snake. In any case, the corresponding note in 2 Kings 18:4 would surely be historically reliable. The creation of the snake is reported in Numbers 21:4–9. If an Israelite was bitten by a snake, he was supposed to look up to the iron snake put up on a stake (compare pic 83) and the venom would not kill him.

Pic. 83: Marble vase from Sidon (4th century BCE), which was originally mounted on a metal post (cf. the drill holes). On the upper rim a snake is visible. On side B is on the carved drawing on the left a snake visible that is mounted on a frame, which could have corresponded to the shape of the iron snake in Jerusalem.

This tale clarifies how much of a danger snakes represented to humanity in those times. There are several incantation texts from the environment of the Old Testament that were supposed to help in case of a snake bite. The iron snake was most likely erected in the Jerusalem temple even though it is not expressed precisely. The snake was saved from the reformatory measures of King Ahaz (see also, on the Sea of Iron, chap 5.4 and to the Potwagons chap 5.5) as the snake was not understood to be a symbol of YHWH. To look upon them meant only that YHWH would send help to the person requesting it. However, it seems to have caused offence in the course of the development of the prohibition of pictures and it was also removed by King Hezekiah.

The long rule of King Manasseh (696–642 BC) brought a time of foreign political peace to Judah. This peace was bought with the agreement of the Assyrians. Manasseh obviously avoided any conflict with the rulers of the land of the two streams. An increase in the use of cylinder seals, as usual for Palestine during this time, hints at a stronger personal presence of the Assyrians. On the seals of this time one can note an increased use of astrological symbols (pic 84). It was obviously a time to be open toward star deities. If the dtr statement is historically accurate, that Manasseh erected altars for the entire heavenly army in the temple area (2 Kgs 21:5), then this mirrors a cultic change in the understanding of the people at this time. As part of the Josianic reform the destruction of these altars is mentioned (2 Kgs 23:12).

Pic. 84: Seal from Tell Kçsân (late 8th century BCE). On the left there is depicted the muðhuððu-dragon, on whose back the symbols of the Babylonia gods Marduk and Nabu can be seen. On the right the crescent standard of the moon god Sin of Haran which is flanked on two sides by branches is to be seen. On the base there is depicted a prayer in front of an incense post; apparently, he prays to the god Sin (crescent of the moon) and Venus (star) as well as the Pleiades (expressed by two points). The branch behind the prayer could display that the gods are being invoked for the thriving of the vegetation.

A much-discussed issue is what to understand from the horses and sun carriages that were also removed as part of the Josianic reformation (2 Kgs 23:11). One thought of horse figurines that were provided with a sun disk attached to the front of their heads and that were found in Jerusalem but also other places. Other scientists are of the opinion that it was live animals that pulled a processional carriage for the Assyrian god Schamasch. In any case, the connection between horses and the sun god is not a Palestinian tradition as it originates from Assyria. The Josianic reform carried out in 622 BC was not just a cleansing of the YHWH belief from heathen elements, it was also a political move away from the Assyrian power that could not longer maintain its hold over Palestine. Josiah used the opportunity and connected the political empacipation with the religious urges of the elite in his country. For this purpose, all Assyrian elements were removed and part of this was also the horses and sun carriages.

In the end the Josianic reformation only led to a partial cleansing of the YHWH faith from foreign elements. Some elements remained rooted in popular piety. In a vision of the prophet Ezekiel, that is dated to September 28, 593 BC (cf. Ezek 8:1), the prophet living in exile in Babylon is being led to Jerusalem and sees women at the entrance to the temple who are crying for Tammuz (Ezek 8:14)[,]. He also sees men immediately in front of the temple praying to the sun (Ezek 8:16). Tammuz was a Mesopotamian god who was honoured as a vegetation god; every year his going away, which was linked to the drying up of the landscape during the summer, was mourned. The territory of the temple remained a place to honour foreign cults even after the Josianic reformation. Due to the increased political dominance of Babylon at that time, there is little surprise that the people of the time oriented themselves more strongly toward the Mesopotamian gods. The temple place was understood as a place of state cult and therefore it seems logical to pray to those gods that were relevant to the interest of the state for the relevant time.

Gerd Theißen

Excerpt from The Transcendence of Texts (2019)

Reading the Bible theologically is motivated by the expectation of finding a "treasure in the field" hidden in the jungle (undergrowth) of words, sentences and texts for the sake of which it is worth giving everything away. This treasure is the Word of God. It enables you to begin a dialogue with God. If that happens, texts will become transparent from God. This is the first meaning of text transcendence. The contributions to *polyphonic biblical hermeneutics* presented here support the hypothesis of a *double transcendence of texts*. Just as in a movement of a sonata, the first theme only gives dynamics to the music by a counter theme and makes it sound, so the Bible only comes to life if we simultaneously understand its context in human life. Added to the theological transcendence of texts is a *human transcendence of life*. In order to understand this, we have to activate all our human scientific knowledge available to us: literary studies, sociology, psychology, ethnology, religious studies, and philosophy of religion. Our thesis is that both of them are inseparably combined. This is anything but self-evident. Both approaches are often in conflict with each other (literal: experience themselves as a conflict).

The research of the human transcendence of texts was sometimes decidedly rejected by the superior position of a theology of revelation, psychology even condemned as idolatry, sociology detected as aberration, which does not find the treasure searched for but destroys it. Something that is self-evident in science was declined with the pathos of the unconditional: (the fact) that we exploit all theories and methods available in order to come to a common understanding of religion. It is worth researching intensively that which people place their confidence in their lives. We are obliged to do that. But for a long time a confessional anti-psychologism and anti-sociologism were seen as part of the identity of many theologians. Within theology, a lack of inner freedom to get involved with these new research questions prevailed. Today it is usually overcome, however not everywhere.

Conversely, the judgments of religious criticism were by no means less harsh: From the perspective of a religious-critical psychology and sociology, all attempts to find an ultimate reality in religion are often considered as illusion or neurosis, repression or resentment. For many contemporaries, the negative opinion on religion has been established. Toward them you will have to solicit patiently to be recognized as a person of intellectual and moral integrity, if you stand up for religion. Especially those likeable modern contemporaries who admit that they have failed to free society from capitalist profit addiction sometimes react to religion with strong defensive reflexes. It seems as if their only consolation is the fact that they have at least consistently separated from religion. Confessional criticism is part of their identity and is often represented by a pathos of the unconditional.

So, there is a profound "hermeneutical conflict" (P. Ricoeur) between the theses that were united in these contributions as search of a double transcendence of texts. This conflict is characteristic of the understanding about religion in our modern society. Criticism of religion has become the medium of the modern religious discourse inside and outside the church. It is precisely for that reason the contributions presented here strive for an understanding where you rely on the fact that it is initiated from both sides. The aim would be to change the hermeneutical conflict into a "hermeneutical polyphony"—not into the harmonious music of old times, but into modern music that unfolds (develops) beyond tonality and therefore meets the needs of our time.

From the theological point of view, you can refer to the double commandment of love for the hermeneutic search for a double transcendence of texts. In it, at the center of the Bible, the relationship with God is treated as equal to that with other human beings. The relationship with God encompasses the whole person. It is explicitly said that this love is meant to encompass the whole heart, the whole soul (*psychē*) and all forces. If you are asked to ethically evaluate both relationships equally, you likely also put both relationships together hermeneutically. The whole human being is researched by psychology, their relationships with other people by sociology. Those who reject these questions with theological pathos do not judge in the sense of the Bible.

From the point of view of religion criticism one can appeal to great critics of religion. They have intentionally strived for the elimination of religion, but their criticism can also have the effect of a better understanding of religion. I have tried to point out that their theses, critical of religion, relativize each other. On the one hand, it is said that religion disagrees with empirical knowledge, on the other hand it is blamed for not being empirically disproved. On the one hand, religion is based on projections into a nonexistent reality, on the other hand it is meant to be a reaction to the predominance of reality. It goes beyond all borders motivated by a desired illusion, it works off incisive limits of life through rituals. It serves the ruling forces to suppress the dominated and the ordinary people as a resentment to domesticate the ruling (forces). Religion is a fire accelerant of human fanaticism but at the same time the engine of "good-doers," which makes it impossible to defend oneself against strangers and enemies. Criticism of religion is precious, because it leads to a better understanding of religion with its theses. Religion is a complex reality. Those who reject the dialogue with the Bible neither act in the spirit of criticism of religion nor in the spirit of the Bible. For criticism of religion is also rooted in the Bible. Criticism of religion has started in antiquity with the prophets in Israel and the philosophers in Greece.

Conflicts are meant to be a stimulus for developments, but only if they are carried out in the course of mutual respect. This is the principle of democracy. The same applies to the hermeneutic conflict between criticism of religion and preservation of religion. To evade this conflict would be a sign of weakness of vitality. It is a great help to realize the following: religions, and among them especially the biblical religion, have encouraged criticism of religion. I interpret the "Mosaic distinction" (J. Assmann) as an obligation not to accept everything in religion. A criterion of what you can accept is ethics. Therefore, an "ethical monotheism" is the center of attention in the Old Testament, and in the New Testament it is the double commandment of love. This is why we are able to transfer antireligious criticism from outside into intra-religious criticism and thus make it fruitful. Also, the Bible has already developed visions of a reformed and modified religion—as the vision of the "new covenant" by Jeremiah. Conversely, it is helpful if you admit: even harsh critics of religion were often encouraged by the dream of realizing on earth what they had recognized as worthwhile in religion—even if they wanted to abolish heaven at the same time.

Theology can refer to the Bible as inspiration for this path. A modern theology which is critical of traditions should therefore be a "Scripture-inspired theology." It is not bound to the letters of the Scripture, but nonetheless to its spirit. This spirit is intently focused on both of the most important criteria by which we have to measure everything written in the Bible: the first one is the "Mosaic distinction," which relates each worship of God to doing good, and the second one is Jesus's double commandment of love, which summarizes this "Mosaic distinction" and expands love to strangers, sinners, and enemies. This spirit, however, includes quite a lot of more precise impulses. This will become apparent if we recognize Scripture as basis of a *sign language*. For religions are sign languages with a grammar of their own. These grammar rules, their *axioms and basic motives*, make up its spirit, which works through the letter but is not identical with the letter. To sum up, theses motifs are mentioned once more: the motifs of creation, of wisdom, of miracle, of the distance between God and human beings; the motifs of hope and renewal, the repentance motif, and the exodus motif; the motif of faith, of incarnation, of substitution, of change of position, of love, of the judgment, and the motif of justification. Those who have internalized these (and other biblical) motives and are inspired by them will be able to create new texts in the spirit of the Bible to make new experience and to gain new insight. All this is "according to the Scripture." The principle of Scripture has to be understood in a new way, of course. Part of this principle of Scripture is that we do not only orientate to the Scripture but to Scripture *and* tradition, experience *and* reason (according to the Methodist quadrilateral). We actually already encounter texts in Scripture itself that were continually written as traditions; already in the Bible we find the expression of rich experience in the Psalms and reasonable reflections in Wisdom. If the spirit of the Scripture stays alive in theology and the church from the Prophets to Jesus and the apostle Paul, we will be able to reasonably find the "treasure in the field." Because the double commandment of love has been supplemented with a small addition. It says: We are meant to love God with all our heart, all our soul, *with all our reason*, and with all our strength (Mark 12:30).

Ruben Zimmermann

Excerpt from The Fiction of the Factual (2015)

How beautiful was the study of the New Testament, when the real words of Jesus were still separated from the unreal by clear criteria, (when) the origin of the first letter of Peter was precisely dated, or we could be told by Josephus how the historical John the Baptist genuinely was. Meanwhile everything has become complicated. Josephus is not anymore considered a fact-oriented historical writer whose information we can set as an objective standard against texts trending toward the New Testament. The questions of origin and introductory questions became uncertain, the validity of the criteria of authenticity has been radically disputed in Jesus research. But with these changes it is not only about the matter of a regular transition of science, in fact, the former fundamental beliefs such as the possibility or theological necessity of the search for origins and facts have been shook.

The change is nowhere more clearly seen than in the question of Jesus, the core question of New Testament studies. Still, here and there, one can hear the farewell to the so-called "third quest," the third round of questions about the historical Jesus. There, the Jewishness of Jesus was emphasized in a politically correct manner, and with an elaborated set of criteria, the historical Jesus tradition was made plausible, or in the Jesus-Seminar of the American Westar-Institute, authentic words of Jesus were determined even by means of a majority decision of scholars. However, the different methodologies, the wider perception of contexts, and also the inclusion of non-canonical texts, such as the Gospel of Thomas, have not at all led to consensual results. Instead, the diversity of scholarly constructions of Jesus was surprising: alongside the Jewish restoration prophet (Sanders), stood the social revolutionary (Horsley), and the Cynic wisdom prophet (Crossan), or the wandering charismatic (Theissen) joined with the wonder healer (Borg) and the exorcist (Twelftree), to name only a few examples. At the end of the third quest, one must plainly acknowledge: the diversity of constructions of Jesus most likely reflected the diversity of Jesus researchers, but they (the diversity of constructions) could not bring the historical truth to light. No wonder that some felt reminded of Albert Schweitzer's résumé of the liberal life of Jesus research a hundred years earlier.

Rightly, it was critically asked whether the search for the historical Jesus beyond the New Testament texts was not at its core mistaken and whether the criteria of authenticity did not necessarily have to get caught up in the hermeneutical circle. This skepticism has been supported by the insight of the historical studies which in the course of the linguistic turn challenged to engage in more self-criticism of its (historical studies) own doing. Historical theorists like White exposed works of the historism (for example, Ranke) of a "narrative plot," that is, a narrative structure although these actually just wanted to say how it really had been. Since it stands as a commonplace what language had all along maintained: "History" becomes only concrete in "stories," "History" does not exist without "Story." Even more so: facts are as the Latin *factum* (= made) plainly reveals, by no means given, but made. An objective reconstruction of events is impossible. And not only, because they are not accessible without language anymore, but because events are always already being construed and interpreted in the moment of occurrence, even by the ones experiencing it and the witnesses themselves. Therefore, there is only the "fiction of the factual." With that the ideology of the reconstruction of facts as maxim of New Testament studies has lost its basis. This had also grave methodological consequences: The traditional rules of the historical-critical search for the origins had to be revised. Or does the historical query even have to be given up completely?

Memory research offered an escape. In so doing, early Christian history was interpreted as remembered history, and the Gospels were appropriately seen as medium of memory, in which the past was preserved and likewise was made relevant for the present. To name one example, the Gospels remember the death of Jesus on a Passover, but with varying chronological details, be it the day before the Passover, on the 14th of Nisan, as in John, or on the 15th of Nisan as in the Synoptics. Historical Jesus research attempted then an unambiguous clarification which admittedly was not to be achieved. Every narrative is factually based on the Passover, but at the same time it shows a theological creative will, which ranks the events in a larger narrative context (the Passover meal in the Synoptics; the slaughter of the Passover lamb in John.) A memory-oriented approach is especially interested in the productive link between historical reference and literary narrative. Within Jesus research this "memory-approach" is praised as a new leading paradigm, in which the question of the historical Jesus had to give way to the question of the "remembered Jesus" (Dunn).

While historical memory research offered few concrete tools for textual analysis, the literary memory research appreciated now texts especially as a medium for remembrance. This equals a "narrative turn" of memory approach. *The remembered Jesus is likewise the narrated Jesus.* Because the texts of the New Testament are the beginning and end points of the analysis, one is well advised, also to especially appreciate their linguistic style. For this, narrative research offered a fully differentiated theory of textual interpretation. A few examples should show how this change of perspective has influence on the classic fields of Jesus and respectively on Gospel research:

In parables, one is not interested anymore in the *ipsissima vox* of the parables of Jesus (Jülicher, Jeremias), in fact, they can be analyzed literarily as metaphorical texts, which capture a memory process as typified remembered media, in which the narrator of the parables himself is staged as the Parable of God and the readers (male and female) are drawn into a dynamic process of quest for current theological meaning.

If for a long time, regarding the miracles, New Testament scholars have worked really hard on the question, which could have rally happened, the view is now directed toward the narrative style, in which a characteristic tension is constructed between a historical demand of reference and a content that breaks into reality. It is especially this paradoxical assignment between connection with the past and the confusion of customary experiential world, which turns the miracles stories as "fantastic reported facts" into a provocative medium of memories of Jesus and the revelation of God.

Eventually also the question of Christology is not anymore reduced to the historical reconstruction of the self-identification of Jesus with a traditional sovereign title such as Messiah or Son of Man. Moreover, it is being investigated how the narrative itself or the transmission of metaphors (such as son) created a "narrative Christology" or "Christo-poetics."

The new perception of the texts obtained a rethinking with regard to their (the texts) linguistic intrinsic values also in other fields of the New Testament studies: The author of the *Lukan double work* does not have to be pulled to-and-fro between the poles of "historian" and "poet", for his work has both historio-graphic as well as poetic-theological aspiration.

If the people of the narrated world were just based on the historical figures and communities, the figurative world in the *Gospel of John*, such as, for example, the "Beloved Disciple," can now be appreciated in its own literary-theological intrinsic value, without having to deny a historical demand. For example, John the Baptist was already remembered as a historical figure in the prologue of the fourth Gospel, but he was likewise presented as the concept of ideal witnesses, which in turn can be set out as model for the audience.

In Paul, it no longer primarily concerns the question whether Jesus actually now was an "atoning sacrificial lamb" or had been "ransomed," but rather with the question of how, for example, the traditional cult or slave experience was used within metaphoric statements, in order to interpret and understand the historical event of the cross.

Or if the question for the pseudepigraphy of the Deutero-Pauline or of the Pastoral Letters had been highly stylized as an act of acknowledgement of the truth, the stylistic device of author fiction is being appreciated in a literary approach, which can be used in order to support the truth of the gospel without any intentions of betrayal in the current process of communication.

The examples could be greatly increased. But now the question suggests itself, whether the historical dimension of texts did not, conversely, get lost with the "narrative turn." Is the historical question not being evaded with the linguistic appreciation of the texts, which belongs to the basic confession of the incarnation theology, (namely) that Jesus lived concretely in space and time?

Although the historical inquiry had to be more reflective and concerning the reconstructability of the past humbler than before, it remains indispensable for the New Testament studies. The texts of the New Testament are no timeless myths, but must be taken seriously in their self-interest to be factual, historically referential texts. In order to understand them, knowledge about the context and time in which they originated is not only helpful, but ultimately necessary.

And here too, intensive research is currently being carried out. Not only have the text finds from the twentieth century from Qumran and Nag Hammadi, which are now more widely evaluated, but also the work on the Corpus Hellenisticum, that is, the Jewish as well as the philosophical Greek writings at the turn of the times created a multifaceted picture of the ancient Mediterranean culture. The discovery of parallels in motive and concept was thereby significantly facilitated by the use of electronic concordance (TLG). Biblical archeology also needs special reference which crucially illuminates the contextual origin of early Christian texts as a nowadays multidisciplinary venture. It is not exaggerated, if one occasionally speaks of a new "history-of-religions school" in which the New Testament is conceived as a (small) part of the ancient culture and textual world.

But the high specialization of different methods, be it the narratological or also the cultural-historical approach, can sometimes give rise to the effect, that they stand unconnected side by side. Both methods harbor opportunities but also limits. The history-of-religions scholar stands in danger, in love with foreign texts and cultures, of losing the texts of the New Testament from sight more and more. The literature researcher, as a terminological and methodological tightrope walker, hardly dares to go into the lower regions of concrete textual interpretation. At the same time, the "narrative turn" of historical science, as also the "realistic turn" of literary science, offer chances of a common perception of history and text, as was outlined above in the example of Jesus research. The texts of the New Testament are historical-literary "reality stories" that can only be appropriately interpreted in the integration of both approaches. The narrative visualization creates a bridge between the first audience and the current recipients and brings New Testament research once more back to its central concern: that is the meaningful interpretation of New Testament texts. The texts of the New Testament are (together with the ones of the Old Testament) developed canon, that is, the standard of Christianity. The interpretation of the New Testament can therefore be content neither with historical archiving nor with narratological description, but aims at current understanding and theological giving of meaning. This needs a revival of hermeneutical reflection including its theological premises. In itself a further differentiating method, New Testament studies were more and more transformed into a subject for experts that got lost in the ramifications of detailed observations of philology or history of religion. It is not surprising that conversely the reference of the current dogmatics or ethics toward the New Testament was reduced to homeopathic dosages.

However, the glance into the history of Bible interpretations emphasizes that the current meaning has always come to fruition by means of completely different approaches, one remembers the fourfolded meaning of Scripture or the viewpoints of Chladenius. The current pluralism of methods can therefore connect with a proven tradition in which interpretation of Scripture had still been understood as "art of interpretation." More honesty regarding the constructivity of their doing, yes even courage for creativity and aesthetics would not only guide New Testament studies more colorful and joyful into the twenty-first century, but make it more interesting as an interlocutor for other theological disciplines and beyond.

Zacharias Frankel

Excerpt from The Jewish Oaths in Theological and Historical Relationship (1840)

To the problems whose solution has been rarely attempted in the field of the free research belongs the question of the Jewish Oath which has been asked for a long time. Even the term which one associated with the word Jewish Oath, and usually still associates today, shows that one assumed a subordinated position and (that one) forwent a free, absolute research; For instead of starting the research on the oath of the Jew according to his dogmas of faith, instead of asking on which basis the holiness and the inviolability of the oath according to Jewish terms of religion rests, one was content to argue about the oath that had to be given by a Jew in front of a Christian authority, drew the circle even tighter and kept an eye on the oath of the Jew against the Christians. Then one quoted a few Hebrew passages that were passed from one author to another and often misunderstood, and it was not in any way taught how the oath was binding, but how the authority had to protect themselves against perjury, for such sacrilege was presumed from Jews without objection. One could therefore, because one passed over every rational theory, not reach an unbiased appreciation of the question. And if even the philologist makes the oath (as it can be found in the Scripture), the subject matter of his research, that way he was content to consider it from the antiquarian point of view without relating the result to the present time, without designing it so that practical use (application on instances in life), arises from it and jurisprudence uses the result as a template. All the more secure had the jurisprudence itself to become: The research started from a point of view that was tarnished by prejudices, therefore the result turned out differently according to each subjectivity of the researchers, and it demonstrated the insecurity, the sway to and fro that makes itself known where the idea is not merged into reality, the general not into the concrete. The starting point had been mistaken with the beginning of the research, there one had to issue the hope from the start to ever accomplish a positive result.

And who had to pay for the false research? The Jew! Because one took the opinion biased by prejudices as a basis that the Jew does not shun the Christian authority and primarily if it stands against the Jew to vow falsely, then it only concerned an accumulation of preventative rules against the one who is afflicted with the suspicion of perjury: one grasped with the elimination of the theory of all superstition and all the spiteful (things) to accumulate bulwark on top of bulwark, fortress on top of fortress against the enemy and to get from him the confession of truth.

Most of the versions of the Jewish Oaths mentioned in this essay show that one went even further, did not stop at the pretended self-defense, but also granted a wide field to the wantonness and the intentional mockery rooted in religious hatred [or: hate of religion]. In them the roughest, uncontrolled fanaticism is voiced, they hold the monument of barbarism of their time: and one does not err if one assumes that religious hatred [or: hate of religion] itself has produced the thought of a self-defense, that the first reason for the offending version of the Jewish Oath has not been mistrust, but the petty joy to mock the followers of other religions and to offend him in his religion. And if at times a better impulse let the indignity of such a practice be recognized, then the fanaticism did not want to let go of its prey and used the wickedness of the Jew as an excuse for such measures. The handling of the Jewish Oath showed itself in the most appalling, mankind degrading shape [or: form]: the wicked wantonness was being practiced, the oath in front of Christian authorities was a desired opportunity to offend the Jew, to scorn him morally: the Jewish Oath degenerated into a naughty game which has been played with the most holy, for these versions lack all dignity, all seriousness becoming such a high act. Though one came to realize that the oath had been degraded in this manner to a despicable toy and one became suspicious of it; but instead of raising above the prejudices in free spirit and to research the source of all evil, one believed in unhappy infatuation which again the Jews had to pay to secure oneself by broader and more selective measures: one outdid the previous age regarding follies, the most ridiculous attempts were made, the insignificant was piled up again on the insignificant, still one was not feeling reassured: for the untruth carries its punishment in itself, and where specific means are being researched which are even based upon inhumanity, there only dishonoring (things) can be achieved: nothing can ever give the truth to the spirit caught in abhorrence and hatred!

For if we turn away from the indignity of the Jewish Oath in its common version and ask, whether it even meets the means intended by it: "to bring to light the truth and to reject the lie," then the wrongness of the unfounded, one-sided research shows itself again: it is confirmed that the Jewish Oath according to its character is to the same extent unsuitable to meet the task it had been given as it violates the emotion through its external form.

If you look at the oath in the first place and which assurance each oath taking can give, then the thought occurs that the oath belongs to the divine, the invisible; therefore, it should basically be an inadmissible means of reassurance for the earthly judge if the requirement would not be allowed to be asserted that the awe of the original principle of truth which is based on the higher ideality, the sensation of our divinity before God lives in the breast [or: heart] of each men. The oath is the bond which brings the earthly in immediate relation to the celestial: it (the oath) is not perceivable to the judge; for the human eye cannot perceive the invisible: and still he is supposed to give information about the doubtful; which belief exists that not in even more doubtful shelter has been taken? The threat that in the event of committing perjury and that if it comes to light strict punishment from a judge follows, cannot be taken as the basis of trust that one bestows to the oath: for the threat reveals the uncertainty and all the more, the threat in the case of the perjury coming to light can rarely create a deterrent effect. Additionally, the threat itself has to be preceded by a principle of the oath and its holiness; for what else should justify the strict punishment? Which (principle) is therefore the principle of the oath, whether it originates from elevation or from fear (as will be discussed further on), at all times the assumption must take place that the oath giver shares with us the belief in a higher judge who perceives the spiritual and may be invoked only for the truth. But that even under these conditions some (things) are still endangered, that some concerns have to be conceded, whether the former does not invoke with other intentions, with another opinion God as a witness for the truth, is confirmed by the precautions made against the so-called reservations by which any cunning circumvention should be prevented. And even these precautions have to be preceded by the assumption that the principle of the oath has general validity. On the one hand because, if the oath is not considered holy by the oath giver, it is of no use to restrict him with boundaries so that he is limited to the point which the judge wants to be confirmed by oath; for the one committing perjury does not recognize the holiness of the oath and thus gives oath to untruth even if there is no excuse for it presented to him. And additionally, from another point of view these precautions looked at per se prove themselves to be fruitless. Reservations are not subject of the sensual contemplation, they are excuses which the mind devises with cunning; and who wants to trace the excuses that he knows to find, who can oust it from all hiding places? Therefore, here again (one) has to return to the idea and to bring the oath giver to see in the moment in which he gives the oath the deity in whose name the authority swears him in and to quasi give oath to that deity. This way the oath gains more importance which has to be kept holy all the more, because one would otherwise have to ban the oath completely from jurisprudence or at least never ought not to consider it as a religious act. The oath will be made holy and the more it can be achieved by distancing human support that the oath taking is tied to the thought that the assurance is given not in front of men but in front of God, the holier the oath becomes, the more it gains in admissibility.

How does the so-called Jewish Oath fulfill this role? Does it aim to raising the emotion? Does it remind, which is colored through and through with hate of humans and degradation, of something truthful, something holy? Does it let the judge appear to be the deputy of the deity, and stresses that in front of whom who checks for heart and kidney and is the original spring of truth and holiness, a vow has to be taken? It only shows the hostile, distrusting judge who wants to penetrate into the innermost despite the human limitations, and does so with a nasty look and in such a manner that the person fulfilling the oath remembers that he is serving an oath in front of humans, for such an oath is not worthy of a deity! What value such an oath has cannot be calculated lightly; it cannot contribute to the establishment of the truth in neither the conscientious nor the less conscientious: it is more an associate of the lie as a means to promote the triumph of the untruth. In the less conscientious the so-called Jewish Oath can only cause derision: the undignified game that is being played with the oath can only lead him to wish to surpass the cunning of religious hate and mockery by greater cunning: it is only shown all too clear to him to view the oath as something human, and he will happily cling on to this to be at peace with his conscience and to find a pretense to reciprocate the injustice that has been done to him with equal injustice. And the conscientious person? He will not serve such an oath even to the truth; he feels his value as a human and cannot betaken of the dignity that is part of the personality of a human; because which insult to honor, which injury does not show the Jews Oath! It is a branding, which the honor loving one can only endure with the deepest reluctance, which he will try to escape even with the loss of some of his rights: he prefers to sacrifice some things before enduring such mockery and the fruits of this sacrifice are enjoyed by the cheater, the wrongful plaintiff or the lawfully accused; and the winning of the oath is—promotion of the unlawful and the untruth!

This about the Jewish Oath as it used to be common practice: and it is painful to realize that even the oath prescribed by the Coder Augusteus with all its formalities often suffered from the above-named shortcomings; that it even contains some things that in part are a wrong oath and in part encourage perjury. The oath of the Coder Augusteus therefore misses its purpose completely and the residuum remains to be injury to humanity and degradation of the court. But also, in some other German state the Jewish Oath showed itself on such a low level, and one only reached this in a few states, to remove all undignified in conducting the oath taking of the Jew. The need to improve the Jewish Oath was commonly known, but it is rightfully demanded that one needs to recognize what should be given instead of the abolished, and which form of oath would provide the state a sufficient warranty in relation to political as well as civil aspects. In regards to this question it would be enough to advise on which basic principle the oath was based for the Jews and what includes this name in Jewish law. However, history also has its demands; it rightfully demands to observe how it originated. Therefore, it becomes an irrefutable duty to proof that only confusing terms mirror images of terror if only one used the terror as a pretense and still does. And this demand is even more urgent as the Jewish oath has not become subject to history, rather more it is still blossoming in history: it therefore shows the necessity to accompany it through its varying phases, its origin, progress and current conformation to honor its value completely.

The research therefore needs to include the following points:

I. About the principle of the oath for the Jews and the way in which it has to be made according to Jewish Law.
II. About the area, which Jewish Law assigns the oath and the relationship between it and the vow.
III. About the inducement of the different forms of the Jewish Oath and how they correspond to their uses whereas the Jewish Oath still current in some states being compared.

And from these investigations the result should be:

Which are most appropriate versions of the assertoric and promissory oaths for the Jews according to today's spirit in Jewish, as well as in common law, and which are the related forms.

Abraham Geiger

Excerpt from Our Worship: A Question that Needs an Urgent Solution (1868)

The restoration of the former conditions—that was our longing and expectation for the future, that it is no more. We do not long for Palestine, do not want to depict a special popularity [or: tradition], (do not want) to establish our own state, we rather recognize in all districts of the earth the great homeland, love the fatherland allocated to us with all intimacy of the soul, look trustingly toward the great promise that the earth will be filled with the knowledge of God, a great sanctuary, and that at every place where we praise God He will come to us and (will) bless us. No lying request for the restoration of a Jewish state, for collecting the scattered into the far corners of the East should cross the gates of our lips, the lament for the former lost glory should be silent, as well! This change has also been mostly carried out in the renewed order of prayer, and rightly so. The dilemma between the reality, not only the conditions, but also the sensations, and the formerly romantically nurtured fantastic constructs that have descended to too-shallow sentimentality, must be extinguished. Jerusalem stays for us the holy spring from which in the past the doctrine of the truth originated, the spring has now become a mighty, fructifying stream, which pours itself over the whole earth. The current heap of rubble (which is) Jerusalem is for us at the most a poetic wistful memory, no nourishment for the mind; no elevation, no hope is tied to it. "The teaching originated from Zion, and God's word from Jerusalem" may be gladly announced by us, and with the changeable expression which ideas of time endure in the Hebrew language the word of Scripture does not mean for us literally that the teaching will originate from there, but that it originates, has originated from there. Jerusalem is for us an idea, not a site limited by geographical boundaries. But where the sense of the word of the prayers lets arise the misunderstanding that we offer tribute to the place, there such (a misunderstanding) has to be eliminated.

It is different with Israel's position and mission [or: vocation]. We would have to stop being Jews if we should believe our mission concerning world history was finished, if we would give room to the thought that the task given to us was already completed, that our unique position as community of fellow believers is merely a legacy from the past, not a still continuing holding together for a specific work of salvation in the present and the future. No, our task is not yet completed, our days have not run out; we are still the witnesses of God's unity, the human nature which is aiming for purity from within itself, the fraternization of peoples in truth, justice, and love, witnesses for all of mankind who first teach through the own loyal holding on in silence, then also announce the doctrine through the bravely declared word. Israel has yet not expired as a spiritual force of life, its importance for world history has not faded, but it only fulfills its mission [or: vocation] in truth if it has the consciousness to affect the whole of humanity, in it and with it. Each barrier, be it a fantastic traditional or a religious, each ostentation and introspection dulls this task, destroys its mission [or: vocation]. It may have been excusable, even necessary and salutary in the days of strong pressure, deep suffering of the soul, where the Jew had to withdraw into himself and to draw comfort and spiritual encouragment from his wounds; but now it is important to give with a free (here in the sense of unencumbered) view, in loving attachment to the entirety (here is the sense of community) just as to receive from it. Expressions of thanks for God separating Israel from the peoples, for—as is in the common version of the "Aleinu"—not making us like the peoples of the countries/lands, "(for) not setting us as the tribes of the soil, (for) not setting our share as theirs, our lot as the one of their mass," these and similar expressions go against our entire sensation, give cause to misjudgment of our entire task. In the possible view toward the past they (the expressions) are redundant, with regard to the present, to whose (meaning the present) interpretation they entice in the whole context, they become conceited complacency. We truly do not want to deny our distinctiveness, we want to hold on to and take good care of the splendid spiritual ground on which we are rooted, but we are nonetheless not allowed to misjudge that it is seriously in need of this care, that the ground has to be cleared from fast growing creeping plants, just like on the other hand the rest of humanity did also not struggle in vain, (that) their efforts have not been for nothing. United with it (distinctiveness) each part of its legacy according to its talent, we want to promote the truth, teach and learn, give gladly and receive openly, but not stand apart in disapproving arrogance, even if it is unintentional, even if it has involuntarily crept in. What purpose serves the perpetual repetition of the phrase: "he who has chosen us from all peoples" or even "raised us above all languages," what is the purpose of this conceited self-praising, even if it were only considered a preamble to our resulting debt of gratitude? Let us at least voice it: who has chosen us, we recognize the mission [or: vocation], which the world history has laid on us and to which we should stay loyal, let us become aware of the duties which he has imposed on us: why then the sideways glace that lies in the comparison and so easily gives the unjustified pride nourishment? Who is secure in his power and efficiency, does not boast with it; only the petty voices it and his doing belies his words. It is no worship of God to spread the seed of separation into the minds day after day where it is unnecessary; the consequence of it is either that the nucleus of true estrangement is nurtured or—what is currently rather the case—that the words are uttered thoughtlessly, here and there with an internal protest or with a superior smile about such childish wording. That is not prayer, not purification of the soul, such impulses have to be cleared away.

Ulrich Volp

Thesis on Patristic Ethic and Its Relationship to the Biblical Texts (2019)

Introductory Thesis

1. In regards of the fact that a considerable amount of preserved literature of the Church Fathers is exegesis, one can assume that the biblical narrative and the anthropological basis of the biblical texts had a formative influence on the development of Christian ethics in antiquity.

2. However, this does not even closely answer the question in which form this significant meaning took place—for example whether the patristic ethics originated "on the ground of the gospel" or whether it was rather "a product of the Greek spirit," or whether the ethics of the church fathers were the result of completely different challenges.

Theses about the Emergence of a Patristic Ethic

3. Efforts of interpretations of patristic ethics in the past usually took three different paths: firstly, it was attempted to reconstruct dependencies to certain philosophical doctrines of virtue (Epicurus, Stoics, Aristotle, Plato). Secondly, an approach was made to understand the ethic based on one or more basic terms that were analyzed to be decisive for patristic ethics (human will, justice, fellowship, belief and love, etc.). The third approach profiled the originality of patristic ethics compared to philosophical ethics or compared against the vulgarity ethics of antiquity. All three approaches are appropriate and have aided our understanding of patristic ethics significantly.

4. Simultaneously the three approaches were not suitable, as they do not sufficiently take up the context (theological, social, ritual, etc.) of the ethics of antiquity. Every research into patristic ethics has to name the questions and challenges that are behind the ethical statements of the Church Fathers.

About the Relationship between the Bible and Patristic Ethics

5. In the research into patristic ethic so far it was justified to indicate the great differences between "biblical ethics" and "philosophical ethics" but also some commonalities between for example pagan popular ethics, New Testament common ethics and their reception with the church fathers.

6. Equally meaningful is furthermore the historical development of central patterns of Christian lifestyle that was neither existing in the philosophical tradition nor in the Bible: martyrdom, virginity, humility as a monastic lifestyle.

7. Also the often-used categories of "intellectualism" and "community ethics" do not alone explain the observed differences and developments.

8. As a consequence it cannot be permitted to easily apply biblical or philosophical ethics to the way of life of Christians of the antiquity directly or indirectly.

9. To put it in positive terms: to determine the relation between biblical and patristic ethics one has to construct questions that ethical concepts and ideas can try to answer.

10. Part of such a context-oriented approach is the inclusion of ethical concepts into the very varying exegetic traditions of the Old Church.

11. Finally, one has to keep an eye on which kind of "Bible" determines the relationship between patristic ethics and the written word. In many cases it can be the Septuagint that constituted the Holy Scripture for the church fathers. In the process of forming canon the context one is trying to relay to changes continuously however. For the

development of a properly differentiated relationship to Judaism, to salvation history, to law and gospel, etc. the constantly changing context during the first century has enormous consequences. This situation also means a basic difference regarding theological ethics today and its relationship to the Bible.

The Meaning of Patristic Ethic for Today's Ethic

12. Research into patristic ethics promises great potential for a better understanding of the ethical and anthropological parameters by which all ethical considerations in Christian-shaped cultures are shaped.

13. A view to those Christian (father)texts that for the first time systematically formulated theological ethic should not be regarded with less significance than the value of the classical ethical texts of ancient philosophy that also for the first time looked at [literal: penetrated] the basic ethical questions in a philosophical way.

14. In some Christian churches, the church fathers own their authority as *doctores ecclesiae* or as the guarantors of orthodoxy. An ethical dialogue with these churches cannot be held afar from the ancient texts. Even the reformers were not without deep respect of the patristic ethic. That is the reason why it belongs for the reformatory theologies to the past and the present of ethics.

Volker Küster

Excerpt from Intercultural Theology as a Vocation (2015)
2. The Vocational Field

According to the three aforementioned dimensions, the vocational field can at first be roughly divided in the encounter with foreign religions, foreign theologies, and foreign churches.

2.1 Encountering Foreign Religions

Christianity shares in Europe a long history with Judaism and Islam. Initially it spread out in the area of the diaspora synagogues, and in the context of the religious policies of the Roman Empire it was initially classified as a Jewish sect, which gave it the status of a permitted religion (religio licitas). Following the final destruction of the temple in Jerusalem in the year AD 70 and the expulsion of the Jews out of the holy city, the Jewish presence on European soil gradually grew by means of migration. By AD 1000, the center of Jewish life had shifted to the West.

Islam spread out aggressively, directly after its emergence in the Arabian Peninsula in the seventh century. It virtually took Europe in its grip. In the south, bands of Muslim troops crossed the strait of Gibraltar. For more than seven hundred years, the Moors settled on the Iberian Peninsula (AD 711–1492). They invaded up to the territories of the

Byzantine Empire at the East and repeatedly sieged Constantinople, which finally fell in AD 1453. Not to mention the Muslim sovereignty over Sicily (AD 827–1091).

Although Karl Martell stopped them in the battle of Poitiers in the south, it would be another five hundred years before Ferdinand II of Aragon and Isabella of Castile finally triumphed and drove back the Muslims over the Mediterranean Sea. At this occasion, the Jews were ousted at the same time, as well. The Conquista should follow the Reconquista, the conquest of the territories in the new world (should follow) the territorial reconquest. Christopher Columbus (1451–1506) in whose name the amalgamation of the Christian faith and the colonial project depicted itself in a mysterious way—nomen est omen—took advantage of the victory frenzy in order to ingratiate himself with the court and (in order) to secure finances for his explorations by promising profit to the crown.

Meanwhile the rulers of Central Europe had started several crusades to the East because of the pressure of the Roman Papacy (1096–1291). The aim of the liberation of Jerusalem and the Holy Lands was already doomed to failure despite all efforts because of the difficulties with replenishment. On the other hand, the Muslims in turn succeeded in settling in Eastern Europe. The long Turkish wars (1423–1878) against the further expansion of the Ottoman Empire (ca. 1299–1923) and the "Turks in front of Vienna" (1529 and 1683) have become virtually proverbial for European Islamophobia. What is often forgotten in the description of this history of conflict is the relative tolerance, with which the Muslim rulers met the "people of the book," Jews and Christians, and the fruitful cultural exchange, the vestiges of which can still be visited today in Andalusia or Sicily. The ambiguities of these religions clearly come to light. Their life-promoting doctrines often stand in stark contrast to the brutal violence, in which they are involved.

During the counterattacks in the East, it also came to riots against the Jews, wherever the murdering hordes met them. Such pogroms and evictions of Jews, the "unbelievers" in one's own land, the "murderers of the Messiah," how they were abused, also shook the spiritual centers of Jewish life on the Rhein—in Mainz, Worms, and Speyer. One still finds in Luther wicked words about the Jews. The centuries-old Christian anti-Judaism eventually ended in the gas chambers of the Third Reich. During the industrialized and organized murder of six million European Jews and the escape of another approximately 280,000 Jews from Germany alone, the Nazis and their collaborators robbed Europe, if nothing else, of a majority of its intellectual and creative potential.

The colonial project and its following, the Christian mission, meanwhile also brought the Europeans in contact with the primal religions of Africa or the Pacific plus the Asian religions, especially Hinduism and Buddhism. The often strict denial of foreign religions and cultures was thwarted by the necessity to translate the Christian message. Without knowledge of the foreign cultural-religious context, this could not be done. That with it (the knowledge) came the recording and translation of foreign holy texts and (that) missionaries sometimes became researchers, is again a clue to the ambiguity of these intercultural-religious exchange processes. The first translations of the Asian holy texts in the nineteenth century inspired the intellectual interest of philosophers like Arthur Schopenhauer (1788–1860). Eventually, Hinduism and Buddhism would manifest in Europe today beyond the migrant communities but above all in the realm of wellness and interior design. A considerable number of conversions have not been recorded.

After the end of the Second World War, the Christian complicity in the Holocaust led to a new consciousness about the relation of the Christian churches to Judaism. From the Catholic side, this was supposed to come about during the Second Vatican Council (1962–1965). However, political intervention from the Arab world ensured that it eventually came to a declaration about the relation of the church to the non-Christian religions (*Nostra Aetate*) in general. This was the birth of the modern theology of religions.

In the World Council of Churches, which represents Protestant and Orthodox churches, the question of the relationship of "Church and Israel" was at first assigned to the Department for Faith and Church Constitution, a kind of inter-Christian "Bureau of Standards/Office of Weights and Measures." Only in the course of the foundation of a secretary's office for interreligious dialogue (1971), was the relationship to Jewry declared a topic for dialogue, indeed it has become in a way the nucleus of the modern dialogue movement.

While the theology of religion looks for a place for other religions in one's [or: its] own thought-system, the theology of dialogue exceeds the boundaries of one's [or: its] own faith and thereby makes itself "vulnerable" to the other—in order to take up the concept from the Hamburg missiologist Hans-Jochen Margull. The theology of religions ultimately stands before a dilemma of exclusivism and inclusivism: Does the religious foreigner fall victim to everlasting damnation if he does not convert to Christianity, or has he always already been included in God's plan of salvation? The postmodern pluralistic theology of religions wanted to cross this Rubicon and to advance from the ecclesiasticism and the Christocentrism of exclusivism, respectively, over the theocentric-inclusivistic (position) to a position beyond Theism/Non-Theism. However, therefore, it ended in a kind of meta-inclusivism. The theology of dialogue in contrast pursues another way, its double commandment reads as follows: Bear witness to one's own faith and learn to understand the other (person), to such a degree that he/she can recognize himself/herself therein. The exclusivism-inclusivism dilemma of any religion is thereby discredited [or: discounted].

The question who has a dialogue with whom about what can only be answered in such a way that the dialogue is an event between followers (male or female) of different religions. They can only speak for themselves, but also perform simultaneously a role as border crossers between the religious communities. There are different types of dialogue: the dialogue of life is pre-conceptual; it focuses on the good coexistence of men on site. It has proven itself again and again in interreligious collaboration, such as during disaster relief. The dialogue of reason on the other hand is supported by the scholars of different traditions. Here allegiances to the concepts of the respective doctrines are at stake. A "we agree to disagree" is therefore often inevitable. Nevertheless, this common quest for truth is indispensable for mutual understanding. The mystics of different traditions meet in a dialogue of the hearts. This sharing of spiritual experiences in meditation and prayer is post-conceptual.

Theology as well as the dialogue of religions requires knowledge of foreign religions. Here religious studies come into play, which today should obviously belong to the curriculum of theological studies. I would, however, go a step further: As we are training religious professionals and not people professionally engaged with religion, guest lectures from scholarly representatives (male or female) of other religions and interreligious encounters should become a normal situation in theological faculties.

Appendix 7
The Mainz Method Checklist

1. Find all the verb forms.
2. Find all commas.
3. Find all conjunctions.
4. Mark the main clause.
5. Identify case and number of all nouns; establish noun phrases.
6. Locate all referent nouns.
7. Look out for participles used as adjectives.
8. Look up all new words and try combining the verb with phrases.
9. Perform a rough translation of the sentence.
10. Polish up the sentence to ensure readability.

Glossary of Terms

[A]

Abendmahl [das] (n.): communion
abgleiten (v.): to divert
Abkehr [die] (n.): rejection, renunciation
Abschnitt [der] (n.): paragraph
ähnlich sehen (n.): to resemble
allein (adv.): solely
allemal (adv.): certainly
Angesicht [das] (n.): face
anheben (v.): to pick up, arise
Ansichreißen [das] (n.): take over
antreffen (v): to meet, to encounter
Auferstandene [der] (n.): resurrected one
auffordern (v): to invite, to prompt, to request
aufrecht (adj./adv.): upright, erect, straight
aufrichtig (adj./adv.): wholehearted, sincere
Aufrichtung [die] (n.): establishment [*in the sense to establish*]
Augenblick [der] (n.): moment; from *Auge*, eye + *Blick*, glimpse

[B]

bald (adv.): soon
befangen (adj./adv.): biased, prejudiced, bashful
Befehl [der] (n.): order, command
begreifen (v.): to grasp [*an idea or concept*]
Beichte [die] (n.): confession
Beispiel [das] (n.): example
Bekenntnis [das] (n.): acknowledgment

Bereitschaft [die] (n.): readiness
Beruf [der] (n.): vocation, mission, calling
Beugung [die] (n.): bending
Bewegung [die] (n.): movement
Bezugstext [der] (n.): reference text
Böse [das] (n.): wicked, evil
Buchstabendienst [der] (n.): religion of the letter
Buße [die] (n.): repentance
bußfertig (adj.): repentant

[C]

Christ [der] (n.): Christian
Christenmensch [der] (n.): the Christian person

[D]

dann (adv.): then
Darstellung [die] (n.): portrayal, discussion
Dasein [das] (n.): existence
denn (conj.): because, for, that
derhalben (conj.): therefore
Deutung [die] (n.): interpretation
Dispens [der] (n.): dispensation

[E]

echt (adj): real, genuine, true
eigen (adj.): characteristic
eigenmächtig (adj.): arbitrary, unauthorized
Einsicht [die] (n.): insight

ekklesiologisch (adj.): ecclesiological
entscheidend (adj./adv.): crucial
entsagen (v.): forsake
Entwicklung [die] (n.): development
Erben [die] (n.): heirs
Erfahrung [die] (n.): experience
ergreifen (v.): to seize, to grip
Erkenntnis [die] (n.): recognition
Errettung [die] (n.): redemption
ertragen (v.): to endure
Erwählung [die] (n.): election
Erzählung [die] (n.): story
ewig (adj.): eternal

[F]

fassen (v.): to grasp, grab
Forderung [die] (n): demand, claim, request
freilich (modal particle): of course
Fremde [das] (n.): the foreign things
Fremde [die] (n.): foreign lands
Frevelhaftigkeit [die] (n.): sinfulness
Frömmigkeit [die] (n): piety
führen (v.): to lead

[G]

Gebiet [das] (n.): region
gebieten (v.): to command
Gefangenschaft [die] (n.): captivity
Gegenstand [der] (n.): object, subject matter
Geheimnis [das] (n.): mystery
Gehorsam [der] (n.): obedience
gelten (v.): to be in place, to apply
Gemeindezucht [die] (n.): church discipline
gemein (adj.): common
Gemeine [die] (n.): congregation
am gemeinsten (adj.): most common
Gerechtigkeit [die] (n.): righteousness
Gesetz [das] (n.): law

Gesinnung [die] (n.): ethos, way of thinking/feeling, disposition
Gestaltungswille [der] (n.): will to design
gestempelt (adj.): stamped
Gewalt [die] (n.): power, authority
gleichen (v.): to resemble, to be like
gleißen (v.): to blaze
Gleißner [der] (n.): a phony
Göttliche [das] (n.): the divine

[H]

Haufe [der] (n.): common people
Heide [der] (n.): gentile, heathen
Heilswirken [das] (n.): work of salvation
Heimat [die] (n.): home [*general sense of*]
Heuchelwerk [das] (n.): hypocritical works
hoch (adj.): high
höher (adj.): higher

[I]

[J]

Jünger [der] (n.): disciple

[K]

Keimzelle [die] (n.): nucleus, seed
Klarheit [die] (n.): clarity, brightness
Konkurrenz [die] (n.): competition
Körperwelt [die] (n.): bodily world
Kreis [der] (n.): circle

[L]

lebendig (adj.): lively, living
Liebe [die] (n.): love
lösend (adj.): saving

[M]

Machen [das] (n.): making
Makarismus [der] (n.): macarism

Menschwerdung [die] (n.): incarnation, becoming human
Merkmal [das] (n.): characteristic feature
sich messen (v.): to compete
mithin (adv.): at times
Mönchtum [das] (n.): monkhood
mönchisch (adj.): monastic

[N]

nahetreten (v.): to get closer, to approach
notwendig (adj./adv.): necessary, needed, required

[O]

offenbaren (v): to reveal, manifest
Organ [das] (n.): part of body, voice, institution

[P]

[Q]

Quelle [die] (n.): source, spring

[R]

Rechtfertigung [die] (n): justification
Reichstag [der] (n.): Imperial Diet
richten (v.): to judge, correct

[S]

Schöpfer [der] (n.): creator
Schöpfung [die] (n.): creation
Schranke [die] (n.): barrier
schuldig (adj.): guilty
Schwärmertum [das] (n.): enthusiasts, simliar to Anabaptists
seelisch (adj.): spiritual, emotional, mental
Selbstverleugnung [die] (n.): self-denial
Seligkeit [die] (n.): blessedness
strafen (v.): to punish

Strom [der] (n.): current, stream (of river, rain, electricity)

[T]

Tatbestand [der] (n.): fact
Tatsachenbericht [der] (n.): factual report
täuschen (v.): to deceive
todgeweiht (adj.): moribund
treiben (v.): to do
Treue [die] (n.): faithfulness

[U]

Übereinstimmung [die] (n.): conformity, accordance
Überlieferung [die] (n.): traditions
umfassend (adj.): including, encompassing
umkehren (v.): to turn, to repent
Unmittelbarkeit [die] (n.): immediacy
unsterblich (adj.): immortal
unterscheiden (v.): to distinguish, differentiate
Untersuchung [die] (n.): examination
Urchristentum [das] (n.): genuine Christianity
Urheber [der] (n.): author
Urstoff [der] (n.): original matter
Urwesen [das] (n.): original being

[V]

verbinden (v.): to connect, to combine
Vereinigung [die] (n.): union
Verfassung [die] (n.): condition, state of being
Vergebung [die] (n): forgiveness, absolution
Verhalten [das] (n.): posture, behavior, attitude, disposition
Verhältnis [das] (n.): relationship, relation
verleihen (v.): to give, to lend
verloren gehen (v.): to get lost, to go missing, to disappear

vermittelst (prep.): by means of

vermögen (v.): to be able to

verpflichten (v.): to obligate, to commit oneself

Verstand [der] (n.): mind, understanding

verunheiligen (v.): to desecrate

verworfen (v.): discarded [participle II of *verwerfen*, "to discard"]

Verweltlichung [die] (n.): secularization

Verzicht [der] (n.): sacrifice, renunciation, dispensation, waiver

vielleicht (adv.): may, might, maybe, possibly

volkstümlich (adj.): traditional

Voraussetzung [die] (n.): prerequisite, presupposition

Vorsprung [der] (n.): head start, lead

Vorstellung [die] (n): notion, idea, conception

Vortrag [der] (n.): sermon, speech

[W]

Wahrnehmung [die] (n.): perception

warten (v.): to maintain

weissagen (v.): to foretell

Weissagung [die] (n.): prophecy

weltlich (adj.): secular

wesentlich (adj.): important, significant, fundamental

wichtig (adj.): important, necessary

Widerspruch [der] (n.): opposition

wiederum (adv.): again, in turn, even though, on the other hand

[X]

[Y]

[Z]

Zeile [die] (n.): line

Zorn [der] (n.): wrath

Zuversicht [die] (n.): confidence

zuwenden (v.): to turn to

Zweifel [der] (n.): doubt

Bibliography

Aberbach, Moshe, ed. *Jewish Education and History: Continuity, Crisis, and Change.* Translated by David Aberbach. New York: Routledge, 2009.

Ames, Edward Scribner. "The Religion of Immanuel Kant." *The Journal of Religion* 5.2 (1925): 172–77.

Baader, Benjamin Maria. *Gender, Judaism, and the Bourgeois Culture in Germany: 1800–1870.* Bloomington, IN: Indiana University Press, 2006.

Baird, William. *History of New Testament Research: From Jonathan Edwards to Rudolf Bultmann*, vol. 2. Minneapolis: Fortress, 2003.

Barth, Karl. *Der Römerbrief.* Bonn, 1919.

Ben-Sasson, H. H., ed. *A History of the Jewish People.* Cambridge, MA: Harvard University Press, 1976.

Blomberg, Craig L. *The Historical Reliability of the Gospels.* Downers Grove, IL: InterVarsity Press, 2007.

Bonhoeffer, Dietrich. *Nachfolge.* München: Kaiser, 1937.

Brecht, Martin. *Martin Luther: The Road to Reformation: 1483–1521.* Minneapolis: Fortress, 1993.

Brown, Stuart, Diané Collinson, and Robert Wilkinson. *Biographical Dictionary of Twentieth-Century Philosophers.* New York: Routledge, 1996.

Clark, Elizabeth A. *The Fathers Refounded: Protestant Liberalism, Roman Catholic Modernism, and the Teaching of Ancient Christianity in Early Twentieth-Century America.* Philadelphia: University of Pennsylvania Press, 2019.

Clarke, Paul Barry, and Andrew Linzey. *Dictionary of Ethics, Theology and Society.* New York: Routledge, 1996.

Cross, F. L., and Elisabeth A. Livingstone, eds. *The Oxford Dictionary of the Christian Church.* Oxford: Oxford University Press, 2005.

Dennison, William D. *The Young Bultmann: Context for His Understanding of God, 1884–1925.* New York: Peter Lang, 2008.

Durrell, Martin. *German Grammar and Usage.* 6th ed. Routledge Reference Grammars. New York: Routledge, 2017.

Eisenberg, Ronald L. *Essential Figures in Jewish Scholarship.* New York: Jason Aronson, 2014.

―――. *The JPS Guide to Jewish Traditions*. Philadelphia: The Jewish Publication Society, 2004.

Erickson, Millard J. *Christian Theology*. 3rd ed. Grand Rapids: Baker Academic, 2013.

Evans, C. Stephen. *Pocket Dictionary of Apologetics & Philosophy of Religion*. Downers Grover, IL: InterVarsity Press, 2002.

Feiner, Shmuel. *Moses Mendelssohn: Sage of Modernity*. New Haven, CT: Yale University Press, 2010.

Fox, Michael V. *Ecclesiastes*. JPS Bible Commentary. Philadelphia: Jewish Publication Society, 2004.

Frankel, Zacharias. *Die Eidesleistung der Juden in theologischer und historischer Beziehung*. Dresden, DE: Arnoldifchen Buchhandlung, 1840.

Galli, Mark, and Ted Olsen. *131 Christians Everyone Should Know*. Nashville: Broadman & Holman, 2000.

Geiger, Abraham. *Unser Gottesdienst: Eine Frage, die dringend Lösung verlangt*. Breslau: Schletter'sche Buchhandlung, 1868.

Gerrish, Brian. *A Prince of the Church: Schleiermacher and the Beginning of Modern Theology*. Philadelphia: Fortress, 1984.

Gillman, Neil. *Conservative Judaism: The New Century*. Springfield, NJ: Behrman, 1993.

Godsey, John D. "Barth and Bonhoeffer," *Christian History* 32 (1991).

Green, Clifford, ed. *Karl Barth: Theologian of Freedom*. Minneapolis: Fortress, 1991.

Greenspoon, Leonard. "Judaism." Edited by John D. Barry et. al. *The Lexham Bible Dictionary*. Bellingham, WA: Lexham, 2016.

Hauser, Alan J. "Friedrich Schleiermacher." Edited by John D. Barry et al. *The Lexham Bible Dictionary*. Bellingham, WA: Lexham, 2016.

Hodgson, Peter C., ed. *Hegel Lectures on the Philosphy of Religion: One-Volume Edition, the Lectures of 1827*. Berkeley, CA: University of California Press, 1988.

Jackson, Samuel Macauley, ed. *The New Schaff-Herzog Encyclopedia of Religious Knowledge: Embracing Biblical, Historical, Doctrinal, and Practical Theology and Biblical, Theological, and Ecclesiastical Biography from the Earliest Times to the Present Day*. New York; London: Funk & Wagnalls, 1914.

Kant, Immanuel. *Beantwortung der Frage: Was ist Aufklärung?* Public Domain, 1784.

Keel, Othmar, and Christoph Uehlinger. *Göttinnen, Götter und Gottessymbole: Neue Erkenntnisse zur Religionsgeschichte Kanaans und Israels aufgrund bislang unerschlossener ikonographischer Quellen*. Afterword by Florian Lippke. Bibel+Orient Museum. Freibourg, Switzerland: Academic Press Fribourg, 2010.

Kenny, Anthony. *Immanuel Kant: A Very Brief History*. London: SPCK, 2019.

Kerr, Fergus. "Book Notes: Barthiana." *New Blackfriars* 79 (1998): 550–54.

Küster, Volker. "Interkulturelle Theologie als Beruf." *Neue Zeitschrift für Systematische Theologie und Religionsphilosophie* 57.4 (2015): 447–63.

Lajoie, Raymond A. "What Tyndale Owed Gutenberg." *Christian History* 16 (1987).

Levenson, Alan T. *The Making of the Modern Jewish Bible: How Scholars in Germany, Israel, and America Transformed an Ancient Text*. Lanham, MD: Rowman & Littlefield, 2011.

Luther, Martin. *Der große Katechismus*. Public Domain.

———. *Von der Freiheit eines Christenmenschen*. Public Domain.

Lutzer, Erwin W. *Rescuing the Gospel: The Story and Significance of the Reformation*. Grand Rapids: Baker, 2016.

MacCulloch, Diarmaid. *Reformation: Europe's House Divided, 1490–1700*. New York: Penguin, 2004.

Mawson, Michael, and Philip G. Ziegler, eds. *The Oxford Handbook of Dietrich Bonhoeffer*. Oxford: Oxford University Press, 2019.

McGrath, Alister E. *Christian Theology: An Introduction*. 5th ed. West Sussex: John Wiley, 2011.

McGriffert, Arthur Cushman. *Martin Luther: The Man and His Work*. New York: Century, 1911.

Mendelssohn, Moses. *Jerusalem oder über religiöse Macht und Judentum*. Berlin: Friedrich Maurer, 1783.

Metaxas, Eric. *Martin Luther: The Man Who Rediscovered God and Changed the World*. New York: Viking, 2017.

Metz, J. B. "Kirche Nach Auschwitz." *Kirche und Israel, Neukirchener Theologische Zeitschrift* 5 (1990): 99–108.

Miller, Kevin, ed. "Gutenberg Produces the First Printed Bible (1456)," *Christian History* 28 (1990).

Nietzsche, Friedrich. *The Portable Nietzsche*. Edited and transated by Walter Kaufmann. New York: Penguin, 1977.

Olsen, Roger E. *The Journey of Modern Theology: From Reconstruction to Deconstruction*. Downers Grove, IL: InterVarsity Press, 2013.

Perez-Alvarez, Eliseo. *A Vexing Gadfly: The Late Kierkegaard on Economic Matters*. Eugene, OR: Pickwick, 2009.

Pinkard, Terry. *Hegel: A Biography*. Cambridge: Cambridge University Press, 2000.

Plaut, W. Gunther. *The Rise of Reform Judaism: A Sourcebook of Its European Origins*. Philadelphia: Jewish Publication Society, 2015.

Raynova, Yvanka B. "Reformation der Kirche oder Reformation durch Kultur?" *Labyrinth* 20.2 (2018): 5–13.

Reid, Daniel G. *Dictionary of Christianity in America*. Downers Grove, IL: InterVarsity Press, 1990.

Ridley, Aaron, and Judith Norma. *Nietzsche: The Anti-Christ, Ecce Homo, Twilight of the Idols, and Other Writings*. Cambridge: Cambridge University Press, 2005.

Roper, Lyndal. *Martin Luther: Renegade and Prophet*. New York: Random House, 2016.

Rusten, Sharon, and E. Michael Rusten. *The Complete Book of When & Where in the Bible and throughout History*. Wheaton, IL: Tyndale, 2005.

Ryrie, Charles Caldwell. *Basic Theology: A Popular Systematic Guide to Understanding Biblical Truth*. Chicago: Moody, 1999.

Sacks, Elias. *Moses Mendelssohn's Living Script: Philosophy, Practice, History, Judaism*. Bloomington, IN: Indiana University Press, 2017.

Salfeld, Siegmund. *Das Martyrologium des Nürnberger Memorbuches*. Berlin: L. Simion, 1898.

Schleiermacher, Friedrich. *Über die Religion: Reden an die Gebildeten unter ihren Verächtern*. Leipzig: F.U. Brodhaus, 1868.

Schlingensiepen, Ferdinand. *Dietrich Bonhoeffer, 1906–1945: Martyr, Thinker, Man of Resistance*. New York: T&T Clark, 2010.

Schorch, Ismar. "Zacharias Frankel and the European Origins of Conservative Judaism." *Judaism* (1991): 344–54.

Schwarz, Hans. *Theology in a Global Context: The Last Two Hundred Years*. Grand Rapids: Eerdmans, 2005.

Scruton, Roger. *Kant: A Very Short Introduction*. Oxford: Oxford University Press, 2001.

Sears, P. Chase. "Karl Barth." Edited by John D. Barry et al. *The Lexham Bible Dictionary*. Bellingham, WA: Lexham, 2016.

Shanks, Andrew. *Hegel's Political Theology*. Cambridge: Cambridge University Press, 1991.

Stackhouse Jr., John G. "Following Jesus in the Dark." *Christian History* 94 (2007).

Theißen, Gerd. *Texttranszendenz: Beiträge zu einer polyphonen Bibelhermeneutik*. Beiträge zum Verstehen der Bibel 36. Berlin: LIT, 2019.

Van Til, Cornelius. *A Christian Theory of Knowledge*. Phillipsburg, NJ: Presbyterian and Reformed, 1969.

Volp, Ulrich. "Thesen zur patristischen Ethik und ihrem Verhältnis zu den biblischen Texten." *Journal of Ethics in Antiquity and Christianity* 1 (2019): 91–92.

Wiender, Max, ed. *Abraham Geiger and Liberal Judaism: The Challenge of the Nineteenth Century*. Cincinnati, OH: Hebrew Union College Press, 1981.

Zetterholm, Karin Hedner. *Jewish Interpretation of the Bible: Ancient and Contemporary*. Minneapolis: Fortress, 2012.

Ziefle, Helmut W. *Modern Theological German: A Reader and Dictionary*. Grand Rapids: Baker, 1997.

Zimmermann, Ruben. "Fiktion des Faktischen: wie der historische und der erinnerte Jesus zusammengehören." *Zeitzeichen* 16 (2015): 17–19.

Zwickel, Wolfgang. *Der salomonische Tempel*. Mainz: von Zabern, 1999. Repr., Kamen: Hartmut Spenner, 2011.

Image Credits

The following list provides the credits for the images found on the chapter headers.

Chapter 1, Bibelhaus Erlebnis Museum Frankfurt am Main

Chapter 2–4, the opening page of the book of Genesis in Martin Luther's Bible translation of 1534, published by Hans Luft, public domain

Chapter 5, illustration of Martin Luther by Hannah Wolf

Chapter 6, illustration of Immanuel Kant by Hannah Wolf

Chapter 7, illustration of Moses Mendelssohn by Hannah Wolf

Chapter 8, illustration of Friedrich Schleiermacher by Hannah Wolf

Chapter 9, illustration of Karl Barth by Hannah Wolf

Chapter 10, illustration of Dietriech Bonhoeffer by Hannah Wolf

Chapter 11–12, Tel Dan Stele © 2018 by Zondervan

Chapter 13–14, Greek text of 1 Corinthians 13 © Nathan Holland/Shutterstock

Chapters 15–16, relief from the Arch of Titus © Matt Ragen/Shutterstock

Chapters 17–18, mosaic of Jesus Christ from the Hagia Sophia © Artur Aogacki/Shutterstock

Author Index

Subject Index